AF819990

21 Years 2025-2005

ICSE

CHAPTERWISE

QUESTION BANK

English Language

(Paper 1)

Class 10

21 Years 2025-2005

ICSE

CHAPTERWISE

QUESTION BANK

English Language
(Paper 1)
Class 10

Author
Srishti Agarwal

arihant
SUCCESS AND NOTHING LESS

arihant
SUCCESS AND NOTHING LESS

ARIHANT PRAKASHAN
(School Division Series)

ADMINISTRATIVE & PRODUCTION OFFICES

Regd. Office
'Ramchhaya' 4577/15, Agarwal Road, Darya Ganj, New Delhi -110002
Tele: 011- 47630600, 43518550

Head Office
Kalindi, TP Nagar, Meerut (UP) - 250002, Tel: 0121-7156203, 7156204

SALES & SUPPORT OFFICES

Agra, Ahmedabad, Bengaluru, Bareilly, Chennai, Delhi, Guwahati, Hyderabad, Jaipur, Jhansi, Kolkata, Lucknow, Nagpur & Pune.

PO No : TXT-XX-XXXXXXX-X-XX

Published By Arihant Publications (India) Ltd.

For further information about the books published by Arihant, log on to www.arihantbooks.com or e-mail at info@arihantbooks.com

PRICE ₹245.00

Follow us on

Achieving 99+
Marks in Board Exams

Achieving 99+ marks in board exams is definitely an ambitious goal, but with the right approach and these 7 tips from toppers, you can definitely increase your chances of success!

Here are the 7 Topper Tips to ace your board exams:

1. Master the art of consistency

Consistency builds understanding and confidence, both crucial for excelling in exams.

2. Build a winning study strategy

Create a personalised timetable that prioritises subjects based on your strengths and weaknesses.

3. Befriend the syllabus

Focus on high-weightage topics and prioritise mastering core concepts before moving on to advanced ones.

4. Embrace active learning

Explain concepts to yourself or in study groups to solidify understanding.

5. Conquer the past

Solve Past years' papers and Sample Papers under timed conditions to practice time management and understand paper pattern.

6. Seek help, when needed!

Don't hesitate to clarify doubts with teachers, tutors, or study groups. Asking questions strengthens your understanding and prevents confusion.

7. Prioritise well-being

Eat nutritious meals, get enough sleep, have regular exercise, practice stress management techniques like meditation to stay calm and focused during exams.

These tips are just a starting point, and you can personalise them to fit your learning style and preferences.

Description of

Exclusive Features

Composition Writing

01

Short Story

Story writing is a creative but difficult art of composition. It requires a lot of innovative thinking, planning and mastery of narrative skills and language. A short story is a narrative of moderate length that revolves around a single incident involving one or more characters. It must have a proper beginning, middle and an end. A story needs to be well-planned and written in an interesting manner.

Steps to Write a Short Story

There are no specific rules for writing a story but there are countless ways to create an interesting one. However, the writer should keep the following steps in mind while writing a short story.

Summary of the Chapter

At the start of each chapter , such as Description, Short Story, Debate, Picture Composition, Narrative, steps to write a composition, and points to be kept in mind while writing a composition are given in simple and easy to understand language.

Examiner's Comment

- Many candidates failed to understand the meaning of 'original' in the given topic. Some candidates indulged in plagiarism and lifted the story 'Hearts and Hands' in entirety from the short stories.
- Most students ignored the essential elements of a short story, which are plot-structure, sequence, setting, characters and dialogues. In some cases, the secret was immediately revealed and the element of shock/ surprise was missing.

Examiner's Comment

The book contains the examiner's comment at various places. This will help the students to understand the common mistakes done by them while answering the questions. It helps the student in understanding how the question needs to be answered.

Suggestion for Students

Understand the distinction between original and lifted stories and insist on originality. Learn about the elements of a short story and plot structure.

Suggestion for Students

Some answers also contain suggestion for students. These are actually tips that would help the student understand how they can develop the skill to answer the question.

Format 1

Jingle Bells Residential School ← Sender' address
Igatpuri - 422 402

10th October, 2018 ← Date

My dear Mummy / Mother, ← Salutation/Customary greeting

I know that you are very disappointed with my half yearly report that you must have received last week. I am truly sorry for a poor performance and I am feeling very depressed at having let you down so badly. I do not want to make excuses but this last term I have been in and out of the infirmary several times. I had a bad attack of malaria and was unable to attend classes for about a week. Barely had I got over this when I broke out in a rash because of the medication and I had to go back into the infirmary. As result of this, I missed many classes and I scored very poorly in three subjects.

I have now picked up health and have requested my teachers to give me some extra assignments. I also plan to do group study with some of the other boarders of my class.

I am sure that this will help me to catch up with my studies and I promise you I will score much better marks in the next unit tests.

Please do not be worried about my health, I am much better. I look forward to meeting you during the mid-term break. ← Body of the letter

Yours lovingly, / Yours affectionately, / Your loving son,
Sanjiv ← Subscription and Signature

Standard Formats

In chapters like Letter Writing, Notice & E-mail Writing standard formats prescribed by ICSE are given. This will help students to learn proper format of each writing task.

Dream, Believe, Achieve

Insights from ICSE Toppers

"Board exams are way easier than you think. It's easy to score if you study regularly for even an hour. Consistency is key,"

DIVYANSH AGARWAL

ICSE Topper (99.40%)

He dedicated time to solving topic-wise papers from the last 10 years, providing valuable practice before his final revision. A planned approach and schedule help to prepare and cover the syllabus better.

ANONDEE SAHA

ICSE Topper (99.6%)

Before the boards, my school had given all students a month to study and I tried my best to study 8-9 hours every day.

I relied on revising the syllabus of each subject at least twice during this period and went through past years' question papers and extra questions that my teachers had sent.

For excelling in the boards I would like to advice students to study regularly from DAY 1. They should refer to previous years Board question papers and should always have a positive attitude and should be confident. But not overconfident

MUSKAN PATHAN

ICSE Topper (99.4%)

"I studied everything independently, which gave me a better understanding of what topics I needed to improve. I studied only 1.5 to 2 hours daily but stayed consistent and regular,"

MIHIKA SANJANWALA

ICSE Topper (99%)

NILOTMA SINGH

ICSE Topper (99.6%)

"I had started preparing, chapter by chapter, right from the beginning of the academic session as we had weekly tests on every topic that was covered in class. However, the hard-core preparation started only in late November 2022 which was about three months prior to the board examination.,"

Previous Years Papers guide me to a great extent as they helped me understand the scope and area of the questions that could be asked. The specimen papers were extremely helpful as we had undergone a change in examination pattern this year.

"While my primary schooling in Shanghai (China) taught me to be a global citizen, my higher secondary schooling at Greenwood High (Bannerghatta) elevated my inquisitiveness and curiosity on various subjects,"

"Personally, POMODORO technique, a time-management method based on 25-minute stretches of focused work broken by five-minute breaks, helped me immensely not only to organise myself better but also to cover a vast syllabus with the least fatigue,"

SHIVANI NEELAMRAJU

ICSE Topper (99.40%)

Please Note that all the information given here is collected from different websites.

Contents

ICSE Chapterwise Solved Papers 2025-2005

PAPER -1 LANGUAGE

Latest Syllabus

Class XII (2025-26)

PAPER I LANGUAGE 80 Marks

All questions will be compulsory.

Question 1 Candidates will be required to write a composition of about 300–350 words from a choice of subjects which will test their ability to: organise, describe, narrate, report, explain, persuade or argue, present ideas coherently with accuracy and precision, compare and contrast ideas and arrive at conclusions, present relevant arguments and use correct style and format.

The topics will be varied and may be suggested by language or by other stimuli such as pictures. The subjects will be so chosen so as to allow the candidates to draw on first-hand experience or to stimulate their imagination.

The organisation of subject matter, syntax, punctuation, correctness of grammatical constructions and spelling will be expected to be appropriate to the mode of treatment required by the subject.

Question 2 Candidates will have to write a letter from a choice of two subjects requiring either a formal or an informal mode of treatment. Suggestions regarding the content of the letter may be given. The layout of the letter with address, introduction, conclusion, etc., will form part of the assessment. Special attention must be paid to the format of the letter with emphasis on vocabulary appropriate to the context.

Question 3 Candidates will be given a specific situation and will be required to

(a) Write the text for a notice based on given directions.

(b) Write an e-mail on the same content as the notice.

Question 4 An unseen prose passage of about 500 words will be given. Uncommon items of vocabulary or structure will be avoided. A question will be set to test vocabulary. Candidates will be required to show an understanding of the words/phrases in the context in which they have been used.

A number of questions requiring short answers will also be asked on the passage. These questions will test the candidates' ability to comprehend the explicit content and organisation of the passage and to infer information, intention and attitude from it.

The last question will consist of a summary that will test the candidates' ability to distinguish main ideas from supporting details and to extract salient points to re-write them in the form of a summary. Candidates will be given clear indications of what they are to summarise and of the length of the summary.

Question 5 There will be a number of short answer questions to test the candidates' knowledge of functional grammar, structure and use of the language.

All the items in this question will be compulsory. They will consist of correct use of prepositions, verbs and transformation of sentences.

ICSE
CHAPTERWISE SOLVED PAPERS

01

Short Story

Story writing is a creative but difficult art of composition. It requires a lot of innovative thinking, planning and mastery of narrative skills and language. A short story is a narrative of moderate length that revolves around a single incident involving one or more characters. It must have a proper beginning, middle and an end. A story needs to be well-planned and written in an interesting manner.

Steps to Write a Short Story

There are no specific rules for writing a story but there are countless ways to create an interesting one. However, the writer should keep the following steps in mind while writing a short story.

- To write an interesting story, the writer must think like the central character to catch their emotions and qualities.
- As a story is a short description of any scene or incident, the details should be mentioned creatively to develop readers' interest.
- While building the plot of the story, the writer should make sure that the sequence of events is proper, to avoid confusion and complexity.
- A very important part of the story is an apt ending to add significance to it. A justified climax is an unsaid expectation of the readers.

Points to be Kept in Mind While Writing a Story

- Before writing, concentrate on the outline of the story.
- Story should be written in an easy and comprehensible language.
- The style of writing should be lucid and logical.
- Events should be chronologically organised in the story.
- Write the story in past tense. However, as per the requirement, present or future tense can also be used.
- Focus should be only on the incident.
- Add a twist to your story to keep the reader's interest.
- Consequences/climax of the story should be clear and satisfying.

PYQs Previous Years' Questions

1. Write an original short story in which two children and their school teacher are the main character. ***ICSE 2023***

Ans. **The Best Friends**

Ramu and Suresh were really good friends. They had been classmates since they started school and loved to create mischief. They always pranked teachers but their pranks never hurt anyone. Though they were pranksters of the school, they were loved by all. One could find them playing sports in the field, working on projects together and even participating in debates taking opposite stands.

Once their English Teacher Mr. Sullivan had read the poem 'The Tale of Custard the Dragon' in the class and started a discussion on bravery. The discussion was healthy till a classmate stated that Suresh was not as brave as he showed and told the class that Suresh was sacred of lightening. Suresh who was sitting quietly got upset when Ramu did not defend him. He asked Ramu to do the same but Ramu did not say a word. Thus, it led to a fight between the best friends.

Mr. Sullivan got worried for he did not want the best friends to fight over something as trivial as this. So, he called the boys and explained the situation to them but in vain. The boys did not even want to talk to each other. So, Mr. Sullivan decided to play a small prank on the boys to prove his statement. He called the boys to the restricted part of their Convent School which was claimed to be haunted.

When the boys reached the area, the door of the room closed and strange sounds came from the room. The boys were scared and started beating the door so someone could hear them. But no one came to help them. They even looked out to find a way to escape the haunted room and saw a window with a broken pane. Together, they rushed towards it and helped each other escape the room. When they were finally out of the room, they hugged each other for both of them were safe. Outside, they saw Mr. Sullivan who was standing with a smile. He told the boys about his plan to reunite them and explained that Ramu had requested him for the discussion so that Suresh learns to defend himself and be bold. Ramu told Suresh how he had heard someone call Suresh a wimp and wanted Suresh to prove them wrong. Suresh easily understood Ramu's explanation and apologised for starting the fight.

2. Write an original short story entitled: 'Lost and Found'. ***ICSE Specimen Paper 2023, 2019; ICSE 2011***

Ans. **Lost and Found**

This happened around the time when I was in the fifth grade. My 13th birthday had arrived and I was ecstatic. My father gave me a new bicycle as a gift. I was very happy to see it. I spent the entire day on it, going to different places. I showed it to all of my friends. They also wanted to ride my bicycle. Once, I drove it to a park nearby. I had a great deal of fun there. In my overjoyed state, I forgot to bring my bicycle home.

When I arrived at my house, I went for a walk with my friends. It is then that I realised that I'd forgotten my bicycle in the park. It had been a long night. I was taken aback. I wondered whether or not to inform my father. I came to the conclusion that if I told him, he would scold me. I also knew that we won't find it that late in the evening.

When I came home, I discovered that my father already knew about my lost bicycle. I couldn't figure out how he knew that it wasn't in the garage. He became enraged and demanded to know where my bicycle was. There was nothing I could do. I told him what had happened and how I had mistakenly left it at the park. His anger only grew on hearing that. He continued to scold me. Late after that, I went to sleep and as soon as it was morning, I went to find my bicycle.

I went to my friends' house and asked for their help. They agreed to help me and said that we should check in the park first. They accompanied me but my bicycle was nowhere to be found. I was afraid that it had been stolen. But, I reasoned to try harder. I inquired of the park's guard if he had seen any green bicycle. He stated that he had found a bicycle there the day before and had kept it in a secure location.

I was overjoyed and went to get it. Soon, I returned home after thanking the guard and showed it to my father. We were both overjoyed. Now, I think a thousand times before leaving my bicycle anywhere. That day, I realised the true worth of my bicycle.

3. Imagine a situation where a child runs away from home but later returns. Why did he or she run away? What made him/her come back? Write an original short story entitled: 'Finding My Way Home'.
ICSE Specimen 2022 Sem II

Ans. **Finding My Way Home**

Freedom and space are two important parts of any teenager's life. We crave it and when we get it, we retaliate. That is exactly what Ramya did about a year ago when she decided to flee, from her home at the age of 14. Ramya's decision was not sudden. It has a reason- her parents' constant nagging. Her mother had always interfered in her life. She had to know where Ramya had been all day, who she was with, what she did and so on. The nagging nature was so overwhelming that Ramya needed her approval for everything. Her father didn't fare any better. He was often nodding his head in agreement with whatever she said and Ramya hated it.

She needed space but her mother refused to give it to her. One day, fed up of her mother's nagging, she thought that she should flee. She had about two thousand rupees, so hurriedly she put her things in a bag. She left for school the next day but arrived at the bus station unsure of where she was heading. She decided to visit her ancestral village, which was a 100 kilometres away from Delhi. She had never ridden a local bus alone before but she got a ticket and ascended the vehicle slowly. After three hours of journey, the bus reached its destination but Ramya could not recognise it. She had visited the village 2 months back and depended on her memory to go her grandparents' home.

She decided to look out for a friendly face to get some help. However, she found none. So, she sat down and started crying. Suddenly, an old gentleman came and sat next to her. After some time, he asked Ramya if she was okay and what the matter was. Ramya told him everything and the man advised her to return to her parents. He suggested that Ramya tell her parents how she feels and that they would listen to her because parents are their children's sole well-wishers. Ramya realised how reckless she had been in running away and decided to go back.

Soon, with the help of the gentleman, she returned home. When she reached her home, she found her parents were crying. They were surrounded by the police and the neighbours. When Ramya made her presence known, her mother ran to her and hugged her. Ramya also started crying and told everyone the matter. She, then, apologised and promised to never do it again.

4. Write a short story in which the main characters are an old woman, a small child and a little puppy.
ICSE 2021 Sem II

Ans. **The Lost Puppy**

A little girl named Sophie found a puppy near a tree when she was going back to home from school. The puppy looked weak and was afraid of people passing by. She went close to him but he stepped back. He tried to hide behind the tree. Seeing this, Sophie took out a water bottle and a packet of biscuits from her bag and offered them to the puppy. Hesitantly, the puppy came out and sniffed the biscuits, sensing no danger, he hungrily ate the biscuits and drank the water. Meanwhile, Sophie was gently petting the puppy who seemed to like it as he started wagging his tail. When Sophie realised that the puppy was not scared, she inspected him for injuries. She found that his leg had a huge cut and so she took him to the nearby veterinary clinic and got him medicines and band aids.

While inspecting the puppy, Sophie had also noticed that he wore a collar indicating that he was someone's pet. However, she could not find the name of the owner on it. So, she decided to look for the puppy's owner herself.

She went to nearby homes but to no avail. Since no one was there to look after the puppy, she decided to take him home.

On reaching home, she gave him a bath, cleaned him thoroughly and put medicine on his injury. Meanwhile, she also put up an advertisement in the locality so that Tabby, the name she had given to the puppy, could be found by real owner. After a few days of advertisement, an old lady came up to Sophie and told her that she was the owner of Tabby. The lady told her that she went out for a couple of days and left her puppy with the neighbours. But he ran from their house and ended up meeting Sophie. Tabby also started licking the lady's face and wagged his tails in excitement. Seeing this, Sophie was sure that Tabby belonged to the lady. He happily his away with her. Sophie would visit the old lady's house whenever she missed him.

5. Write an original short story entitled 'The Secret'.
ICSE 2020

Ans. **The Secret**

Rohan was a fun-loving teenager. He was fourteen years old and a student of eighth standard in a reputed school. His happy family included his parents and his seven-year-old sister, Rhea. His father was a doctor and mother was a homemaker. One day, Rohan found a diary in their storeroom while playing with his sister. The diary had an attractive leather cover with golden border. He took it and kept it with his books. The next day, Rohan opened the diary and found that it was an secret old diary that belonged to his mother. He started reading it. It contained beautiful descriptions of his mother's childhood, her village, ancestral home, etc. Next, he found the description of the marriage ceremony of his parents and their new life. But the real surprise still waited for him. After few pages, it was written that he was the adopted child of his parents. They adopted him from an orphanage five years into their marriage. This secret left him absolutely shattered. He felt betrayed and ran away from home immediately.

Rohan roamed for many hours. Being exhausted, he sat on a bench in a park. There, he saw an old lady coming with a large tiffin-box. She distributed puri-aloo to all poor children. All the children called her 'Amma' (mother). After finishing their meal, they started reading. Looking at those children, Rohan got into thinking about his parents, how they treated him and fulfilled all his demand. He realised that his parents loved him unconditionally. They never differentiated between him and his sister, who was their biological child. He realised his mistake and returned home. His anxious mother asked him where he had gone for such a longtime. He replied that he was very busy with his cricket match and forgot the timing. She served his favourite meal Rajma-chawal. Rohan realised it was his real home and decided that he would never think about the 'secret' anymore.

Examiner's Comment

- Many candidates failed to understand the meaning of 'original' in the given topic. Some candidates indulged in plagiarism and lifted the story 'Hearts and Hands' in entirety from the short stories.
- Most students ignored the essential elements of a short story, which are plot-structure, sequence, setting, characters and dialogues. In some cases, the secret was immediately revealed and the element of shock/ surprise was missing.

Suggestion for Students

Understand the distinction between original and lifted stories and insist on originality. Learn about the elements of a short story and plot structure.

6. Write an original short story in which two children and their grandfather are the main characters.

ICSE 2019

Ans. **What Sarita Did with Grandfather's Coins**

Every month, Sarita and her younger cousins would go for Sunday lunch at their grandparents' house. The children would always wait excitedly for the moment their grandfather would give them a few coins, so that they could buy something for themselves. Then, all the children would run off to buy chewing gum, ice cream or potato chips. The adults in the family felt that the children would never learn to manage their money. So, they told the children that they would have to show, over a period of one year, just what they could manage to get with those few coins.

The two smallest children paid no attention to this and continued spending the coins on sweets. However, Ajit, all of ten years old, had a will of iron. He saved all the coins he was given. At the end of the year he had collected more money than anyone. He won the competition hands down. His cousins learnt from him the advantages of knowing how to save and be patient.

The eldest cousin was 12-year-old Sarita. Poor Sarita didn't enjoy the end of the competition because even though she had had a wonderful secret plan, she had spent her money without giving her plan enough time to work. But that didn't stop her from continuing with her plan.

When she was about to complete the second year of her plan, Sarita surprised everyone by turning up at her grandparents' house with a guitar and a lot of money. Her playing was even more impressive. She played the guitar really well.

Then, Sarita told everyone how she did it. She had got to know a poor guitarist who played in the park. She offered him all the coins her grandfather had given her, if he would teach her how to play. On seeing Sarita's excitement, the guitarist agreed and taught her happily for months. Then, the guitarist loaned her a guitar so they could play together in the park, as a duo. They were so successful that gradually she managed to buy her own guitar.

Sarita would always tell people how it was possible, with just a few coins well spent, to make your wildest dreams a reality.

Examiner's Comment

- Most candidates ignored the essential requirements of a short story, which are plot-structure, sequence, setting, characters, dialogues.
- Some students found it difficult to link the question with the story. Many failed to understand the meaning of 'original'.
- Some indulged in plagiarism and wrote in entirety the story- 'After Blenheim' from poetry.

Suggestions for Students

- Be original. Do not lift stories from textbooks, movies, poetry, etc.
- Focus on the importance of writing original story in every short story writing practice session.
- Understand Plot structure.

7. Write an original short story entitled 'The Gift'. *ICSE 2018*

Ans. **The Gift**

The series of events that I will narrate today has been taken from the immediate past of my very own life. The story begins about two months ago when I had given the final exams for my degree in computers. I would become a graduate in about two-month time when the results would be declared. After this, my father wanted me to take over the business of our family's computer sales and service showroom as he wanted to retire and live a peaceful life. In addition, my birthday was also coming up soon for which I knew what I wanted.

For a few weeks, I had been admiring a new model of a Royal Enfield Bullet bike in a dealer's showroom. I had told my father that it was all I wanted for my 21st birthday. On the morning of my birthday, my father called me into his office in the computer showroom. He first wished me a happy birthday and then told me how much he loved me. He opened his desk drawer, picked up a gift wrapped rectangular box and presented it to me. Curious, but somewhat disappointed, I opened the box and found a leather-bound Bhagwad Gita in it. I got very angry at him so I blurted out, "With all your money, you gave me such a book!" Then, I decided to start my own business and stormed out of the house, leaving the gift on his desk.

I went to live with one of my close friends who was staying in an independent flat. After the final exams, I started looking for a job while awaiting my result. However, after a month, I got a call stating that my father had suffered a heart attack and was hospitalised. I rushed to the hospital but it was too late. He had passed away.

Soon, our family lawyer phoned and told me that in his will, my father had left me all his possessions including ownership of our computer business. With a heavy heart, I went through his papers and soon found gift wrapped the Bhagwad Gita he had given me. In tears, I opened the packing and began to turn the pages. Suddenly, a key taped to a small envelope dropped from the book. It had a tag with the dealer's name, the same dealer in whose showroom I had seen the bike I wanted. On the tag was the date of my birthday and the words 'Paid in full'.

Examiner's Comment

- Some candidates wrote in a narrative form even though the question asked for an original short story. Ideas were borrowed form movies and books.
- Some of them wrote about 'nature' and 'life' as gifts. In many cases, the direct impact of the gift on the receiver was missing.
- Some students got distracted and shifted their focus to describing the gift.

Suggestion for Students

- Developing reading habit to improve vocabulary.
- Differentiating between a story and a narrative.

8. Write an original short story that begins with the words: ''It was raining hard that night. In my hurry to get into the house, I didn't notice the black car parked across the road. I realised something was wrong when.........'' *ICSE 2017*

Ans. **A Pleasant Surprise**

It was raining hard that night. In a hurry to get into the house, I didn't notice the black car parked across the road. I realised something was wrong when I heard strange muffled voices coming from inside the car. Was I being followed? Were there some robbers sitting inside that car ready to rob any one of the houses or what was it? Who exactly was sitting in the car and why were they parked here?

I was really terrified when suddenly I saw a man all dressed in black getting out of that car. While I was trying to observe him, he started walking towards me. "He must've noticed me", I thought while I was shivering from the chill in the rain and most probably because I was wet. As soon as I tried to ring the bell of the house, that man called out, 'Excuse me.'

I was terrified at that man's call and wanted to run away but could not. The man asked me if I knew a mechanic nearby as he was a stranger to this city and was heading towards Delhi, where his mother was admitted in a hospital. I was still not sure whether I should trust that man but, at the same time, my father opened the door as I had rung the bell.

I just decided to go inside the house when my father happened to have a glance at that stranger. Suddenly, my father screamed with excitement, "Oh Shreekant! How come you are here? You had disappeared suddenly." That man looked at my father and came running towards him and screamed "Oh Pulkit, is this your house? Are you settled in this city?" My father replied him in affirmation and further asked him to come inside as the weather was really bad. I was totally confused as I didn't know the stranger and my father was asking him to come inside. My father introduced me to that man, who was his class fellow some 22 years back.After finishing college, they had not been in touch with each other. My father was really excited meeting his old class fellow. he called a mechanic to get his car repaired and invited him to stay and rest till the rain got over. So, initially what was scary for me, turned out to be a pleasant surprise for my father.

9. Write an original short story which illustrates the truth of the statement 'One lie leads to another'.

ICSE Specimen Paper 2017

Ans. Saira was a sixteen-year-old girl belonging to a middle class family. She went to a really expensive private school as she was smart in academics. She were friends with many rich students but her best friend was Anna, who was very good at studies and was also interested in extra-curricular activities. Besides studies, she talked to Saira about fashion, jewellery, concerts and parties, etc. Although Saira was not really interested in these things before, hearing about them made her want to do all the things that Anna did. One day, Anna told her that she was going to The Towers with some friends and asked her to join them. Saira knew that her parents would never allow her to go with Anna but she really wanted to have fun so she decided to go with them.

Next day, Saira told her mother that she would be late from school as there was an extra class and took some money from the college savings. She felt uneasy about lying to her parents but forgot all about it soon. When her parents asked her about the extra class, she again lied that she had been working on a project with her science teacher.

After some days, Anna again asked her to join them somewhere and Saira agreed. And thus, these excuses continued. As a result, her studies were affected while her college savings were getting reduced.

One day when Saira's mother was cleaning her cupboard, she noticed that the money Saira had saved for college had reduced significantly. When she asked Saira about it, the latter got afraid. She did not want her mother to find out that she goes out with Anna. So, she lied and said she did not know about it.

Her mother started scolding their maid thinking that she was the culprit. The maid was terrified and started crying which made Saira feel guilty. She was frightened but she also wanted to save the innocent maid so she decided to lie yet again. She told her mother that she had taken the money to buy some books. Her mother was surprised and doubtful. So, she asked Saira to show her the books but Saira couldn't.

Finally realising that she cannot escape the situation, Saira told her mother everything. Her mother got angry and scolded Saira. She decided to take the rest of the saved money so that Siara could not spend it recklessly. She also told Saira that she wasn't allowed to stay back in school until her teacher informs her of the same. Saira realised that her one lie led to several others that she had lost the trust that her mother reposed in her. She promised that she would never lie again and apologised to her mother.

10. Write an original short story that begins with the words : "The day started off well enough, whoever thought it would ...."

ICSE 2016

Ans. The day started off well enough, whoever thought it would end otherwise. We were going to Mumbai to spend one week with my elder sister who is settled there. We had booked the plane tickets in advance. My younger sister and myself were very happy and excited to meet her for not only were we meeting her after three years but also she was expecting her first child. Finally, the flight time approached and the formalities were completed. We were just about to board the plane when a loud announcement terrified us. "All passengers about to board Indigo flight 753 should immediately deboard and gather in the waiting hall. The flight is cancelled". The announcement was repeated many times. We were all very shocked, disappointed and somewhat enraged. I, along with my sister, came down in the hall and sat in a corner chair.

It was 11p.m. and I could see the dark airport road outside. I was thinking of my mother's premonition that it would be an unlucky hour for a journey. As I was so excited about the Mumbai trip, I never paid any attention to my mother's words. Suddenly, an old lady came rushing and said that a time bomb had been found and some terrorists were suspected to be inside the airport. We all were very scared and prayed for our safety. Suddenly, there was a commotion as security personnel were seen running after someone. As the person was running with great speed, they were not able to apprehend the suspect terrorist.

He was holding a gun in his hand and as he passed the hall he started shooting randomly. An old lady who could not move or act very fast became his first victim. I was very terrified but kept my cool. As the terrorist was shooting and running, it became very difficult to catch him. Suddenly, I had an idea. I bent down and slowly started crawling towards the terrorist. As his back was turned towards me, I gestured to the security personnel to come closer.

Still bent down, I pushed him hard in the legs, his gun fell down and immediately he was overpowered by two security personnel. He was very angry and tried to catch hold of me but before he could do anything he was captured and taken to a secret place where they would interrogate him. I was surrounded by people in the hall who congratulated for my presence of mind and courage. As our flight was cancelled and we were too terrified to travel the next day, we decided to return home. I had been so excited that morning but never knew the breathtaking adventure I would go through by the end of the day.

11. Write an original story that begins with the words "He was the funniest boy I had ever met. He would make everyone laugh .... " ***ICSE 2015***

Ans. He was the funniest boy I had ever met. He would make everyone laugh even in the most trying times. Blessed with great humour, Varun was one of the most wanted person in our parties for he could make everyone forget their worries. No amount of sadness could dampen his spirit.

I remember once when the three of us friends including Varun had failed the chemistry exam badly. Our parents had been called and we were told that most certainly we would have to repeat a year. That was a very hard time, but even then no look of worry could be spotted on Varun's face or in his behaviour. His cheer was undiminished even when his father suffered a major financial loss in business. Even during that time, Varun was known to spread cheer around. He always pushed his worries to the backseat and dedicated himself towards making others happy.

However, the loss of his pet dog Veeto, some months ago, immersed him in grief. That was the only time that robbed him of his smiling face. For days, he did not speak to anyone and shut himself up in his room. We could not see him like that so all of us friends decided to do something to dispel his gloom.

One day, we all went to his place and rang the doorbell of his house. There we kept a little box, slightly open from one side and hid ourselves so that he could not see us. When he opened the door, he was surprised to find no one. He picked up the box with a look of amazement on his face. He took the lid off and there came out a puppy, quite like Veeto. He held him in his hands and started to play with it. It brought the smile back on his face. Then, we all came into his sight and uttered with excitement, 'Surprise!'

Indeed, that little effort from our end, helped Varun come out of his sorrow.

12. Write an original short story that begins with the words: ''It's not my fault'', he shouted .... ***ICSE 2014***

Ans. **Misplacing of Camera**

"It's not my fault", he shouted as he went across to the opposite bank of the river in the boat. He was very annoyed with his friends, who accused him of forgetting the camera at a coffee shop.

He seemed a teenage boy, who came with his friends on a school trip. I came here because this place was a famous tourist spot. It was famous for its water scenery and numerous water sports besides their cultural dances and music. It was really fascinating to see how one could enjoy a whole world of entertainment here.

However, I was curious to know more about that teenage boy. Many questions came in my mind – Whose camera it was? What made him forget the camera? Did he try to find it? Therefore, to settle my curiosity, I enquired about him from the children who came on the same school trip. I came to know that his name was Rohan. He belonged to a middle class family and was passionate about photography. Another child informed me that some of his friends were quite rich. One of his friends brought his camera on the trip. Because Rohan clicked beautiful pictures, his friend gave his camera to him. After every click, Rohan used to return the camera back to his friend, Ankit. But Ankit was very irresponsible. Although, he brought his expensive camera, he did not want to shoulder any responsibility of keeping it safe. After clicking pictures in the coffee shop, Rohan placed the camera in Ankit's hands. Ankit, however, kept it on the table. They sat there for a while and left from there. When they crossed a beautiful temple, they thought of getting some pictures clicked.

It was then that everyone realised that the camera was missing. Ankit and others started blaming Rohan. Rohan felt humiliated and left his group.

I felt pity for Rohan and wanted to help him. I went to the coffee shop and narrated the entire incident. The manager of the coffee shop was a genuine man. He ordered his staff to find the camera. Suddenly, one of the staff members remembered that one of those boys went to the washroom while leaving. The camera was found in the washroom. I took it and returned it to Ankit. He then realised his mistake and apologised to Rohan.

13. Write an original short story that begins with the words: ''In the background, I could hear an awful commotion, men's voices raised and women screaming''. **ICSE 2013**

Ans. **Tremulous Fire**

In the background, I could hear an awful commotion, men's voices raised and women screaming. I was at loss to understand what the matter was. I tried to ignore and sleep. But the voice was too loud to let me sleep peacefully. I was so irritated that I threw my sheet and rushed towards the window. I was aghast to find that thick black clouds of smoke were emanating in the sky. I was sure that something terrible had happened.

The whole scenario was one of chaos and hundreds of people had come out of their homes with buckets full of water. They tried to extinguish the fire, but to no avail. Huge flames of fire from a nearby apartment complex leapt into the sky making the scene look tremulous and terrifying.

I rushed into my parents' room and woke them. They were fast asleep as their room was in the rear. They too were totally bewildered after I gave them the news. We rushed downstairs and joined the crowd which was besirk with shrieks and clamours. While some people were running desperately for water, some fainted due to suffocation.

On enquiring, we came to know that the multi-storeyed building of the complex was caught in a blazing fire due to a short circuit. I could see a lot of smoke rushing out of its many floors but nothing seemed to be clearly visible.

Finally, the fire brigade arrived and many fire fighters rushed to the spot. Water was thrown at a tremendous speed and in a huge quantity. The people trapped were asked to move to one side of the building. Slowly, they all were rescued from the demolishing fire which was ready to swallow each and everyone at sight. Everyone rescued was taken to the hospital immediately for treatment and checkup. Fortunately, no one died.

I have never had such a bewildering experience in my entire life. It was the most devastating and dangerous life experience I witnessed.

14. Write an original short story that begins with the words: "It wasn't going to be easy she knew… but somehow she had to confront him. She took a deep breath and walked into the room". **ICSE 2012**

Ans. **Confessions**

It wasn't going to be easy she knew but somehow she had to confront him. She took a deep breath and walked into the room.

She came across a dark corridor and saw the room as the light came. He was sitting right in front reading newspaper. His back was towards her. She was nervous as she knew why she was called. She also hesitated but somehow she ignored the lump in her throat and called for him.

Dad!

Hearing her voice, he turned towards her and kept the newspaper aside. He was wearing spectacles which he suddenly took out and put on the table. His eyes were somewhat bulging out as though they were supported by the spring and could anytime pop from the sockets. He asked her about her school report card. She kept looking down as she did not have the courage to look him in the eye. He waited for her response but when there was no answer, he lost his calm and shouted with anger. It made the poor girl rattle with fear. Scared, she dropped her report card on the floor hoping her result would pacify her father. She hoped her father would not scold her for her marks.

Her father picked up the report card. As he opened it, he saw that his daughter scored all the marks in nineties. A smile came upon his angry face. His eyes turn towards his daughter who was still trembling with fear. He went towards her and hugged her.

She was aghast at her father's behaviour. Although out of words, she felt the love of her father for her. This was all that she ever desired after the death of her mother.

Two months before her boards, her father made it very clear that she must score full marks in order to get into the best college in the city. But when her result came, her score was 92.5% which was not enough to get her a seat in the best college of the city.

She was scared that her father would be disappointed. Thus, she feared to reveal her marks to her dad. He, however, jumped with excitement as her daughter had worked hard and scored in 90s. A chill ran down her spine and suddenly all the fear disappeared. Now, she could enjoy her result.

15. Write an original short story, beginning with the following lines:
"The water was cold. I took a deep breath and jumped...". *ICSE 2010*

Ans. **Irrevocable Mistake**

The water was cold. I took a deep breath and jumped. There was no alternative left. The police was very close. It was a very complicated case. I wished I hadn't broken into this mad run. I wish I would have had the courage to stay back and explain that it was not me who killed that boy. But then who was listening? Did the Sub Inspector have patience to listen to me? As I tried to swim across the ice-cold water, needles of shivering cold darted across my limbs. If I stayed too long in the water, I would freeze.

It all began just a week ago. A new student entered the college. He wanted to join our group. Being seniors, we took it as an opportunity to make him do odd things. Although ragging was totally banned in the college, we did not obey the rules and wanted to have some fun.

We asked the new boy to meet us near an old fort late in the night. The fort was near the highway and not many people went there. Infact, it was popular for its horror stories. The new boy, Raman, was from a different city and did not know much about the fort. When we reached the fort, it was already 12:30 am. Raman was waiting for us all alone. He was looking so pale as if he had seen a ghost.

We went towards him and explained his task to him. The fort had a huge water compound. He was instructed to climb up the steps and jump into the water compound. His passive reaction and unwillingness spoilt our plan. So, I climbed with him up the steps and assured him that I will jump with him. He was still reluctant. I convinced him that we all have done this many times.

As we were about to jump, I stepped backward and he jumped alone. We all enjoyed the scene and bursted into peels of laughter. But soon our laughter gave way to panic. We saw Raman's body floating on the water. No sooner had we rushed to pull him out, than we could hear the blaring of police sirens.

The police was on its usual patrolling and saw my friends rushing out in panic from the fort. I was caught holding the boy. I trembled with fear as the police began to approach me. I broke into a run. I ran as fast as my legs could carry me, not stopping, not thinking. But now, I have crossed the river and run safely on the other side of the river bank. I have now decided to go to the nearest police station and tell them the truth, the whole incident as it actually happened. I am sure that nothing but the truth will set me free.

16. Write a short story entitled : 'Escaped'. *ICSE 2009*

Ans. **Escaped**

John wanted to escape from the world. He had nobody in the world. One day, he went to the city to get some food. On his way, he shot 16 zombies who wanted to attack him. Then he saw a girl who was being followed by a zombie. When she saw him, her eyes glanced. There was hope in her eyes. John shot zombie that was following the girl. She got scared. He stopped the car and the girl ran to him. John took her home. Her name was Jane. She had lost her whole family to the zombies. But, now she felt safe with John. One day, John went to the forest but while he was coming home to the farm, he saw thousands of zombies at the farm. He ran as fast as he could but he couldn't help it anymore.

The zombies had got Jane. He screamed and cried. His new found hope was gone as he lost Jane in the zombie invasion. The zombies got attentive because of John's screams. But, his eyes were closed. He opened them when he heard some strange noises in front of him. He saw all the zombies coming towards him. He ran to his car and turned on the engine. He drove away from the farm, crying. After hours of driving, he didn't know where he was. He drove along a lonely highway. Every hundred metres, there were some crashed cars with dead persons or zombies. He knew he was lost.

After days of only driving around he stopped the car on the highway. He took his gun and held it to his head. His eyes hurt and were red. There was no other way to escape the zombies. He lost his only hope and he had no food for days and as a result, he began to get crazy and started conversations with himself.

He pulled the trigger. A loud noise came out of the gun and he escaped the world. He took his life, when he was only two miles from the military base where he could have been safe with other people who gave up on their hope. But, he didn't make it and escaped his life.

17. Write a short story in which twin siblings and the school bully are the main characters. ***ICSE 2008***

Ans. **Tears of Repentance**

Rachael and Riya were ten-year old twin sisters who looked exactly like each other. It was hard to tell them apart. Blessed with good looks and beautiful curls, they had wonderful hearts which any parent would feel proud of. They were known for their kind words and good deeds. Further, they always carried million dollar smiles on their innocent and beautiful faces. In short, the twins were loved by one and all.

Also known to everyone in the school was Jack—the school bully. Rudeness, disrespect, tormenting and teasing other students were his quality traits. He had a little band of supporters to boot. Sly by nature, he always carried out his mischief behind the teacher's backs. Rachael and Riya were a common target. They were subjected to all kinds of comments and ridicule. They bore it all patiently. Not even once did they retort in anger. Jack could not comprehend and endure their behaviour.

As Christmas was around the corner, the teacher asked all the students to indulge themselves in different tasks in order to spread the message of Christmas to others. While some wrote poems on love and peace, some made handmade cards and others packed gifts for their dear ones. Rachael and Riya got busy in decorating the little tree in front of their class. While everyone was doing something, Jack was looking at the twins with malicious intent. He and his supporters were all chuckles while the duo were at work. The twins went about their task assiduously, smiling and humming carols. From their teacher to the headmaster, everyone applauded their effort.

Jack, like a hawk, was waiting to swoop down and seize the opportunity to destroy the twins' labour of love. He could not see everyone praising them. His moment came soon when Rachael and Riya left the Christmas tree on its own. Jack and his gang crawled, unnoticed towards the tree. When they reached close to the tree, Jack thought that it was a pretty ordinary effort on their part.

Seemingly, plain bits of paper, strung up on the boughs. They began to pull off the rolled pieces of paper. However, before tearing them up, Jack thought about opening the rolled paper and see what was written. On one of those many bits of paper was written – "Happy Christmas Jack. We love you. Jesus loves you too. God bless, Rachael and Riya."

Jack's heart melted. Tears of repentance began to flow down his cheeks. He quickly rushed off to the twins and apologised to them for all his mischiefs.

18. Relate an incident or write a short story which has as its central idea 'Advice not Taken'. ***ICSE 2007***

Ans. **Advice not Taken**

The ability to make effective decisions is a fundamental requirement for both professional success and personal happiness. A teenager is restless, keen to learn, willing to try new flavours of life and finally, aggressive in behaviour. As a teenager, we feel that our decisions are right and perfect and so we do not prefer to listen to advice of our elders.

Teenagers are friendly and so am I. I would prefer to be in a park with all my friends than in Mauritius with my family. Once, my friends and I decided to go out and watch a movie at PVR. On the other hand, there was a family function that day. I asked my mother if I could go out with my friends that day and the clear and obvious answer was, No! "How can you be out when there is a family event?" she said. I stood hard on my decision and compelled her to stand with it.

The difficult part was over as I had convinced my mother and did not have any pressure of missing the event. Like all mothers, my mother advised me not to go out to crowded places and insisted on carrying a cell phone. We all left earlier than the scheduled time as we decided to roam around and spend some time in the gaming centre. After that, we went to book tickets for the movie. Luckily, we got the tickets of the show and all our seats were in the same row. But, little did we know that our luck would stay with us for a while. Hardly had the movie began, when a group of men barged into the theatre hall and started creating a chaos.

They asked all of us to leave the screening hall. Then, they began damaging the chairs, lights and were creating a rampage. All of us were suddenly taken aback. Some panicked, some rushed out, some stayed in their places and some were confused like us. The exit doors got jammed as all the audience started rushing out. It was almost like a panic scene.

Soon, the police arrived and the situation was under control. They took us aside and made sure that we were safe. They asked us why we had come without our parents and advised us not to go to such places without them. Disappointed, I came home and also felt guilty for not taking my mother's advice. If I had taken my mother's advice, I would not have to go through all this.

19. Write a short story which illustrates the truth of the statement ''Rumour is a Great Traveller''. *ICSE 2006*

Ans. **Rumour is a Great Traveller**

Once upon a time, a hare was resting under a banyan tree in a forest. He had an intuition of doom and thought, "What would happen to me if the earth broke?" Suddenly, he heard a weird striking sound. He said, "It's happened, the earth is breaking up." He jumped up and ran madly without even observing the direction.

When he was running through the forest, another hare saw him and asked, "What happened?" The hare cried, "The earth is breaking up. You better run too." The second hare ran so fast that he overtook the first hare. As they were passing the forest, they shouted, "The earth is breaking up, the earth is breaking up." Very soon, thousand of hares were running through the forest.

On seeing hares running through the forest, the other animals too got frightened. The news spread from one mouth to another and soon everyone came to know that the earth was breaking up. It didn't take much time before all the animals joined the race. All creatures from reptiles, birds, insects to four footed animals, everyone was trying to escape and their cries of fear created chaos all around.

A lion standing on a hill saw all the animals running and thought, "What is the matter?" He ran down the hill rapidly and positioned himself in front of the crowd. He shouted at them, "Stop! Stop!" The powerful presence of the lion curtailed the rising wave of fright among the animals.

A parrot yelled, "The earth is breaking up", alighting on a rock near him. The lion asked, "Who said this?" The parrot replied, "I heard it from the monkeys." When the monkeys were asked, they replied that they had heard it from the tigers. When the tigers were asked it was found that they were informed by the elephants. The elephants told that the buffaloes formed their source. Finally, when the hares were caught up, they pointed one to another until the one who started this menace was recognised.

The lion asked the hare as to what made him think that the earth was breaking up. The hare wavering in fear answered that he heard it cracking. The lion investigated the matter and discovered that the sound that the hare had heard has been caused by a large coconut falling from a tree.

The lion said to all the animals, "Go back to your homes. Next time onwards, confirm a rumour before acting on it."

20. Write an original short story that concludes with the sentence, ''After it was all over, I realised that every cloud has a silver lining''. *ICSE 2005*

Ans. **Every Cloud has a Silver Lining**

"You are under arrest." I looked back and saw the police officer accompanied by his juniors. I was whisked into a car and taken like a high profile criminal. The car stopped not in front of the police station but at the Crime Branch Headquarters where the SSP and other senior officers were waiting for me. As I stepped out of the car, newsmen flashed their cameras. There was a chaos. However, I was taken inside a room for interrogation. I was frightened and had no idea about the happenings and was totally disordered.

At last, someone dressed in civil uniform came and started questioning me. "How do you know Dawood? What are your plans?" The questions pouring in caused a more puzzling environment. The police was already issuing statement mentioning the details of how they had trapped Chetan, Dawood's man in Pune. All kinds of stories were circulated within hours. The evening newspaper had splashed my photograph on the front page and every channel worth its name had footage of me as breaking news.

I told him that I was innocent but no one paid any heed to it. I also heard some of the police officials talking about using third degree on me so that I reveal the truth. I was terrified at the thought of it. But, the truth was that I was innocent and no one wanted to believe that.

After great difficulty, I understood the entire situation. The much talked about criminal, Dawood was sending orders to his counterparts in India. These orders were given on a mobile number which was similar to mine. The police had intercepted some messages and played them for me. I said the voice was not mine. They recorded my voice and sent the record for the audio and voice forensic analysis. Finally, it was proved that the voice was not mine. Then they went into the details of the number again and enquired whether it was 98919XXXXX. I told them that my number was 989981XXXX. Only then they realised their folly.

Eventually, I was allowed to go and all the charges levelled against me were removed. I was also interviewed by many news channels. I became a star overnight. After it was all over, I realised that 'Every cloud has a silver lining'.

02

Debate

A debate is a formal discussion or an argument on a subject on which people have different opinions. It is used as a means of putting your points forward to convince the audience about the point of view. In this type of composition, the person is free to express his/her views by writing either in favour of or against the topic. In Argumentative/Debate composition, the person arrives at a conclusion through reason to persuade the listeners of the speaker's point of view.

The following expressions can be included to enhance your debate to make it more emphatic

- I support the motion whole heartedly
- I strongly oppose the motion
- In my opinion
- I'd like to present my views
- I fail to understand why my worthy opponent feels
- I totally disagree with the view
- Let me explain my point
- My worthy opponent has just pointed out… But I feel
- I reject/submit/sympathise/agree
- It may sound strange but
- My knowledgeable opponent has submitted that

Points to be Kept in Mind While Writing a Debate

- Prepare the debate properly by considering both the positive and negative aspects of the topic.
  Remember you have to write either for or against the topic.
- Make it clear in the beginning whether you are speaking for or against the motion.
- Debate should always have a good introduction to grab the audience's attention and garner their interest in the topic.
- Bridge the gap from opinion to reason.
- Try some examples in support of your view.
- In the end, sum up your opinion.

Format of a Debate

Worthy Chairperson, respected Principal and dear students

Formal Address
Greet the audience.

Today I, Puneet, stand before you to speak against the motion 'Teenagers today are more worldly wise than their parents'.

Against the Motion
Take your stand for or against the motion.

The teenagers knowledge may be significantly more on a particular subject, but with respect to being worldly wise, they are far behind their parents. This is for parents have knowledge blended with years of experience. This makes them more worldly wise then the teenagers, who are on the threshold of life.

Years of experiencing the many ups and downs of life make parents a better judge of human character and nature. They can therefore judge people more accurately and are not waved by superficial factors. On the other hand, teenagers are swayed by superficial, irrelevant factors which may just be a facade and far away from reality.

The information explosion in the print and electronic media, may give more information to teenagers. This however cannot make them more worldly wise then their parents for advice, in important decisions relating to their work or career.

Moreover, teenagers being young are more enthusiastic and optimistic by nature. This is for they have seen the brighter side of life only, being protected from its harsh realities by their parents. They are therefore prone to taking decisions in a haste. Parents on the other hand, being seasoned and cautious, make more rational decisions. They take a balanced view of things as they know the virtue of patience and tolerance. They are therefore in a better position to evaluate options more logically and practically, before arriving at a firm decision.

Besides being optimistic and rash, teenagers have a tendency to follow the dictates of the heart, rather than their mind. They are easily moved by superficial considerations like colour, looks or aesthetic appeal. On the other hand, parents take decisions on merit, with sound time tested logic, using their mind. They are therefore less prone to error.

Arguments against the Motion
- Present your arguments in a sequence.
- Support your claims with facts, statistics, etc.

Thus, teenagers even today are not more worldly wise than their parents. They lack experience and wisdom which comes with age.

Conclusion
It should be dramatic and effective.

Thank you.

Formal Thanks
Don't forget to thank the audience.

PYQs Previous Years' Questions

1. School examinations do not test intelligence. Express your views for or against this statement. ***ICSE 2023***

Ans. **For the Motion**

Evaluation is the key to testing one's academic knowledge and not intelligence.

Good morning to one and all present here. We all know that evaluations or pen-paper examinations have been accepted by everyone as one of the best ways to tests a student's knowledge, understanding and learning. But does it test the practical skills that are required in the world? Does it test a student's presence of mind or precisely state the positives of one's personality?

The answer is no. Hence, I stand in favour of the motion that school examinations do not test intelligence. While success in school examinations may reflect the knowledge and hard-work of a student, it may not necessarily reflect their intelligence levels or their potential. It only tests the factual knowledge that the student learn from books and in classes.

We all agree that each individual is unique in their own way and there is not one particular pattern of defining intelligence. The school examinations, however, do have a particular pattern and those who fit the mould tend to succeed in it. History is full of examples of such individuals who didn't particularly fit in the pattern of school or examinations but went on to become great individuals in their fields. The great Mathematician, Ramanujan, was so fond of Mathematics that he failed most other subjects. Albert Einstein generally didn't like lectures or tests. It would not have been possible for either of them to be considered as intelligent had they been judged based on their examination results only. The complexity and intelligence of their minds is reflected in their groundbreaking theories and research work. It was only when they were allowed to think freely instead of being restricted by the education system that they could achieve their true potential.

It is also important to understand that academic success isn't the only form of human intelligence. Some students are great at other activities like sports or art. These activities involve just as much effort and intelligence as conventional academics and examinations. For example, the strategies involved in playing sports, the detailing required to complete a painting or the imagination required to write a novel are all different forms of intelligence. Hence, the human intelligence cannot be limited to just school examination.

Against the Motion

Evaluation is an essential criteria that tells us the level of learning possessed by a child.

Good morning to one and all present here. We all learn a variety of subjects in our school. But do we check if the child has understood and learnt the basic ideas or concepts that are crucial to life. The answer is examinations. Therefore, I stand against the motion that 'school examinations do not test intelligence.'

While I agree that examination does not completely test a student's intelligence, it cannot state that intelligence and examination have no relation. We know that some students work really hard and do not often get the best results, while some can get top results by working less than others. This kind of a situation shows us that intelligence does have a role in examination.

It is also important to take into consideration that many universities and schools provide scholarship on the basis of the examination results. Some universities also consider the examination scores of a student before accepting them. This helps us understand that examinations can be extremely helpful for teachers to assess the students. Especially because there are generally many students at the same level, it may not be possible for a teacher to individually assess each student. Examinations can help them to find out the students that are able to understand the subject and those who need more help to improve.

It is generally believed that school is helpful to lay the foundation for the things that we do in our future lives. Examinations are important in this regard as they help the students to test how much they learnt from what was taught to them. This can reflect the knowledge, dedication and work put in by a student to their studies and acts as a crucial indicator of their general level of intelligence. Thus, good examination result is a reward that a student receives in return for their effort and speaks volumes about their intelligence.

2. Democracy cannot survive without education. Express your views for or against this statement.

ICSE Specimen 2023, ICSE 2019

Ans. **For the Motion**

Respected judges and my honourable opponents, today, I am here to present my views in favour of the motion 'Democracy cannot survive without education'.

Thomas Jefferson said, "An educated citizenry is a vital requisite for our survival as a free people." In a democracy which is believed to be the best way for realising human rights, one cannot survive without education. Democracy is a form of government in which all the power lies in the hands of the citizens and the representatives chosen by them. But, its true realisation can only come with proper education.

The total adult literacy rate around the world in 2010 was 84.1%. This means that there were nearly 785 million illiterate adults in the world. This kind of ignorance and lack of knowledge can be very harmful, especially considering the number. For instance, let us take a look at plebiscites. It asks the voters only one question that can be answered only with a 'yes' or 'no'. Will every voter be aware of the possible consequences of their choice for the whole nation? How can they make informed decision? It is only possible to make a serious decision like this when every single voter is properly educated.

Education should be provided right from childhood because without it, a person's ignorance and vices would cost the nation dearly, creating a need to correct them later on in life. On the contrary, if children are educated, they would imbibe virtues which would enable them to contribute as responsible citizens to their nation. They would be able to make correct choices for the country. Along with providing children with the right information, it will also teach them honesty and integrity and for a democracy to prosper, it needs people with truth and integrity in all the departments.

Thus, the key to a rich, progressive country is not democracy in itself, but proper and informative education. An ignorant crowd, if given the right to choose from a number of options, can inflict more damage to the state than a well-educated monarch or dictator.

Against the Motion

Respected judges and my honourable opponents, today, I am here to present my views against the motion 'Democracy cannot survive without education'.

Imagine the ancient Greek Democracy which only considered its citizens to be Athenian men of age, thus excluding everyone who was not Athenian. Now, compare it with today's democracy, where everyone has a right to vote and get represented as a candidate to fight in the elections. During those days, great thinkers like Aristotle and Plato thought about educating the masses by educating their mind and in this way, giving them power through education. For this, they had to democratise the government.

Democracy is a process which took time to reach its goal of equality and even now we have not achieved it, though we are closer to it. For this purpose, we have to be educated enough to understand the political structure of our government. I do agree with this fact. But, this does not apply to the Indian Democracy, where political literacy matters, but education might not.

How can we judge a politician by their educational qualifications? There have been many great leaders who were uneducated but did fantastic work for the country and the Indian people has succeeded in recognising them. Take, for instance, the current Prime Minister of India. Mr. Modi, though not highly educated, has proven to be a great and capable leader. He is the person India chose for two consecutive elections to be the nation's Prime Minister. He has proven to be a far-sighted visionary who has worked to improve the Indian economic growth globally. And, he was chosen by the masses of India. Several people, both educated and uneducated, vote to choose him as the leader of the country. They did so because they realised his potential, through his past works and his tenure as the Chief Minister of Gujarat.

So, according to me, though education helps in making wise decisions, democracy itself can survive without education. If a person is hard working, simple, honest, devoted to his service and has a far-sighted vision of future, then democracy also will outshine without education.

3. "More learning happens outside the classroom than inside it.''

Express your views either for or against this statement. ***ICSE 2022 Sem II***

Ans. **For the Motion**

Learning cannot be simply equated to marks, grades, degree or job. It is a life-long process. Good morning to one and all present here. We all agree that getting a good education is just a key to enter the society. It does not ensure success in our lives. To be successful, we must experience the world outside the classroom as school days are just a small chapter in our lives. We learn the realities of life only when we enter the society. Thus, I agree with the motion "More learning happens outside the classroom than inside it."

Learning is the primary as well as one of the most important things we do in life. It starts pretty much when we're born. In fact, many say learning begins even earlier. An unborn baby listens to the outside sounds and gets used to the different patterns of intonation. This is when we first start learning a language. As soon as a child is born, he/she spends time doing nothing but learning. He/She learns from family and the society as well as school books. While school books teach formal and factual things, it is the world outside that teaches a child the best ways of life.

Education in a classroom is like petrol to a car, whereas education outside is like the engine with propels the car forward through the boulevard of life. Hands-on learning and community involvement often allow young minds to expand their horizons and explore topics that are not offered in school. Learning outside the classroom can help raise achievement, improve classroom behaviour and improve the engagement of students, including those who are hard to engage in the classroom environment. In a classroom scenario, the routine is fixed and predictable which spare the students from changes needed to adapt oneself into the world. A student can read about a culture or watch a video about the ocean, but it does not have the same impact as seeing the sculptures and paintings live or enjoying the marvels at an aquarium. This can hold especially true when it comes to learning and experiencing science.

So, in my opinion learning outside the school helps us a lot in our learning style. Although, people learn in different ways, I'm sure that they will learn much faster when they experience from outside world. Schools are just the microcosm of the real world, as the real world is bigger and more diverse.

Against the Motion

Good morning to one and all present here- Today, I will present my views against the statement "More learning happens outside the classroom than inside it". Learning is arguably the most important activities that human beings engage in. It is through learning that we are able to acquire new knowledge and skills. It can therefore be said that learning is integral for the development of the society. Due to the importance of learning, many societies have come up with formal institutes where learning takes place. These institutes include schools where students attend and gain information on a wide variety of subjects.

Students can interact with one another when they learn in a classroom setting. All students are learning and teaching others at the same time. All of the experience outside starts with the classroom. Students can build on each other's ideas and produce better final results. In addition to this, students are more motivated to learn when other individuals who are also engaged in the same learning surround them. But when children learn outside the classroom, they may remain deprived of this experience and end up learning alone. Learning outside the classroom can surely give them new experiences but those experiences can be both positive and negative for which students may not be prepared to handle.

Contact with the teacher in classroom learning leads to better learning outcomes for the student. Teachers are a very important part of the learning process since they act as informative guides and make children disciplined. Interaction with the teacher also increases the concentration level of the individual. Students have to learn on their own outside the classroom. No one is there to guide them and make them learn the importance of discipline in life to become successful.

Learning requires a significant amount of time to be dedicated to the activity. Classroom learning is well-structured and the teacher has a program of what the students should learn. This is not the case with leaning outside the classroom. There are no prepared schedules and life teaches lessons in its way. Although we gain a lot of knowledge outside the classroom, this knowledge can only be implemented due to what we learn inside the classroom. Therefore, classroom learning can provide in-depth knowledge on how to be prepared for life.

4. Parents can never be friends with their children. Express your views either for or against this statement. ***ICSE Specimen Paper 2022 Sem II***

Ans. **For the Motion**

The first authority figures in our lives are our parents. The primary goal of their lives is to help us grow into the finest versions of ourselves while simultaneously guiding us to accomplish the same for ourselves.

Good morning to one and all present here. Today, I am going to present my views in favour of the motion "Parents can never be friends with their children". The parent-child relationship is a special one. A positive parent-child bond plays a crucial role in raising confident and resilient children. A parent's role is to discipline and guide children. So, while being friends with your child may seem very attractive, numerous studies state that it's really not the best idea for either parent or child.

Parenting is one of the most difficult tasks in the world. It takes a herculean effort to give birth to human beings and mould them so that they are ready for the world. They will always try to provide their child with the best of everything, even if it means sacrificing their own happiness. However, many a times in making sure that their little one is getting the best and becoming the best, parents become an overbearing authority who children are scared of.

A parent-child relationship is an unequal one because parents are in a position of authority, are more knowledgeable and exert more influence than the child. As a result, parents often forget that children have their personality. They perceive their child to be an extension of their own personality and then anticipate their child to grow up to be how they want them to. They impose their own unfulfilled aspirations and ambitions on their children. They forget that their children have the right to their own set of likes, dislikes, ambitions and goals, which they should support as long as the goals are real, honest and positive. Consequently, children are often afraid of being criticised, harmed or misunderstood if they confide in their parents. All of these imply that they are not always able to be friends with their children.

Against the Motion

Whenever we are sad, angry, happy or anxious, we only look for a few people to help support in our life and the first one among these people is our parents.

Good morning respected Principal, teachers and my dear friends. The given statement is true for all of us. Our parents are our safest havens. With our parents, we can disclose all of our anxieties and secrets. Even when we are upset with them, they never leave us alone. And hence, I stand against the motion that parents can never be friends with their children.

Our parents are our first friends with whom we share everything. When we talk to our parents, we find the answer to all of our issues. Through thick and thin, they keep our hands in theirs. The emotional role of the parent is built on love, affection and esteem. It's an essential part of being a parent and it's a beautiful thing to behold. Parental attention is a cure and a tonic to the growing mind in the otherwise tense and tattered social life in today's world.

A parent who is approachable, accessible, and has their kids' best interests at heart grow a close bond with children. A child with such a parent would never seek company elsewhere. Thus, parents are our best friends providing us with unwavering affection.

5. 'A family without pets is an incomplete family'. Express your views either for or against this statement. ***ICSE 2020***

Or Every home should adopt a pet animal. Express your views either for or against this statement.
ICSE Specimen Paper 2017

Examiner's Comments

- Many students strayed from the proposition. They focused more on grooming of pets than giving their views on the proposition.
- Majority of the candidates lacked ideas to develop the essay.
- Some candidates mistook 'pet animals' for 'domesticated animals'. (cow, goats). Many candidates failed to take a stand and argued both sides of the motion. At times, the number of arguments given were inadequate.

Ans. **For the Motion**

Good morning to one and all present here. We all have seen many movies which have moved us with a representation of great bonds of love between a family and its pets. In fact, many of us might have come across families who share great love with its pets. If you talk to such families, you would realise that a family is incomplete without a pet. Hence, I fully agree that a family without pets is an incomplete family. Pets provide companionship and help to reduce our loneliness. Sometimes playing with pet reduces our stress level and makes us emotionally well. Hence, the presence of a pet in the family ensures a great physical, emotional and mental well-being of its members.

Having a pet delivers a great sense of responsibility to the child. Feeding and caring for pet encourages childhood responsibility. Children with pets display improved impulse control, social skill and self-esteem. Kids with a pet go outside more frequently to go for walks, run and play in the park. Research shows children who live in homes with a dog can possibly have fewer ear infections, respiratory tract infections and require fewer antibiotics. The exposure to animals at a young age stimulates the immune system. Children who grow up in homes with pets have less risk of developing common allergies and asthama. Thus, pet owners require fewer doctor's visit.

Pets also teach kindness and compassion. Pets are a perfect stepping stone for teaching children empathy and how to take care of another living being.

A pet offers unconditional support when anyone in the family is sad, angry or upset. We can always trust our pets as they would never betrays us. Pets like dog give safety to our family and lots of entertainment to family members. There are lots of benefits of owning a pet. Pets teach adults as well as children valuable life lessons which have great significance in our life.

Against the Motion

Good morning to one and all present here. Today, I would present my disagreement with the view that a family without pets is an incomplete family. First of all, maintaining a pet is an expensive affair. You have to maintain their health which includes expensive food items, immunisations and visits to the Veterinarians.

Today, we are leading our lives with a very busy schedule. Who has enough time to look after the pet? Most parents professionals and the children are busy with their schools and other activities. Nobody has time to play with pets or look after them. Pets have to spend long hours in home without any companion. It makes them anxious and irritated. To solve this problem, some family appoint servants to look after pets. But these paid persons are not kind enough to the pets.

Sometime pets like cats and dogs carry infections diseases. It is not good for the child below 10 years of age. Thus, parents have to be cautions while selecting pets for their family. A pet can also not be good for your family if you do not get the right kind of pet. If someone buys a dog like, German Shepherd or Saint Bernard while living in a small flat, it is harmful both for him and the pet. These large dogs need atleast 2 hours of exercise and need large space to run and play. If you cannot provide this, it will ruin the health of the dog.

The family with young children should be very careful about getting a pet. If the child is too young, sometimes he/she may be hurt by the animal accidentally. Finally, we should remember that bringing a pet home means we also have to adjust with them. Pets like cat, dog or bird can make a lot of noise in the middle of the night. So we have to prepare ourselves to take these challenges positively, when we decide it's time for a pet, otherwise being a pet owner only creates problem for us.

6. "Closed Circuit Television (CCTV) must be installed in every classroom". Give your views either for or against this statement. ***ICSE 2019***

Examiner's Comment

- Some candidates mistook CCTV camera for television. Many candidates failed to take a stand and argued both sides of the motion.
- Some gave inadequate number of arguments .e.g., most centred around classroom indiscipline and slothfulness of the teachers being curbed.
- Some candidates deviated from the necessity of installation of CCTV in schools to CCTV in public places like malls and shops.

Ans. **For the Motion**

Good morning to one and all present here. We have all heard or read stories of children being ill-treated by unsympathetic teachers at schools around the world. These incidents happen, as they are reported regularly in the media. Accordingly, everyone has their own opinion on whether a school should have CCTV cameras installed or not. I wholeheartedly agree with the idea that a CCTV should be installed in every classroom.

There are many advantages of installing CCTV cameras which the Principal can monitor. The first one is that this move will deter bad behaviour, both by the students as well as the teacher. If the students know they are being watched, they might be better behaved. This might prevent bullying and intimidation.

Further, teachers and students can be protected from false accusations later on. If there was an incident regarding safety (for instance, a fight, bullying etc), CCTV cameras will capture the incident and the recording can be used as evidence. A lot of times incidents like these happen and there is no evidence against the perpetrator, but with closed circuit cameras we would easily know what is happening and take suitable action quickly.

The teachers can also use past recordings for improving classroom management and also work on their problem areas. Even the Principal can evaluate a teacher's effectiveness by analysing the video footage.

The most important advantage is the trust generated in parents' minds when they come to know that the Principal is monitoring every classroom. Parents will feel more secure if they know that the classrooms are being constantly monitored. Parents of new students being admitted to the school will be put at ease when they discover that the classrooms have cameras. So, it encourages them to send their children to one school over another.

For all these reasons, I believe CCTV in the classrooms at our school can be a good thing. Parents can come in, see the footage and any problem situation can be settled faster than it could have been previously without the cameras.

Against the Motion

Good morning to one and all present here. I disagree with the view that CCTVs must be installed in every classroom.

The biggest problem with installing CCTV cameras in classrooms is that teachers and students would feel that the school principal does not trust them. Teachers will be afraid of using innovative methods of teaching due to the fear of being misunderstood by the Principal. They would be afraid to take up any classroom activity other than the accepted thing, as they may fear that it may be used against them. This could lead to a 'guilty until proven innocent' attitude. It will create an authoritarian atmosphere and students may come to school with a sense of apprehension.

Another important issue which goes against installing CCTV cameras is that of intrusion of privacy of the students and teachers. Teachers and students would be worried whether there are any hidden cameras installed in places other than classrooms which could invade their personal privacy.

A further issue is regarding the cost to the school of such systems compared to the benefit they will give. The whole system will need not only the cameras. The associated equipment includes a Digital Video Recorder (DVR) to record information from the cameras, a switcher to view scenes from different cameras, power supply for the system and the extensive cabling involved. With such a large expenditure, the school Principal and Management will definitely want a commensurate return in improved learning, better security and, ultimately, better results of the students. It means that the Principal will be overworked unless he hires an assistant to help him with the monitoring. This will again bring up the matter of intrusion of privacy, as the assistant will not be of the same stature as the Principal.

Thus, if we do a cost-benefit analysis of installing CCTV cameras in classrooms, it is doubtful whether the benefits will outweigh the costs.

7. 'Money is important for happiness'. Express your views either for or against this statement. ***ICSE 2018***

Examiner's Comment

- Many students wrote arguments both in favour as well as against the proposition, failing to take a clear stand and not following the rubric.
- Some essays took the form of a narrative, where points were repeated and logical arguments were lacking.
- A striking error noticed was the inclusion of short stories to illustrate the point.

Suggestions for Students

- Students must know how to establish an argument with as cohesive link between points.
- Explore interesting introductions with suitable quotes and do not accept stories in argumentative essays.

Ans.

For the Motion

Everybody in the world needs money for not only their basic needs but also for many other needs. Hence, there is no harm in earning money as per capacity and need. Swami Vivekananda once said that earning money is a duty for the family men. But need is a relative term. There is no limit to need. 'Give me more', has become the philosophy of this age. This never-ending demand makes many persons just money-earning machines and forever unhappy. But we don't mean this amount of money. Happiness comes from fulfilment of physical, emotional and mental needs. These are fulfilled by the three equal and independent parts of wealth: economic, social, intellectual. Money is the main component of the economic part of wealth. So, money is one of the important resources that is needed for happiness.

Indian philosophy always teaches us how to be satisfied with limited resources. A man needs some minimum amount of wealth for survival and to lead a dignified life. So we should be satisfied with whatever money, amenities, power and resources which are available to us as per our highest capacity. There is no trouble in trying our best for all out success and upliftment. But when the final outcome is decided, we should accept it with satisfaction that we have done our best. This will also make us happy.

We should also remember that many people have less money or resources than us. They have less food, clothes and other basic needs for survival and for leading a dignified life. But they are still happy. You may wonder why. It is obvious that they are happy with the money they have. They thank God and are always obliged to Him for what wealth they possess. They never blame anybody or compare themselves with anybody. They are contended and satisfied with what they have. However, if they did not even have this much of wealth, they may have faced various issues in life which could bring unhappiness. They may lose the opportunity to fulfil their aspirations and always regret this matter later on in life. An example is a typical rural farmer who cannot progress in life due to his inability to get loans from financial institutions, as he cannot furnish collateral to guarantee the loan. Thus, lack of such wealth will cause permanent unhappiness.

Thank you.

Against the Motion

Most individuals are of the view that a good amount of wealth results in happiness, while some believe that being very rich has its own curse. I completely agree that a lot of money always brings with it many unforeseen problems as well.

Money and its vicious power to attract humans to fulfil their various wishes, at any cost, has always been debated. Earning sufficient money for one's basic needs and amenities, as well as to fulfil their family obligations and provide them with suitable comforts of a modern life, are very much justifiable. However, the issue arises that more wealth leads to a feeling of greed and a sense of invincibility amongst family and peers. As a result, a sense of suspicion, envy and jealousy creeps in within social relationships and takes a heavy toll on family matters as well. For instance, the recent war of words in public between two wealthy brothers, due to differences of opinion, for sharing and taking control of the vast business empire left over by their father. Such instances, due to fear of personal financial loss, lead to a permanent damage in relationships and splits between members of a family.

Secondly, gaining more financial clout, and enjoying the material luxuries the world has to offer, comes with its own set of sacrifices. Many high-earning corporate CEOs and senior level management at most large companies struggle with their daily hectic work schedules and get overburdened by the responsibilities, with the only aim of maximising the profit at any cost. This results into them not being able to devote enough time to their family and friends, as well as a deterioration in their physical and mental well-being, and later lead to life-threatening diseases. A recent survey showed that more than 40 per cent of top executives in India are suffering from high-blood pressure and stress related issues. In conclusion, I believe that having too much money not only leads to issues in personal and family relationships, but also deprives one of a healthy and peaceful way of life that can be enjoyed with just sufficient money.

Thank you.

8. "School days are the happiest days of our lives." Express your views either for or against this statement.

ICSE 2017

Ans.

For the Motion

Respected Principal Sir, staff members and dear students; today, I am going to speak in favour of the motion ''School days are the happiest days of our lives.''

Yes, I agree with the statement that school days are the happiest days of our lives. We are surrounded by our own group of friends and enjoy every moment of school time. Be it Sports or Yoga, Maths or English period, there is giggle and laughter over matter which may not be laughable for others. We are free from worries which adults face and enjoy life as it comes. These are happy carefree days. Friends are plentiful and life is all about fun, fun and more fun.

Moreover pretending to be sick, playing pranks on the teachers and not doing homework are some of the naughtiest things, we remember of our school days. In our school days, we have no tension of earning money as whatever we need, is provided by our parents or we are given money to buy that thing. A healthy competition among the students also makes school life a fun. No matter what kind of competition it is whether of studying, playing or speaking in debate, all inculcate us the spirit of determination and self-confidence without gorging the feelings of enmity for anyone.

School days are happy not only in the context of fun, but also in the context of learning. We learn very important lessons of life, like respecting our elders be it our teachers or staff members, sharing our things with our friends, helping one another and many more. We do make mischief and get punished which also do not go in vain as with them, we learn bad things are always bad and always bring bad results.

During school days, holidays are best realised. For us, they are like a gift from God himself as we do not have to get early and get ready like machine. We can have fun of playing cricket or football in the morning or watch our favourite programme on TV. The picnic spots that we visit in our school trips are the most memorable ones and cannot be forgotten throughout our lives because they are the trips where we do not have to arrange anything and the company of our best school buddies and teachers adds the happiness.

During school days, we get different experiences with different teachers. As our class changes, our teachers change too. Some of these new teachers are good and some are strict. This experience also becomes a fun and a learning lesson as it is only the teachers of our class or school that let us live the days of school to the fullest. They may be strict or ignorant, but always remain our well wishers and make our school days happy.

So, the time spent in school is the golden period of one's life as one does not need to pay heed to the worldly problems rather one needs to realise the happiness that each moment provides one during one's school days.

Against the Motion

Respected Principal Sir, staff members and dear students; today, I am going to speak against the motion ''School days are the happiest days of our lives.''

I do not agree with the statement that the school days are the happiest days in our lives. To support my point, I will give you the following reasons.

My first point is the unnecessary competition that we have to face during school days. We have to compete for everything from occupying a seat in our school bus to secure the top position in the class. We are supposed to give our best performance and get the best regardless of our own choice. This makes our life stressful and full of tension and worries. My second point is the less time we are given to play and for recreation. No sooner do we go out to play than our mothers call us back home on the pretence of coming exams or of some activity in school. And if by chance which usually happens with most of the students, we do not score or perform as expected by our parents and teachers, we are made guilty and are made to feel that we are nothing, turning our days nightmare.

My third point is toward the discrimination on the ground of performance in the exams. When it comes to scoring marks in exams, everybody becomes our tormentors. These tormentors include our parents, our teachers, tutors and even our siblings who want nothing from us but the highest marks in exams. Their behaviour toward us changes according to the marks we score. More marks affectionate behaviour, less marks rudest behaviour as if we have committed a crime.

The behaviour of some of the classmates is also very disturbing as they trouble all the class and fight with the weak students. They behave as if they were hooligans and always ready to fight. They create such an atmosphere in the class as one feels unsecured. Even the teachers do not pay heed to their mischief. The tension of homework is always looming as all the teachers give a lot of homework which has to be completed on the same day and on being it to be incomplete, the students have to face punishment. Even the holidays are not free. The students are given homework that consumes all their time. Some of the teachers are of the habit of using abusive language and beatings. They make their students' life hell if they are not followed. Besides all these we are left with no choice but to curse ourselves, an experience that no one wants to go through. So, each day we pass at our school is full of stress that does not let a child live free rather he feels confined. Thus, I do not agree with the statement.

9. "The use of mobile phones must be allowed in schools." Express your views either for or against the statement. ***ICSE 2016***

Ans. **For the Motion**

Good morning honourable judges, teachers and my worthy opponents.

Shakespeare has very wisely said: "There is nothing either good or bad, but thinking makes it so." Similarly, mobile phones in themselves are neither good nor bad; however, how we use them makes them good or bad. I strongly feel that mobile phones do not harm a student and should be allowed in schools. Hence, I will speak for the motion.

Cell phones or mobile phones have become an important part of our daily lives. Today, it is difficult to imagine our life without a cell phone as most of our work is done using cell phones. They provide an easy access to information which is a boon for brilliant students. Knowledge that was earlier limited to books and libraries is now at finger tips.

With mobile phones, you can communicate with anyone from anywhere at any time. Thus, a student can easily connect with his/her parent at any time of the day from anywhere. Day-by-day, these devices are getting smaller in size and lighter in weight. Such features make them easy to carry. They are not just to help you in making calls but also allows self-learning with thousands of application promoting learning.

So, it is better to make the students use the cellphones constructively. Cellphones can make the children organise, can improve their safety as they will be able to contact people in medical and safety related incidents. If we trust our children with computers, we must trust them with cellphones also.

Against the Motion

Good morning honourable judges, teachers and my worthy opponents.

We all are living in 21st century which is the age of science and technology. All the scientists of the world are inventing new technology to ease our life and give us comfort. Mobile phones or smart phones are invented to give us comfort and to keep us updated with the knowledge of the world, at a fingertip away.

However, these devices have become a source of major distractions for the students. Young boys and girls seem to have become inordinately addicted to them always scrolling though social media sites and continuously texting. They are thoughtlessly and uselessly wasting their precious time on them neglecting their studies. Children get hooked to the gaming apps, social media sites, becoming passive and killing their creativity. They spend less time in playing sports, exercise and outdoor activities. A major issue related to mobile phones is that it has become a means of flaunting social status. The overuse of mobile has posed serious health issues.

Radiation caused by network towers as well as mobile phones, affect not only eye sight but also causes difficulty in concentration, fatigue, headaches and sleep disturbance that can further trigger health complications. Owing to late night use of mobile phones, the youngsters skimp on sleep which has made them aggressive and irritated. Another major disadvantage of the increasing use of mobile is the spread of undesirable information. Not only is such information confusing but they are also not age appropriate.

At this age, the mind is tender and gets influenced easily. Cellphones can be seen as a means used by students for cheating during examinations. They can simply text anyone and ask for assistance. Moreover, mobile phones spoil the healthy and learning school decorum. Schools are meant for imparting education, knowledge and life skills. Thus, the cellphones should not be allowed inside the school ground.

If teachers have to make a call, they can use school landline or if a kid needs to call his/her parents, he/she would be allowed to use the landline. The children must be guided and counselled by the teachers and parents about how to use cellphones judiciously. School authorities must monitor children. Discussions can be done to make the children aware of the advantages and disadvantages of using mobile phones in schools.

10. "All girls or all boys schools provide a better learning environment than co-educational schools". Express your views either for or against the statement. ***ICSE 2015***

Ans.

For the Motion

Good morning to one and all present here. We all know that it is our duty to ensure that our children feel a sense of security and freedom at school. In this light I agree with the statement that all girls or all-boys schools provide a better learning environment than co-educational schools.

It has been observed that all-girls or all-boys schools can provide a more structured learning environment for both boys and girls. Boys and girls differ in the way they act, how they learn and their interests and abilities. They need an educational environment tailored to meet their unique needs. In general, boys are more physically active, assertive and comfortable learning in a more chaotic environment than girls. Girls are able to sit still and prefer a quiet, focused and orderly classroom.

In all-girls or all-boys schools, the curriculum and course offerings provide advanced work in areas of the children's greatest interests and natural abilities. Moreover, single-sex schools encourage children to take risks in expressing themselves as they learn without the fear of embarrasssing themselves in front of the opposite sex.

A study conducted states that single-sex schools develop greater self-confidence and broader interests especially among adolescents. Girls report that they feel more comfortable, they can interact more with teachers and develop move favourable attitudes towards subjects such as maths and science.

In addition, single-sex schools for boys allow adequate time for male maturation and benefit the boys by giving them more structure and discipline due to their tendencies of restlessness and aggression.

Furthermore, separating girls and boys fosters an environment of non-stereotyping and encourages learning. It also promotes interest for boys in humanities courses and they feel more at ease because they do not feel the peer related societal pressures. It benefits girls as co-educational schools foster obsession over hair and clothes and tend to make them distracted. The students in the all-girls or all-boys schools also feel the freedom to attend classes usually associated with the opposite sex.

Thus, in my opinion, all-girls and all-boys schools provide a better learning environment than co-educational schools.

Against the Motion

Whether to admit their children into all-girls or all-boy schools or co-educational schools has always been a problem that parents are disturbed with. It seems to be a dilemma, but I would say there is absolutely no difficulty in making this choice. Good morning to one and all present here.

Coming from a co-ed school, I stand against the statement that "All-girls or all-boys schools provide a better learning environment than co-educational schools."

Education in the general sense is a form of learning in which the knowledge, skills, values and beliefs are transferred from the teacher to his students. The modes of education do not vary as per the sex of the students. Thus, education cannot be divided on the lines of sex.

When it comes to schools, there are many more important issues than having same sex schools. In fact, the age-old belief of same sex schools being better than co-educational schools has been long dismissed by the impressive results of the latter. Not only have the students of co-educational schools done academically well but also, it has been seen that they are more confident beings than the students of same sex schools.

When girls sit along with boys in the same classroom, it helps develop cordial relations among students and instils in them mutual harmony and brotherhood. Moreover, co-educational schools offer a diverse curriculum that is available to all students, deemphasising gender-linked stereotypes related to course work. Co-educational schools encourage all children to explore a broad range of career opportunities. Today is especially an age when men and women work together and compete with each other in offices, homes etc. Thus, co-education teaches or prepares them to interact with the other sex in the future. Boys and girls learn to respect one another and cooperate as equals. As such, this system of study helps both the boys and girls to improve their confidence and also provides for an excellent foundation in developing realistic and meaningful relationships.

In society, males and females are members, functioning as workers or decision makers or whatever role they get to play. There is no way to avoid contact with the opposite gender, and it is essential for one to learn the proper way to interact with others so that one can develop healthy relationships with people around. An all-girls or an all-boys school cannot provide such an environment to its students within the campus. This may lead to the development of a negative response to the approach of the opposite gender. It is the accumulated experience from interacting with the opposite gender and observing others interact with the opposite sex that enables one to be apt and able in communicating with others, whether male or female. This is certainly an important advantage of studying in a co-ed school.

Last but not least, students studying in a co-ed school can enjoy the advantage of building a set of balanced moral values, more easily than those studying in a single-sex school.

11. ''Working women make better mothers.'' Express your views either for or against this statement." ***ICSE 2014***

Ans. **For the Motion**

"The hand that rocks the cradle is the hand that rules the world." It is very true that mothers play an important role in the growth and development of the future generation. These days, there is a fight between two kinds of mother, working and non-working. Mothers are constantly fighting and debating to figure out who is the better parent. In my opinion, an educated and a working woman will have a more positive impact on the child and hence, is more capable of moulding the destiny of the future generation.

Respected Principal, honourable teachers and my dear friends. Today, I am here to express my views in favour of the motion 'Working woman are better mothers'.

Now, when the women are moving shoulder to shoulder with men and moving ahead in life, debating if they are better mothers is like emotionally blackmailing and making them weak.

It is also like accusing them that they are neglecting their responsibility of bringing up their children well. They should not be made to feel small for wanting and working to move forward in their professional life. In the age of equality, women are increasingly encouraged to 'have it all' by balancing their career, children and marriage in order to be seen successful. And still, they are accused.

It's like maintaining a double face. On one hand, people talk about the necessity of a woman to actively participate in the country's economic growth and then when she steps out, they shout that she is not balancing her home and office with the result that her children are running astray.

It is also not necessary that the women who stay at home prove to be perfect or better mothers. The children of mothers who stay at home are more pampered whereas a working mother's children are more disciplined. Also, working mothers are able to guide their children better by providing them with the right amount and kind of exposure.

I think it is not right to constrain and limit women to house-keeping and child-rearing and waste the abundant potential which is within them. We should not, thus, be stuck in tedious arguments about whether women, especially mothers, should or should not work. What is noteworthy is that it is the happiness of a woman we should really be talking about.

Thank you

Against the Motion

Respected Principal, honourable teachers and my dear friends. Today, I am here to express my views against the motion 'Working woman are better mothers'.

If a woman is working outside the home, she can only feed her baby once or twice a day and that is not enough for the well-being of the child.

A child learns by example and so the first school of the child is the home and his first teacher is the mother. If a woman works outside the home, how would she have the energy to tell bed-time stories and moral lessons to the child?

She may not be there at meal-times and the child would have to be kept in the care of a maid. Such a mother won't be able to ensure that her child gets proper nourishment in his all important formative years.

When a woman is at home, she has enough time to spend with her children not because she has less work to do but because, being at home, she is there for the child whenever needed. The children get time to share their problems, happiness, fun and curiosity with their mother. She teaches them manners, traditions and customs. A child's best friend is its mother but if she is too busy taking care of both the home and her job, how would she have the time and energy to be there for the child?

A working woman has to leave her child when it is barely a month old. She remains constantly worried about her child. A child cannot be looked after properly in her absence. As a result, baby-sitters are hired, who often turn out to be a fraud. Moreover, a woman who works outside, suffers from the guilt of not being able to spend enough time with her child. This affects her relationship with the child. She either over-indulges with the child to compensate of the lost time or becomes very strict because she does not want the child to get spoilt.

Hence, I would like to conclude that non-working women make better mothers than working women. If a woman stays at home and looks after children, it is definitely more beneficial for both to her own well-being and that of her children.

Thank you

12. "Boarding schools are far better than day schools for the all-round education of a child." Express your views either for or against this statement. ***ICSE 2013***

Ans. **For the Motion**

I agree that boarding schools are far better than day schools for the all-round education of a child.

Students in a boarding school show better progress and are supposed to be more disciplined. Furthermore, there are many special help programmes available there such as mentor-mentee programme in a boarding school. The purpose of this mentor-mentee system is to provide guidance to students about academic matters and to foster a close and constructive professional relationship between students and the staff of the faculty.

While all lecturers in the faculty are potentially academic advisors to all students who seek their advice, each teacher who is a mentor, is assigned particular responsibility to a small group of students which are the mentees. In day schools, programmes like this are not present.

Moreover, by staying in a boarding school, children will learn to be independent and deal with difficult and tough situations on their own. This will help them grow as an individual and bring out the best in them.

This is because students, who are in boarding schools, are mostly far apart from their parents. They usually have to make their own decisions, unlike day school students who always depend on their parents.

Boarding school can also produce individuals who are very creative. This is because they can make students do things that day school students cannot do such as dorm decoration. They need to decorate the dorm with some challenging themes. Moreover, small class size, diverse curricula and individual attention from faculty and advisors give boarding students many distinct advantages so that students can focus on their education well.

At the same time, the teachers can give more attention to individuals who do not understand a topic as the number of students in the class is less. Boarding school reduces compartmentalisation, because academic studies are blended with other activities, such as sports. This natural juxtaposition increases the appeal of both pursuits.

As the conclusion, I want to emphasise that boarding schools are better than the normal day schools because it produces individuals who can tackle the real world where their attitude and discipline, determine their success.

Thank you.

Against the Motion

In my opinion, day schools are better than boarding schools. Many day schools offer co-educational facilities and this is an important requirement in terms of today's world. Interacting with the opposite sex in the early years, will enable children to be comfortable in the presence of the opposite sex when they reach a stage where they might have to work alongside them in an official environment.

Although, there may be a few boarding schools that offer co-education, day schools clearly outnumber the boarding schools doing this and co-education in day schools is a much more accepted and existent structure, especially in India.

Day schools are a preferred option as they are much less expensive than a boarding school. Tuition fee in day schools is cheaper. Most of the good quality day schools are relatively cheaper than boarding schools and this is another reason why parents opt for day schools over boarding schools.

Day schools allow parents to admit students in private tuition of their choice as well, in case their children need extra coaching. Most boarding schools in India have fees that is a bit exorbitant and unless parents are willing to fund a new experience and style of education for their children, most average Indian parents prefer day schools. Day schools are a better option for those parents who wish to have close supervision over their children.

Day schools also enable constant parent-teacher contact and this helps the parents monitor the progress of their children in terms of both academic and extracurricular activities. This is also an important aspect of a day school. Parents can provide moral guidance if they are in constant contact with their children and this is possible only if the children are admitted in a day school.

Moreover, if children are used to the comforts at home, they might find it difficult to survive in a boarding school. Day schools enable the children to relax a bit more than boarding schools. In a boarding school, students are required to take part in many events and many students find it difficult to deal with this schedule.

Furthermore, in case of any sickness or injury, parents can be with their children immediately if they are admitted in a day school.

Thank you.

13. "Money causes more harm than good." Express your views either for or against this statement. ***ICSE 2012***

Ans. **For the Motion**

It is a common saying that "Money is the root of all evils." Idealists wonder why we cannot live in a world where everyone is equal and where there is no greed or jealousy resulting from status differences.

Unfortunately, they overlook the fact that our desire to have higher status than others is part of our human nature and nothing can change it.

Money comes and goes but what stays are memories with our family and friends. Man kills man for money. Abundance rarely brings anything other than increased sorrows, wars, crimes and robbery which is happening because of money. More and more people are finally realising that money cannot bring them the happiness they crave for. A person is not willing to sacrifice his happiness and freedom to obtain economic status. We want certain things and money is necessary to enjoy them happily.

Moreover, money is only needed to provide us with a safe and comfortable home, food to eat and the ability to visit friends and family other than that one doesn't need more money at all.

There are things that are far more important than having money, things like spending time with family and loved ones and enjoying what you like to do. Time is more valuable than money, you can get more money but you cannot get more time. If one has to work fifteen hours a day and never gets time to spend with family, friends and spend that money, then what good does it do? You have not lived a perfect day, even though you have earned your money. While money can't buy happiness, it certainly let you choose your own form of misery.

Once our basic needs are met, we find richness in being together and enjoying the simple things. We certainly have to be careful to set our priorities correctly to avoid regrets later in life. Money can help fill a loss of material needs. But, learning to be content is far more important. Though money can buy status, friendship or even save you out from a sticky situation but all these evaporate, once your money vanishes. However, time invested in love and quality friendship lasts eternally.

Thank you.

Against the Motion

I strongly condemn the motion that "Money causes more harm than good."

In my opinion, money is an essential commodity that helps us run our life. Without money, people will stop working with eagerness.

When there is equality everywhere, the determination to work will decrease. A person, who works hard, will get the same benefit as a person who is lazy. Hence, it will be wrong. Ultimately, everyone will stop working and there will be no progress, no development and everything will come to a stand still.

I would like to state that though money is not everything but money is something very important. Beyond the basic needs, money helps us achieve our life's goals and support the things we care about the most—family, education, healthcare, charity, adventure and fun. It helps us get some of life's intangibles—freedom or independence, the opportunity to make the most of our skills and talents, the ability to choose our own course in life, financial security and much more. With money, much good can be done and much unnecessary suffering can be avoided or eliminated.

However, with money people choose these positions because they are not motivated or qualified enough to do anything else. Money is simply a representation of the value of work. Certainly work doesn't cause more harm than good! People do misjudge the value of some work compared to others but this is a fault of our values and assessment of how to value work–it's not the fault of money.

Moreover, it is the money that creates respect and honour for someone. It is the money that tames the most shrewed one. Money can give us the power to make a difference in the lives of others. It gives us the time to develop and nurture our relationships.

Thus, I would like to conclude by saying that it is a requirement of life in a society to be able to exchange goods, ideally through a universal token such as money, just like it is a requirement of life as an individual to be surrounded by air to breathe.

Thank you

14. "Private tuitions are a necessary evil." Give your views either for or against this statement. ***ICSE 2011***

Ans. **For the Motion**

Respected Principal, honourable teachers and my dear friends. Today, I am here to express my views in favour of the motion 'Private tuitions are a necessary evil'.

Private tuition is a part of the learning process that has become a backbone and a big part of our system of education. Private tuition has existed for decades and will always exist because we have a system of education which is coupled with competition.

Without that additional coaching, it is not easy for a student to compete with their classmates. Very often what they get in class is highly inadequate for them to clear the competitive exams. To be successful, they are compelled to seek extra coaching outside school hours to stay in the race to pass the finishing line.

Today, the syllabus taught in class is not sufficient for those who are in quest for knowledge or who are on the competitive track. Very often, the teacher finds themselves in front of an uncooperative class who deliberately puts a spoke in their wheel and makes their work a real ordeal. A teacher, in spite of all the skills and competence, if does not get the cooperation of the class, is utterly unable to make progress and is never able to deliver good.

Therefore, those who are in search of knowledge, are compelled to have recourse to private tuition. Moreover, private tuition helps in improving the performance of the child. It can be complementary when the lessons done in the class have not been fully understood by the student.

Generally, a classroom is not conductive to individual teaching. The teacher-pupil interaction highly spoken of is not possible in the class due to large class-size. A teacher normally tries to avoid a dull student. So, such a student may fail to catch the eye of the teacher. In such cases, private tuition may be helpful. The pupil may not only be taught, but also made to work at exercises which they would normally avoid in class.

If the tuition teacher is earnest, the pupils can progress and improve gradually.

Some of the topics that are not covered in the class or which require supplementary reading could very well be done in the tuition hour. Additional exercises could be done, better reading is possible which may lead to better understanding. Thus, private tuitions are necessary as they provide the needful things to the students.

Thank you

Against the Motion

Respected Principal, honourable teachers and my dear friends. Today, I am here to express my views against the motion "Private tuitions are a necessary evil".

In earlier days, tuition was not necessary as education was not so emphasised. But, now-a-days, many students prefer to go to tuition because they believe that it helps achieve success in examination. They may sign up for tuition either because they are forced by their parents or just out of their own willingness. Some students decide on studying by themselves. However, deciding on taking tuition has great pros and cons on student's achievement and life.

Private tuition makes a child depend more on the teachers and the notes they give rather than on himself. Children, who take tuitions, give stereotype answers because they don't use their own mind to produce answers rather they become machines of learning answers.

Private tuition can be a financial burden to parents who are poor. Taking tuitions is very expensive as well and not everyone can afford to send their children for extra private tuition.

According to research, those children, who take tuitions, don't study seriously in the class because they feel that they can learn and grasp the topics while taking tuitions. This way they disturb the whole class and also waste the time of serious minded students. Now a days, we can see that lots of teachers are more inclined in giving private tuitions as it has become a source of extra income for them but this is completely against the noble profession of teaching. Teacher should make a target to set the maximum output in the class/school so that the tuition trend fades away and every child can get an equal opportunity to learn from his teachers.

Moreover, tutors provide additional homework on top of those given by the teachers in school. Sometimes, tutors do arrive at the wrong timing. For instance, students are not in the mood to learn or have gone through a hard day work in school and are, therefore, mentally tired. Despite such a bad timing, the tuition sessions may still have to carry on, which make it unfruitful.

Some students treat their tutors as a walking dictionary, expecting them to furnish answers to the homework given by school without thinking through the solutions by themselves over time. This can make them mentally lazy.

Thus, in my opinion private tuitions are not mandatory.

Thank you

15. "More lessons are learnt on the sports field than in the classroom." Express your views either for or against this statement. ***ICSE 2010***

Ans. **For the Motion**

I do agree that more lessons are learnt on the sports field than in the classroom. In a student's life, extracurricular activities empower him to make his own active decisions and also help him gain an accurate experience skills and confidence to lead him on the path of his future.

It is considered truly that through participation in sports and different games, students learn cooperation, teamwork, leadership skills and time management. If you consider deeply, the sports field is a minifield of life.

Whatever we experience or learn here, serves to be an invaluable experience to us for life. Sports foster friendship and cooperation. Sportsmen forget caste and religious differences and become friendly with one another.

Often sportsmen have to live together while undergoing training and participating in competitions. They understand one another and learn to make the adjustments for corporate life. In other words, they learn the virtue of tolerance. Moreover, when they go to other countries to participate in international competitions, they are not merely competitors but the messengers of goodwill. This way, they spread goodwill and love throughout the world.

Furthermore, young people have surplus energy and if this is fruitfully utilised, the foundations are laid for a healthy society, where people are fully aware of the need for discipline, cooperative effort, team spirit etc.

They also learn to cultivate the vital quality of learning how to work as a team, to become not only good winners, but also good losers. The statement "The battle of Waterloo was won on the play fields of Eton" implies that playing games and the spirit of sportsmanship helps inculcate lasting values, which make us good citizens, apart from promoting 100 per cent physical fitness. Life teaches us "Failures are stepping stones to success."

The same is true with the sports field. Here, too, one failure does not mean absolute doom. It simply gives us the courage to rise and fight again. Perhaps failure makes us tougher for the next round of fight. Moreover, the sports field naturally instructs people to play the game of life with its right spirit, which is what matters most, not victory or defeat.

Thus, in many ways, the education we receive and the lessons we learn from sports outnumber what we learn in our classrooms.

Thank you.

Against the Motion

I do not agree with the statement that more lessons are learnt on the sports field than in the classroom. As more time is spent on sports field, no time is left to pay attention to the academics. The person gets stressed due to non-performance in the academic field and many times his frustration can be noticed in his playing strategy.

Due to tough competition, every team wants to win. Instead of learning tolerance, the players develop a habit of recoursing to unprofessional tricks so that their team could win.

So, many times, instead of being tolerant and full of competition spirit, the player adheres to unethical practises, which in longer run harms him.

Sports does teach lessons to the children but not always good ones. Many children are not naturally talented and only come across failure and embarrassment on the sports field. This may hurt their confidence and may put them off any sort of exercise for life. Many other activities can teach team work and other life skills e.g. hiking and camping, playing in a land or raising money for charity etc.

Sports make people too competitive and encourage the worst side of human nature. Apart from this, sports encourage cheating, disrespecting opposite team members and referee and drug abuse. These problems are worse in professional sports where the need to make money adds further pressure to win by any means. Too much competition can lead to stress and depression and thus affects a person mentally and physically.

Thank you.

16. "The use of mobile phones has lowered active social life and has become an addiction." Express your views either for or against this statement. ***ICSE 2009***

Ans. **For the Motion**

Good morning to one and all present here.

Mobile phones, undoubtedly, are one of the most spectacular developments, ever to have taken place in the field of telecommunication. They offer the easiest and simplest way to stay connected, with our near and dear ones, thus augmenting and invigorating our social life. However on the contrary, they have actually lowered active social life and have become an addiction for the youth of today.

The young generation is enamoured by this latest gadgetry. Smart phones undisputedly offer many conveniences, like access to the Internet, entertainment, social networking and the ability to use idle time, (time spent in travelling or in leisure) to best use. It is however some of these conveniences that have actually eroded social life.

The urge to stay connected with our own circle of friends and relatives, has made us a social outcast in the society in which we live. It is quite common to find a group of youngsters sitting together in a place talking on phone to people far away, unmindful of the presence of others around. They are thus more concerned and connected to people far away, than to those around them. Such behaviour dissuades them in cultivating new friendship, in the mistaken belief that they are more secure by staying connected to their known circle of friends. This virtual networking, actually weakens their active social life.

The convenience of utilising the idle time also affects us socially. Business executives and professionals are the worst sufferers. They have no time for leisure as they can be called for work whenever the need arises. This not only affects their social life, but also their family life. The ringing of a mobile is a real nuisance on occasions like an important meeting, praying or participating in a funeral.

Nevertheless it is now becoming indispensable and an addiction because of many value added features that provide social networking and entertainment. These features have caught the imagination of the youth who spend hours on their smart phones. According to psychiatrists, this causes compulsive disorders and is one of the biggest non-drug addiction in the 21st century. Spending excessive time with mobiles isolates the person from the society.

Mobile addicts tend to neglect obligations towards family, work or study and drift away from friends. Being victims of low self-esteem, they have problems of developing social relations and are more comfortable in the virtual world. They feel insecure without their phones. In its absence they suffer from anxiety, irritability and sleeplessness. Besides the addictive influence of mobiles, medical research has proved that it can cause serious health hazard for the frequent user.

Undoubtedly mobile phones have made our lives more safe and comfortable. However, like all good things their excessive use has adversely impacted our social life and has now become an addiction.

Against the Motion

Good morning to one and all present here.

I do not support the motion, ''The use of mobile phone has lowered active social life and has become an addiction.''

In my opinion, mobile phones keep one in constant contact with people they consider important. Active social life in the hectic pace of life today has been lowered by our busy schedules, not by our mobile phones. On the contrary, mobile phones help us to stay connected with our family and friends, whichever part of the world we may be living in. In days gone by, letters and telegrams were the major means of communication. A letter sent from India to a person in the US took minimum of three weeks to reach and an equal amount of time was taken for the reply to reach. Even if one tried to call from the landline, one had to use ISD and STD facilities which may or may not be working and which were prohibitively expensive. Now the rates are so low and the connectivity so good that we can talk everyday through our mobiles, as we wish.

Moreover, it is much easier to visit our loved ones today because all we have to do is call and find out if they are home and visit them. Coordinating a party is much easier with the use of mobile phones. Whether, it is reserving ticket for the railways or for the airplane, one need not stand in a long queue or call an agent. It can be done easily using the internet on the mobile phones. Our life is becoming more and more convenient and the mobile phone has become an indispensable and inseparable object. Nothing more than a cell phone comes to great help in emergency. If you are driving by the freeway and the vehicle jams, the cell phone comes to your rescue.

You are stuck in a lone place, again you can call somebody and ask for directions. Moreover, parents can be little less worried about their kids by being in constant touch with them.

Using mobile phones distributes our communication to make it easier than before. The more you talk, the more you know how to talk and the better your communication skills become. This is applicable if you're a sensible person and keep note of your interacting habits over the phone. It can be a communication tutorial. Thus, mobile phone has become a crucial part of our life. It has made communication easier and quicker. It is not an addiction but a necessity.

Thank you.

17. "No other subject taught in school is as important as Moral Science." Express your views either for or against this statement. ***ICSE 2008***

Ans. **For the Motion**

Good morning to one and all present here.

In today's rat race values are eroding fast. There is a total decadence in social and moral values. Children go to schools daily thinking how to scale heights they will reach, how rich education can make them. In today's cut throat competition even the parents instruct their wards that they should top in the class. Hence, I stand in the favour of the statement.

Childhood is a very impressionable age. The mind is like soft wax, so whatever one is taught at a tender age it leaves a deep impression. Therefore, Moral Science must be made a compulsory subject in school curriculum. It is also a science of human soul, it's a mirror of one's inward mind, one's ethics. Moral Science inculcates values in mankind and this value education should be taught since childhood.

Therefore, schools should shoulder the responsibility of imparting moral values to them. In order to make them self-reliant, confident and responsible citizens, they need to be imparted with value based education, which only Moral Science can do. After all, ''Todays' child is tomorrow's citizen.''

Moral Science is not a religion based subject. Rather it eliminates fanaticism, superstition and violence. It preaches 'Love All Serve All'. This value is lacking in todays' generation. It helps child to pay heed to his conscience and not to be led away by worldly show. However, theoretical knowledge is not enough. Teachers should make their life exemplary to their students. The lives of great patriots or spiritual leaders must be brought to the forefront. Only Moral Science can stem the tide of rapid value erosion and motivate the students towards a healthier life. A child is then trained emotionally, mentally and physically how to be a responsible citizen or a good son or a daughter. They can resist wrong peer pressure, intolerance and through right conduct lead forward their nation.

Furthermore, Moral Science helps a person to become a better human being. One becomes more understanding, patient, pious, decent and wise. One learns to do things without any selfish motives. Pleasure is derived in doing things for others as one feels that one is doing it for good. The end result is that the world can become better and happier place to live in. Peace and contentment can be found.

Therefore, there can be no doubt about the fact that no other subject taught in school is as important as Moral Science. Let the light of spirituality shine through the eyes of the little ones.

Against the Motion

Good morning to one and all present here.

I stand before you to contradict the statement, "No other subject taught in school is as important as Moral Science". I would rather emphasise the point that knowledge is big power and this power comes through learning not merely Moral Science but all other subjects even more seriously and intensively like Geography will unfold the mysteries of the different regions on the globe. The study of applied Sciences like Maths, Chemistry, Physics, Biology will unravel the vast potentialities that can enrich our life and resolve many mysteries about the atom and element, land and sky, stars and planets.

Whereas not much effort is required to learn ethics and morality, much mental labour is involved in learning subjects dealing with different branches of learning. Moral Science teaches us about moral good or bad which can be learnt spontaneously and instinctively by watching the behaviour of the elders we come across daily.

The great advancement in technology in conquering time and space has been possible because much more emphasis is being laid on the study of science. Now, environmental studies is being given more importance and it is made compulsory subject at all levels of school education. The global warming is threateningly increasing, posing unimaginable danger to our hard gained advancement in civilisation. More and more stress is being laid on protecting the environment and saving the fast depleting resources for our coming generations.

Man's march to higher and higher ladder of civilisation will remain unhampered only if he keeps himself abreast with the changing scenario and copes with it on the strength of knowledge which empowers him to fight against any eventuality.

The harmonious development of a student's personality can be possible with equal emphasis on the study of all subjects and not just becoming an island into himself by simply meditating on God, Life and Death. Let such things be special subjects of religion and metaphysics to be taken up only by those exclusively interested in this particular branch. The more we learn about other subjects, the richer will be our knowledge.

18. "Cinema, both entertains and educates the masses." Express your views either for or against this statement. ***ICSE 2007***

Ans. **For the Motion**

Good morning to one and all present here.

Cinema today has come a long way from the early days of 'silent pictures'. The true to life sets, dramatic screen plays, photographic techniques, acting histrionics, and their portrayal on a 70 mm screen, with digital sound effect, in plush multiplexes, have made cinema an ideal medium for entertainment and education. Its close affinity to the people, mirrors their social values and ethos often showing the true picture of life. The evils that plague the society vividly portrayed on screen, makes it a powerful medium for social change that not only entertain but also educate the masses.

There is no disputing the fact, that cinema offers an easy and affordable means of entertainment to the masses. For some, after a day of hard work it is an escape from the tension and worries of life. To others it is a respite from boredom. The true to life portrayal of characters, evoke our emotions, moving us to tears, laughter, thrill or even shock. It is this ability of catering to a variety of tastes, interests and moods which make it an ideal medium of entertainment.

It is also a very powerful tool for education. The audio-visual mode of presentation leaves an indelible mark on our mind and makes learning a pleasant experience. This is for we get to see, and hear about different people, places, and customs leading to a better understanding and assimilation of ideas and knowledge. Historical movies bring to life the dead pages of history. Pictures like Gandhi, Shaheed Bhagat Singh and Mughal-e-Azam give valuable insight about these great people, their struggle, aspirations, and ideology. Such films promote nationalism, brotherhood and communal harmony. They remind us of their sacrifices and our rich cultural heritage.

It is also an excellent medium for advertising and propaganda. The advertisements and endorsements help in promoting the sale of goods and services. The government also uses it to promote social harmony and health care. Documentaries create awareness for prevention of aids, polio eradication and other information to benefit the society.

Realising its significance the government has set up the film division, under the Ministry of Information and Broadcasting for the production and distribution of good films for the general public. This is a conclusive proof of the significant role that cinema plays in entertaining and educating the masses.

Against the Motion

Good morning to one and all present here.

Today, cinema is by no means a source of entertainment and it certainly does not educate the masses. Today cinema houses are packed with either low class people or with anti-social elements that go to the cinema only to pass comments, tease the fairer sex or to pick a fight. Today, no decent respectable person wishes to go to the cinema to watch a movie. They would prefer not to have any entertainment at all than to go through the harrowing experience of being pushed around in long queues or to hear the abusive language used.

Cinema is largely responsible for the depravity in society today. The vulgarity and the shameless exposure of the human anatomy have driven the teenagers towards forming an unethical society where all morals have been thrown out of the window. Violence packed films have given a new meaning to violence in society. Today teenagers walk about with guns in their pockets ready to implement what they have witnessed on the silver screen. Children have become disrespectful and disobedient. There was a time when children were afraid of their parents and teachers but today it is the other way around.

Cinema is having a tremendous negative influence on society. It is not only teaching you how to commit the crime but also how to dodge retribution successfully. Ideas are generated in the minds of the young and the reckless and then ruthlessly implemented.

Today a poster displaying a man holding the national tricolour would hardly draw an audience, no matter how good the plot and the picturisation of the movie may be, but a skimpily dressed beauty would draw enormous crowds even if the movie has no plot. Such is the change cinema has brought about in the taste of the audience. Movies with nudity and violence sell while movies on patriotic themes or religious themes become super flops. Cinema has thus played a major role in the degradation of the society and must not be considered means of entertainment or education for the masses.

19. "The computer will soon replace the Book." Express your views either for or against this statement. ***ICSE 2006***

Ans. **For the Motion**

Good morning to one and all present here.

Computers have already taken a major role as an information resource today. Computer technologies such as hypertext and the internet remove the geographical constrains of print media and allow for a new method of distributing and reading documents.

Books have always been affordable, concrete sources of information, but the next ten years will bring computers that are faster to access, as convenient to use and that hold more information than books. Hence, I stand in favour of the motion that computers will soon replace books.

In next 20 years, print media may not be able to keep up with the exponential growth of information simply because of the presence of a computer and internet. With the internet, a book can be availed by every person using a computer. Hence, instead of the hassle going to the market to buy a book, people are taking to using a computer and finding it there. Further, the density of information on a computer is far greater than that of a book. A typical computer hard drive can hold around 2000 novels giving it an seemingly unlimited storage capacity. In addition, computers also provide much faster access to information. *For example,* looking upwards in a dictionary might take a few minutes while computers can give the definition for any word and pronounce it for you, immediately. The computer's speed and space will make it a necessary technology as we move into a new millennium.

The future will bring even greater advantages to the computer over the book. Soon, computers will have screens that are crisper and more comfortable to view than a printed book. With new technology, computer screens will no longer strain the eyes and it will become feasible, even desirable to read an entire novel on a computer screen. Technology will soon produce a computer that is as compact, durable and comfortable to read as a book, but that could contain thousands of books in electronic form. Although, computers will never completely supplant books, but we may soon rely on them more than print media. Computers will meet our needs for information storage and distribution and will be a convenient way to hold more information in less space than todays' book.

Against the Motion

Computer will never replace books. However, useful the computer may be, it is absurd to imagine it replacing books. Computer, any day, is far more expensive than books and do not work on fresh air. It needs power through batteries and mains to work. One cannot lie in bed and read them leisurely and of course if milk or syrup spills on them the damage could be much more. Computers have viruses and are not completely dependable but a book in a shelf is very dependable. It does not make you strain your eyes as computers do. A book somehow has a sense of belongingness. We can make our notes as well as turn to specific pages without really having much problems. One can even sleep with a book on one's bedside and wake up in the morning to read it.

Moreover, with the help of computers, students simply copy-paste and the matter is complete. The pride of a library and collecting the first edition as well as autographed books of an author will have no relevance. A book reveals the nature of a person but with a computer no one knows who is an avid reader and who is not.

The printed book can easily be read and stored. Students can write their notes and refer to them at any time. The computer troubles its users, while a book is perfect relaxation. The joy of placing your hands on a book and reading through its pages is ecstatic and can never be replaced by computer. No one is going to put computers into the hands of kindergarten students and then not everyone can afford to have a computer. So, lets forget about such an idea and live realistically. Books may have their limitation but they can never be superseded by computers. No one wants to lose the joy of reading a book and at the end pronouncing to himself that, 'It is finished'.

Thank you.

20. "The commercialisation of festivals has eroded their real significance." Express your views either for or against this statement. ***ICSE 2005***

Ans. **For the Motion**

'Man is by constitution a religious animal' said the great scholar Edmund Burke.

Good morning to one and all present here. We all agree that it is religion that makes him more loving, humane and sociable. Festivals are associated with religion and are basically celebrated, to commemorate a special occasion. These are pious occasions, for religious ceremonies and merry making. However, their significance have now degenerated to only merrymaking, because of commercialisation.

Companies marketing consumer products have usurped such pious occasions, to enrich themselves. They launch new products and also create discount schemes well before the onset of festivals like Deepawali and Christmas to create an urge to splurge, thus propping up their sales. They induce people to buy costly presents for friends, relatives and children which have made festivals very materialistic. Gone is the joy, love and compassion one experiences on meeting friends and relatives during such festive occasions.

The religious rites and customs observed have also undergone a sea change. Thus, we now use decorative lights instead of the traditional diyas during Deepawali. Similarly during Christmas the carol singing and the hymns have been replaced with Christmas ball, and other forms of merry making in prestigious hotels and clubs.

The commercialisation is playing havoc with our culture. An important factor in diluting the essence of festivals is our mistaken notion of modernity and the convenience offered by Information Technology. So great is the pressure of time that we do not have the energy or the inclination to visit our near and dear ones on a festival that comes once a year. Instead, we send them e-mails and prefer to go shopping at Deepawali melas.

Indeed commercialisation of festivals has eroded their real significance. This is because festivals have been reduced to only celebrations and merry making. Corporates have succeeded by their ingenuity, to convert such pious occasions, to enrich themselves. There is however an urgent need for us to pray and introspect, during festivals, for this can only enrich us socially and spiritually.

Against the Motion

Good morning to one and all present here.

I do not support the motion that commercialisation of festivals has eroded their real significance. The world is increasingly getting more cosmopolitan and secular. Many festivals which were once restricted to specific communities have assumed a pan-Indian character. No doubt, this promotes national integration.

But today's world has also opened the flood gates of the commercialisation of festivals. Festival time is a boom time for opportunity seeking businessman. As the number of revellers willing to splurge increases every year, wily business houses come up with more ideas to cater to them and thus we witness the rich variety of greetings cards, the plethora of speciality items related to a particular festival, the festival feasts at restaurants and the festival themed shopping malls and super markets.

It is not necessary that everyone should celebrate a festival in the same way, or that it should have the same significance for everyone.

This depends on what is considered to be the basic aim of a festival. In case of Christmas, is it simply to praise God or is it to have a good time? Festivals in the middle of winter were as much to banish the long nights with merriment as to praise the God (s) for the day beginning to get longer again. If it is simply about having a good time then commercialisation makes little difference. Commercialisation can even make having a good time easier as there will be more variety and the festival is likely to get more spectacular.

Fairs and festivals are like the ornaments on the soul of India. A vast range of fairs and festivals are celebrated here, ranging from those of national eves, to those of cultural eves like Holi, Diwali, Eid, Rakshabandhan and many more without any differentiation of caste, creed, sex, race etc.

With the changing times, these festivals are also changing in terms of the ways they are celebrated and the values which they hold though the basic legendary story behind the celebration of any such eve remains the same, the generation gap can very well be noticed over here. Oldies still stuck to the traditional ways of the celebration whereas, the youth blends liveliness to the event along with their innovative ideas of having unlimited fun.

In my opinion, commercialisation of festivals has made them all the more interesting and spectacular.

03

Narrative

A narrative composition is an oral and written description of an event or series of events that take place in one's life, which is presented to its readers and listeners in the form of a story or an essay, providing them with the necessary details in proper order so that the message is conveyed thoroughly.

A narration is similar to storytelling, with a simple difference in context-of fact and fiction. A story can be based on imagination while a narration is based purely on the real life experience or incident.

Purpose of Writing a Narrative

Narrative writing is very important in our day-to-day life. It helps in sharing our stories of personal experiences with others and allows us to gain empathy. It also helps the most shattering incidences to reach out to the world.

Points to be Kept in Mind While Writing a Narrative

- Create an outline of the basic parts of your narrative.
- Use the past tense to describe a past incident.
- Use contrast and comparison to add variety and interest.
- Describe your narrative using vivid details, recreating the experience for your readers or listeners.
- Narrate your experiences keeping in mind the small details that are important for your readers or listeners to know.
- Identify and remove any information that seems to distract from the focus and main thread of the narrative.

Sample Narrative

Write a narrative comparing life to riding on a roller coaster.

Ans

Heading or Title — The heading of the narrative should be short in a word or a couple of words.

Corkscrew

I have never really liked roller coasters.

Unfortunately, I have come to the conclusion that life is very much like one.

The first and only time I rode a roller coaster, I was fifteen and naively excited. I lacked the foresight to remove my glasses before boarding- a silly mistake, especially considering the beast in question is called "The Corkscrew," a monstrous structure that, as the name implies, loops up, down and upside-down in a giant corkscrew.

Like a lamb brought to slaughter, I am calm, innocently curious about what lies next.

Soon, I am at the very top with the entire amusement park spread below my feet. As I am confronted with the vertical descent below, all spidery dark metal curving sharply down and away, my stomach starts twisting uncomfortably. The realisation that this is definitely not where I want to be right now becomes a solid block of panic tearing at my chest as the coaster pauses for a moment and then slices downward as it curves into a corkscrew, straining to throw us off.

I want to scream, I really do, but the whole of my mental capacity is focused on somehow preventing my glasses from slipping off my face using sheer willpower.

Somehow the ride is over, and I make it off and onto the nearest bench, sanity and glasses still surprisingly whole and present. I breathe a sign of relief that I survived.

The experience taught me like any well-designed coaster, life has twists and turns and steep drops, but it also has ups. Agony is inevitable, but it does not last forever, and we are stronger and wiser for having lived through it, even if only by a little bit.

So, perhaps while I do not plan on getting on a roller coaster anytime soon, chances are I may end up on one but I will not panic or be scared by the memory of my last coaster ride, because I'll know and believe that it gets better.

Expression — Expression is the way in which the narrative is expressed or the way in which the writer puts forward his thoughts. It covers the entire body of the narrative.

Content — It consists of the matter of the narrative. It begins after the title and ends before the conclusion. It contains the core or central idea of the narrative.

Conclusion — End the narrative with a conclusion, which is the narrator's perspective on the experience he underwent.

PYQs Previous Years' Questions

1. Imagine a situation where you get an opportunity to change one thing in your school. What would it be? Why do you want to change it? How would you bring about the change? ***ICSE 2023***

Ans. Modifications and updations have become the norm of the era. We can always find things for improvement and change. Hence, if I get the opportunity to change one thing about my school, I would change the way of communication which leads to the wastage of paper. There are times where I feel that my school is too reliant on using paper even for small things. For instance, the school library still puts up the issue slips on the books to keep record of issuing history and find out when a book is due to be returned. They also use the issuance register book for recordkeeping. The teachers also use attendance register books for marking attendance in the classroom. Further, any message to be passed within the school premises is written on a paper and then passed.

I personally feel that in the modern day and age where certain alternatives are available, we should try and minimise our usage of paper. Global warming is a serious issue and trees are helpful in protecting our environment from the climate change. The environmental effects of paper production include deforestation, the overuse of energy and water as well as air pollution and waste problems. Given the situation, it is important to consider methods that are more environment-friendly.

I would like to digitise all the recordkeeping in the school, including the library and class attendance. This could be easily done with the help of any smart-device, such as a tablet or laptop. I would also like to encourage the school to switch to recycling the used paper and using recycled notebook for work. Students should also be given the option to email their assignments and homework. If my school can reduce the unnecessary use of paper, it can contribute in protection of our environment and its resources.

2. Imagine a situation where your mother has been unwell and you had to help her. Explain what you did to help. What did you learn from the experience.

ICSE Specimen Paper 2023

Ans. We might not realise it but mothers play a very vital role in a family, whether it be keeping the family together or by helping everyone with their work. We might often fail to understand how hard they work for us. I got an opportunity to realise her responsibilities when she became sick. It was during when I was in Class IX with my mid-term examinations just around the corner. She couldn't go to work or do household chores at all. It was then that my father and I took over her responsibilities.

My father took leave from office during those days. Our daily routine included my father cooking breakfast for us in the morning, with me getting up early in the morning to revise for some time and mop and clean the house. Then, I would get ready and after giving medicines to my mom I would go to school. After coming back from school, I would help my father in preparing lunch, following which we ate together.

In the evening, I used to talk to her and help her with whatever she needed. Then, I made sure that she was taking her medicines on time. My mother did not want me distracted from my studies right before my examinations. So, I didn't forget to do that. She had become so weak. And she would have trouble relaxing at night. Sometimes, I used to give her a head massage so she would get better sleep.

She did not get any better in the first two days, so I took her to the doctor. I did her laundry, putting all the clothes in the washing machine and then putting it out for drying. She started getting better on the third day and by the fifth day, she was completely fine, carrying out with the household chores and her job.

This incident taught me to be more helpful and now I make sure to contribute, by doing all my work myself and being more organised and cleaning my room myself. I think that lessens half of her work. I am trying to be less dependent on her so that she gets time to rest. We realise that she has her own individuality and she deserves some time alone. On holidays, I try to help my mom with nearly everything.

3. It is very important for young people to spend time quietly or alone for a short while every day. If you were given an hour to spend on your own, how will you spend it? What will you learn from the process?

ICSE Specimen Paper 2022 Sem II

Ans. In this pro-social world, we are strongly influenced in favour of being with people, or at least constantly interacting with others, be it through social media or other electronic means. We are always going somewhere, doing something or at least chatting to someone about going somewhere or doing something. In this constant interaction setup, we often forget to spend some alone time thinking it to have many negative impacts.

While there is a wealth of research pointing to the psychological downsides of loneliness, there is an increasing of an individual. amount of evidence suggesting that a certain amount of quality time alone is critical to well-being of an individual. In fact, research finds that there are many positive impacts of some alone time.

It allows one to learn more about oneself and become self aware. It empowers one to become comfortable with oneself. This confidence, in turn, will project in the future decisions one will make. It boosts creativity. It gives one an opportunity to plan life. It improves your mental wellbeing, makes one happier, experience lower levels of stress and less likely to suffer from depression.

Hence, if I were given an hour to spend on your own every day, I would either start journaling or learn to play violin. Journaling would help me reflect on how I had spent the day, the people I met, the words we shared and the activities we engaged in. I'd like to understand how my activities and the people I encounter affect me and my viewpoint. I'll consider whether I could have done or said something better, or whether I could have said or done nothing at all. It will assist me in comprehending my errors: whether or not I could have avoided them and if so, how? How could I get out of it if I even made it? How could I make it less likely that I'd do it again?

Because we learn from our experiences and, conversely, we are constructed from our experiences: both joyful and painful, I believe it can help you become a more thoughtful, compassionate human.

4. Have you ever said or done something that changed the life of another person? Give an account of your words or actions that led to this change and describe how the experience made you feel. ***ICSE 2020***

Ans. Most things that change a person's perception happens to be an experience that they have gone through and learned from. And of all these experiences, there are some rare instances when an individual becomes the agent or the cause of bringing change in someone's life.

Recently, I had the opportunity to become a medium of bringing such a change in somebody's life. It so happened that I accidentally bumped into a very old friend of mine. It look us some moments to recognise each other as both of us had changed a lot but when we did, we exclaimed with joy.

She had left the city because of her father's transfer and had come back to attend a family function. We decided to sit in a coffee shop and spend some time with each other while discussing our lives. She was very happy because her father had been recently promoted and they were prospering financially. I was so happy to see her enjoying life.

We had been sitting there for an hour, when we realised that it was getting dark. When the bill came, she insisted upon paying my share as a treat for her father's promotion. I hesitated at first but then gave in. She paid the bill and gave the remaining amount as a tip to the waiter. I was a little surprised but didn't say anything. Just as we stepped out of the coffee shop, it started raining. Since both of us had to go in the same direction, we decided to take a rickshaw.

However, because of the rain, we couldn't find any. Suddenly, a rickshaw pulled in front of us. We asked if he would take us to Pandav Nagar.

He agreed and said that he would charge fifty rupees. I was about to get on the rickshaw when my friend told the old man that she only give him thirty rupees. I was surprised to hear this. It had been three years since she left the city and the prices had increased. What the old man was charging was fair enough.

But my friend kept on arguing. And it was at that moment that I said, 'Isn't it strange that we tend to spend extravagantly in places where we have to show off our prosperity, but when it comes to pay a fair price to a hardworking man, we start negotiating?" My friend immediately realised that I was referring to her gracious tip in the coffee house. She felt ashamed and quietly got on the rickshaw. The old man safely dropped us home and happily took the money.

I saw that my friend had understood the real meaning of happiness when she saw the gleam in the eye of the old man as he held the fifty rupees note in his hand. This episode made my friend a little more humble and compassionate.

Examiner's Comment

- Most candidates simply produced memorised essays. Several students wrote on the same theme.
- Some candidates misunderstood the question and wrote an account of the impact of the other person's words/actions on them (candidates) rather than the other way around.
- Good vocabulary was also lacking.

Suggestions for Students

- Perform adequate reading and vocabulary building exercises.
- Avoid plagiarism
- Use all senses to accentuate the composition.

5. Imagine that you have changed your school recently. Narrate your experiences on your first day in the new school. How did you feel at the end of the day. ***ICSE Specimen Paper 2019***

Ans. The first day at a new school can always be scary and nerve-wrecking. Starting a new school can seem stressful as we have to give a first good impression to one and all and also make new friends. However, a new school calls for new experiences and new friends which is exactly what I had though when I was to go to the new school XYZ School.

I was in 11th grade when my parents had recently bought a new house in a nice quite neighborhood. I was ecstatic as I always wanted to move to a new house. I was happy but at the same time realised that I had to switch schools and make new friends. The prospect of entering a new school sacred me a little but I bore with it.

It was finally the first day of school; I was excited yet nervous. I hoped I would be able to make new friends.

The school itself was very elegantly constructed with black and white theme, a large playground, swimming pool, badminton and basketball court and large classrooms. When I reached the reception, my class teacher was already waiting for me to guide me to the class. My class had 35 children who were looking at me as if I was an alien. Now, by this time, I had gained some confidence but seeing the others look at me like that made me nervous. After gathering as much courage as I could, I introduced myself and took my seat with a boy.

The class went on normally with no one talking to anyone else and only focusing on studying till it was lunch. I thought I was going to have lunch alone but was surprised when everyone came and huddled together beside me. One-by-one they introduced themselves and started talking to me as if they had known me for years. I was shocked by soon found myself becoming friends with them. All my nervousness had dispelled now for I had friends and teachers- the few that I have met- seemed to like me.

At the end of the day, I was happy and satisfied that it was a great first day at my new school.

6. Narrate an incident from your own experiences when you helped in preparing a meal. Explain what you did and what you gained from the experience. ***ICSE 2018***

Ans. When I was in Class 10 and it was the summer holidays, I thought I would help prepare a meal. It was early morning, mother had gone for grocery shopping, my sister was asleep, and no one else was at home. I decided to help in preparing breakfast by making an omelette. I had seen mother making it many times, so how difficult could it be?

I took two eggs, two tomatoes and a large onion. I chopped the onion on the work surface just as I had seen chefs do it. Then came the tomatoes. I washed them and started chopping them. Suddenly, I cut my finger in my hurry. There was no bleeding but it was just as painful.

It took me two or three attempts to crack open the eggs and drop them into the whipping bowl. The spices were next. Mother always kept the spices on the top shelf in the kitchen. I couldn't reach them, so I got a stool and, climbing on it, got the chilli powder and salt. I put all the ingredients in the bowl with the eggs and whisked them. I lighted the stove, put the big frying pan on it and poured some oil in it. However, some oil spilled on the floor too.

Till the pouring of the batter into the pan, everything was going perfect. Then, I wondered what was used for turning the egg upside down in the pan. Soon, I was running all over the kitchen, searching all the shelves and drawers to find the cooking spoon; all the while the omelette was sizzling in the pan. Finally, I found the spoon and made a rush to turn over the omelette. I managed to do that without breaking or spilling it out of the pan, only to see a very nicely browned, or rather burnt, side up.

While I was busy taking it out in a plate, someone came up behind me. It was mother. I was dumbstruck. She was angry at seeing the kitchen in a mess, the drawers all open, and some salt and chilli powder on the stove and countertop. She found a fit punishment for me: I had to eat the burnt omelette. Sitting on the table and eating the omelette, I realised it didn't taste as bad as it looked. My first cooking experience had turned out to be a minor disaster.

Examiner's Comment

- Most candidates ignored their personal involvement in the preparation of meal.
- Some candidates wrote about how they were helped by a family member.

Suggestions for Students

- Practice narration in the chronological order of the events.
- Perform adequate reading and vocabulary building exercises.

7. Narrate an incident from your own experience when you helped a friend who was in trouble. Explain what happened. What did you do to make the situation better? ***ICSE 2017***

Ans. I still remember what happened when we had gone for a picnic. Everything was going fine when suddenly, my friend Kaushal got a call from his sister that his parents had met with an accident. Kaushal was devastated and did not know what to do. As he belonged to a lower middle class family, he did not have enough money to hire a taxi and reach home fast. I assured Kaushal not to worry and left the picnic in the middle. I took out whatever money I had in my savings account, called a taxi and left for the spot where his parents had met with accident. Kaushal is the eldest in his family, he has two younger sisters.

He was unable to take any decision as the unexpected tragedy had left him too shocked to react. Kaushal had a very few relatives and most of them were unwilling to render any help. I called up all my friends and requested them for help. Kaushal's parents were admitted in a hospital and the surgery could take place only after the required amount had been deposited. I called my father and explained him the situation. As he himself was a doctor, he reached the hospital and talked to other doctors about Kaushal's parents. Meanwhile all my friends gave away not only their pocket money but also reserved money and an amount of ₹ 25000/- was arranged. I bought some snacks and juice for Kaushal and for his sisters who were crying miserably. The next two days were very crucial. Kaushal's father needed some blood which was voluntarily donated by my parents and the parents of my friends who had come there at the hospital. I didn't leave Kaushal alone even for a minute. My mother took his sisters to our home as there was nobody to look after them. After the surgery was done, Kaushal's parents survived and Kaushal relaxed a little.

In those days of need I spent most of my time with Kaushal, reassuring him that everything was going to be alright. Kaushal, till today, remembers this help. He had returned the money but he says he can never pay back the cooperation and help given by me, my family and our friends. Kaushal's whole family treats me like their own son and loves me dearly. I feel very proud of myself.

8. Write about a time when you were late for an important function. What lesson on punctuality did you learn? ***ICSE Specimen Paper 2017***

Ans. Being late can be a stressful and embarrassing situation, but unfortunately, it's something that happens to all of us at some point. I remember a time when I was running late for an important meeting, and it was a situation that I found particularly challenging.

Around a year ago, my passport had reached its expiry date and I had to get it renewed urgently. For the same, I had made an urgent appointment at the Passport Seva Kendra in Chandigarh. I vividly remember, my appointment was scheduled at sharp 1 pm. I had already finished all tasks before hand to reach the centre before time. I had even decided to go by my car. While travelling to Chandigarh, I saw an upturned car with passengers inside it. From what I could see, there was a family of four stuck inside.

Without thinking, I stopped my car at the corner and went out to help the injured. I took out my pocket knife and cut the seat belts and, then with the help of a few other people, succeeded in getting the injured out. Then, I rushed to take them to the nearby hospital and informed their family. As soon as his family came at the hospital, I began my journey again. It was 11 and I still had some time to reach my destination. However, I was almost half an hour late. After reaching there, the gatekeeper denied my entry because I was not there on the given time. I explained to him the whole situation but he was also helpless due to official procedure.

He suggested me to make a new appointment in emergency for the same day with some extra fees. I did the same through the official website and got my new appointment timing. It was 4.30 pm. I took lunch from a nearby restaurant thinking about whether I regretted being late. I didn't for if I hadn't stopped the car and helped the family, their condition would have worsened. So, that was a time when I was late.

9. Narrate an incident from your own experience when you expected to do very well, but for some reason were unable to do so. Explain what happened and why it happened. What lesson did you learn from it? ***ICSE 2016***

Ans. Very recently, I learnt a lesson for life which I am never going to forget. I live in a locality with independent houses. Recently, a man shifted to a house close to my house. He became quite friendly with my children and often used to give them sweets and toys. He became friendly with my parents also. Suddenly, he stopped coming in the park. He did not meet anyone for many days. One day, my sister Kavya and I were playing with the bat and ball and the ball went into this neighbour's house. We were very sure that our neighbour would allow us to pick up the ball. We rang the bell which was answered after a long time. We asked him, if he could give us our ball but that man very sternly said "No" and closed the door. We were really surprised at his behaviour. He was so friendly but his sudden change of behaviour perplexed me.

Suddenly, one idea struck me when I saw the water tank behind his house. We wanted to get our ball so we climbed the water tank and jumped inside our neighbour's house. The door was open. Nobody was there. We went inside and tried to look for the ball under the bed.

I saw the ball. Hurriedly, I took the ball and along with it came a gold bar. We took out both the ball and the gold bar and climbed up the water tank again. Reaching my house, I found my father watching a news on TV.

I couldn't believe my ears when the news reader read that 20 gold bars were stolen from a jewellery shop. They showed a picture of the gold bars and it was exactly like the one we had found. I quickly told the whole story to my father who immediately called the police. The police came and searched this neighbour's house and gold bars were recovered and he was arrested.

The police informed my parents that the man was a thief, a smuggler and under his pleasantness wanted to carry on illegal activities.

I realised that this person should not have been trusted and I should have thought over the reason that he was trying to be so friendly with his neighbours. I learnt the lesson that we should never trust a stranger.

10. You had booked a ticket on an early morning train. However, you woke up late and missed it. You then decided to run to catch a bus to the next station where you hoped to catch up with the train. Narrate the entire event, how you felt, the effort you made and how you finally caught the train. What did you learn from this stressful experience? ***ICSE 2015***

Ans. The alarm bell buzzed at 3:00 am to wake me up from my sleep so that I could catch my train which was to leave for Udaipur at 5:00 am. However, I put the alarm off and went back to sleep.

Around 3:45 am, my phone rang. I reluctantly answered, half asleep. On the other end of the call was my cousin who enquired whether I had got ready to leave the house for the station. Her question "What time will you reach the station?" made me wake up at once. I looked at the watch and rebuked myself for sleeping extra, when ideally I should have been getting ready. I told her that I would reach the station at 4:30 am and hurriedly put the phone down. I got up from my bed and rushed to the bathroom.

By 4:10 am, I reached the cab stand. However, there was no cab to be found.

In a state of panic, I called up my friend who stayed nearby. Thankfully, he answered my call and rushed to help me. He drove as fast as he could and we reached the station exactly five minutes before the scheduled time. However, to my utter shock, I was on the wrong platform. I hurried to the platform where my train was waiting. Unfortunately, by the time I reached the platform, the train was rolling on its wheels. My cousin was shouting at me from inside the train and asked me to run. I ran as fast as I could but missed it. I couldn't believe what had happened. I did not know what to do. Other passengers were looking at me and some were mocking at my carelessness. However, an old couple came and suggested me to catch a bus to the next station where I might catch up with the train.

I hurried to the bus stand which was nearby. Thankfully, the bus was about to leave. I found myself a seat and prayed to reach in time. To my relief, the bus dropped me an hour prior to the scheduled timing of the train. I bought water, drank some and splashed the rest on my face.

This stressful experience taught a very important lesson to me of punctuality. Time and tide wait for none. It's better to be early than late.

11. Think of a time when you found yourself in an embarrassing situation. Narrate how you got into that situation, how you dealt with it and the lessons you learnt from it. ***ICSE 2014***

Ans. The proverb 'Pride comes before a fall' became very apt for me. I was also good in academics and managed to come in the first three ranks in the class with the minimum of effort. The result was that I became egotistic and started making fun of my classmates especially because some of my class fellows laughed at my witticism. This encouraged me on and I started misbehaving when some lenient teachers were present.

One day, when the Hindi period started, our teacher walked into the class just as the bell rang. I had just sat down when the previous teacher had left and I did not notice our Hindi teacher coming in. All the children around me stood up and wished her. I was still sitting and before I could get up, she saw me seated and thought that I was trying to insult her. As a punishment she made me stand the whole period on the chair. The whole class kept looking at me, whispering and laughing. Instead of stopping the children, she asked me how I felt to be at the receiving end for once. I had never felt so humiliated in my life. On the top of it, she pointed out at my hairstyle and compared it to the one we see in the promotional advertisement for the candy 'Centre Shock'.

Everyone burst into peals of laughter. I felt ashamed and realised how other children felt when I ridiculed them. Thankfully, I was made to sit down in the next period. No one was in a mood to study as it was the last period of the day. One of my friends imitated the way our Sanskrit teacher spoke but in a very exaggerated manner. I could not help and burst out laughing.

My teacher got so furious at me that she lost her temper and took me to the Principal's office. There, I stood outside the office for almost twenty minutes. To add to my embarrassment, there was a football tournament in our school that day.

Children from other schools were also participating. One of them happened to be my neighbour with whom I never got along. When he passed by me and snickered, I wished the Earth to crack and swallow me up.

What an embarrassing day! I shall never forget it. I resolved that I would never behave like that ever again.

12. Teaching someone else how to do something can be a rewarding experience. Think of a skill that you have helped someone to develop. Perhaps you taught someone how to swim or to bake a cake, or helped someone learn how to study more effectively. Narrate the events that made up the process of teaching the skill, and say what made the experience important and memorable for you. ***ICSE 2013***

Ans. It really does seem that children are becoming interested in cooking again. I don't know if it's due to the success of cooking shows on television, such as Masterchef and Junior Masterchef, that my brother's kids are definitely more interested in what's for dinner, what's in it and even ask that "Can I cook tonight?"

Cupcakes, in particular, give reasonably quick results and the children enjoy frosting and decorating. So, I decided to teach them how to make cupcakes.

Cupcakes are so quick and easy to make that they are ideal for children to bake. I always think the best cupcakes for kids to make are those where all the ingredients are put in the bowl together. Whether they mix with an electric mixer or with a wooden spoon, there is very little mess.

When I taught them how to bake a cupcake, these are the following steps I asked them to follow.

First, I listed all the ingredients that were needed—butter, caster sugar, plain flour, baking powder, salt, eggs and vanilla extract. I also told them the exact quantities that were required. Once all the ingredients were in place, I instructed them to preheat the oven to 180°C/350 F. Then, I instructed them to line the muffin tin with paper cases.

I explained to them how the batter or mixture is made and all the tricks involved to make a good batter, the consistency needed and how to correctly mix all ingredients without over mixing the batter or incorrectly whipping the eggs.

After the mixture was ready, the next step was to teach them how to grease the paper cases and spoon the mixture into them. After that, the cupcakes were kept in the oven for 18 to 20 minutes until risen, golden and firm to touch.

Once the cupcakes were out of the oven and ready, I told them to let them cool completely. It was time for the decoration of the cupcakes. The kids were overjoyed at it. They decorated the cupcakes with colourful frosting and sprinkles.

The kids made very creative cupcakes. The delighted look on their faces was truly wonderful to see. It was a memorable experience for me. Their tiny little hands served me each of their cupcakes and we relished eating them together.

13. Relate a special incident or experience in your life which you still recall with happiness. ***ICSE 2011***

Ans. It was the last week of May. My Class X examination result was to be declared that day. I had been waiting for this day with anxiety and curiosity. I got up at six o'clock in the morning, took bath and prayed to God to grant me success. I was somewhat uneasy and restless. My mind was swinging between hope and fear. It was a strange mix of anxiety and expectation. I was not sure what was in store for me. My parents had high expectations from me.

At one moment, I was sure that I would score good marks while at the next, I feared what would happen if I performed badly or failed. At ten o'clock, I went to the school with my mother to get my result. Other children also came with their parents. My hands were shaking and heart was throbbing.

My class teacher handed over my result to my mother. Immediately, a wide smile spread across her face. She hugged me tightly and told me that I had stood first in the class with 98.9% marks. Soon, I met the Principal and other teachers. They all congratulated me. In the evening, when I returned home, I saw many of my relatives and friends had come to congratulate me. My father welcomed them cordially. He seemed to be very proud of me. We spent the whole day cheerfully.

The whole atmosphere of the house was at once changed. Friends and relatives kept pouring in to congratulate me. Tea and sweets were served to all who came. Many of my relatives brought sweet boxes for me. All were in a jolly and happy mood. My mother prepared nice dishes for dinner. I also invited two of my friends for dinner.

Never before had I been so happy. Even today, when I recall this incident, it brings immense joy and happiness to me. It was indeed one of the happiest days of my life which I shall remember for many years to come.

14. Recall a time in your life when you were certain about something but were later proved terribly wrong.

ICSE 2009

Ans. We make many mistakes but by learning from them, we work better in the future. After all, we are all human and can make mistakes.

My school used to be my home. I hardly had time for my own family. Every moment was spent in the extra curricular activities which made me the most popular girl in school.

The importance I placed upon being the most popular girl was absurd though I did not think so at that time. I felt proud when my juniors recognised me by my name and when they, with respect and admiration in their eyes and voices, asked for my advice. Even my seniors envied me. It was crucial to my popularity that I continued to win all the athletic medals, be the conductor of the school choir and be the best tennis player in the under—15 category.

My name was associated with all these achievements. With all these distractions, which took up most of my time, I did not heed the warnings of my teachers. It annoyed me when they pestered me about my grades.

As weeks passed and the examinations approached, everyone began spending their time in the library, studying. I, instead, spent my hours in the swimming pool. I sat for the papers, confident that I could at least scrape through.

I was certain that I will pass the examinations but was later proved terribly wrong when my parents were unexpectedly asked to see the Principal. I could not imagine what the reason could be. My cheeks burned when I learnt that I had to repeat the whole academic year as I had failed my examinations badly.

Word spread around the school like wildfire. My name was now associated with failure. Being so busy with my numerous activities, I never had any time to make any good friend. As a result, I had no sympathetic friend or confidante to fall back on. The loneliness I felt was unbearable.

I learned my lesson the hard way. At the expense of my studies, I had enjoyed short lived popularity. I was a disgrace to my family and myself. Nevertheless, I picked up the pieces with determination. Now, I have excelled again, but this time, in the academic field as well. Never shall I repeat the mistake I made.

15. Recall a remarkable event of social importance in your city or locality. Give a little of its background, the event as it occurred, and its impact on the lives of people.

ICSE 2007

Ans. In December 2012, the brutal rape and subsequent death of a 23-year-old female student in Delhi quickly gained attention in India and abroad.

The woman was beaten and raped in a moving bus. Medical reports later said that the woman suffered serious injuries to her abdomen, intestines and genitals due to the assault. In the days immediately following the inhumane incident, protestors staged large demonstrations at Delhi's India Gate and outside government buildings including Rashtrapati Bhavan, the official residence of the President of India.

People no longer wanted to sit back and wait for the government's action. They knew very well that 'Justice delayed is justice denied'. Thus, thousands of protestors clashed with police and Rapid Action Force units.

Demonstrators were *lathi* charged, shot with water cannons and tear gas shells and arrested. Similar protests occurred throughout the country. Thousands of people silently marched while others started a hunger strike. Protests also occurred online on social networking sites like Facebook and WhatsApp, with users replacing their profile images with a black dot symbol. Tens of thousands of people signed petitions protesting the incident and demanding justice.

Many of the mourners carried candles and wore black outfits and some pasted black cloth across their mouths. Some of the protestors drew slogans on papers spread on the road, condemning the incident and demanding stricter laws and speedy judgement. The incident made breaking news all across the globe. It sparked protests across South Asia, including marches and rallies in Nepal, Sri Lanka, Pakistan and Bangladesh.

The demand for severe punishment for the perpetrators led to the death sentence for four of the accused while one died in the police custody and one was a juvenile who was given the maximum sentence of 3-year imprisonment in a reform facility. The incident left a deep scar on the minds of everyone. This was a remarkable event of social importance where the entire world stood together and demanded justice.

04

Description

A description is a piece of writing that elaborates a person, place, thing, feeling or state of mind. It outlines the understanding of a person about the thing to be described. The person who is describing must know all the concerned facts about the object to be described. The language should be kept simple so that the information can be conveyed in an easy way.

Points to be Kept in Mind While Writing a Description

- Make sure that you note down some ideas before you begin describing it.
- Use clear and concise language.
- While describing something, appeal to the senses of the reader. Explain how the thing smells, fells, sounds, tastes and looks.
- Use simple language and avoid writing very long sentences.
- Leave the reader with a clear impression. It should evoke a strong sense of familiarity and appreciation in the reader.
- Always present an organised, objective and logical description.

PYQs Previous Years' Questions

1. You are a regular visitor to your school library. Describe your library. Give details of the familiar sights. What do you see and feel as different students come in and check out the books? Why is this place so important? ***ICSE 2023***

Ans. Books are called a man's best friends and best place to find them is a library. I, as a bibliophile, love books and you would often find me sitting in the library reading one of the detective mysteries there. Thus, it is safe to say that library is my favourite place to go to in the entire school and I relish my time there. The shelves are stacked with thousands of books that the school has accumulated over many decades. There are many kinds of fiction, non-fiction books and academic books available for students and teachers to choose from. I am personally fond of the fiction section, with books ranging from classics, horror, crime to fantasy fictions and much more. The library also has some interesting non-fiction categories, such as biographies. Mrs. Chawla, the librarian, can often be seen sitting behind her desk, waiting for students to return or issue books.

I often feel amazed by the whole idea of a library where students can come and take the books without worrying about having to buy them. Whenever I see the students selecting the books they want to read or take like with them, I find they have a sense of excitement and anticipation just like me. I often feel like none of this would have been possible had the library not existed. It feels as if the knowledge of the entire world, everything that each of us would need to know to be successful in our lives awaits us in the library. I often think of how the books that people check out can help them in their future and if they would look back and think of how this present moment changed their perception or sparked their interest in a particular thing. It all starts with one book.

The place is incredibly important for all the students as it gives them the freedom to read what they wish, a freedom that course books don't often provide. It also gives them the opportunity to learn and grow their knowledge of things outside the curriculum and get inspired by the lives of others through selected biographies. Moreover, Mrs. Chawla is incredibly kind and helps the students with finding books and often ignores the fines when the students tell them why they couldn't return the books on time.

2. You are a regular traveller in your school bus. Describe what you see on your way home from school each after noon. Give details of the familiar sights and sounds you experience each day.

ICSE Specimen Paper 2023, ICSE 2019

Ans. As soon as the bell rung, announcing the end of the day in school, voices of school children could be heard from every corner. I have been regularly using the bus service since nursery to Class 10th. Every year the bus number, driver and conductor keep on changing though my route remains the same. Even children keep on changing every year. Travelling by school bus is sometimes interesting and at the same time, it can be boring and tedious.

The bus I travel in picks thirty students from the school and stops at ten places, picking and dropping children. In the morning, my mind feels fresh, enjoying morning scenes. Everything seems peaceful and even the roads remain clear. But the scenario is completely opposite when we return home in the afternoon. All my bus mates become very energetic, during that time. They talk and shout nonstop. Some even fight while others are busy relating their whole day's school experience with their friends.

Due to the peak hour, the streets are packed with people. This is increasing air and noise pollution and causing us to remain stuck in the suffocating traffic jams. While waiting at signals, both the students inside and the people outside make funny faces and wave to each other.

At times, we get hungry and thirsty, so whatever we have, we share with each other. While passing through the vegetable sellers, some of us ask the rates of vegetables to irritate them. Then, all of us laugh together. Sometimes, we even play games to entertain ourselves. Travelling from school in the afternoon is definitely a mixture of experiences and a lively time, even though it is also annoying.

3. Describe a time when all the lights in your locality went off. What were the sounds you heard as you sat in the darkness? How did you feel when the lights came on?

ICSE 2022 Sem II

Ans. Have we ever wondered what happens in the nights? What kind of sounds can we hear in the night? I did and was shocked to discover how nature is alive even at night when we humans are sleeping and resting. It was a warm summer evening and my summer vacations were going on. I had just returned after many hours of playing cricket with my friends in the locality and was enjoying the cool air of the AC when suddenly the lights went off.

All of us initially thought that it would come in an hour or so as was the norm. But we all were wrong. The lights would not come back until 4 am and till then we had live without any chilled air, sweating and finding way to beat the heat. The first hour was fine but after that it was a terrible torture. My parents had lit many wax candles near us so that we could see but the heat was killing us. So, we all made paper fans to dispel the heat.

The time was passing really slowly and everyone in my house decided to try to sleep. I also went to my room but could not sleep. Sitting idle by the bed, I realised that the night was not so silent. One could hear even the slightest of movement in the night. I heard the slick movements of the lizards outside the windows, the rustles created by the winds and the thap thap of the guard's stick could also be heard with great clarity. I could even hear the tick-tock of the clock.

The night and the sounds made me wonderstruck. For a moment, I forgot all about heat I was feeling and tried to listen as many sounds as could. I don't know how, but I fell asleep while doing so. And when I woke up, the light was back.

4. If you were granted a special wish what would you choose? Say why you would make this choice and how it will be useful to you and your loved ones. ***ICSE 2022 Sem II***

Ans. Wishes are indeed something special in one's life. Wishes are the special desires which one likes to be fulfilled to see their life dwell in happiness. I would like to make a wish which could make the world a better place to live in.

My wish is very simple but hard to attain, I want to see a peaceful world. Every day, we hear news of killings, rapes, murder, one country attacking another, etc. Such things have become so common. The statistics vary for ongoing conflicts in the world right now but it would be safe to say that there are at least thirty conflicts in the world involving countries and hundreds of tribal and sectional conflicts or uprisings that cause injury, death and hostage situations in the world. This amount of violence in the world creates upheaval and tension for generations to come. People often hold onto prejudices, fears and hatred for many years. This creates a world of hatred rather than cooperation and peace.

In the last 5000 years of civilisation, there have been more than 50,000 wars and uncountable instances of violence which have brought about nothing but loss, destruction and remorse to mankind. Development would have definitely been at a much higher scale if wars had not taken place and mankind would have been much happier and peaceful. Along with scientific progress, weapons of destruction and violence have also advanced. These are unfortunate developments. Due to the unmitigated spectre of violence and war compounded by the nuclear arsenals, the very existence of mankind is threatened.

A wish for world peace would mean a global environment where people share ideas and resources. Tolerance for differences in race, religion and cultures would prevail. This would be a world where people worked together not against one another. My generation would be free from wasting time with disputes and conflicts. I could live a life with my family where I could travel without fear to any part of the world. The destruction from violence and war would be eliminated which would let my generation truly see the wonders of the world before these places are destroyed through warfare. This wish is one I feel well worth requesting if given the opportunity.

5. Describe an area in your city or hometown which is famous for its street food. Give details of the familiar sights and sounds you would experience on this street. ***ICSE Specimen Paper 2022 Sem II***

Ans. A city does not comprise only of the infrastructure or the people residing there but it also comprises its food, festivals, styles, traditions and customs of the city. Every Indian city is with its own differences. For instance, the existence of Kolkata is itself an art. Not only due to the appreciation and thriving of the literal sense of art and culture, but there's also more to it. Each and every location has its own style and type of food, which is also influenced also the creed and sect of people living in majority in that area.

I belong to Kolkata, Old Lake Town region which is very peaceful yet thriving locality. The planned locality was earlier not very developed with only street food and small local stores. But, it is now full of important food and leisure hub having many famous local as well as international fast food chains and a shopping mall along with many street food stalls. One can find many local sweetmeat shops with tasty *sondesh* of many varieties and *mishit doi* served in mud pots. One can also find small stops to eat the spicy and tangy *puchka*, *churmur* and *jhaalmudi*. It is not uncommon for these stalls and shops to be brimming with customers.

One cannot forget the many varieties of rolls sold here. The stalls selling these rolls are always surrounded by people waiting for their turn to get their delicious rolls. The streets are completely busy with people thronging around hawkers haggling to buy their wares. One can also find stores selling biryanis, macher jhol and many other dishes.

Apart from Lake Town, there is the area of Park Street and adjoining areas like Bow Barracks which are famous for wine, cakes, cookies. One can also look out for an area called Territi Bazar which is famous for its variety of Chinese breakfast! Out of all, the area of New Market or Esplanade has some of the best and unique street food. The list can go on-and-on, such is the grandeur of Kolkata.

6. Which do you prefer-morning, afternoon, evening or night?

Describe your favourite time of the day. What are the sights, sounds, smells and feelings that you associate with your favourite time of the day? Why do you like this part of the day better than the others? ***ICSE 2020***

Examiner's Comment

- Most candidates misunderstood the topic and gave an account of all parts of the day rather then focusing on their favourite time.
- Poor use of language was seen in some cases while some candidates had described seasons instead.

Suggestions for Students

- Plan before attempting question
- Perform adequate reading and vocabulary building exercises.
- Use all senses to accentuate the composition.

Ans.

Morning

My best time of the day is early morning. Usually, I get up at 5 o'clock in the morning. Getting up early makes me feel pleased as I can offer prayer to God and exercise which enhances my energy. I start my day with a refreshed mind. It is still dark in the early morning. The birds seem to just start to wake up. It's pretty calm and quiet all around our locality. It is the perfect time for me to breathe in the fresh air and take my tea while standing in my balcony. At this time, the sky is like a canvas where God paints a streak simply dividing the dark from the light. Gradually, more colours come out, red being the first.

The clouds float like cotton balls circling the nucleus of sky, the Sun. The sun rises spreading yellow-golden colour all over the sky. In the meantime I finish my tea, following which my mother asks me to take bath. So I prepare myself for school. While I am getting ready, my mind comes at peace as the devotional music from adjacent temple starts to play. Then when I am eating my breakfast, I plan the day's schedule.

Sometimes, (on the days of school holidays) I also go for a walk. It is a pleasure for me to see the activities in early morning. Generally, there are students and parents on the side of the road, waiting for their school buses. Sweepers are busy cleaning the roads. Grocery shops are just opening their shutters. Fresh cold air is blowing. Newspaper boys are busy distributing papers and there are only a few vehicles on road.

Afternoon

The best time of the day for me is afternoon.The afternoon is the time that starts in mid-day and ends in evening. It is the time when the Sun is descending from its daytime peak position. During this time, the sun moves roughly from the centre to the Western part of the sky. Sunlight becomes bright and glaring. It is also the time when I return from school at 2:30 pm and relax after a hectic schedule. Everybody is busy with their work; there are lots of vehicles on the road, sometime this creates traffic jam. Often, I get late in reaching home. After reaching home, I feel relaxed. I change my clothes. It gives me a feeling of freshness. Sometimes, I watch television for a while.

Then, I read the newspaper as I do not have time to read it in the morning. I also play with my pet dog it gives me a sense of pure joy and relaxation. I chat with my mother and tell her about my whole day. While I eat my lunch, she advices me about my study. Sometimes, my mother makes my favourite dishes for me. While I take my lunch, my pet dog sits before me expecting food. I give him some food inspite of my mother's disapproval. After lunch, I usually take a nap. It refreshes my body muscles and my mind. Scientific research proves that the ability to remain alert is associated with proper resting time. So, taking rest in afternoon rejuvenates me to study properly in the evening. We can also nurture hobbies like music, painting, etc. during afternoon. As it is considered relaxing time, we can fully utilise this time for our extra-curricular activities. In the afternoon, I attend my guitar class twice a week. It gives me immense pleasure and enhances my mind. Thus, afternoon is the best part of my day.

Evening

For me, the best part of the day is between five to seven in the evening. It is truly a relaxed and peaceful time for our family after a hectic morning at school or at the office. My mother whose day started at 5:00 am would be relaxing in our balcony with a cup of coffee and some snacks and I would be sitting by her chatting about the whole day activities in schools and tuition centre. It is the best time when we can share our views about everything. My father would be in his favourite chair reading the newspaper or watching news on the television.

After a while, I play with my dog who loves to run around with me. Sometime, I go to the nearby park to play with my friends. We have great fun on the swings, often screaming or singing which reduces our tiredness and rejuvenates us.

Later, as I sit on the grass to rest, I admire the scenery around me. There are lots of flowers blooming in our park. Now, it is time for sunset. The Sun, a golden ball of fire, is sinking behind the buildings. Gold, pink, orange and yellow colours are displaying in the sky, making it a huge painting of our artist. Birds are seen flying back to their nests. All the plants and trees are looking beautiful in the twilight.

The stillness and quietness of the evening make me feel at peace with everything. It is the time when the crickets start to chirp and the surrounding becames quiet. Now, it is the time to return back home. Coming back home, I take some light snacks and prepare myself for doing homework.

Thus, evening is my favourite time of the day, a time of beauty and quietness when we can relax after a hectic day schedule.

Night

The favourite part of the day for me is night. After taking the dinner, it is the time which I can spend according to my wish. In the night time, my surrounding is most peaceful, noise-free and distraction free. During this time, I can study attentively. I can learn a topic with just one attempt and that retains longer in my memory.

I prefer night time as it signifies that I can just relax and study. There is no stress. I feel comfortable to do my work watch tv and eat. Literally, night is my comfort zone when I can do anything I wish to do.

It is always good to relax at home. After spending the whole day in school, in coaching centre, in hobby centre my full body requires rest. It is only possible during the night. Lying on my own bed with my favourite pillows makes my body muscles relaxed. This helps me to boost up my energy.

Scientific studies suggest that the brain works actively at night; thus, it is more effective to study before I go to bed. Studies also suggest that a good amount of sleep at night also helps good memory retention. So, I take atleast 7 hours sleep every night. This proper resting time helps me to start my next day with energy.

7. Your class had to conduct a Morning Assembly. Write an account of how you prepared for it, what your role was and what you gained from the experience. ***ICSE 2019***

Ans. I am the class monitor for Class X in our school. One week before Teachers' Day, our school Principal informed me that my class will conduct the Morning Assembly on Teachers' Day and we should start preparing for it.

That day, I asked my classmates to wait in the classroom during the short morning break and announced this decision of the Principal. I also informed two classmates that they would look after the public address system and lighting arrangements. The remaining students of our class (35 in number) would ensure that all the school students were seated in their respective places well before the 'Principal' arrives. I was to act as the Principal.

The programme decided was that after I made the announcements for the day, one student would speak on a topic of interest for five minutes. We chose a highly vocal girl, Rashmi, of the class to speak on the importance of Teachers' Day. For the next two days, we rehearsed our roles in the auditorium. I made some improvements in what Rashmi had prepared by using simple words. I also asked her to speak slower than her normal speed as students of junior classes should also understand what she said. The two boys in charge of the sound and light arrangements also checked that all the equipment was in working condition one day before the important day.

The day finally arrived. My classmates came 15 minutes earlier than normal and ensured that all students were seated. When the bell rang for the start of the Assembly, I came out from behind the curtain and walked up to the podium. Simultaneously, all the students stood up. After we had greeted each other, we sang the Vande Mataram. Then, I told the students to sit down and made two announcements. After that Rashmi spoke very enthusiastically on her topic. The rehearsals had paid off handsomely in her case. After singing the National Anthem, I announced the end of the Assembly.

From the experience of conducting the Morning Assembly, I have gained the knowledge that conducting any important event successfully requires proper and detailed planning. I also learnt that it is important to conduct rehearsals to iron out any flaws before the actual event.

8. Summers are becoming hotter with each passing year. Write a description of one such very hot day. What did you see and hear as you walked outside? How were birds and animals affected? ***ICSE 2019***

Examiner's Comment

- Many candidates' focus had completely shifted to global warming.
- Most students confused between a hot summer day and the summer season.

Suggestions for Students

- Perform adequate reading and vocabulary building exercises.
- Think in a sequential and logical pattern.
- Get familiar with the structure of a formal composition.

Ans. I was spending the summer holidays in my small native village. It was the beginning of June when I had to go out to the post office in the nearby village for some work. The morning was very stuffy. There was not a single cloud in the sky or any breeze to dry my sweat as I walked the three-kilometre distance on the cart track. As the Sun rose higher and higher, it shone more strongly. Although I was wearing a cap, I felt the Sun's heat. However, I walked on the ground that seemed as hot as a furnace.

Then, hot winds began to blow and the dust started swirling around me. I saw that the condition of birds and animals was as bad as mine. The birds were trying to seek shelter in the trunk of leafless trees. I saw some black buffaloes which had lain down in a pond which still had some water, although the water was very dirty. The trees and bushes looked withered. The grass was yellowed and totally dry. The cart track was deserted, as all people were indoors. I did not meet anyone during the 30 minutes I walked to the post office.

By the time, I finished the work at the post office, it was 2 p.m. I was dreading the trek back home.

However, I was lucky to find a small dhaba in this village where I could eat lunch and relax till the evening in the shade. As I had nothing to do back at home, I decided to do back just that. After eating a delicious lunch, I dozed off while sitting under the fan in the dhaba.

The heat continued till evening. When I woke up, I found that the Sun was about to set. After having tea at the dhaba, I started the walk back home. People had begun to move about. The silence of the village was broken by the shouts of some hawkers. The village was coming to life. I hastened my steps and was soon back at home. The first thing I did was to have a bath and change into fresh clothes. I was feeling comfortable again.

9. You had been waiting outside the examination hall. Describe what you saw and the sounds you heard when you arrived at the place. What were your feelings? Describe how the scene changed once you entered the hall and the examination started. ***ICSE 2018***

Examiner's Comment

- Many candidates' failed to base the composition on their personal experience.
- Some candidates missed the description of noise, chatter and last minute rush.

Suggestions for Students

- Perform adequate reading and vocabulary building exercises.
- Think in a sequential and logical pattern.

Ans. Examinations sap the examinees of energy and make them sleepless for nights. But then, it has not so far been possible to devise a better way of judging their ability. So, they are a necessary evil which all students have to face.

Students have to work hard for months. As the crucial day arrives, they reach the examination hall in tension.

I had a similar experience during my Board examination. A few minutes before the start of the first paper, I saw a strange scene outside the examination hall. An eerie silence prevailed there. The examinees were carrying their books and notes in their hands which they had already mugged up and were now trying to revise. Most of the examinees were not inclined to talk to anybody. But a few, sitting or standing in groups of two or three, were seen discussing some points. I did not form a group, rather stood alone to wait for the Supervisor to turn up.

Even the dullest students appeared to be great scholars outside the examination hall. They were reading their books most attentively. Some of them may have been thinking of devising some means of copying or how to behave if they were caught copying.

Most of the students reached the examination hall well before time. They looked at the notice-board to find out their room and even tried to locate their seats. As soon as the bell rang, all the students entered the hall. A few examinees reached the hall late and entered in a state of great excitement. The supervisor was lenient and accommodated them. Soon, everyone was seated in silence. The only sound was that of the supervisor who was getting ready to distribute the papers and announcing the rules of the exam. No one talked or tried to recall anything, rather everyone prayed and prepared to do their best.

10. There has been heavy rain in your city/town. You went to school but found that it was closed because of the rain. Describe the sights and sounds near the school and narrate how you finally reached home and spent the rest of the day. ***ICSE 2017***

Ans. It had been raining very heavily since last night with lightening and sound of thunder terrifying us. In the morning, the streets and roads were flooded but still I got ready for school. I took a raincoat and left.

While walking, I saw that there was water everywhere. At some places, it was knee deep. Fewer people could be seen on the roads. The roads had disappeared under the water and one could cross it only by walking through it. I saw no student of my school on the way except Mr. Sharma . He teaches Maths at our school and rarely takes leave. Though the rain had stopped, water drops were falling from the tree leaves as if it were raining. The sky had again become dark with heavy clouds suggesting that it could rain anytime again, so I was walking at an escalated speed.

When I reached the school, I found a big notice announcing that the school was closed for the day as water had entered the ground and some classrooms. There were some other students who had ventured to the school inspite of all odds.

Some of them left after reading the notice while others stayed back, talking and playing with their friends. I decided to go back home since the weather looked uncertain. As I was leaving, I saw Rishi, a friend of mine, enter the school campus. I greeted him and shared the news with him.We live nearby so we decided to go together. He told me that the road he took wasn't submerged in water, so we took that path.

On the way, I saw a few huts which were in a very bad condition. The tin sheets on top of a few had fallen down. They were being put back in place by people. Nearby, a couple of trees were struck by lightning and had fallen on the footpath. The road, however, was cleaner than the one I took and thus, I reached home in little time.

My mother was waiting for me. She told me to change into clean clothes as soon as she saw my wet trousers. I was given a hot cup of milk and told to study at home. Soon, it started drizzling again. Looking out the window, I wondered how the rain had troubled people and prayed it would stop soon.

11. You walk home from school one afternoon to find the door unlocked and on entering you are shocked to see the house in total disarray. You call out but get no answer. Describe in detail what you saw, the reason behind your house being in total disarray and how you found your family. Mention also, how the experience ended and what impact it had on your life. ***ICSE 2016***

Ans. I returned home from school in the afternoon. When I reached home, I found the door unlocked. I went inside and was shocked to see the house in total disorder. I called my mother, who would usually be home at that time, but nobody answered. When I entered the drawing room, the whole furniture was turned up side down. Every bag and almirah was emptied, throwing everything on the floor. It seemed that the whole house was searched for something. What was more disturbing and strange was that nothing was stolen; even the i-phones and i-pods were on the desks, along with my mother's wallet.

As I was worried about my mother and younger brother, I enquired all my mother's friends and our relatives. She was at one of her friends' house. Hearing about the incident, my mother arrived home in ten minutes and was equally horrified to see the house in such a condition.

My mother informed me that she had gone to meet her friend who had got a lottery of one crore. She might have not locked the house properly in a hurry. Later, after much investigation, it was found that some small children, who were playing outside, were chased by some monkeys. In panic, the children, seeing the door unlocked, entered the house to hide but the monkeys followed them. A long hide and seek game ensued between the children and the monkeys. The monkeys were responsible for throwing everything out of the closets and the furniture was turned upside down by the children.

Somehow, the children managed to hide themselves in the store adjacent to our bedroom. Monkeys left and went outside the house. We all breathed a sigh of relief that there was no theft or robbery. It took at least two hours to set the house again in order.

It was really an unforgettable day in my life as I got really scared looking at the condition of my house and not one member of my family member present. But, I thanked God that my mother's mistake resulted in saving small children from being bitten by monkeys.

12. Describe in detail the view from your bedroom window. Does your room overlook a park? A busy street? What are the sights, sounds and smells that you would typically see, hear and experience at different times of the day? ***ICSE 2015***

Ans. My bedroom is the zone of maximum comfort for me. The mere sight of my bed, study table, almirahs, etc. dispels all my fatigue and freshens me up. The view from the window is very beautiful. My window overlooks a park. The park has tall and wide trees which attract a variety of birds like parrots and white pigeons. The grass and bushes are neatly trimmed and the little plants bear flowers in many colours. There is a jogging track too built inside it. Indeed, just one look outside the window has such a soothing effect on me, which is beyond description.

In the morning after waking up, I see people running and jogging on the track. I also hear the sounds and hoots of birds. Besides, the breeze of dawn coupled with the aroma of trees, prepares me to kickstart my day on a positive note. I, however, enjoy the evening view the most.

When I return home in the evening, the sweet smell of the trees and the sight of little kids playing in the park rejuvenate my soul. The rays of the setting Sun are scattered all over the sky giving it the most radiant look. The birds are seen returning to their homes and there is a pleasant and calm aura all around.

I gaze at all the trivialities and activities that are visible from my window while taking my evening snacks and tea. Sometimes, my sister joins me and we chat and discuss the various things and people we see in the park. We also miss the regular visitors of the park if they do not turn up. The comfort that one draws at one's home is unmatched by all the luxuries of expensive hotels and buildings. Even more comforting is that little corner which one calls one's bedroom.

Therefore, the window of my room and the view of the park are seemingly little things but together they make up an integral part of my daily routine.

13. Describe an early morning walk through your city or town in winter. Give details of the smells, sights, sounds and feelings you experienced. ***ICSE 2014***

Ans. A morning walk is very rewarding. It is only at this time in the cities when the roads are not crowded as there is hardly any traffic. One can enjoy the walk in the lap of nature. As one walks, the worries and anxieties vanish away. The sheer delight of the movement is enough to make the day. In the morning, the nature is at its best.

I go for morning walk with my friends to the nearby park where we take two or more rounds of the walking path. As we set out from our home, we see the street deserted except for a few walkers like us. There are couples in track suits and sports shoes walking briskly along. There are also groups of elderly men gossiping and laughing among themselves. Youngsters are seen wearing ear phones and jogging to their favourite songs.

In the quiet of the morning, I can hear the chirping of the birds, parrots and pigeons. They are seen flying from one branch of a tree to another. Amidst the sheet of thin white fog, the colourful flowers in the park give solace to the heart and are a feast to the eyes. The fragrance of the sweet smelling flowers fills my mind with a freshness which cannot be compared to anything in the world.

The park is filled with people of various age groups. The cold winter has not prevented these health conscious individuals to stay back in their cozy beds and to put off going for the morning walk, the most important nutrient for the healthy body.

The pure fresh air of the morning, devoid of the poisonous gases exhaled by the innumerable vehicles running to and fro in the city streets, gives a boost to the body to battle the days' hectic schedule.

Gradually, penetrating through the dense fog, the first rays of lights glimmer and shine across the park. Now, the body begins to respond well to the movements of the limbs and the flow of fresh, cool air one breathes. The momentum now sets in and the legs appear to walk effortlessly. One feet glides over the other as if trying to be the first to land ahead. An hour later, it is time to stop as the empty stomach demands attention.

By the time we return from our walk many tea-stalls and sweet shops are open making fresh sweets and snacks. We stop at our favourite shop where we indulge in hot tea and samosas.

Words are insufficient to describe the feelings one undergoes during winter morning walks and the experience of indulging in hot and tempting snacks.

14. You were on a school trip and were on your way back to the hotel late one night when your school bus, full of children, broke down in a lonely area. Describe what you saw and experienced as you looked around. How was the problem solved? ***ICSE 2013***

Ans. We had been looking forward to our school trip from the very first day in Class X. Every year, school plans tours for every class and it is always a special affair. This year, we went to Nainital for three nights and four days. We left for Nainital late in the night. We reached our hotel in the morning and after breakfast, our teachers advised us to take some rest.

After some rest, we got ready and gathered for lunch. After lunch, we left for local sight seeing and shopping in the local markets. It was evening then and our teachers gathered us for dinner. We dined at a local restaurant which was famous for its food.

It was dark when we left for our hotel. Singing songs, we had hardly reached half way when suddenly the bus broke down. It was 11 pm and we were in a deserted place. The driver left the bus to find a garage so that he could get it fixed. It was totally dark and cold too. The hills and trees outstretched on both the sides. It was an eerie feeling.

Our teachers were also worried but they kept their calm and instructed us to remain quiet and not to make any noise, least we drew attention of anti-social elements. At a distance of 200 metres, we saw some light, for there were lamps burning. We all moved towards it with some hope. On reaching there, we saw a group of friends who were camping there. They were singing, dancing and enjoying themselves around the bonfire. When we approached them, they were shocked and asked the reason of our approach. We told them our predicament. They asked all the students to use their tents. We all had such a nice time dancing, singing and sharing some of our school experiences with them. It became the most memorable trip ever.

Then, noodles were prepared and everyone enjoyed their late night maggi around the bonfire. We were awake until the first rays of the sun indicated that it was morning. The bus was redeemed and so we all bid our goodbyes to the lovely people who helped us and made our trip an exciting adventure to be cherished life-long.

15. People play a very important role in our lives. Describe in vivid detail, any one person and show how he/she has been a very special influence in your life. ***ICSE 2012***

Ans. When reflecting on personal influences in my life, no one has had a greater impact than my father. He is a role model for me. He always stands by my side. Whenever I fall down, he encourages me to stand up by myself. I have always admired his open mind, compassion and sense of understanding. He is a very reserved man, but has a great sense of humour, and always knows how to put a smile on my face. One good lesson my dad has taught me is that you most likely won't have the answer to everything, but that is what life is for, to learn from your mistakes and find those answers you are looking for. From him, I also learned that to make people hear you, you need to speak.

My father has always taught me the right behaviour. I still remember the day that my father sat next to me and said that, "Hey son, the most important thing to help you become a successful person is your honesty. Never lie to anyone and never lie to yourself." After saying that, he slowly explained the value of honesty. He told me that every bad situation in the world began with a lie. When a person steals something, he lies to the law, or when a husband cheats on his wife, he lies to his wife. I always think back on these words whenever I am in trouble.

In every aspect of my life, my father continuously pushes me to excellence. Whenever I feel like giving up, or have a question or a concern, I know I can always call on him for advise. His teachings are a cure for my selfishness. He taught me to consider everyone a part of my family and taught me how to love people by sharing and giving. From him, I have learned that sometimes you have to put other's needs ahead of your own, but not to the point that they begin taking advantage of you. His strength seems to be unbreakable during hard times. He is also extremely determined to accomplish anything he sets his mind on. I hold great esteem for how he stands up for what he believes in and never back down. I am what I am because of him and whatever I will achieve in my life will be credited to him.

16. Think of a time when you achieved a personal goal. Say why the goal was important to you and how you achieved it. Describe how you felt on achieving it. ***ICSE 2010***

Ans. Learning something new is a very scary experience. One of the most difficult things I have ever had to do in school was to learn cycling. I was mortally afraid of falling and injuring myself. I watched my friends with disdain as they cycled to school, while I trudged along with my school bag on my shoulder. Occasionally, a friend would give me a lift on his bicycle which would make me feel even more awkward. One day, I finally decided to learn this important skill and requested my father to help me.

New situations always made me a bit nervous and my first cycling lesson was no exception. Early Sunday morning when everyone was fast asleep, I crept out of bed, put on my full sleeves shirt and trousers. As I wheeled out my brother's bicycle on to the driveway, my father called out to me. He was glossing over the newspaper which he put aside as he came towards me. We steadily made our way to the park adjacent to our house.

Reaching the park, he made me sit on the cycle holding the seat from behind. My legs barely touched the lower pedal. A stream of instructions followed, "Hold the handle straight", "Look straight ahead", "Don't stop peddling,'' etc. He gave an initial push to the cycle from behind. I found these coordinated instructions quite difficult to follow, and soon I was down with the cycle over me.

However, the strong grip of my father softened the fall and I escaped with minor bruises. My father was patient. He encouraged me and boosted my confidence. So, I got up and holding the handle of the cycle firmly, I pushed the pedal down with my legs, at the same time trying to retain my upright position. In about an hour's time, I learnt to coordinate the movements as my father ran behind holding the seat of the cycle.

The next day, we repeated the entire exercise, completing one round of the park. During the second round, I felt more free and easy. To my surprise, I found my father standing right in front of me smiling and waving. He had intentionally let go of my seat after the first round. I had indeed mastered the skill of cycling. From that day onwards, it became my hobby and later fetched me the Inter-School Championship Trophy.

Learning to cycle was not easy for me. However, my persistence in achieving this personal goal finally paid off. Now whenever I am faced with a new challenge, I am not nervous. This is because I know that as I practice more, my skills would get better. This has made me more confident and bold. It is indeed a wonderful feeling when you achieve a goal, you have set for yourself.

17. A school carnival or fete is a great occasion for fun with friends. Describe one such event in your school. **ICSE 2010**

Ans. The word 'carnival' itself brings forth tremendous excitement in the hearts of kids and adults alike. The word spells enjoyment and an occasion of fun with friends and family. Every alternate year, our school organises a carnival for students, their families and friends.This year, our school organised the carnival in the month of December and aptly called it the 'Christmas Carnival'. A lot of preparations and hard labour went into making this carnival a successful event.

This year, we had fifteen game stalls and seventeen food stalls. The junior and senior students were divided into groups and deployed at each stall in such an organised manner that they not only got an opportunity to shoulder the responsibility of the stall but also got time to visit other stalls and enjoy the carnival along with their friends.

Amongst the game stalls, the most popular ones were Nine Pins, Ring the Duck, Shoot the Basket, Test of Strength, etc. However, the greatest attraction was The Golden Goal stall, where one had to kick a football into a three-foot ring suspended in the air, grossed the highest amount of money.

A large variety of fast food items was served at the various food stalls. There was a persistent rush at the *Chaat* stall, the *Pakoras* stall and the *Dosa* stall. The coffee stall also turned out to be a huge favourite. As the evening progressed and the chill increased, everybody wanted to grab a cup of coffee. The people also enjoyed many rounds of 'Housie' while many of the senior students interacted with the crowds in the guise of clowns and other cartoon figures and held the interest of little kids.

The carnival came to an end late in the evening with the prizes for the 'Lucky Draw' being announced. The first prize was a LCD Television and was won by a student of Class VI. The second prize was a 230 litre refrigerator and the third prize was a Samsung Washing Machine. There were also ten consolation prizes which consisted of ten Titan wrist watches. This year, the carnival was a grand success with a record breaking fifteen thousand people attending the event, hats off to our dedicated team of teachers and the able guidance of our Principal.

18. The waiting room at a railway station presents a wonderful opportunity to observe human behaviour. Describe an experience when you were early for a train and had to spend some time in the waiting room with different kinds of people. **ICSE 2009**

Ans. If you ever want to observe human behaviour closely, I think one of the best places to do so is the waiting room of a railway station that accommodates a huge variation of our modern day society. I was enroute Delhi to Kolkata and due to an unfortunate misunderstanding, was forced to switch trains at Lucknow. The time gap was two hours between both train hence, I had no other option but to take refuge at the waiting room of the railway station. As I entered the waiting room a foul smell tickled my nostrils but I soon became accustomed to it. The announcement of the arrival of a train caused some seats to get vacant and I quickly occupied one and made myself comfortable. Opposite to me, a family of five was busy haggling over some petty issue. Apparently, the wife had forgotten to complete some household chores before leaving and the husband was reprimanding her for the same.

Their three children, the eldest being not more than eight years old, were chasing each other around the waiting room and the mother was screeching her head off trying to control them.

On another bench sat an elderly couple who was hardly talking to each other. They seemed to be too lost in a world of their own, probably weighed down by the worries of this relentless world. Suddenly, the old lady said something which brought a smile to the otherwise serious face of the gentleman and he keenly began to observe the three little ones playing with each other.

Another young newly married couple sat in the farthermost corner of the room talking in hushed voices to each other. Fortunately, the next announcement was for their train and they were replaced by a contingent of women hockey players who were returning from a match. By their upbeat mood and excitement, one could easily guage that they had won their match and were now eager to get back home.

It was indeed a very interesting two hour wait. Isn't it strange that when a person sits idle, he notices a variety of human behaviour which normally a troubled mind would have overlooked? Such was the case with me and believe me, I enjoyed every moment of it till the arrival of my train was announced.

19. A village fair is very different from a city one. It is usually held annually and is connected with a religious festival or harvest. The purpose of such fairs is usually trade and to exhibit and sell village handicrafts. Describe one such fair. ***ICSE 2008***

Ans. A village fair is very different from one in a city. The village folk seek entertainment in fairs and festivals. It is usually held annually and connected with a religious festival or harvest. The purpose of such fairs is usually trade and to exhibit and sell village handicraft. The shopkeepers open temporary stalls in the open ground, while the magicians and jugglers entertain people and make money.

Punjab is a land of vibrant people who celebrate festivals and other occasions with great zeal and zest. Baisakhi is one of such occasion as it marks the beginning of the harvesting of crops, signifying reaping the fruit of their labour.

Last year, I went to visit my maternal uncle in Punjab. I was overjoyed to see the fair which was spread over a large tract of open land. The stalls were tastefully decorated with ribbons and buntings. Young girls in beautiful bright dresses were being irresistibly drawn towards the stalls where bangles of all colours were displayed.

The greatest attraction of the fair was the wrestling bouts being held in a big open ground surrounded all round by the spectators. Big prizes had been announced for the wrestlers winning over their respective rivals.

There was a vast variety of sights that attracted the attention of the visitors. A motor cyclist was running his vehicle on the walls of a pucca pit. A magician was showing his tricks. There was a snake charmer, a monkey show and a bear dance. Children were specially interested in buying balloons and toys. The shopkeepers who had put up their stalls of eatables were having a hay day. Pakoras and jalebis could not be missed by anybody as they are the favourite with the Punjabis. However, the greatest attraction of the fair was 'Bhangra', the folk dance of Punjab, which was being performed enthusiastically by a few young boys. The cattle fair was a sight not to be missed since the best breeds of cattle – the cows, bulls, horses, buffaloes etc. – were brought for sale. In this way, fairs show the world their rich cultural heritage.

20. You are a spectator at a cricket match. Trouble erupts suddenly in the stadium and you witness a riot among the crowd. Give a vivid description of the scene. ***ICSE 2006***

Ans. 'Dhoni Dhoni,' shouted the crowd as Mahendra Singh Dhoni, the Indian cricket captain, faced the fast bowler of Pakistan. There was dead silence as the ball failed to strike the bat and hit Dhoni's pad. The bowler and the entire Pakistani I team jumped with joy, appealing to the umpire for an LBW.

Not convinced, he signalled to the third umpire. A tense silence followed as the crowd waited for the decision. As the board flashed NOT OUT, the entire stadium reverberated with joy. The situation seemed hopeless for India was trailing by 33 runs with only two overs to spare, in the World Cup's final match at the Feroz Shah Kotla ground in New Delhi.

The tension in the crowd increased as the run rate per over mounted. Unhappy with the slow scoring, a section of the crowd started raising slogans and hurling bottles into the field. This was objected to by others, and soon a melee ensued.

In the free-for-all that followed, people ran helter skelter for cover, causing a stampede. Women and children caught in the stampede cried out for help. Utter confusion prevailed in the stadium for well over fifteen minutes. The match was halted and the organisers appealed to the audience to remain calm and maintain order, for the match to continue.

In the meantime, the local administration immediately swung into action, the police used mild force to quell the rioters. They rounded up some mischief mongers and herded them out of the stadium. The injured were provided first aid by the paramedics while the seriously injured were carried away on stretchers to the ambulance. Some semblance of order being restored, the umpires decided to continue the match.

Not losing hope, my friends and I started waving the Indian tricolour and shouting, "We want four, We want four." Soon, the entire stadium reverberated with this slogan. Taking a cue from the crowd, Dhoni in the very first ball of the over struck for a four. This was followed by two consecutive fours and a six. This proved to be the turning point of the match. Now with victory in sight, the crowd became ecstatic, bursting crackers and beating drums.

There was pin drop silence as the over progressed, with just ten runs coming of the first five balls. The tension became palpable as the last ball was bowled. He valiantly lifted the ball over the long on boundary, with bated breath we watched as a fielder ran after it and to our dismay, took a brilliant catch just as his outstretched leg crossed the boundary rope. The third umpire's decision was called for and with the light blinking green, bedlam broke loose in the stadium. The crowd went berserk with joy and happiness. I embraced my friends, jubilant at India's victory.

21. You have returned to your city after spending five years in a foreign country. The city has changed during your absence. Describe the changes that have affected the life of people in the city. Give your personal views regarding the changes. ***ICSE 2005***

Ans. I returned to my city after almost five years. A lot has changed in these years while I was completing my studies abroad. I boarded the taxi available outside the airport. The taxi was very comfortable with AC and GPS fitted. The taxi driver spoke in English and then excused himself as he steered the vehicle to the side and answered his cell phone. It had been five years and India had changed considerably. My city was different. Now, it seems everyone has a cell phone. The most unexpected thing happened when the taxi driver asked me whether I would like to pay by cash or card. I almost gave a jaw-dropping reaction to him.

On my way, I noticed that the roads were wide and vehicle were less. New and improved versions of motor vehicles decorated the roads. The road itself spoke of so much change. Traffic lights now indicated the time you have to wait or pass. The broad roads and flyovers with green signboards of international standard dazzled me. I could see all new DTC buses fitted with AC and of international look.

But what caught my attention was the tremendous progress made by the Metro. Every nook and corner of Delhi was touched by the Metro.

When I reached home, it was completely transformed. The walls were no longer painted but were decorated with tasteful wallpapers. Photo frames had given way to elegant and modern paintings. The rooms were spacious. The furniture matched the European contemporary style. Modular kitchen with in-built microwave looked tremendous. Digital cable on TV offered numerous national and international channels to choose from. This was just too much to take in.

I also met some of my friends in the evening. They took me to the nearby mall. As we passed through, I could see the market completely transformed. Restaurants serving fast food and international cuisines with neon lights and flashy signboards covered the landscape. I treated my friends at a restaurant serving authentic Japanese cuisine. Everyone relished 'sushi', the famous delicacy of Japan. I could observe that not only the attitude but the tastes of the people have also changed. Five years ago, the only restaurant we used to go was Pizza Hut or McDonald but now everything has changed.

05

Picture Composition

Picture composition is usually divided into three patterns. A student is asked to describe a given picture, to make a story out of it or to express and elaborate upon the thoughts and feelings suggested by the given picture. The picture can be a photograph, an action scene, a quote written over a picture or a scene or a sketch of a famous personality. The composition is written in three different forms so as to highlight this uniqueness.

It requires a wide range of imagination, creativity, good hold on vocabulary and the ability to sequence all events together.

Following points should be followed while writing picture composition

- The student should look at the picture carefully to ascertain the basic plot or the theme.
- The picture should be studied carefully with a view to identify the specific and minute details.
- The focus should be widened to take into account the other or peripheral details, given in the picture, i.e. facial expressions, postures, clothes, etc.
- Design the factors or causes which have an impact on the details.
- A strong conclusion is required at the end of the composition.
- If the picture doesn't suggest anything evidently, the student is advised to invent a theme which bears a direct connection with the picture.
- After identifying or deciding the theme, attention should be paid to the designing or moulding of the characters of the story.

PYQs Previous Years' Questions

1. Study the picture given below. Write a story or a description or an account of what it suggests to you. Your composition may be about the subject of the picture or you may take suggestions from it; however, there must be a clear connection between the picture and your composition. **ICSE 2023**

Ans. Dog was the first animal that humans tamed when they settled down and started practicing agriculture. They have been rightfully called a 'man's best friend'. Dogs have always been very helpful to humans and have always shared a special relationship with us. These fluffy creatures protect us from dangers, are the most loyal creatures and stand by our side in thick and thin.

Regardless of their role in helping humans over the generations, a lot of dogs are stray and lonely in the streets. They often don't have anyone to help them. People even behave rudely to them at times. Since they can't voice their emotions, it is important for humans to try to understand them and help them by providing any sort of assistance they may need, as is shown in the given picture.

It is important to be compassionate towards them and all other animals because they are living beings and need help, just like humans. Just by treating the dogs well, we can make sure that those animals who on the streets are able to survive and lead a good life. Even a little act of kindness such as protecting them from the rain or the cold can act wonders.

Dogs are amongst the most loyal creatures, and they would go to any length to protect the people they care about. They don't need money or any material possessions, only to be treated with kindness, care and compassion and they would be some of the best companions.

Their symbiotic relationship with humans is the reason why we have co-existed together for many years and the dogs on the streets have survived for many years even without proper resources. It is our duty, to help them, to do our part and preserve the bond that exists between our species, the foundations of which were laid thousands of years ago when the first dog became a part of the human community.

2. Study picture given below. Write a story or a description or an account of what it suggests to you. Your composition may be the subject of the picture or you may take suggestions from it; however, there must be a clear connection between the picture and your composition. ***ICSE Specimen Paper 2023***

Ans. Hunger is a long existing and draining problem in India. People, mostly children, from poorer backgrounds might go days without eating. This has burdened India with the huge problem of child malnutrition.

Children who do not get food end up suffering from a lack of nutrients, which weakens them, causes diseases and can even stunt their growth. India, in fact, has the world's highest burden of child malnutrition. Low income has become the primary cause of the issue of malnutrition.

Although investments are made and money is directed towards child welfare, there is only a marginal growth. However, it has rightly not stopped anyone from trying. Several initiatives have also been taken by the Indian Government, including Narendra Modi's vision of 'Kuposhan Mukt Bharat' and various NGOs to put an end to this problem.

One such NGO is the No Hungry Child Organisation. It works for underprivileged background children providing them the Nutritious meal and Education support. They feed hungry children in a clean and open environment, providing food in adequate quantities and simultaneously ensuring that no food goes to waste.

India has the maximum number of children in the world suffering from malnutrition and the claimed aim is to increase awareness on the issue. The first 1000 days of a child are critical for cognitive development, physical growth and immunity. In an attempt to achieve this, Horlicks launched the 'Horlicks Mission Poshan' with actor Amitabh Bachchan as the campaign ambassador. The focus is that during the first 1000 days of a child, they will be addressing the issue of malnutrition, stunting and infant mortality.

In addition to these organisations, we can also play our part in ensuring an end to hunger and child malnutrition. We need to connect and reach far and wide as it is critical for mass awareness to bring in these positives change in the society.

In addition to raising awareness, we must raise funds and actively engage on-ground to make child hunger a subject of mass movement. It is only through everyone's contribution that we can eradicate this social evil.

3. Study the picture given below. Write a short story, description or an account of what it suggests to you. Your composition may be about the subject of the picture or you may take suggestions from it. ***ICSE 2022 Sem II***

Ans. I was passing by a motor garage when I saw him working. I was stunned to see a 12-year-old boy, covered in dirt and car oil trying to repair a car. I went to him and asked him his name.

He told his name was 'Chhotu' as his employer used to call him that. I asked him why he was not at school at that time and was instead working there. Chhotu got emotional and told me his story. He told me that a few months age he also went to a nearby government school.

But one day, his father died in a road accident and his mother had no money left to send him to school. He had to become the bread earner of the family to support his mother and 3 younger siblings. As a result, he dropped out of the school and started doing menial works, and then joined this garage a few months ago. I was so touched by his story that I wanted to do something for him.

I held his hands and told him that he would be going to school from the next day and that he could work in the garage part-time. I also told his employer the same and he agreed. Next day, I went to Chhotu's house and talked to his mother and got him ready along with his siblings to get them admitted in the nearby school.

They felt so happy knowing that they would be going to school. Their mother thanked me a million times. I tried to help their mother by getting her associated with a famous NGO who helps women in distress. They impart them vocational trainings free of cost to make them self-reliant. Chhotu also promised me that he would work hard to become a respectable and learned man in future. I felt so content after helping the child. My soul was filled with happiness.

4. Study the picture given below. Write a short story or description or an account of what the picture suggests to you. Your composition may be about the subject of the picture or you may take suggestions from it.

ICSE Specimen Paper 2022 Sem II

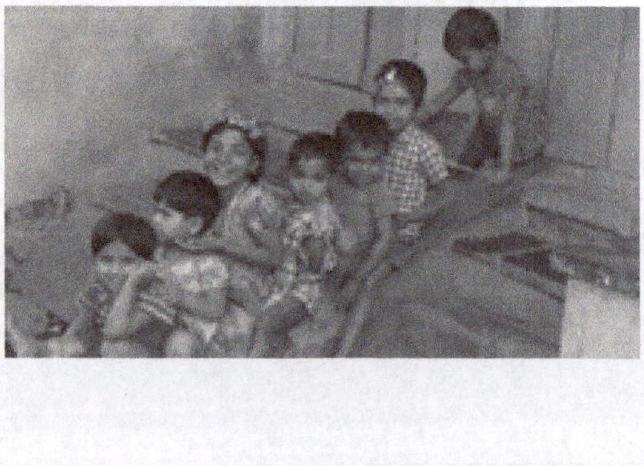

Ans. I have often seen the little children in the nearby slum going to the nearby bangle factory to earn a meagre living. The small, frail-looking children always seem to be distressed going into the dingy region and while coming out, their faces tell nothing but a story of misery and helplessness. Many-a-time, I had wanted to help the children but never came up with an idea of how I would do it and honestly I forgot about it until a few days before my birthday. I had wanted to do something different this year for my birthday and was looking for ideas. I did not want to throw a party this year and did not know exactly what I wanted. One day, while returning from school, I saw those children playing in the dirt and was immediately struck with an idea. I wanted a day of fun and frolic for these children and so went to my parents with the idea.

At first, they were surprised but soon they rejoiced that I wanted to bring joy to those underprivileged. The next day, my father went to the slum and talked to their parents for it. It took him a while but with a promise that the money of the day will be paid by him, the parents agreed. Next, he went to the factory owner who apparently was my father's friend. He also agreed and finally the day arrived. I along with the children went to the nearby park where we played a lot of games. Then, we came to my house and played some more. We also clicked a lot of pictures and watched a movie. After that, we ate Mcdonald meals which was loved by all of them.

It was noon and we decided to go to the nearby zoo. All of the children were very happy and I felt elated for not only was I satisfied on seeing the little children happy just like me but I was also very pleased with the fact that I got to bring that joy on their faces.

5. Study the picture given below. Write a story, a description or an account of what it suggests to you. Your composition may be about the subject of the picture or you may take suggestions from it; however, there must be a clear connection between the picture and your composition.

ICSE 2020

Examiner's Comment

- Most candidates failed to form a composition which would connect with the picture. They mentioned and focused more on the negative impact of mobile phones.
- Some candidates focused shifted to child labour.

Suggestions for Students

- Practice picture composition and discuss with other students how a story or description can be built properly on a picture.
- Improve vocabulary.

Ans. The given picture shows five children, seemingly from a humble background trying to click a selfie. The only difference is that they don't have a mobile phone. But there is one thing that they have that strikes out invariably irrespective of the fact that they are just pretending to take a selfie. That thing is the genuine smile on their face. They may not have the perfect tool for clicking a selfie but they have smile that indicates their joy. In this century, no one can refuse that money has become a deciding factor for the quality of life we are leading. But the problem is that nowadays people have started linking money with happiness. We will have to understand that money helps us in acquiring the comforts and luxuries of life but it does not guarantee happiness.

Money doesn't make you laugh when you are lonely. Indeed, money can help you buy a mansion, a fancy car or branded clothes that might make you happy, but these things don't last for long. Soon, you will start seeing that your neighbours have a better house, more cars and many other things that you don't have. At that moment, money will no longer be a source of happiness.

Happiness isn't a quality like height, weight or income that can be measured easily. It is a complex, indistinct state that is developed by momentary simple pleasures. It is the tendency to feel positive emotions and holding a sense of purpose.

Happiness is not having a lot of privilege or money. It's a broader thing. It is our ability to connect with others, to have meaningful relationships and to have a better community. People who say they are happy have strong connections and communications with other people. That is a sort of recipe for happiness.

This picture of these children smiling with pure innocence reflects their happy souls and gives us the clear message that we should stop searching for happiness in materialistic things. All we need is a big smile from within the heart and the world will be a happy place.

6. Study the picture given below. Write a story, a description or an account of what it suggests to you. Your composition may be about the subject of the picture or you may take suggestions from it; however, there must be a clear connection between the picture and your composition. ***ICSE 2019***

Examiner's Comments

- In several cases, the link between the picture and the essay was missing as many strayed from the central theme conveyed by the picture.
- Some candidates focused on merely listing of 'element seen in the picture' or as a sight viewed on a journey without any reference to the picture. In many cases, the essay did not conclude logically.

Ans. When I went to the local market outside my office during the lunch break to eat something, I observed a very common sight at the nearby small shop which sold all kinds of packaged food items such as chips, sweets, etc.

The nearby primary school had just got over and there was a crowd of students around this shop, who were jostling each other to buy food items. I realised that the children were simply wasting their pocket money on such snacks which are tasty but have very little nutritional value.

In fact, such snack items are harmful to the health of children. This is because they are generally deep fried and spiced heavily, thus being high in calories, fat, sugar and salt.

Children and teenagers these days are more prone to eat such foods daily while they neglect homemade food. They are leading their lives towards danger through their unhealthy lifestyle.

These foods affect their health adversely, whatever may be their age group, weight and health condition. The foods are considered as high in calories; however, one who eats them ends up getting easily exhausted and needs more food frequently. These items do not provide an appropriate level of energy which is required by children of this age.

Thus, the child develops the tendency of craving for food more frequently. What the children acquire from these foods are unhealthy fats, but not healthy nutrients. Thus, they feel a lack of oxygen, which causes poor functioning of the brain. They absorb cholesterol from such types of foods. The cholesterol causes plaque formation in the arteries and creates problems for the heart to pump its normal amount of blood. That's why they feel fatigue.

A high level of bad cholesterol damages their liver and also increases their weight. According to research, such children are overweight or obese and are highly prone to heart and liver disorders. They are more prone to become diabetic and lethargic because of the high amount of sugar collecting in their body. They also get high blood pressure because of the high amount of sodium in the salt. Thus, such children should be trained by their parents to follow healthy eating habits and not waste their pocket money on such items.

7. Study the picture given below. Write a short story, description or an account of what the picture suggests to you. Your composition may be about the subject of the picture or you may take suggestions from it; however, your composition must have a clear connection with the picture. ***ICSE Specimen Paper 2019, 2014***

Ans. Lakshmi was the third child in the family of five children. Her mother was a poor labourer who worked at the nearby construction site along with her father. Lakshmi was 7 years old and used to accompany her parents to the construction site. One day, the manager at the construction site offered to employ Lakshmi at a meagre pay. Her parents accepted, considering it an additional income for their family.

The small girl was forced to do hazardous work without proper compensation. She was risking her life just to keep her family's body and soul together. So tragic is her condition that she had turned into a physical and mental wreck. Her weak and fragile body seemed to suffer from disease. Lakshmi would keep breaking stones in a corner, crying and regretting her fate. Such was her misery that in the days when she should be going to school and playing, she had to work hard. Such was her irony that instead of smiles and carefreeness, her face was writ large with a worry for earning her bread. Child labour is another name which can be given to this picture. It is a serious blot in the efforts to project our nation as a dynamic country. The root cause of child labour is poverty and to some extent ignorance. This girl Lakshmi has become symbolic of all child labourers who are exposed to the difficulties of the world at such a tender age. It is a pity to see her shouldering the responsibilities of her family.

The government should thus, realise the grimness of the situation and take strict actions to ban child labour. Additionally, adopting a multi-prolonged problem-solving approach is required. Furthermore, this should be incentivised by the provision of education and vocational based skills training for each child in the poor families. The combination of the right information complemented by the right rewards will combat child labour and in the longer run, poverty.

8. Study the picture given below. Write a story, a description or an account of what it suggests to you. Your composition may be about the subject of the picture or you may take suggestions from it; however, there must be a clear connection between the picture and your composition. ***ICSE 2018***

Examiner's Comment

- A number of candidates who attempted this question focussed on Women's Cricket in India or on girl child and women empowerment without any reference to the picture.
- In several cases, the essay did not conclude logically. Clear link between the picture and the essay was missing as many strayed from the central theme suggested by the picture.

Suggestions for Students

- Students should learn to link the essay with the given picture.
- Use pictures and encourage students to interpret the pictures from different perspective.

Ans. While I agree that girls from all corners of the nation are coming out of shells and taking positions that were denied to them, I had never expected to see a women's cricket match cheered by all. But I did see the image. Last week, a cricket match was held in Muzaffarnagar, my friend's village. I was in his village because both of us were going on a road trip together and I had to pick him up. While there, he told me about the match and I went to watch the game him thinking it to be an all- boys cricket match. But I was in it for a surprise when I saw three girls playing with the bat and ball as if warming up. I thought maybe they were just kidding. But no, the girls were actually parts of the team that were paying the match that day.

My shock was just wearing off when I found another shock in the forms of the entirety of the villages coming forward to support the girls. My friend, looking at my face, told me that this was how it was in their village. Girls were not discriminated. In fact, girls were told to go to school, get educated, work and participate in all extracurricular activities, especially sports.

Soon, the teams were ready to play the game and what a game it was. The girls were astounding. The first teams totaled at 215 runs in 15 overs while the second team took the lead by 218 runs in 12 overs. While the girls were playing, the village elders were cheering and complementing the girls for their improvement and performance. I was stoked. The image of Indian villages being orthodox, limiting and traditional was completely shattered by the village. Contrary to my opinion, my friend's village was more open and accepting of its female population than many communities residing in cities.

9. Study the picture given here. Write a story, a description or an account of what it suggests to you. Your composition may be about the subject of the picture or you may take suggestions from it; however, there must be a clear connection between the picture and your composition. ***ICSE 2017***

Ans. In the modern world, where the talks of animal rights had taken the world by storm, we talk about cruelty to animals. Human beings taking advantage of their intelligence treat animals in violent and immoral ways. But here what we see is a close bonding between a baby elephant and daughter of Mahendra the caretaker of the elephant.

Mahendra lives in a small house on the outskirts of a jungle near Bengaluru. Herds of elephant are seen in jungles and Mahendra is employed at a plantation where elephants root out stumps with their heavy feet. So, many times Mahendra has taken the baby elephant to his house and his daughter Kavya has developed a great affinity with it. Both it seems have become really good friends.

Kavya roams around in nearby areas surrounding, plantation and spends her time enjoying the company of the baby elephant. Who says man is an enemy of animals. Kavya and the baby elephant are a living example of close bonding between man and animals. What animals need is love and sincerity and they will prove more faithful and helpful than other human beings. This bonding proves that 'Haathi is Mera Sathi' or the elephant is my friend.

10. Study the picture given below. Write a story or a description or an account of what it suggests to you. Your composition may be about the subject of the picture or you may take suggestions from it; however, there must be a clear connection between the picture and your composition. ***ICSE Specimen Paper 2017***

Ans. It is plight of the India that even after 76 years of independence the country can still find a large number of children employed to earn money. Child Labour is a curse that the nation is facing since long. The curse is most rampant in the agricultural sector wherein the illiterate parents find in pair children an extra pair of hands to work in farms. Once can find many children carrying large haystacks on their heads when they visit any farm.

It is sad that even with many governmental efforts that ban child labour, it is still rampant in many places. The reason for child labour essentially springs from one root cause- Poverty. The lack of proper or enough livelihood is directly connected to a limited access to quality education, inadequate agricultural technology, and traditional attitudes towards children's participation in agricultural activities.

Child labour in the agriculture industry can easily be divided into hazardous and non-hazardous. Hazardous child labour is majorly health and opportunity destroying. The constant exposure to pesticides, long working hours, the vulnerability to cuts from sharp knives and other health issues along with the inability to get proper education destroy the future of the child.

None-hazardous child labour highlights that participation in some agricultural activities is not always child labour. Age- appropriate tasks that are of lower risk and do not interfere with a child's schooling and leisure time can be a normal part of growing up in a rural environment. Especially in the context of family farming, small-scale fisheries and livestock husbandry, some participation of children in non-hazardous activities can be positive as it contributes to the inter-generational transfer of technical and social skills and children's food security. Improved self-confidence, self-esteem and work skills are attributes often detected in young people engaged in some aspects of farm work. Therefore, it is important to distinguish between light duties that do not harm to the child and child labour, which is work that interferes with compulsory schooling and damages health and personal development, based on hours and conditions of work, child's age, activities performed and hazards involved.

11. Study the picture given below. Write a story, a description or an account of what it suggests to you. Your composition may be about the subject of the picture or you may take suggestions from it, however there must be clear connection between the picture and your composition. ***ICSE 2016***

Ans. Everybody is waiting for the rains to arrive. The city has already had a long dry spell. The weather has been very hot, the power cuts and water shortage have added to the misery. A lot of people have fallen ill due to the intense heat and few have died also.

Not only the humans, but the animals also are having a hard time in this burning heat. The monsoons were scheduled to arrive in the city, but the wait is still on for the season's first rain. A few people are organising *havans* so as to please the rain god. Some have left the city and gone to the mountains to get respite from the heat. Finally, the rain came when we least expected it. It seemed that people had lost hope after waiting for too long. It was afternoon time and suddenly it started raining. The downpour was very heavy and lasted for 2 hours.

I was studying for my class test when it rained when I saw a girl and a boy playing in the rain from my window. Although they had umbrellas, they threw it away and were enjoying getting wet. Everyone was joyous and enjoyed the rain. Children were dancing and playing in the rain. They also made paper boats and floated them in the water. This reminded me of my childhood days. I also used to come out in the rain and play with my friends. The weather had become cool after the rain. When I finished studying, I had a cup of tea with *pakoras*. Everyone in my home was very happy as finally, it had rained after a long wait. It was such a great relief for everyone!

12. Study the picture given below. Write a short story, description or an account of what the picture suggests to you. Your composition may be about the subject of the picture or you may take suggestions from it, however, your composition must have a clear connection with the picture. ***ICSE 2015***

Ans. The world's population of tigers have some basic necessities in order to survive. These are water, food which comprises of only preys as tigers are carnivores and forests where these animals can conceal themselves. When any of the above-mentioned requirements are not available, their chances of survival diminish naturally. Today, world over, tigers face this situation.

As human population and exploitation continues to grow, the forest cover tends to shrink. As more and more space is needed by the human population and the infrastructure they require–towns, roads, buildings, etc., more and more forests and other natural habitats are being destroyed to make room for it.

Human beings are rapidly encroaching into wild areas which were once ruled exclusively by the tigers. Loss of habitat is only driving this animal to the verge of extinction. Without tall trees or grass, this animal can be easily hunted down by anyone. Moreover, as without the forests, even the tiger's prey cannot survive, so the former will ultimately die of starvation.

However, the government has taken a view of the grim situation and has reserved some essential forest covers as wildlife sanctuaries and national parks. This particular percentage of the reserved area is not to be touched by man and his activities.

Thus, we as humans, must realise our social responsibility and make an effort to let the tigers and other wild animals have their natural habitat intact. For if they are robbed off their home, the ecological balance gets disturbed.

13. Study the picture given below. Write a story, a description or an account of what it suggests to you. Your composition may be about the subject of the picture or you may take suggestions from it; however, there must be a clear connection between the picture and your composition.

ICSE 2013

Ans. School is perhaps one of the best experiences of life. This makes me recall an incident from my life. An excursion was planned by my school when I was in the 9th standard. The news camc as a surprise to me. We all were too excited to go. We were informed that we were going to Jaipur for two nights and three days. When I went home, I very cautiously told this to my mother who did not stir a bit. I had to try very hard to convince her. Finally, she gave her consent and advised me not to do anything reckless on the trip.

Once we were in Jaipur, we visited beautiful forts. We also saw peacocks and could not stop ourselves from admiring their beauty. As we were about to click some pictures of the peacocks, we heard some school kids screaming. The noise was so loud that we moved towards the direction from where screams were coming. To our surprise, we saw three of our school children sitting on an elephant. That was not the usual scene of an elephant ride because the animal was crossing the lake with all these four people sitting on it. The lake surrounded the fort and was deep. The water was also quite cold that day and so the elephant was slightly uncomfortable crossing the lake.

The elephant was losing its balance and this was the reason that the kids were screaming. Everybody present there was only looking at the helpless kids as even the elephant's master was unable to control the balance of the animal. Although the kids were holding each other, they seemed to be very afraid. Suddenly, the elephant lost its balance and all its passengers fell in the water. All the children started yelling for help. My friends and I knew swimming, so we jumped into the lake to their rescue. By God's grace, we were successful in saving their lives. On coming back from the trip, we were praised by our school Principal and were also awarded with the bravery award. Our parents felt so proud of us.

14. Study the picture given below. Write a story or a description or an account of what it suggests to you. Your composition may be about the subject of the picture or you may take suggestions from it; however, there must be a clear connection between the picture and your composition. ***ICSE 2012***

Ans. The intense and clear study of the picture in question describes a girl's poor state. She is sitting with her younger sister at a popcorn stall. There are a lot of packets spread around her and a heap of popcorn is under the process of roasting and cooking in the pan. While the girl is roasting the popcorn, her younger sister is anxiously waiting for the customers. They look quite innocent and poor.

It is the story of a 9-year-old deprived girl child, Gudiya. According to her friends and teachers, she was extremely good in studies. Unfortunately, she could not go to school anymore because she had to earn money for the family after the sudden demise of her father. Her father was the sole bread earner of the family. His demise led her to choose between her books and starvation. The choice was obvious. She decided to help her mother by earning a livelihood to support her family.

The second time, I met Gudiya after 6 months of our first meeting. This time was different from the last time. I was disturbingly shocked to see the adverse changes that had forced her into such an ill fate. Those little eyes that once twinkled with the gleam of becoming a doctor, sparkled no more. She now worked at a roadside popcorn stall, selling popcorn with her younger sister, only to earn a square meal for her struggling family. Childhood should be a time of enjoyment, discovery and learning. Child labour is a reprehensible practice that steals children of their childhood. Like Gudiya, many others are out there, who are forced and exploited due to circumstances. Poverty, hunger, starvation etc turn them into child labourers. They are considered useful as labourers because they are easier to manage and control and perhaps, most importantly, could be paid less than adults. Child labourers are often made to work for long hours in dangerous conditions. This practice is considered exploitative and is illegal.

However, India itself is a home to a quarter of the world's working children. Although Indian law prohibits the employment of children under 14 years of age, child labour remains widespread in India. This is all due to public indifference, poverty and lack of political will and proper implementation of law.

15. Study the picture given below. Write a story or a description or an account of what it suggests to you. Your composition may be about the subject of the picture or you may take suggestions from it; however, there must be a clear connection between the picture and your composition. ***ICSE 2011***

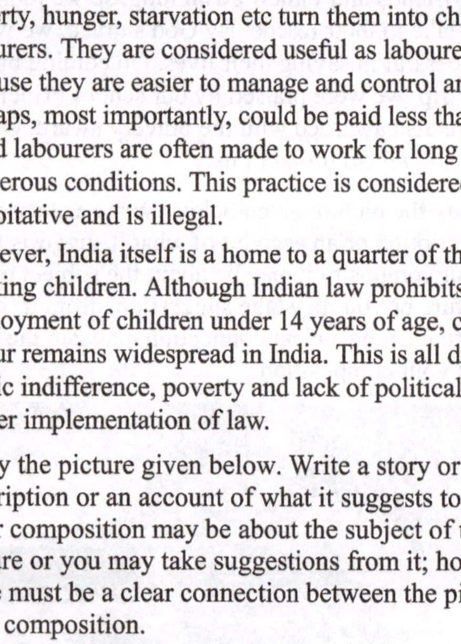

Ans. Due to the heavy downpour, the city of Kolkata is completely flooded. All the streets are waterlogged which makes commuting hazardous.

Life in Kolkata seems to move pretty smoothly for everyone till the rains descend. The rains are the only time when vehicles lose their power of transporting people from one end to the other end of the city.

The best and the only available mode of conveyance is the cycle or hand-rickshaw. When most of the people are seen stranded in the city, believe it or not, in these trying times the rickshaw pullers come to their rescue.

The hand rickshawalas actually call it their season. Everyone is eager to get a ride on a hand rickshaw and is even eager to pay more. Thus, the rickshaw pullers earn more than 8 to 10 times of their usual wages during this period and some of them thank the rain Gods for this bounty.

Sujit, a hand-rickshaw puller, had been out of luck for many days. He was not able to make enough money for there was much competition on his route. He was a native of Kolkata but he always found that people from outside came and dominated the rickshaw pulling trade. Sujit needed money and he knew that things were getting tough.

Although it had rained and the roads were flooded, he was not getting many customers. At the corner of the road, he saw two ladies stranded. They looked poor with an umbrella and had a worried look on their faces. They had left their home and were going to meet their family. When the auto driver dislodged them from his vehicle, they could not wade the flooding waters.

Sujit offered to help them and allowed the ladies to sit in his rickshaw. One of the ladies said that she would pay, but Sujit just wanted to help them. It took him more than an hour to take them through the flooded water to their house. There family members were waiting anxiously for ladies to arrive. The family members had tried all means of communication to contact them.

On seeing the ladies, their families were extremely happy. Sujit did not expect anything, but the delighted father gave him a five hundred rupee note with tears in his eyes and expressed his gratefulness to Sujit. Sujit realised that 'God rewards the noble people'.

16. Study the picture given below. Write a story or a description or an account of what it suggests to you. Your composition may be about the subject of the picture or you may take suggestions from it; however, there must be a clear connection between the picture and your composition. ***ICSE 2010***

Ans. Life is nothing but a series of dramatically charged situations that choose to change when least expected. Often great courage is demanded to adapt oneself to these situations which are more than often cruel and rarely generous. It is to one of these cruel situations that Aarti found herself subjected to.

Aarti was a 10-years-old girl born to a poor family of nomads that wandered from city to city performing various acrobatics and earning their daily bread. Unfortunately, her father was paralysed when he was hit by a speeding car and lost the use of his legs. Being the only child of her parents, she was left with no other option, but to help her mother to earn their daily bread. Aarti was an excellent tight rope walker and people would marvel at her performance. Ever since she was 8 years old, she had earned a name for herself in this field.

Aarti had always aspired to perform in the city. Her mother was very apprehensive about this, being common village people and having never visited the city. When Aarti did get an opportunity, her mother refused to go, but sent Aarti along with her uncle. In the city, Aarti performed at many places and earned a name for herself.

On the way back to her village, she was dumbstruck to see the destruction caused by the flood. A few survivors informed a distraught Aarti that her family had been swept away in the devastation. She felt her whole world crashing in, had it not been for the reassuring presence of her beloved uncle and aunt, she felt she could have died.

Aarti, however, got on with life with great fortitude. She continued with her tight rope walking. Soon, she was chosen to be one of the many performers at the centenary celebrations of one of the most prestigious colleges of Delhi. Her performance was very much appreciated and applauded and she was awarded a special prize of ₹ 1 lakh.

Being in the limelight, she was immediately noticed by the owner of a prestigious circus who offered her a very lucrative job which she accepted. Today, Aarti is a famous performer. Her dedication towards her work and her perseverance were the ultimate winners.

17. Study the picture given below. Write a story or a description or an account of what it suggests to you. Your composition may be about the subject of the picture or may take suggestions from it; however, there must be a clear connection between the picture and your composition. ***ICSE 2009***

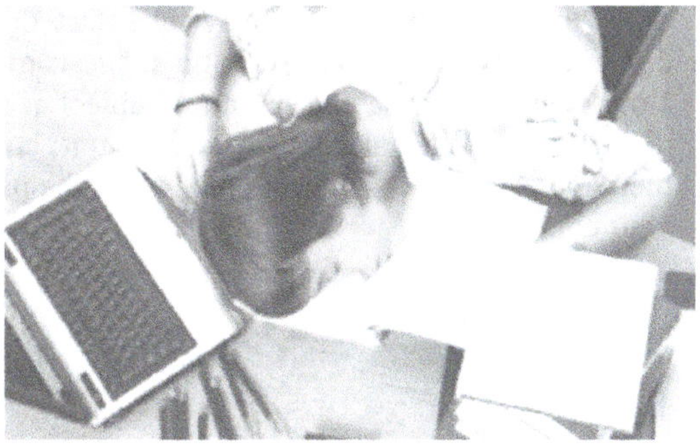

Ans. Today, the world has become so competitive that it has caused a sharp rise in the expectations of parents. Expectations always cause pressure and this pressure is borne by the child. This pressure sometimes acts as a catalyst but very often it proves fatal, resulting in a child trying to eliminate himself or developing an inferiority complex. This in turn causes them to withdraw into a shell. The picture depicts an overburdened student.

Very often, children are found falling off to sleep while studying due to sheer exhaustion. The parents expect their child to wake up at 4 am and get down with their studies, get ready and then attend school, again get down with their books at night and prepare their subject for the next day.

During the examination period, it gets even worse. The child is expected to perform miracles and is goaded to despair in a quest for obtaining a high rank and percentage. The child, on their part, tries hard to live up to the high expectations of their parents and in doing so, mentally and physically wears themselves out. Some succeed while others are not so fortunate.

Parents are only concerned with their expectation but have no time to understand the psyche of their child. They don't take out time to understand their child's mentality, their weaknesses or strengths and their interests.

They don't even know if their child would be able to cope up. At times, they try to fulfil their unfulfilled ambitions through their child and here lies the problem. Every child is a gift of God and is born to achieve greatness in their own way. Children should be nourished properly in order to prepare them for the burden of studies.

It is, therefore, strongly recommended that the parents should understand the fact that a child must be allowed to grow up according to their natural instincts. Parental discretion and direction is definitely a must, but to mould a child according to your own ambitions is wrong.

18. Study the picture given below. Write a story or a description or an account of what it suggests to you. Your composition may be about the subject of the picture or you may take suggestions from it; however, there must be a clear connection between the picture and your composition. ***ICSE 2008***

Ans. Bordering India in the North-East, I came upon a lot of poverty stricken people. The leaders were corrupt and ruthless. The people were forced to live in abject conditions and work for meagre incomes.

What made my heart bleed was the sight of thousands and thousands of poor people everywhere. The faces of these people showed sorrow, pain and hopelessness.

I decided to go to the countryside. Everywhere, there was greenery and serenity. Scores of poorly clad people worked in the fields. Hunger and starvation stared them in the eyes. Children were left to fend for themselves.

I decided to go and talk to one poor little girl. She had her baby brother on her back. I asked her what her name was. She could not understand the language in which I was talking to her. Thankfully, an elderly person came to my rescue. He started interpreting for me.

He told me that the girl's name was Ritu. Her little brother's name was Kapil. Then, the elderly man started to unfold the little girl's life story to me. She came from a very poor and large family. Her parents were too poor to send them to school. Her other siblings had gone out to do odd jobs.

Her duty was to look after her little baby brother while her parents tilled the land. I felt heart broken to see how poorly she was dressed. The weather was cold and she hardly had enough clothes to keep her warm. There was a blank, lost and vacant look on the little fellow's face.

When I observed her closely, I could see a beautiful face. A soft, rosy blush and a smile beginning to break forth. The little boy behind her back was trying to hide his face at intervals. The man, who had stopped to help me, went his way. I thanked him for his kindness.

I stood there for long trying to befriend the little girl. I offered her a few sweets which she shyly accepted. I thanked God and my lucky stars for the many blessings I have received in my life. I wondered what was the fault of these innocent little children? Why did they have to suffer for no wrong doing of their own? The injustice of it all only baffled me further.

19. Study the picture given below. Write a story or a description or an account of what it suggests to you. Your composition may be about the subject of the picture or may take suggestions from it; however, there must be a clear connection between the picture and your composition. ***ICSE 2007***

Ans. The Delhi Race Course is getting all geared up for the summer racing season. People fly from all over the country to witness the glitter and glamour that surrounds the great spectacle. As the great day arrives, the race course is decorated with cheerful crowd comprising fashionably dressed men and women. It becomes the central hub of activity. Owners, participants, jockeys, fans and the green grounds before them make it a perfect picture.

I visited the race course and was amazed with the magnitude of what I beheld as I walked along with my uncle. He is the owner of a large number of horses. I was directed to the 2nd row of seats with a great view. I glanced around in amazement to see ladies with umbrella to protect them from the afternoon sun. Men were in three piece suits. The fragrance and aroma, a blend of flowers and perfumes filled the air. Finally, the pistol fired in the air, the gates flew open and the 10 massive creatures broke free in a mad chase. There was cheering and an indescribable excitement in the air. The jockeys were taking the race well and were tightening every muscle to make every stride of their horse with ease and perfection. These riders are thorough professionals and the animals are extremely well bred. The first race is won by 'Watergate'. The experience was gripping and it left me speechless. 'Watergate' is paraded in along with its rider and the owner. They receive a big trophy and also a cash prize. I was so thrilled at the spectacle that I settled down for the next race.

At this moment, a thought passed through my mind. I have heard wild stories of people betting on horses and becoming millionaires in a day. Even my uncle is a multi-millionaire. I secretly wish in my heart to be able to earn a fortune by betting on these horses. However, my thoughts are quickly rejected by the moral values of hardwork and honesty inculcated in me by my father.

20. Study the picture given below. Write a story or a description or an account of what it suggest to you. Your composition may be about the subject of the picture or may take suggestions from it, however, there must be a clear connection between the picture and your composition. ***ICSE 2006***

Ans. The light of the dying Sun was shimmering on the sand. The beaches of Lakshadweep Islands were illuminated by the showers of beautiful and peaceful light. My grandpa lived at Kadmat island in Lakshadweep and we visited him along with my younger brother, Vaasu.

This season as well, the Lakshadweep Adventure Sports Championship was going to be organised. I like wind surfing a lot and so I got my name registered immediately. At last, the day arrived. I had practised for it day and night and thus, was quite confident of winning it. Vaasu also infused a lot of confidence in me.

The day dawned bright and clear as I took my grandpa's blessings and set out for the starting point with Vaasu on my tail. The spectators crowded the beach, moving their handkerchiefs and throwing flowers.

At last, the trumpet sounded and the whistle blew up. I trapped the wind in my sail and the board lurched forward. I could hear Vaasu, 'Di, you can do it!' Hearing this, I zipped through all the contestants.

Everybody was dumbstruck but cheered madly. The track was not an easy one. After 2 km, I saw a boy approaching me very fast. It appeared as if he was determined enough to overtake me. The last 3 km route was the toughest part of the race. Sometimes, he left me behind and sometimes I left him behind. Then, there came a steep turn and unfortunately for him, a lot of turtles clogged his way.

He was a bit confused and tried to scrap past them. However, he could not control the speed and crashed down. Before he could recover from the blow, I crossed the finishing line.

My grandpa and Vaasu came walking through the water and hugged me. The first prize was a real big trophy and along with that I got a beautiful new surfboard and gear.

SECTION TEST

01 Short Story

1. Write a short story related to the given prompt. At a Chinese restaurant, your character opens his fortune cookie and reads the following message: "Your life is in danger. Say nothing to anyone. You must leave the city immediately and never return. Repeat: say nothing."
2. Write an original short story beginning with the following words. She was delighted to find the sealed envelope lying on her table. As she reached for it ....
3. Write a short story titled 'A Terrible Collision'.
4. Write a short story in relation to "It was a hot day. A blind man was crossing the road, suddenly a car came ……..".
5. Write a short story titled 'The Keyhole'.
6. Write a short story titled 'The Three Lessons'.
7. Write an original short story which ends with ….. 'Admission to the nearby school as a present.'
8. Write an original short story with a sibling pair and an adventure as central to the story.
9. Write an original short story that begins with the lines: With a look of supreme confidence, she walked onto the stage ....
10. Write an original short story which has for its ending : ………… You may print this if you like.

02 Debate

1. "Success depends on character and not on opportunity" Express your views for or against the statement.
2. "The most important thing in life is to be successful." Give reasons why you agree or disagree with the statement.
3. "The best things in life are free." Give your view for or against the statement.
4. "Teenagers should be allowed more freedom?" Give your views for or against the statement.
5. "The wealthy are not happy". Give your views for or against the statement.
6. "A world without rules is a happier place." Argue against this proposition.
7. "Academics and extra-curricular activities must be given equal importance in school." Write for or against proposition.
8. "The only way to minimise human suffering and pain is to control our needs." Write for or against the topic.
9. "Rising prices can be controlled only by the government." Write for or against the topic.
10. "Everyone should become vegetarian." Write for or against the statement.

03 Narrative

1. You had a nerve-wrecking experience when you fell into a ditch with a snake which was later identified as Cobra. Narrate the incident and how you came out of that situation.
2. You have been living in your ancestral house since your birth. The house has been given to the government by your father because the Delhi Metro line has to pass from there. Narrate the incidence of how they broke the news to you and describe your feelings about moving out of this house.
3. Narrate an incident that you would aptly title as 'The Unusual Summer Vacation'.
4. Narrate an incident when you travelled by an overcrowded bus.
5. Narrate an incident that was very disappointing for you.
6. You got involved in an event unintentionally. This experience helped you discover a hidden talent/interest. Narrate the incident and write how this discovery enriched your life.
7. Imagine a situation where you meet your favourite movie character. Write the meeting in detail.
8. Narrate an incident from your own experience when you helped a friend who was in trouble. Explain what happened. What did you do to make the situation better?

04 Description

1. Describe one embarrassing / awkward incident about you that your family found really amusing.

2. You went to a national park on a holiday with your family. During the safari, a wild animal walked across your path when you least expected it. Describe the animal's behaviour, your family's reactions and your feelings during this encounter.
3. Describe the scene at a busy railway station during the holiday season when your uncle saved a young boy.
4. Write a description of the day when everything went wrong in school.
5. Describe the wedding ceremony of your friend in which you took an active part.
6. Recently you had travelled by bus. Describe your experience of your visit to the bus stand.
7. On a train journey you detect a bomb in the compartment, you help in evacuating and rescuing the passengers and in the confusion lose your baggage. Give a detailed account of your adventure.
8. "Society is influenced more by show than by substance". Relate an incident from your experience, which brings out the truth of this statement.
9. It was a long awaited climax to your period of training for the parachute regiment - the day of the first jump! Describe how you prepared yourself for the parachute drop, the drop itself and your feeling after the event.
10. You have been on a flight recently. While going through a cloud the plane develops engine trouble. Describe what took place in the plane and how you were saved.

05 Picture Composition

1. Study the pictures given below. Write a short story or description or an account of what the pictures suggest to you. Your composition may be about the subject of the pictures or you may take suggestions from it.

1.

2.

3.

4.

5.

6.

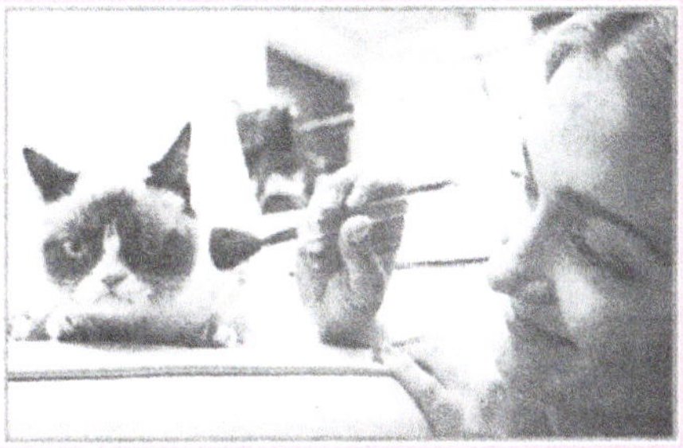

06

Letter Writing

Letter is a written message that we send to people who are far away from us. It is meant to convey our message to them in a clear manner. We usually write letters to our friends and relatives. Although with the advent of telephones, mobile SMSs and chat–the importance of personal letter writing has become less popular, this art is still required in most forms of formal communication. The art of letter writing is no more an ornamental accomplishment but something that every educated person must acquire for practical purposes.

Types of Letters

Letters can be broadly classified into two main categories–Formal letters and Informal letters

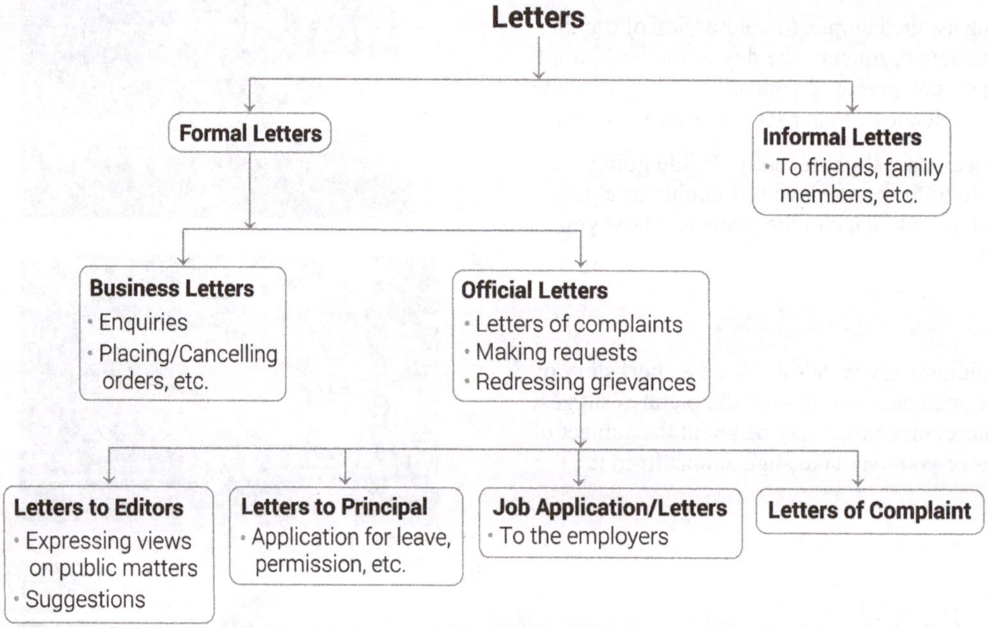

Formal Letters

Formal letters are meant to be addressed to the heads or managers of civil, public or private companies, such as the Police Commissioner, Director, Branch Manager, Chairman, Mayor etc. Hence, the tone of such letters must be positive, polite and formal. Also, the message must be to-the-point and short. Informal language and jargons should be avoided in these type of letters. Formal letters are written to serve the following purposes

- To ask or give information
- To register complaints
- To apply for job
- To apply for leave
- To redress grievances (to bring into notice public/social issues)
- To persuade customers, etc.

Steps to Write a Formal Letter

1. **Sender's Address**

   This portion includes the sender's full address. It is written at the top of the page. Specify the house number first, followed by the street, town/state and pincode.

   Example 2334/31, Mangal Pandey Nagar
   Ekta Park
   Meerut-250002

2. **Date and Receiver's Address**

   While writing date, always remember the day is written in figures, month in words and year in full figures. The receiver's address comprises of the receiver's name/designation and the complete address.

   Example 12th December, 20XX
   The Editor
   The Times of India
   Daryaganj
   New Delhi–110002

3. **Salutation**

   The salutation, used in formal letters, is a greeting to whom the letter is addressed. The salutation is written below the subject line and is never followed by any other word.

   - Dear Sir/Madam

4. **Body of the Letter/Message**

   This is the main part of the letter. The writer's message or purpose of writing the letter comes in this part. So, it must be drafted carefully so as to create a convincing and appealing impact on its readers.

   The message can be divided into paragraphs to distinguish or mark the subject matter properly. If the matter is too short, it is not required to divide it into paragraphs. The body of the letter can be divided into the following parts–

   - **Introductory Paragraph/Sentence** State the purpose of writing.
   - **Information Paragraph** Give details of the issue, problem (cause, effect, solution, etc.)
   - **Concluding Paragraph** States your hopes, request, comment, etc.

5. **Subscription/Leave Taking**

   A letter should not be ended abruptly with only the writer's name or signature for that may look rude. So, there should be proper leave– taking followed by your name. It is a courteous way of ending the letter. The expression used must match the salutation.

   For example,
   Thanking you
   Yours sincerely / Yours faithfully/ Yours truly

   Note: The first letter of the second word (here 's', 'f', 't') is never written in capital letter.

6. **Name and Signature**

   It is written just below the subscription and includes the sender's name and his/her signature. If applicable, the sender's designation may be added in brackets.

Points to be Kept in Mind While Writing a Letter

- Read the information carefully to understand it properly.
- Write the key points for establishing good content and make sure that the body of the letter is in sync with the main theme.
- Your letter must be coherent and not begin or end abruptly.
- Keep your letter brief and to-the-point.
- Use simple language so that the letter is easy to understand.
- These letters are written in a crisp and clear pattern, and in a matter-of-fact style.

Suggested Specimen of Formal Letter (Issued by Board)

Format 1

Q. Write a letter to the Police Commissioner of your city drawing his / her attention to the menace of hawkers outside your school. Tell him / her what dangers they pose and offer solutions for their rehabilitation.

Flat 236, Black C,
Hill Crest View Apartments,
Salem Street,
Coonoor-26. — Sender's Address

23rd February, 2018 — Date

The Police Commissioner,
Police Commissioner's Office,
6, Cavalry Road,
Coonoor-3 — Receiver's Address

Dear Sir, — Salutation

I write to draw your attention to the menace of hawkers outside St. Paul's School in Nehru Nagar of our town. I am the Secretary, Swach Bharat Club, St. Paul's School. — Introduction: In describes the purpose of writing.

The hawkers sell open food and cheap toys. A number of our school students cluster around them and the lane in front of our school is blocked, dirty and congested.
I would request you to look into this problem and have the hawkers move into the field behind our school. This would ensure that they are not deprived of their livelihood and the area in front of our school is kept clean and congestion fee.
The hawkers must also be warned about the importance of necessary hygiene and the sale of clean food. This will ensure that students do not fall sick after eating food sold by the hawkers. — Informative Paragraph: Always change the paragraph while making a new point.

I trust that you will consider my suggestion and take the necessary steps as outlined in my letter to you to deal with the menace of hawkers outside the school. — Conclusion: Having hope/comment/request.

Thanking you,
Yours faithfully, / Yours truly,
Santosh Haldar — Salutation and Complimentary Closure.

Format 2

Q. Write a letter to the Police Commissioner of your city drawing his / her attention to the menace of hawkers outside your school. Tell him / her what dangers they pose and offer solutions for their rehabilitation.

Ans.

Flat 236, Block C
Hill Crest View Apartments,
Salem Street,
Coonoor-26.

23rd February, 2018.

The Police Commissioner,
Police Commissioner's Office,
6, Cavalry Road,
Coonoor-3

Dear Sir,

I write to draw your attention to the menace of hawkers outside St. Paul's School in Nehru Nagar of our town. I am the Secretary, Swach Bharat Club, St. Paul's School.

The hawkers sell open food and cheap toys. A number of our school students cluster around them and the lane in front of our school is blocked, dirty and congested.

I would request you to look into this problem and have the hawkers move into the field behind our school. This would ensure that they are not deprived of their livelihood and the area in front of our school is kept clean and congestion fee.

The hawkers must also be warned about the importance of necessary hygiene and the sale of clean food. This will ensure that students do not fall sick after eating food sold by the hawkers.

I trust that you will consider my suggestion and take the necessary steps as outlined in my letter to you to deal with the menace of hawkers outside the school.

Yours truly,/Yours faithfully,
Santosh Haldar

PYQs Previous Years' Questions

Letters Based on Format 1

1. A certain book/chapter has been included in your syllabus. You have heard that a film version is now available. Write a letter to the Manager of a film theatre near your school requesting that the film be shown. Tell him/her why it will be beneficial to the students. **ICSE 2023**

Ans. XYZ School,
PQR City,
New Delhi-02

21st September, 20XX

The Manager,
Cinepolis,
PQR City
New Delhi-02

Dear Sir/Ma'am,

It is to inform you that I am a student of the ABC School, PQR City. Recently, our syllabus has been altered and the book Pride and Prejudice by Jane Austen has been added to it. Since it is a new addition to the syllabus, most of the students have very little idea about the novel.

It has recently come to my knowledge that the film version of this book has also become available. The movie is considered to be a good adaptation of the book and has received positive reviews. It has also been commended for its brilliant performances, great direction and above all its great portrayal of the late nineteenth century England. I feel that the movie would be helpful to most of the students in understanding the culture, customs and norms of those times. By watching the movie, they would also be able to learn the pronunciation of the words that they find in the book. Also, a lot of the students prefer to watch movies over reading books. They confess that watching a movie makes them concentrate much more and it would be helpful to them in understanding the novel and doing well in the exams.

Therefore, I request you to show this movie for the students of our school in your film theatre. It would be extremely helpful for the students and it would increase their knowledge of the story considerably.

Thanking you,

Yours sincerely,
Abhishek

2. Break time at your school is only for a duration of fifteen minutes. Write a letter to your Principal requesting for an extension in the break-time from fifteen minutes to half an hour. Given reasons for your request and explain in what way an extended break would make a difference to you as a student. **ICSE Specimen Paper 2023, ICSE 2015**

Ans. The Principal,
St. John's School,
Dwarka,
New Delhi

21st September, 20XX

Dear Sir/Ma'am,

Respectfully, I would like to inform you that I, Anant Sharma, am a student of Class X in your school. This letter is intended to make a request to extend the fifteen minutes break to half an hour. The purpose of a break time is to provide students with some time to relax and recharge their minds and fifteen minutes is not enough for that. We barely finish our lunch in that time. If we get a half an hour lunch break, we will able to take a walk and even play few games. These physical activities will benefit each student as they spend the entire day in a stationary position. Some physical activity will be good for both their body and their brain.

Kindly grant us an extension in our break time.

Thanking you,

Yours sincerely,
Anant Sharma
Class X

3. You are being considered for a Head boy/Head girl position in the school. Write a letter to the Principal explaining why you think you would make a good Head boy/Head girl. Why does the role interest you? Describe ways in which you would carry out your responsibilities. ***ICSE 2022 Sem II***

Ans. The Principal,
XYZ School,
New Delhi

22nd July, 20XX

Dear Sir/Ma'am,

This is to inform you that, I, Neha Sharma, of Class X I have been nominated as the Head Girl of the school. A Head Girl is a mature, hard-working and talented person who is seen as someone with a friendly and positive approach to work. It is a role that requires patience, respect, care, the ability to work well in a team and to support the reputation of the school. Being open-minded and being able to talk to the younger students on a one-on-one the level are also important qualities required.

I firmly believe I have the skills and qualities necessary to represent the school as the Head Girl. As can be seen by my contribution in the last term, I was able to continue all of my extra-curricular activities both during and after school, in addition to completing my homework on time and performing well in the Mock examinations. Moreover, I would personally benefit by becoming the Head Girl. It would give me an opportunity to develop my public speaking and leadership skills, which will be useful later on in life.

Therefore, I am confident that I will be able to balance additional school activities with schoolwork.

Thank you for the consideration,

Yours obediently,
Neha Sharma
Class X-A

4. You have planned to organise a health camp at school. Write a letter to the Manager of a supermarket requesting sponsorship for the event. Name the event and explain how it will benefit both the community as well as the supermarket. ***ICSE Specimen Paper 2022 Sem II***

Ans. ABC School,
PQR City

14th March, 20XX

The Manager,
ABC Supermarket,
PQR City

Dear Sir/Ma'am,

Every year, we at ABC Public School put in a lot of effort to help individuals and improve their lives. We are currently striving to generate funds in order to host our upcoming health camp school at our school for the people in our neighbourhood. That is why we are currently seeking sponsors to assist us in achieving our objective.

Therefore, I would like to request you to be one of our sponsors by contributing to a fraction of the overall project costs. If you agree, your name will appear on printed materials and signage for our event which will get your name across many people residing in our neighbourhood. Your generosity means the world to us.

Hoping for a positive reply.

Thanking you,

Yours sincerely,
PQR

5. Some taps in your locality are left open all day resulting in a tremendous waste of water. Write a letter to the Municipal Commissioner of your town / city, complaining about the problem. Suggest ways in which this waste of water can be prevented. ***ICSE 2020***

Ans. House No. 222,
Shakti Nagar
Amritsar, Punjab

15th September, 20XX

The Municipal Commissioner,
Punjab

Dear Sir/Ma'am,

This is to bring to your notice the tremendous wastage of water occurring in our area. The Municipality has installed various public taps to facilitate the water supply. It is especially helpful for those households which do not have submersibles at their homes. But this facility has now become a source of trouble for the people. Due to lack of maintenance, most of the taps have worn out and as a result they keep on running. This has caused two problems : first, there is a lot of wastage of water and second, this water gets collected along the roads leading to waterlogging. This has caused a lot of inconvenience for the residents.

I, therefore, request you to look into the matter and get the taps repaired. Also, to prevent the excessive wastage of water, these public taps could be replaced by underground water pipelines with connection to every household. This would provide people water twice a day and there would not be any wastage of water. Until then, these public taps should be repaired and replace at regular intervals.

I hope you will take the matter into consideration and act accordingly as soon as possible.

Thanking you,

Yours faithfully,
Pragya Sharma

6. You want to start a new club in your school.

Write a letter to your Principal requesting permission to start the club, explain your role in it and give reasons to prove that the club will be beneficial for the school. ***ICSE 2019***

Ans. The Principal,
Sunlight Public School,
Ghaziabad

8th July, 20XX

Respected Sir/Ma'am,

This is to inform you that we, the students of Class IX, have written this letter to request you to allow us to start a nature club in our school. The objective of the club will be to inform as many students as possible about our environment and to study animals, birds, flowers and plants and how to conserve them. We plan to hold weekly excursions and meetings on Saturday afternoons when school gets over. I myself have experience of running such a club in my previous school last year. It has helped to increase our general knowledge about these and I am sure that it will benefit the school.

We hope you will permit us to start the nature club for the students whose activities can be monitored by a teacher whom you nominate.

Thanking you,

Yours obediently,
Rahul
Class IX, Section A
Roll No 20

7. You have accidentally left your suitcase behind when you got off the train. You only realised it after the train left the platform. Write a letter to the Station Master reporting your loss and request that the suitcase be located and kept till you claim it. ***ICSE Specimen Paper 2019***

Ans. XYZ Apartments,
PQR City

21st May, 20XX

The Station Master,
PQR City

Dear Sir/Ma'am,

This is to inform you that I, Shivam Shah resident of Mumbai, came to Kolkata by the ABX express PNR No. 12345 seat 23C. I have forgotten my suitcase on my reserved seat. The suitcase is dark blue in color and had some Marvel stickers on it.

Therefore, I request you to find my suitcase and keep it with you safely till I can claim it. I am hoping to come and collect the suitcase in a day or two.

Kindly understand and oblidge.

Thanking you,

Yours faithfully,
Shivam Shah

8. The traffic outside your school is very heavy and chaotic. Write a letter to the Deputy Commissioner of Police (Traffic) pointing out the danger of such heavy and chaotic traffic in a school zone. Suggest possible solutions for the problem. ***ICSE 2018***

Ans. Brahma Public School,
Hindu Colony, Dadar,
Mumbai - 400014

17th October, 20XX

The Deputy Commissioner,
Mumbai Police (Traffic),
Mumbai – 400009

Dear Sir/Ma'am,

This letter brings to your kind attention the regular harassment our school students face on Bhadkamkar Marg due to regular traffic jams at the time when school opens in the morning and when it closes in the afternoon.

We all are aware that the number of vehicles and commuters on the roads is continuously increasing and that there is no proportional increase in the width of the roads to accommodate this increased traffic. Consequently, traffic jams are bound to happen if the traffic is not disciplined.

We observe that jams occur because of all kinds of vehicles being parked irresponsibly for long periods of time on the road near our school. Then we can see drivers getting into ugly arguments, indulging in rash driving etc. Further, as this is a school area, it is a Silence Zone which is clearly stated in the signboards put up by your department. However, there is no silence, as some motorists continuously honk when there is a traffic jam.

If your department arranges two traffic constables on duty at the time of the school's opening and closing, they can create awareness among the drivers about traffic rules and regulations. Further, they can regulate the traffic at that time to improve the situation. If the necessary action is not taken soon, it may lead to accidents.

We have faith in the Traffic Police Department. I believe that the department will fulfill its duties to combat this problem of traffic jams in our school zone.

Thanking you,

Yours sincerely,
Ramcharan Mohapatra
(Head Boy)

9. A number of loose electric wires are hanging from a lamp post near the main gate of your school. Write a letter to the Municipal Commissioner explaining the problem, the danger it poses and suggest a quick solution. ***ICSE 2017***

Ans. Apeejay School,
New Delhi

20th April, 20XX

The Municipal Commissioner,
New Delhi

Respected Sir/Ma'am,

This is to inform you that I, a student of Class X, Apeejay school, Saket, New Delhi, have written this letter to bring to your notice the precarious situation all school students and staff members face everyday when they enter the school. Near the main gate of our school, a lamp post had been erected a few years prior. But it was not maintained. But recently, some loose electrical wires are hanging out of it and are extending to the main gate of our school.

We have requested the local authorities to repair these wires as they pose a literal threat to the lives of students and staff members. There is always a fear of getting electrocuted if any one unintentionally or intentionally touches them.

Inspite of repeated requests, nothing has been done so far. Therefore, it is requested to treat the matter urgently and get the wires set at their proper place to avoid any calamity or loss of life.

Thanking you in anticipation.

Thanking you,

Yours faithfully,

Mukesh

(Head Boy, Class X, Apeejay School)

10. Write a letter to the Editor of a local newspaper telling him/her what you think about global warming, its effects and what people should do to prevent it from getting worse. ***ICSE Specimen Paper 2017***

Ans. XYZ Apartments,
PQR City

30th April, 20XX

The Editor,
The Times of India,
PQR City

Respected Sir/Ma'am,

Through the columns of your esteemed newspaper, I would like to make everyone aware of global warming, its effects and what we people should do to prevent it from getting worse.

One of the most common news in the present world is the sinking for many cities due to rapidly rising sea water levels. We all know he cause- global warming or the long-term heating of Earth's surface observed. We also know that our planet is heating up due to human activities, primarily fossil fuel burning, which increases heat-trapping greenhouse gas levels in Earth's atmosphere. As a result, now-a-days we are experiencing sudden and unexpected climatic conditions. Sometimes, we experience extreme heat; In the other we encounter rains in the most unexpected season while monsoon has become just a dry spell.

It is because of our carelessness towards the environment that has caused this increasing global warming and its dire effects. It is high time that we understand the harmful effects we are causing to our mother earth. To prevent the situation from getting worse, we can reduce our energy consumptions and reduce the exploitation of the resources that we are using. Use less electricity, try to travel from public transport and follow the Reduce, Reuse and Recycle policy.

I request you to highlight this issue on your esteemed daily to spread awareness among citizens and stop the unjust abolition of greenery in localities.

Thanking you,

Yours sincerely,

ABC

11. Your class wants to visit a well-known historical monument in a nearby town. Write a letter to your Principal seeking permission and say why you would benefit from the visit. ***ICSE 2016***

Ans. The Principal,
Happy School,
Daryaganj,
New Delhi-110002

16th March, 20XX

Dear Sir/Ma'am,

This is to inform you that I, a student of Class X-B of your school, have written this letter to request you to organise a trip to the Taj Mahal, Agra. We have chosen the destination by conducting a vote among the class students. The trip would take two days and would be organised on weekend so that the classes are not affected. Our class teacher has agreed to accompany us on the trip. The trip would help us in learning about our cultural heritage. We would also be able to see one of the seven wonders of the world. We are very excited about this visit and have been reading about the Taj Mahal and Agra on the Internet.

Hence, I most humbly request you to permit us to visit Agra.

Thanking you,

Yours obediently,
Saloni Mishra
Roll No. 10
Class X-B

12. You are the President of the Nature Club in your school which is hosting the Earth Day celebrations. Write a letter to the Principal of a neighbouring school inviting the school to participate in the event. State when, why and how you plan to celebrate Earth Day. ***ICSE 2014***

Ans. The Principal,
Queensland Convent,
Azadpur Delhi

10th March, 20XX

Respected Sir/Ma'am,

With great pride and honour, I, Sakshi Saini the President of the Nature Club of Vivekanand Memorial School, extend a humble invitation to a team of teachers and students of your school to participate in the Earth Day celebration being hosted by our school. The celebration will take place in our school ground on 22nd April from 9 : 00 am onwards. The chief guest and the judge for the event is the eminent environmentalist and scientist Mrs. S Lakshmi Subhramanyam. She will enlighten the students on the importance of preserving our planet earth. There will be an exhibition, poster making competition and slogan writing. The best ones will be sent to an All India Level and prizes will be given.

A documentary will also be shown to the students focussing on environmental issues. Then, there will be an interactive session followed by lunch.

It is hoped that the students of your school will actively participate in the event. This activity hopes to bring an awareness among the students about the problems and dangers faced by the planet earth and the measures that need to be taken to preserve the ailing planet.

Looking forward to a positive reply.

Thanking you,

Yours sincerely,
Sakshi Saini
(President, Nature Club)

13. The children in your neighbourhood are forced to play on the street for want of a proper play area. Write a letter to the Editor of a popular newspaper pointing out the need for a playground in your neighbourhood. Give reasons why you think a play area is necessary and point out how it would benefit everyone who lives in that area. ***ICSE 2013***

Ans.

Flat No. C-72, Aakash Towers,
Rohini, New Delhi

31st July, 20XX.

The Editor,
The Times of India,
Daryaganj, Delhi

Respected Sir/Ma'am,

Through the columns of your esteemed newspaper, I would like to to draw the attention of the concerned authorities towards the problem of lack of a proper playground in our neighbourhood.

As you know, children are our hope for a bright future. So it is our duty to provide them with all the basic facilities of life. This includes a proper area to play safely and securely. However, you locality lacks a park which forces them to play on the busy streets. This can prove to be hazardous for their lives. Moreover because of the lack of parks, children don't come out of houses and enjoy the sports and games which are essential for their proper growth and development.

Therefore, I want to request the authorities to construct a park in our neighbourhood. This will allow the children some open area where they can go and refresh, relax and revitalise for their all round development.

Moreover, the adults will be motivated to come out and get some fresh air. They can interact with their neighbours and become friends. They can overcome their sedentary lifestyle by walking, running, doing yoga and relaxing.

I strongly hope the concerned authorities to provide a play area immediately.

Yours sincerely,
Deepakshi Taneja

14. Many areas near your school have been affected by floods. You are President of your school Social Service Club. Write a letter to the mayor of your town/city telling him/her what you plan to do for the relief of the victims. Suggest ways in which you can combine with other organisations to bring about better distribution of relief items. ***ICSE 2012***

Ans.

Srinivas Public School,
Ganjam District, Orissa

6th July, 20XX

The Mayor, District office,
Ganjam, Orissa

Dear Sir/Ma'am,

With all due respect, I, the President of Social Service Club of Srinivas Public School, would like to draw your kind attention towards complications and miseries of various areas and people affected due to the floods. The condition of flood victims of our district is pathetic and relief measures by the government are falling short.

Many areas near our school have been declared as some of the worst affected regions in the flood. Seeing the sad state of our people, the Social Service Club of our school would like to focus our efforts to lend a helping hand in this aspect. Our aim is to mobilise people to provide immediate relief to the flood victims. With the cooperation of local NGO's, we can successfully raise funds by personally visiting several educational institutions in the city, through social media and through word of mouth. Our dedicated team of volunteers would request the public to contribute whatever they could. They would also help in conducting the relief operations more efficiently.

A chamber of traders and industrialists are also with us to support and supervise the aid programmes. Teams of NSA and Scouts are also preparing their cooperation for this cause. A team of veterinary doctors is also with us to avoid the calamities of animals, birds and cattles.

I hope you will give our Social Service Club a chance to put into practice what we have dreamt of and through our joint efforts carry out the relief work.

Yours sincerely,
Abhishek Awasthi
(President, Social Service Club)

15. Write a letter to the Chairman, Local Municipal Corporation complaining about the malaria epidemic in your city. State the causes and suggest ways to deal with the problem. ***ICSE 2010***

Ans.

70, Model Town,
Roopnagar

16th July, 20XX

The Chairman,
Municipal Corporation
Roopnagar

Dear Sir/Ma'am,

As a responsible citizen, I would like to bring to your notice the rising outbreak of malaria in our city. Many people have already been suffering from malaria and the situation is getting worse.

The reason behind the surge in malaria cases are easily visible to the naked eye. Roads are left uncleared for days together resulting in the accumulation of garbage here and there. Because of this, bad odour is emitted which is engulfing the entire area. Moreover, the drains in our locality are not covered and they remain eternally waterlogged. It has resulted in innumerable cases of diseases like dengue and malaria which has taken an epidemic form in the city.

Most painfully, I have to mention here that our repeated requests to the local civic authorities have failed to evoke any response from them for the redressal of the pathetic situation. To improve the situation, the drains need to be cleared regularly. People should be made aware about the necessary precautions against the disease and the measures they should take. Free health camps should also be set up so that the epidemic does not outbreak into more quarters.

I would also request you to take immediate action to prevent further outbreak of malaria.

Thanking you
Yours faithfully,
Ravi Shankar

16. Write a letter to the Director of a television channel complaining about the quality of the programmes telecast. Suggest ways to improve the programmes. ***ICSE 2010***

Ans.

Flat No. 704, A-wing,
Nexus Apartments,
Tardev, Mumbai

13th November, 20XX

The Director,
Colors Entertainment Channel,
Mumbai

Dear Sir/Ma'am,

This is to bring to your kind notice the deteriorating quality of programmes that are being telecast on your channel. It is surprising to note that the channel 'ABC', that was once famous for being thoroughly entertaining and educative, has now deteriorated to the level of only family serials where often the women are portrayed as the villains. These serials are undoubtedly having an adverse effect on human relationships within the household.

Youngsters watching these programmes are inspired to use filthy language, scheming and plotting against their own family members. Besides this, degradation of values and too much of wealth and opulence teaches youngsters to acquire quick wealth through fair or foul means.

It would be much appreciated if you would take note of the above mentioned issues and change the outlook of the programmes that are being telecast. I would suggest adding on some variety in the programmes by introducing some Quiz/G.K. programme, comedies, cooking shows, interviews and some educative programmes to make the channel more interesting.

I am sure that this letter will not go unheeded. We sincerely look forward to better aired programmes in future.

Yours sincerely,
Shraddha Nigam

17. You are the President of the school's Nature Club. Write a letter to a well-known social worker or Environmentalist inviting him/her to be the Chief Guest at the Annual Function of the club. Give some details about your club and the Annual Function. ***ICSE 2009***

Ans.

The Nature Club, St. Xavier's School,
Mall Road, Bengaluru

7th July, 20XX

Ms. Anita Sinha
The Director,
Social Welfare Association
Bengaluru

Respected Ma'am,

This is to inform you that the Nature Club of St. Xavier's School will be celebrating its 10th anniversary on the 31st July, 20XX. It would be our honour if you preside the Annual Function of the club the Chief Guest and increase the grandeur of the day.

We are a ten-year-old club and are very active in the field of social services and environmental awareness. We have also been awarded for the most active participation in the 'Green Drive Project' organised by Environment Association of India. Very often, we organise camps on conservation of nature.

We are aware of your time constraints and will not take much of your precious time. We would indeed be honoured if you could kindly grace the occasion with your presence and shower your blessings upon us.

Yours sincerely,
Sikander Rajput
(President)

18. Traffic jams in your city/town are getting worse day after day. Write a letter to the Deputy Commissioner of Police (Traffic) complaining about the problem and offering suggestions for improvement. ***ICSE 2008***

Ans.

H.No. A-41,
Phase-IV, Ashok Vihar,
New Delhi

22nd November, 20XX

The Deputy Commissioner of Police,
Police Headquarters,
New Delhi

Dear Sir/Ma'am,

This is to inform you that I, Aashutosh Sharma, have written this letter to bring to your notice the chaotic condition of the city on account of severe traffic jams which have become too frequent these days causing unimaginable harassment to the people. We know that the number of vehicles on the roads is on rise and that there is no proportional increase in the number of roads. So, traffic jams are bound to happen.

However, it stretches one's tolerance to the ultimate limit when a difficult situation is aggravated due to the irresponsible behaviour of a few rash drivers. The buses and autos show an appalling disregard for any kind of traffic law. Buses stopping here and there, autos, coming and going through and into every corner and side of the traffic imaginable, drivers getting into an ugly argument on the middle of the road, etc. cause havoc for the daily commuters.

Frequent processions, demonstrations by employees and workers and nagar kirtans add to the already chaotic conditions. Then, there are encroachments and vendors all along the road. The marriage season makes the situation even worse.

The solution lies in being responsible. Traffic rules must be dealt with promptly and strictly. More of public transport should be used, car pooling should be encouraged. During peak hours, efforts should be made by avoiding travelling. Teenagers should not be issued driving licence. The authorities should be strict in removing encroachments and vendors.

I do hope that you will be kind enough to take necessary and stringent remedial steps to arrest the chaotic traffic jams in the city before long.

Yours sincerely,
Aashutosh Sharma

19. A company has been marketing spurious medicines behind claims that its product could be effective in preventing the avian flu or other forms of influenza. Write a letter to the Drug Controller General of the Directorate of Health Services examining the claim of the company and explaining the harm these kind of claims could cause. ***ICSE 2007***

Ans.

24/7 Pharmacy Stores,
Andheri West,
Mumbai

2nd December, 20XX

The Drug Controller General,
Directorate of Health Services,
Mumbai

Dear Sir/Ma'am,

Through the medium of this letter, I, Deepa Mehta, wish to draw your attention towards the marketing of a spurious medicine – 'Oxeprazole capsules and injections' by Collective Pharmaceuticals India Ltd. It claims that these medicines are effective in preventing the avian flu and also other forms of influenza. Such huge claims have attracted the doctors who are readily prescribing these medicines to their patients.

Many patients of the avian flu have used these medicines and their condition has further deteriorated. Some of them have developed severe side effects. Many have even been on the brink of losing their lives.

I, therefore, request you to thoroughly examine the claims of this company and prevent any more such medicines from flooding the markets so that innocent lives may be spared.

Moreover, a ban should be issued on the production of more such medicines. Your immediate action in this regard would be highly appreciated.

Yours sincerely,
Deepa Mehta

20. Your cousin is missing from home. Write a letter to the Superintendent of Police of your locality requesting him to trace your cousin. Give all relevant details that may help the police department. ***ICSE 2006***

Ans.

H.No 222, Shakti Nagar,
Amritsar, Punjab

15th September, 20XX

The Superintendent of Police,
Police Station No. 5,
Amritsar, Punjab

Dear Sir/Ma'am,

This is to lodge a complaint regarding my missing cousin, Mayank Talwar, twenty one years of age, studying in Punjab Technical college, Amritsar.

He went to his college yesterday morning as he informed by one of his friends that the final year result was out and it was displayed on the college notice board. It was like any other day for his mother who had never dreamed of his uncanny disappearance.

We also inquired about his result from the college staff. He scored third position in the entire college. So, we were sure that the result could not have been anyway responsible for his sudden disappearance. All the family members were shocked to hear the sudden disappearance of their family member.

In spite of all our endeavours, we have been unable to resolve the mystery of my missing cousin. Some witnesses have informed us that he had a plan of accompanying some of his friends to Shimla. In case we come to know of any new development related to the case, we would surely inform you.

I would be very grateful if you could kindly pursue the matter with the utmost urgency. My family and I would be glad to provide whatever help might be necessary.

Yours sincerely,
Shivam Arora

21. Write a letter to the Director of the Archaeological Survey of India complaining about the damage caused to a historical monument in your city due to negligence. Suggest steps that the civic authorities should take to preserve the monument.
ICSE 2005

Ans.

H.No. 78/B21,
Civil Street,
Kolkata

7th August, 20XX

The Director,
Archaeological Survey of India,
CGO Complex,
Salt Lake City,
Kolkata

Respected Sir/Ma'am,

This letter intends to bring to your notice that the grand edifice, Victoria Memorial, is threatened by the impish acts of certain uncivilised individuals.

It has been stained by a generous dose of betel juice and burnt out ends of cigarettes. As if these were not enough, I found to no small mortification that some brutes have even etched their names on the walls. This is nothing but extreme cultural sacrilege.

I hereby make a sincere appeal to you to give the concerned authorities a rousing shake so that the rogues who indulge in such mutilation of cultural treasures are taken to task.

It is expected that the rules prohibiting the visitors, the management and the staff from using any kind of tobacco - related products or betel leaf within the memorial or its gardens would be strictly enforced. Similarly, anyone found daring enough to carve personal identification marks on those walls should also be severely penalised.

I hope you shall look upon these humble suggestions in the right spirit.

Yours sincerely,
Aananya Roy

Informal/Personal Letters

Informal letters are letters written to family and friends. The style of writing may depend upon an individual's nature and mood.

An individual should keep the following points in mind while writing informal personal letters.

- An informal letter should be **polite** and **creative**.
- **Casual** or **everyday** expression can be used.
- Rules of spelling, punctuation and grammar must be adhered to.

Suggested Specimen of Informal Letter (Issued by Board)

Q. Imagine that you are in a boarding school and have performed poorly in your terminal examination. Write a letter to your mother, explaining the reasons for your poor performance and tell her how you plan to do better in the forthcoming examinations.

Format 1

Jingle Bells Residential School ← Sender' address
Igatpuri - 422 402

10th October, 2018 ← Date

My dear Mummy / Mother, ← Salutation/Customary greeting

I know that you are very disappointed with my half yearly report that you must have received last week. I am truly sorry for a poor performance and I am feeling very depressed at having let you down so badly. I do not want to make excuses but this last term I have been in and out of the infirmary several times. I had a bad attack of malaria and was unable to attend classes for about a week. Barely had I got over this when I broke out in a rash because of the medication and I had to go back into the infirmary. As result of this, I missed many classes and I scored very poorly in three subjects.

I have now picked up health and have requested my teachers to give me some extra assignments. I also plan to do group study with some of the other boarders of my class.

I am sure that this will help me to catch up with my studies and I promise you I will score much better marks in the next unit tests.

Please do not be worried about my health, I am much better. I look forward to meeting you during the mid-term break.

← Body of the letter

Yours lovingly, / Yours affectionately, / Your loving son,
Sanjiv

← Subscription and Signature

Format 2

Q. Imagine that you are in a boarding school and have performed poorly in your terminal examination. Write a letter to your mother, explaining the reasons for your poor performance and tell her how you plan to do better in the forthcoming examinations.

Ans.

Jingle Bells Residential School,
Igatpuri – 422 402.
10th October, 2018

My dear Mummy / Mother,

I know that you are very disappointed with my half yearly report that you must have received last week. I am truly sorry for a poor performance and I am feeling very depressed at having let you down so badly. I do not want to make excuses but this last term I have been in and out of the infirmary several times. I had a bad attack of malaria and was unable to attend classes for about a week. Barely had I got over this when I broke out in a rash because of the medication and I had to go back into the infirmary. As result of this, I missed many classes and I scored very poorly in three subjects.

I have now picked up health and have requested my teachers to give me some extra assignments. I also plan to do group study with some of the other boarders of my class.

I am sure that this will help me to catch up with my studies and I promise you I will score much better marks in the next unit tests.

Please do not be worried about my health, I am much better. I look forward to meeting you during the mid-term break.

Yours lovingly, / Yours affectionately, / Your loving son,
Sanjiv

PYQs Previous Years Questions

Letters Based on Format 1

1. You have had to shift to a new house recently. Write a letter to your grandmother telling her what you miss about your old house. Tell her also what you like about your new house and what you plan to do to make it comfortable for yourself. ***ICSE 2023***

Ans. XYZ Apartments,
PQR City

17th November, 20XX

Dearest grandmother,

I hope you are in the best of health and taking your medication on time. I miss you and the rest of the family more than I can describe in words. Ever since I left our house, I have felt alone. When I was there with all of you, I was always having fun. It was good to always have some company. In our house, I enjoyed walking through the spacious corridors, spending time sipping tea in the balcony with the family members and playing on the roof with my siblings. One could always find food in the kitchen and it was possible to watch television with the rest of the family.

In my new house, there is no television, roof or balcony. While I do miss those things, I have found that not having these distractions helps me focus on my work. The house is tiny and that makes it easier to take care of. I can clean it pretty easily too. Also, I have a personal bedroom and study, as well as an entire wall that I can use for posters without having to share it with my siblings. However, the house still needs a lot of work to make it more comfortable. I am planning to install a kitchen chimney, which helps with the smoke from cooking. I also have to buy new covers, cushions and blankets for my bed to have a comfortable sleep. I am also planning to have a window installed so that the house could have some much needed sunlight. I hope you would visit me once I have made the house more comfortable.

Yours lovingly,

Anuj

2. Your friend has been unwell and unable to attend school for two weeks. An interschool drama competition took place during the period. Write a letter to your friend telling him/her about the event and your role in it.

ICSE Specimen Paper 2023, 2019

Ans. 3-397/B, Kavita Vihar,
New Delhi

17th November, 20XX

Dearest Anamika,

I hope you are doing better now. It's been a long time since you got sick and you have missed a lot in the school during this time. For one, you scored the highest marks in the Internal Assessments. I heartily congratulate you. Second, there was an Interschool Drama Competition organised on Children's Day by the school. The play chosen by our school was Shakespeare's Macbeth and I got selected for the role of Malcolm.

Had you been there, I am sure you would've nabbed the role of Lady Macbeth. I missed you on the day of the audition and afterwards but I also knew you would've wanted me to give my best so I worked diligently. Finally, on the day of the competition, everyone performed elegantly and tried their best. Our school won the first prize. My happiness knew no bounds. The drama team went for a party after school and everyone talked about how much we missed you.

Keeping that in mind, I pray that you will get well soon. Hoping to see you soon.

Yours lovingly,

Rehan

3. Your favourite aunt/uncle has asked you what you would like as a gift for your birthday. What gift would you choose (specify) and why would you choose this? Write a letter to your aunt/uncle thanking her/him for the kind thought and telling her/him about the gift of your choice. ***ICSE 2022 Sem II***

Ans. 25/89-B, Ground Floor,
Laxmi Nagar,
Delhi

1st June, 20XX

Dear Uncle/ Aunt,

I hope this letter finds you in best of your spirits and health. I am good here and want to tell you that I was overjoyed to receive your present. A big thank you for sending me the gift of such a beautiful camera.

I know you couldn't attend my birthday party due to your busy schedule but I missed you. I was overjoyed at receiving your blessings and the DSLR Camera on my birthday. It is the best present I have ever received. All my friends have also liked it very much. The camera works so well. I took a lot of pictures on my birthday which I will show you on your next visit. I have a keen interest in photography and would like to pursue it as my professional career. I am even planning to join a professional course in the same during summer vacations for which I have already taken permission from mummy and papa. I'm so excited that I'll be able to learn to use the camera professionally.

Once again, thank you very much for the gift. It is really a lovely present.

I am looking forward to your visit.

Yours lovingly,
ABC

4. You have been given a small sum of money to buy a gift for a friend. What gift would you choose (specify) and why would you choose this? Write a letter to your friend telling him/her about the gift and how it will benefit him/her.

ICSE Specimen Paper 2022 Sem II

Ans. XYZ Apartments,
PQR

14th March, 20XX

Dear ABC,

I hope this letter finds you in the best of health and spirits. I am really excited for your birthday party and guess what I have finally bought your gift. From the time I heard that you are about to head to London for your higher studies, I had an idea of what I wanted to gift you. I wanted to give you something which will allow you to remember us all. I decided to buy a Fujifilm Instax camera for you. It comes with film sheets so that you can get polaroid pictures instantly. It also has a selfie mode and is easy to carry and use. With this, you can click artsy and beautiful snaps of beautiful locations, yourself and your near and dear ones. You can prepare cute diaries and boards with the pictures and look them up as and when you wish.

Do let me know if you love my idea and I will place the order for the same so that I can meet you up with your gift! Meet you soon.

Your loving friend,
AQZ

5. You have changed your school recently. Write a letter to your friend in your old school telling him/her what you like about your new school but also what you miss about your old school. ***ICSE 2020***

Ans. House No. 125,
Sector 1, IMT,
Manesar, Gurugram,
Haryana

24th March, 20XX

Dear Yug,

Hope this letter finds you in good health. I am writing this letter to tell you about my new school. It has been a month since I joined this school after my father was transferred here. The name of my new school is Modern Public School and it is a lot bigger than our school. It has the playground twice the size of the one we had in our school. Even the library is much bigger. There is also a spacious cafeteria that serves good quality food. The teachers are extremely knowledgeable and teach very well.

Every Saturday, we have house activities in which the students compete with each other in various sports, literary and cultural competitions. I have also made some new friends.

But I still remember the fun I used to have in my old school. I especially miss those hobby classes that were conducted every Thursday. What fun we used to have during the dance class! I also Miss Sangeeta ma'am and I am grateful to her for teaching English so well. But most of all, I miss you. Although I have made new friends, nobody can replace you.

I hope I will be able to see you soon. Eagerly waiting for you!

Yours affectionately,
Harshit

6. Your friend has not fared well in the recent examinations.

Write a letter to him/her expressing your concern. Give him/her some advice on how to score better marks and offer to help him/here to improve his/her performance. ***ICSE 2019***

Ans. B-103, Sajeevani Society,
MG Road,
New Delhi–110019
27th March, 20XX

Dear Mohit,

How are you? I came to know from your brother, whom I met yesterday, that you had not fared well in your Class IX final exams. I am very concerned about this because you were always serious about your studies and I did not expect this.

I miss you so much now that you are away at boarding school. When you come here to spend the summer holidays, we will have lots to talk over.

I am sure you can do much better in the Boards next year if you learn to study without help from coaching. I feel you had adjusted yourself to coaching till you studied here upto Class VIII. In boarding school, I know that there is no coaching and thus. I don't attend any coaching either. I study by myself every day in the evening and revise each lesson taught in class that day. This keeps the lessons fresh in my mind. At the time of exams, I just need to go through my notes to refresh my memory. You can study using my method when you come here and obtain as good results as I get.

More news when we will meet. Take care of yourself. I look forward to meeting you in the second week of May.

Your loving friend,
Ravi

7. Your uncle has offered to get you a pet for your birthday. Write a letter to him telling him what you like, give reasons for your choice and tell him how you take care of your pet. ***ICSE 2018***

Ans. House 365 - E,
Malviya Nagar,
Patna - 800003

15th February, 20XX

Dear Uncle,

Namaste. How are you? I am sure you are healthy and fine. Even I am doing well here.

As you know very well, next week is my birthday. You know your gifts are always valuable to me and delightful. I remember you were telling me, when you visited our home last month, that you were planning to give me a puppy as my birthday gift.

Uncle, I am eagerly waiting for this give from your side. I am quite excited about it. Since a long time, I have been interested in looking after a puppy and you are fulfilling my wish. As you very well know, dogs are very faithful pets and can also guard a home against intruders. I can train up the puppy to be a good guard dog.

I understand that keeping pets in the house is not easy. We have to take good care of them. I assure you that I will take good care of it. I will keep writing to you regularly about its training and progress.

I am eagerly awaiting its arrival. I am making preparations for its stay in my room.

Thanks once again.

Please convey my respects to Aunty and regards to Sunny.

Yours affectionately,
Arvind

8. You were a part of an organising committee for an inter-school event which was very successful. You and the other committee members were congratulated and praised at the school assembly by the Principal. Write a letter to your grandmother telling her about the event and your feelings at being recognised and praised in front of the school. ***ICSE 2017***

Ans. St. Thomas Boys Hostel,
Roorkee

20th April, 20XX

Dearest Grandmother,

How are you? I miss you everyday. I am very excited and happy right now. Last week, my school had organised an Inter-School Quiz Competition in which six schools had participated. An organising committee was formed by our school principal. The committee's function was to chalk out the programme and to look after the participants and accompanying teachers coming from other schools. I was also selected as a member of that organising committee. The event went off smoothly and the guests were looked after properly. Timely distribution of snacks, water and serving of lunch was all responsibilities of the members of the organising committee which were taken care of with minutest details.

Next day during morning assembly, the principal congratulated all the members of this organising committee. The principal praised our efforts in front of the whole staff and students. It was a proud moment for all of us. As I was also a part of it, I was very happy as everyone appreciated our work. It was a great feeling to be recognised and praised in front of the whole school and staff members.

I wanted to share this proud moment with you. I know you would also feel very proud of me and bless me for future.
With loving regards,
Mukesh

9. Your school recently held a Silver Jubilee celebration. Write a letter to your friend who was unable to attend, giving details of the function and your role in it. ***ICSE 2016***

Or

A friend of yours has been out of station for a month and there was an important event function held in the school while he/she was away. Write him/her a letter describing the event/function and your role in it and why your friend was missed. ***ICSE Specimen Paper 2017***

Ans. WZ-1263, Nangal Raya,
New Delhi–46

5th March, 20XY

Dear Rashi,

How are you? I hope that you are enjoying your trip. While you were on leave, we celebrated the Silver Jubilee of our school. A special function was organised to celebrate the Silver Jubilee. We gathered in the auditorium for the function. The Principal gave a small speech before the function started. He told us about the history and the founders of our school.

The function started with a cultural programme. It was organised by the students of Class XII and depicted the diverse culture of our country. The next programme was a fashion show. I also participated in that show and represented our class. Everyone cheered for me when I came on the stage. I was adjudged the best dressed female by the judges.

The party was followed by a small snacks where we also got a chance to meet the honourable Chief Minister of Delhi, who was the Chief Guest on the occasion.

We enjoyed the celebrations a lot. It would have been a more fun if you also had been present on that day.

I wish that you come back soon and join school.

Yours best friend,
Nisha

10. You are to be awarded a special prize at the Annual Prize Day ceremony of your school. Write a letter to a lady relative giving her the news. Be sure to include details of the prize that you are to receive and tell her why you have been chosen for this honour. ***ICSE 2015***

Ans. 87, Gole Market,
New Delhi–110001

18 March, 20XX

Dear Sister,

Hope this letter finds you in the best of health. It has been a long time since we last spoke. How have you been all this while?

Anyway, I have some news to give. I am to be awarded a special prize at the Annual Prize Day ceremony to be held on 25th March. I am going to be awarded with the trophy for "The Most Bonafide Student" of the year. My teachers are very happy with me for my excellent behaviour in school and so have chosen me for this special prize. Throughout the year, I had not been involved in any fight with any student or argument with any of my teachers and I have willingly helped everyone everytime. Moreover, I have been constantly improving my grades. I was also a member of the basketball team of the school that had won the inter school trophy and brought laurels to the school. My participation in the extra-curricular activities, also added to my credentials. Furthermore, my teachers praised me for starting the literary club for the school. It is indeed a matter of pride for me to receive this award. Mother is also very happy at my achievement.

I plan to meet you after the annual day and show you the trophy. Wishing you lots of happiness.

Yours affectionately,
Ravi

11. Your uncle has promised to give you a gift of ₹ 1000. Write a letter thanking him for the offer, tell him how you plan to spend the money and why you wish to spend it in this way. ***ICSE 2014***

Ans.

25/247, Bagla Kunj,
Khandari, Agra

12th December, 20XX

Dear Uncle,

I hope this letter finds you in the best of your spirit and health. I wish to thank you for the gift of ₹ 1000 that you have promised to give me if I score above 80% in my final exams. It is really very thoughtful of you. I am thrilled that I would be able to spend the money as I like. Moreover, this incentive is pushing me to study very hard and give my hundred per cent.

There is a book 'The Alchemist' by Paulo Coelho which I have been wanting to buy for a long time. Everybody has been praising this book. One of my friends has read it and she found it truly inspiring.

The other day when I went shopping with my mom, I found a beautiful set of painting colours. You know how fond I am of painting. My art teacher has always praised my sense of colour and wants me to join her workshop for five days in the winter vacation. Although the workshop is free of cost, I need painting material. So, I will use the rest of the money for paints and brushes which I saw in the supermarket.

Once again, thanks for your kind gesture and the thoughtfulness behind it. I hope you will be happy to hear the way I plan to spend the money.

I am looking forward to your visit.

Yours lovingly,
Shruti

12. You will soon have to make a decision about the subjects that you wish to study in Classes XI and XII. Write a letter to your Grandfather telling him about the subjects that you plan to take up. Be sure to explain the reason for your choice and how you think these subjects would help you in the future. ***ICSE 2013***

Ans.

808, Galleria Apartments,
DLF Phase-IV,
Gurgaon, Haryana

30th March, 20XX

Dear Grandpa,

I hope this letter finds you in the best of your spirit and health. I am good too. My final examinations have just got over and I was thinking about the stream of subjects which I would have to pursue in Classes XI and XII. I am still very confused regarding the same. I know that I would not take up Science for it does not match up with what I want to do in life. You know I had wanted to be an Entrepreneur since childhood. This dream of mine is related to both Commerce and Humanities.

As I did not know which stream will suit me the best, so I decided to opt for one week trial classes. After attending them I thought I should go for Commerce with Maths stream. Although the subjects are new, they are quite interesting and offers a practical approach. It is quite fun to solve accountancy questions, draw balance sheet, etc. There is so much to explore in Business Studies and Economics as well.

I feel that I have taken the correct decision because it will enhance my interest and aptitude towards becoming an industrialist in the future. Moreover, you and dad are always there to guide and assist me in my future endeavours.

I am sure with a lot of diligence and motivation from both of you, I will do very well and will realise my ambition soon. This stream would greatly benefit me in the future.

Hope to see you soon.

Yours affectionately,
Armaan

13. You were taken by your school to visit a place of historical interest. Write a letter to your classmate who was unable to go on the trip telling him/her about the trip, why it was important and what you gained from the experience.

ICSE 2012

Ans.

H.No. 18/5,
New Rajender Nagar,
New Delhi

18th December, 20XX

Dear Parth

I hope this letter finds you in the best of your spirit and health. I am good too. You might be curious to know about our trip and I am also very excited to tell you all about it. I must say that it was really fun and full of excitement which you unfortunately missed.

We left early morning at around 7 am from the school and reached the railway station to board the train to Amritsar. We reached Amritsar in the afternoon. After settling in the hotel, we had our lunch and went to Wagah Border. It was immensely beautiful sight and the parade enthralled us to no extent. After paying our respect and honour to the martyrs of Indian Army, we left for the the hotel. The next morning, we went to the Jallianwalla Bagh and were told about its history. After spending an hour there, we left for the Golden Temple. First and foremost, the temple was marvelous in the shining Sun. The peace and serenity felt there was relaxing. We sat there till our lunch and then left for shopping in the nearby market. I bought Punjabi Pappads, Jutti's and a beautiful suit for my family. While in the market, we were mesmerised by the beauty of the monuments. Some of the students also entered into gol-gappa competition and gulped as many as 60-70 of them. The scene left all of us in peels of laughter.

All in all, it was a fun trip.

If you would have been with us, you also would have enjoyed it.

Yours lovingly,
Shantanu

14. You have just acquired an unusual pet. Write a letter to your friend telling him/her about it. Give details about the care you have to take in looking after and feeding the pet.

ICSE 2011

Ans.

22, Bhawara Vihar,
M.G. Road,
Agra

3rd April, 20XX

Dear Parul,

It's after ages that I'm writing to you again. I am quite eager to tell you about my newly acquired pet. You can't even think what it is. It's neither a dog nor a bird in a cage. It's a baby monkey which I got from my uncle. He rescued it from the jungles of Assam. He was just a month old baby when I got it. He was too young then to have his normal diet of fruits and breads. He, thus, survived on milk. We had to feed him through a feeding bottle. Sometimes, we also gave him cerelac. My sister found him quite funny and named him 'Bunny'. After a few days with us, Bunny took a special liking towards me and we soon became best of pals.

Bunny is more like a family member now. But he is still only 6 months old. So, we don't allow him to eat anything from outside. My mother cooks for him. He eats boiled rice and vegetables mashed into a paste. Everyday after his meals, he needs a banana. He is more pleased if it's provided by me. I have also cut a portion of a discarded mattress and made a soft bed for him too.

Come soon to my place and visit Bunny. You will find him very lovable and he is quite friendly too.

Yours lovingly,
Sara

15. Your class was taken to visit an Old Age Home where you spent half a day with the residents. Write a letter to a friend telling him/her what you saw, how you felt and in what way you have changed since the visit. ***ICSE 2010***

Ans.

6/66, Chandni Chowk,
Delhi

22nd December, 20XX

Dear Aastha,

I hope this letter finds in best of your spirits and health. I am good too. I wrote a letter to you just two weeks ago and you may wonder why I am writing another letter without waiting for an answer. Well, the reason is simple! Yesterday, our class was taken to visit an Old Age Home where we spent half a day with the residents as a part of the social work project of our school.

During our visit, we were merely expected to chat with the senior citizens for some time and serve some snacks to them. The cultural team of our class was supposed to perform for them. But we were deeply moved when some of the caretakers told us about the cruel manner in which these parents and grandparents had been treated by members of their own family.

Some of them live under the perpetual illusion that someday their sons and daughters shall come back and give them some space in the house. Even our teacher was choked to tears when she heard their experiences. Such things are not new for us but witnessing someone's misfortune right before your own eyes is different.

I have decided to stay in touch with these wonderful and lively senior citizens for the rest of my life. Now, I will not look at them with impatience and irritation but in a more understanding and mature manner. This experience left a deep impact on me and made me realise the true worth of our parents whom we often take for granted and expect them to perform miracles for us.

I hope this letter has left a positive impression on you too.

Yours affectionately,
Natasha

16. You have recently read a book which has greatly impressed you. Write a letter to your cousin telling him/her why you were impressed. Advise him/her to read the book. ***ICSE 2009***

Ans.

H.No. 2/355,
Mall Road, Manali

2nd March, 20XX

Dear Esha,

I hope this letter finds in best of your spirits and health. I am good too. I received your letter yesterday and was glad to know that all is well at your end. I just can't wait to share with you the fantastic experience I had of reading the book 'Art of living'. The book is so mesmerising that once you start reading it you'll really find it impossible to put it down. The book is spell-binding from the very first page. It has taught me some very important lessons on how to live my life effectively. It has also helped me improvise in certain aspects of my life to make me more effective and better at things. This fabulous insight into living a worthy life is very easy to accept and highly appreciated.

I would not like to go into details but would definitely like you to read the book. I assure you that you will not be disappointed. I bet you will feel a drastic change in your life after reading it. Do let me know how the book appealed to you when you do read it.

Yours lovingly,
Aahaana

17. Write a letter to a friend who was absent from school on a day when a really comical incident took place. Describe the incident, say what was so funny about it and what you learnt from it. ***ICSE 2008***

Ans.

Flat No. 771,
Mayur Apartments,
Mayur Vihar,
New Delhi

5th May, 20XX

Dear Pallavi,

School days are full of fun and comedy. Today was also one such wonderful day when a really comical incident took place but alas! You were absent.

Today, we had a double period of Mathematics coupled with an extra class. It was a horribly boring period and all of us dreaded it. But thanks to the circumstances, we enjoyed it a lot.

As our Mathematics teacher stepped into the class, he found us sitting with downcast faces. But the moment we looked at him, our boredom was swept away and a smile went up on every face. We looked at him and then at each other and couldn't stop our laughter. Noticing this, he asked us what the matter was but nobody would tell him anything. He smiled and tried to laugh with us to avoid his awkwardness. But that made us laugh even more. At last, he started teaching us. There was a question which involved some calculation on the number of teeth. On reading it, we again couldn't stop ourselves and laughed loudly. What a scene it was!

You might be wondering now what was the reason behind our laugh. Well, sir had forgotten to wear his upper dentures and as a result, his mouth looked really funny without the boundary of one set of teeth. I know it was bad of us but we couldn't help. But sir was in jovial mood and told us that it seemed as if we had inhaled laughing gas. So, he stopped teaching and left us free to get over our fits of madness! Coincidentally, that was all we wanted and we enjoyed a lot!

I hope you will come to school soon otherwise you might miss out on another dose of laughter.

Yours affectionately,
Priyanka

18. One of your grandparents has completed one hundred years of age. Write a letter congratulating him/her expressing gratitude, praise and admiration for the way he/she has lived his/her life. ***ICSE 2007***

Ans.

H.No. C-24,
Kamla Nagar,
Near Vikas Market,
Agra

14th February, 20XX

Dear Grandpa,

I hope you are well. I am good too. First of all, heartiest congratulations on your 100th birthday! What a lovely bliss for all of us! Today, you have travelled far enough and completed a span of one hundred years giving us all reasons to enjoy and celebrate. I am really disappointed as I could not join your 'Centurion Birthday Bash' but I am always with you-even at the moment.

You must have thrown a lavish birthday party to your 'younger' friends on the lawn of your villa with my parents too. Your active life has taught me a lot— "Be a fighter against all odds: Never give up and you'll win". Your life is itself a brilliant example of hard work, patience and firm determination. You stand like a hero in every season- quite fearless and determined. I really admire you and wish to follow the same virtues of life.

You have been my ideal since my childhood. Whenever I had a problem, I looked at you to find out how you would have handled the situation. Even a blow of shocking pain or a touch of defeat could not deter me from the path of struggle because of your inspiration and glamour for tireless work. It is simply astonishing to notice the way you have maintained your health and balance of mind. You have achieved so much in your life that I am willing to admit the same as an impossible venture for me. The countless trophies in your drawing room are inspiring, to say the least, especially for me.

Once again, I congratulate you on this grand occasion and pray to the Almighty to keep you fit and fine in the years to come.

Your granddaughter,
Divya

19. Recently, you went to a restaurant for dinner and there you saw your favourite sports star. You had an opportunity of spending some moments with him or her. In a letter to your friend give a brief account of your memorable meeting with the sports star. **ICSE 2006**

Ans.

H.No. 221/A,
Lajpat Nagar,
New Delhi
16th August, 20XX

Dear Amrita,

The most amazing thing happened to me during dinner. I got to meet "King Kohli" and I couldn't wait to tell you all about it. I know you won't believe me because I couldn't believe my eyes either that it was really him there in the restaurant.

I was dining at Radisson with my friend Anjali just for fun when he popped up. He was wearing a pair of blue denim and a white T-shirt. Both of us jumped out of joy because he didn't seem to find a free table and here was an open chance for me. I rushed and requested him to join us.

After thinking it through for sometime, he joined us and smiled and allowed some minutes to lapse till our breathing returned to normal. Then, he began chatting amicably. He asked our name and hobbies and became very happy when he came to know that he was my favourite super-star. Slowly, we began feeling comfortable with one another.

He told us about various interesting episodes of the cricket team. He said that Prithvi is the naughtiest member of the team. He can't sit quiet even for a moment and always teases everybody in the dressing room. Rishabh is very sensitive about his batting and really enjoys hitting bowlers out of the field. The three of us rolled with laughter clutching our sides. It really was a great day!

Yours affectionately,
Suhaani

20. Your pen-friend from Japan plans to visit your school and attend classes and activities for the duration of a month. Write a letter briefing him/her on your school routine. Give any other information that you think your friend may need. **ICSE 2005**

Ans.

H.No. 72/4-B,
Chitranjan Park,
New Delhi
25th June, 20XX

Dear Akira,

I hope this letter finds you in the best of spirits and health. I am good too.

First, let me give you the good news. The matter of your joining us has been cleared by the Board of Management of our school. Now you'll be my classmate for the whole of August! From what I know of you, I don't think you'll have much of a problem adjusting to our school. Your outgoing nature and your fluency in English will help you make friends very fast.

Like yours, our school begins at 8 am and we finish classes at 2 pm. In this duration we have 8 periods comprising of 40 minutes each devoted to subject teaching. Recess is only for 40 minutes after the fourth period. We have two terms in a year, and you'll actually be joining us in the latter part of our first term. Saturdays are usually most exciting days and we look forward to them as it is a half day and most of the activities take place on this day. It is usually a day for students to compete against each other in house activities. This helps to bring out the hidden talent of the students.

I know your favourite sport is baseball. Unfortunately, we don't play the game here. Although Football is as popular here as I've heard it is in Japan. And then, there is Table Tennis, Cricket and Badminton.

I must tell you that on 15th August, we celebrate our Independence day. So, much of the first half of the month goes into preparing for it and other co-curricular activities are pushed to the background. But I think the preparations themselves will be quite an experience for you.

As for studies, I know Japan has a very high standard and it will be interesting to see how you feel about the standard of academics here.

Well, Akira, I can't wait to meet you!

Yours faithfully,
Samaira

CHAPTER TEST

Formal Letters

1. Write a letter to the Commissioner of Raipur Corporation complaining about poor sanitary conditions and mosquito menace in your locality.
2. Write an application to the Collector of your district for imposing restrictions on the use of loudspeakers during examination period.
3. You have lost your original certificates of Classes X and XII. You want to get their duplicates issued but you do not know the procedure. Write a letter to the Chairman enquiring about the fee to be deposited, mode of payment, time taken by the board for issuing duplicate certificates and any other formalities.
4. You placed an order with Regent Computer Accessories House for the supply of laptop tables, computer stationery, etc. However, you felt disappointed when you opened the consignment. Two out of the eight tables ordered have wobbly legs and two reams of paper contain defective sheets. Write a letter in 120-150 words to the manager requesting him to replace the defective supplies.
5. The youth of the country are very vigilant these days and feel concerned about the problems being faced by the people. Write a letter to the Editor of a national daily urging him to highlight the role of the youth in eradicating the problems of poverty, unemployment and corruption.
6. As a regular commuter by bus from Noida to Delhi, you have been witnessing rash driving by the bus drivers daily without an exception. Write a letter to the Editor drawing the attention of the General Manager, Delhi Transport Corporation to this problem.

Informal Letters

1. Write a letter to your friend Rakesh/Rakhi inviting him for to attend your sister's marriage.
2. Write a letter to your friend congratulating her/him for topping the board examinations.
3. Write a letter to your friend Rama/Raman requesting him/her to spend the summer holidays with you.
4. Write a letter to your father requesting him to increase your pocket money.
5. Write a letter to your cousin telling him about your recovery from illness.
6. Write a letter to your uncle telling him about your recent visit to Kerala.

07

Notice Writing

A notice is an important form of written communication used by individuals and organisations to convey information about functions, events and occasions or to announce something that has happened or is about to happen. It is direct and formal language. Its style is straight forward.

Points to keep in Mind while Writing a Notice

- Content includes :
  - Target group (to whom it is addressed)
  - Details of the event like date, time, venue, duration
  - Other details

Suggested Specimen of Notice (Issued by Board)

Format 1 Your school is hosting an interschool debate competition. Write a notice for your school informing them of the event.

Ans.

War of Words

Inter-School Debate Competition
on 8th December, 2017
from 9.00 a.m. to 12 noon
at Centenary Hall, St. Hilda's School
All pupils from Classes IX & X who wish to participate are to give their names to Mrs. T. Baker on or before 1st December, 2017

Format 2 Your school is conducting an inter-class talent search. Write out a notice to be put up in your school informing students about the event and inviting them to participate.

Ans.

EVERYBODY'S GOT TALENT

Inter-class Talent Search
Date: Tuesday, 24th July, 2018
Time: 9 a.m. to 4 p.m.
Venue: The Auditorium of St. Agnes' School
Interested students from Classes 8, 9 and 10 may register with the Vice Principal on or before 14th July, 2018.

TYPE 1 Notice for Meeting

This type of notice requires the following details

- Purpose of the meeting or agenda
- Date and time/duration of the meeting
- Details of persons to attend/departments to attend
- Venue, specific instructions for the persons called for the meeting

Sample Notice

You are Abhishek/Avantika of Class X, Translam Academy, Kanpur. Being an Activity Coordinator, draft a notice to all the other Activity Council Members to discuss and plan the activities for Christmas Day celebration.

Ans.

IT'S CHRISTMAS TIME!

Meeting regarding activities for Christmas Celebration

on 23rd December, 20XX

at 10:30 a.m

in Biology Lab, Translam Academy, Kanpur

All the Activity Council Members are hereby informed to attend the meeting with the purpose of discussing activities for Christmas Day celebration.

TYPE 2 Notice for Events

These notices include invitation for competition, tour, celebration, annual sports, cultural event, etc. It includes

- Who can participate in it
- Number of days (in case of tours/visit)
- Last date for depositing the advance (tour/visit)
- Occasion should be mentioned
- Expenditure estimate
- Any specific instructions

Sample Notice

You are the Secretary of the Environment Club of Dharmik Sandhya Public School. Write a notice to invite students to the tree plantation drive organised by the Club on the World Environment Day.

Ans.

Plant it up

Tree Plantation Drive

Date: 5th June, 20XX, Monday

Time: 9.00 am to 4.00 pm

Venue: School Playground

All are invited to participate.

TYPE 3 Notice for Lost or Found

- Article/Object should be mentioned lost or found
- Where you lost or found it
- Description of the article like colour, size, model, etc.
- Date, Time, Day when you lost it/found it
- Whom to contact
- A suitable gift/reward for the person who returns that article/product
- Writer's name and designation/class

Sample Notice

You are a student of Class X of Vanasthali Public School, Ludhiana. You have lost your hall ticket for the Board Examination. You have to put up a notice on your school's notice board.

Ans.

Vanasthali Public School, Ludhiana

1st March, 20XX

Loss of Hall Ticket

Students are informed that a Board Examination hall ticket was lost in the school playground. It contains a photograph along with the Roll No. 1234567. Anybody, who finds it, is requested to give it to the Administrative Officer. The person finding it and handing it over will be rewarded.

TYPE 4 Notice for Seminar/Workshop/Debate or any other Literary Event

- Speakers/Chief Guest/Honourable Persons should be mentioned
- Who can attend it
- Date/Time should be mentioned
- Specific instructions should be mentioned
- Duration of the programme should be mentioned

Sample Notice

You are the Captain of Meerut Public School, Shastri Market, Meerut. Write a notice informing the students about a guest lecture by Mr. Rajiv, an environmentalist, on the topic 'Conservation of Water'.

Ans.

SAVE WATER!

Guest Lecture on Conservation of Water

on 3rd November, 20XX

from 10:30 a.m. to 11:30 a.m.

in the Auditorium, Meerut Public School, Varanasi

Chief Guest–Mr. Rajiv, a renowned environmentalist

Attendance of Class X students is compulsory. For more information, contact the school captain.

TYPE 5 Notice for Appeal/Warning

- Whom to appeal/warn
- Issuing authority (if different from the person signing the notice) should be mentioned
- A slogan or message
- Important instructions
- Courteous way to appeal
- Name and designation of the issuing person
- Any punishment (if required, in case of warning type only)

Sample Notice

Recently, it was in the news that a hurricane hit Odisha and around 13 districts were affected. Being the Head of Environment Society of your school, draft a notice to the students and staff appealing for donations of relief products like clothes, money, books and other articles.

Ans.

GIVE TILL IT HURTS!

Appeal for Donations

Date : 5th December, 20XX

Time : 10:00 a.m. to 1:00 p.m.

Venue : Auditorium, Deewan Public School, Mysore

Students can donate money, clothes, books, articles like blazers, etc. for the victims of the hurricane. Certificated will be given to the highest contributors.

Type 6 Notice for Change of Name/Residential/Company Address etc

- Whom to inform about the change
- Reason for change can be mentioned
- Existing Name/Current Residential/Company Address should be mentioned.
- New Name/Residential/Company Address should be mentioned.
- Your name and signature should be mentioned.

Sample Notice

You are proprietor of a company which has changed its office address from 2A, Phool Bagh Colony to Mangal Pandey Nagar. Draft a notice to be inserted in the local newspaper informing people about the change of address.

Ans.

Change in Address

25th March, 20XX

This is to inform all that we have changed our office address from 2A, Phool Bagh Colony to 334/3, Mangal Pandey Nagar. All are requested to contact us at our new address.

Our phone no. 0121-248276X remains unchanged.

Vinay Sharma

PYQs Previous Years' Questions

1. Write a notice to be put up in your school informing the pupils of Classes IX and X about the Remedial Classes to be held after the school hours and asking them to register their names for it. ***ICSE 2023***

2. Your school is hosting an inter-school music competition. Write a notice informing your school the event. ***ICSE Specimen Paper 2023***

3. March 22nd is World Water Day. The school Dramatics Club is planning to stage a one act play to mark the occasion and create awareness. Write a notice to be put up on the school notice board giving details of the event. ***ICSE 2022 Sem II***

4. You are the President of the school Science Club. You and your team are planning to organise a creative mask-making event using renewable materials. Write a notice to be put up on the school notice board giving details of the event. ***ICSE Specimen Paper 2022 Sem II***

5. Your school is organising a fete/carnival to raise funds for victims of the recent floods in your State. Write a notice to be put up on the school notice board giving details of the event. ***ICSE 2020***

6. Your school is hosting an Inter-School Quiz Competition.
   Write out a notice to be displayed in your school giving all details for the event. ***ICSE 2019***

7. You are the President of a children's club in your locality. You and your team are planning to organise a programme to celebrate Teachers' day. Write a notice to be put up in the local supermarket giving details of the programme to create an awareness of the event. ***ICSE Specimen Paper 2019***

8. You are the Secretary of Tours and Trips Society of Translam Academy International, Meerut. The school is organising a 20 days historical tour to some important places in South India. You have been asked by the Activity Coordinator to put up a notice inviting students interested in visiting those places. Write this notice to be put up on the school notice board.

9. You are Secretary of AVM Housing Society. You are going to organise a Blood Donation Camp. Write a notice urging the members of your society to come in large numbers for this noble cause. Invent all the necessary details.

10. You are School Pupil Leader of Rani Laxmi Bai Senior Secondary School, Gwalior. Draft a notice for your school notice board inviting the names of the students who want to participate in the cultural programme organised in aid of the victims of the recent Assam floods.

Answers

1.

Remedial Classes

For Classes IX and X

Days: Monday to Friday
Timing- 2 : 30 to 4 : 00 pm
Venue - Respective Classes
Register your names with your class teacher.

2.

Inter-School Music Competition

Day : Monday
Date : 20th September, 20XX
Timing - 11 : 00 am to 2 : 00 pm
Venue - Respective Classes
Participate and win exciting prizes!

3.

Save Blue. Live Green.

World Water Day Celebration

On 22nd March, 20XX (World Water Day)
from 1:30 p.m. to 3:00 p.m.
in Auditorium, Delhi Public School, Meerut

All the students are hereby invited to the one-act play, to mark the occasion and create awareness. The play will be followed by an interactive session.

4.

Creative Mask Making Event

Day : Wednesday
Date : 22nd March, 20XX
Time : 9 : 00 am to 1 : 00 pm
Venue : Science Room

Event Details

- Use only renewable material
- Come dressed traditionally

All of you are hereby requested to attend the event and honor the contribution made by children in our formation.

5.

For the Ones in Need

Fund Raising Carnival

on 8th April, 20XX
from 11:00 a.m. onwards
in Vidyasagar Public School, Bihar

Students are requested to be a part of the fest, and bring their parents and friends. There will be various food stalls, games and rides. A lucky draw will also be organised. The coupons for the luky draw can be obtained from the reception.

All are invited to participate and help the victims of the recent floods in the state.

6.

Puzzlers

Inter-School Quiz Competition

on 5th September, 20XX
4 p.m. onwards
in Auditorium, Sunlight Public School, Ghaziabad

The events of the function is as follows

- Welcome to the Chief Guest, Ms. R Shastri, MLA
- Announcement of the rules, introduction of the teams and the Quiz Master
- Actual conduct of the quiz
- Presentation of prizes to the winners and runners-up
- Address by Chief Guest
- Vote of Thanks by the Principal
- Refreshments

All faculty, staff and students are requested and welcome to attend.

7. **Thank you Teacher!**

A cultural programme to celebrate Teachers' Day
on 5th September
from 5 : 00 pm to 7 : 00 pm
at Community Centre, South City Mall
All teachers who are residents of the South City Complex are cordially invited

8. 20 Days Historical Tour
(A visit to Chennai, Mysore, Rameshwaram, Kanyakumari and Bengaluru)
Date : 1st April to 20th April
Fare : ₹ 2500
Interested students need to submit
- Parents' approval letter
- Fees by 24th March

For further details, contact Ms. Saini.

9. **DONATE BLOOD! GIVE LIFE!**

Blood Donation Camp

on 15th March, 20XX from 11 a.m. onwards in
Community Hall AVM Housing Society, Ghaziabad
Residents above the age of 18 and below 50 years with good medical health are urged to volunteer in large number for this noble cause.
Qualified doctors will be available to carry out the procedure.

10. **Cultural Test**
(A charity event to aid the victims of Assam floods)
Day : Sunday
Date : 25th December, 20XX
Time : 11 : 00 am onwards
Venue : School Auditorium
All students are requested to give your names to volunteers.

CHAPTER TEST

1. Draft a notice as Secretary of Lion's Club, Dwarka to inform all the members about the Diwali Mela and sale of items.
2. As Librarian of Crescent International School, Gwalior, draft a notice asking all students and teachers to return the library books they have borrowed, two days before the commencement of the examination.
3. You are Cultural Captain of your school. Write a notice for singers to compete for the HM Award. Winners will get a chance to visit London for a song sequence for the HM Album.
4. You are the Principal of St. Thomas School. Write a notice informing students and parents about the 'Obesity Camp' to be organised by Jessa Ram Hospital.
5. Young astronauts have to be selected for 'Mission NASA'. The preliminary round will be conducted in Modern School. Write a notice inviting students who wish to become astronauts to take the preliminary round for final selection. You are the Director of Science Research Centre.
6. You are the Cultural Secretary of RM Public School, Alkapuri, Vadodara. You have been asked to inform students of Class IX to XII about an Inter-School Dramatics Competition. Draft a notice for the students notice board with all necessary details.

08

E-Mail Writing

E-mail or electronic mail is a message distributed by electronic means from one computer user to one or more recipients *via.* a network. With the advent of the digital age, e-mail plays an important part in everybody's life. It is one of the most popular and fastest way of sending messages anywhere in the world and can be used in formal as well as informal contexts.

Hence, a student should be well-versed with the various features of an e-mail like composing an e-mail, attaching files/documents adding Cc and Bcc recipients, formatting, etc. The knowledge of e-mail and internet makes a student up-to-date with today's technologies and prepares him/her to be ready for the future. E-mail are generally written for formal communications.

Parts of an E-mail

- **Recipient's Address** The first thing you need to enter when composing an e-mail is the recipient's address. An example of e-mail address is: sakshiwrites@gmail.com. When sending a message to multiple recipients, be sure to separate all addresses with a comma.
- **Cc and Bcc** Another option when sending a message to multiple recipients is to use the Cc or carbon copy and Bcc or blind carbon copy fields. When using the Cc feature, all recipients can see the e-mail addresses of everyone the message was sent to. If you want your communication to be more private, choose the Bcc and the email address of the other recipients will not be shown.
- **Subject Line** The subject line is the second part of your e-mail that the recipient will see. It essentially tells what the e-mail is about.
- **Body** The body is where you actually write the message that you want to send.
- **Attachments** Attachments are similar to enclosures in a traditional mail. If you have files that you want to share with your recipient(s), you can include them as attachments to the e-mail.
- **Signature** Some e-mail systems allow you to enter a signature that will appear automatically at the bottom of every message you send. This feature is optional and can be turned off and on as needed.

Steps for Writing an E-mail

1. Type the e-mail id of the recipient(s) in the 'To', 'Cc' and 'Bcc' fields.
2. Compose the subject of the e-mail in the subject line.
3. Attach any files that you want to send with the e-mail using the 'Attach' or 'Insert' option.
4. Write the proper salutation (like Dear Father, Hi, Bhawna, Sir/Ma'am, etc.)
5. Write the body of the e-mail.
6. End the mail with a proper close.

E-mail Etiquettes

It refers to the do's and dont's of the things to be kept in mind while writing e-mails.

1. **Do not Leave the Subject Line Blank**
2. **Include Proper Salutation as per the E-mail type** One must include proper salutation before starting to write an e-mail. The salutation used should depend on the recepient of the email.

   Example- Sir/Ma'am
3. **Avoid using Abbreviations and Acronyms**
4. **Grammar and Language** The message should be conveyed using correct grammar and simple language. The traditional rules for punctuation is to be maintained in the e-mail.
5. **Add Appropriate Closing** One should use proper closing of the e-mail before hitting the send button. The closing of the e-mail should be appropriate.

   Examples

- Yours obediently
- Yours sincerely
- Yours faithfully

Suggested Specimen of E-mail (Issued by Board)

Format 1

Write an e-mail to the Principal of a neighbouring school informing her of the event and requesting her to send a team to participate.

Ans. principalbluebellschool@gmail.com
Inter-School Debate Competition

Dear Madam,
Our school is celebrating its 50th anniversary this year. As part of the celebrations we are hosting a series of competitions and we are beginning with 'War of Words', an Inter-School Debate Competition.
It will be held on 8th December, 2017 from 9.00 a.m. till 12 noon in the Centenary Hall of St. Hilda's School.
Please do send your senior debate team to participate in the event.
The topic will be given to the participants an hour before the start of the competition. They may bring their laptops for use during the preparation time.
We look forward to your school's participation in the competition.
Thanking you,

Yours faithfully,
Ashish Roy
Debating Secretary

Format 2

Write an e-mail to the General Manager of the Supermarket seeking permission to display the notice and requesting a sponsorship for the event.

Ans. rmsouthcity@gmail.com
Teachers' Day Celebration

Dear Sir,
Teachers' Day is around the corner and we, the residents of the South City Complex, would like to express our gratitude to our teachers by hosting a brief cultural programme on the 5th September between 5.00 p.m. to 7.00 p.m.
There are about 25 teachers in our complex and we would be grateful if you allow us the use of the foyer in the Supermarket for the celebration.

We also request you to please sponsor a cup of tea and light refreshments for the teachers and a few guests, about 40 in all.
We look forward to a favourable response.
Thanking you,

Yours faithfully,
Ashish Roy
Secretary, Youth Club, South City Society

Format 3

Write an e-mail to the Principal of a neighbouring school requesting him / her to send a team of teachers to judge the event.

Ans. To : principal@stflorence.org
Subject : Request to appoint judges for a talent search event.

Dear Madam,
I am Maya Gilani, the Cultural Secretary of the Student Council, St. Agnes' School. We are conducting a talent search contest for the students of Classes 8, 9 and 10.
This is to be held on the 24th of July, 2018, from 9 a.m. to 4 p.m. in Music, Art, **Dance, Magic, Acrobatics and Stand-up Comedy**.
We request you to send a team of three teachers from your school to judge the talent search, Everybody's Got Talent.
Anticipating a positive response,

Yours faithfully,
Maya Gilani
Cultural Secretary, Student Council
St. Agnes' School

Format 4

Write an e-mail to a prominent basketball coach of your city who has agreed to be the referee at the event giving all relevant details.

Ans. To : coachformidable123@gmail.com
Subject : Invitation to Referee Dribble Stars – Inter House Basketball Competition.

Dear Sir,
I am Sam Sequeira of Berkeley High and I write with reference to my telephone call to you earlier. We are conducting an inter- house basketball competition on 4th July, 2018 from 9 a.m. to 1 p.m. on the Main Basketball Court, Berkeley High Sports Complex. Thank you for having accepted our request to referee the event.

The schedule is as follows
• Ruby vs Emerald Match 1
• Sapphire vs Topaz Match 2
• The Battle – For third place – Match 3
• The Grand Finale – The Final Match

We will arrange to pick you up by 8.15 a.m. from your residence and you will be dropped back after the Basketball Competition.
We look forward to seeing you at Berkeley High.
Thanking you,
Yours faithfully,

Sam Sequeira
Games Captain
Berkeley High

PYQs Previous Years' and Other Important Questions

1. Write an email to the Principal of a neighbouring school inviting their pupils to attend the classes if they so wish. Give all details of the classes to be held. ***ICSE 2023***

2. Write an e-mail to the Principal of the neighbouring school informing him/her of the event and requesting him/her to send a team to participate. ***ICSE Specimen Paper 2023***

3. Write an e-mail to the Principal of a neighbouring school requesting him/her to send a team of children to participate in the interactive session which will follow the play on 'World Water Day' celebration. ***ICSE 2022 Sem II***

4. Write an e-mail to the General Manager of a local hospital requesting him / her to send a senior doctor to talk to the participants at the event about the quality of mask which would give them the best protection. ***ICSE Specimen Paper 2022 Sem II***

5. Write an e-mail to the Principal of a neighbouring school inviting him/her to send their students to attend the fete/carnival. ***ICSE 2020***

6. Write an e-mail to the Principal of a neighbouring school requesting him/her to send a team of three members to participate in the Quiz Competition. ***ICSE 2019***

7. Write an e-mail to the General Manager of the Supermarket seeking permission to display the notice and requesting a sponsorship for the event. ***ICSE Specimen Paper 2019***

8. As a member of your residential society, write an e-mail to Inspector of Local Police Station, Mr Sharma, informing him about miscreants who ride their bikes rashly every evening outside your society.

9. You are the President of the Nature Club of your school. You wish to subscribe to the 'Nature for All' magazine for the school library. Write an e-mail to the Subscription Department of the magazine requesting them to send the details of the subscription plans.

10. Write an e-mail to the Manager of Smart Automotive Company, Mr. Ahmed, regarding the poor quality of service facility available in the city.

Answers

1. principal.dps.2013@yahoo.co.in

Invitation for students to attend foreign language classes

Dear Sir/Ma'am,

The school is going to organise Spanish, German and French classes for the students of Classes IX-XII from the 20th of September, 20XX. The school has invited teachers and language experts from embassies to help the students in spoken as well as written languages. The classes would last three months and would take place after school hours (2: 30 pm - 4 pm) from Monday to Friday. This is a great opportunity for the students to get acquainted with foreign languages.

The students of your school are welcome to attend these classes if they wish. Each student can pick one language to learn from the three given languages. Kindly send the interested students to our school for the same.

Thanking you,

Yours faithfully,

Anita Kumar (Head Girl)

Vidya Public School

2. principal.dps.2013@yahoo.co.in

Request to send a team for participation in the Inter-School Music Competition

Dear Sir/Ma'am,

The school is going to organise an Inter-School Music Competition on the 20th of September, 20XX. Five schools from the city will be participating in the competition. The winning team will be honoured with Gold Medals and prize money.

Kindly send a team from your school to participate in the event.

Thanking you,

Yours faithfully,

Anita Kumar (Head Girl)

Vidya Public School

3. principal.abc@xyzschool.com

Interactive Session on World Water Day

Dear Sir/ Ma'am,

This is to inform you that Delhi Public School, Delhi is going to organise a one-act play on World Water Day, i.e., 22nd March, 20XX in the School Auditorium to mark the occasion and create awareness. The play will be followed by an interactive session on the same. You are requested to send a team of children to participate in the interactive session. It will be a great opportunity for students of both the schools to interact with one another and improve their knowledge.

Kindly send the names of the participants by 4th March, 20XX.

Thanking you,

Regards,

PQR

(Principal)

Delhi Public School

4. GMHospital@sthospital.com

Request to send a team of doctors to discuss the mask quality.

Dear Sir/Ma'am,

This is to request you to kindly send a team of doctors to our area for health meeting against Covid-19 protection including mask quality. People here are living below the poverty line and are unable to afford a health checkup. This health checkup would be very beneficial for them because then they may approach their concerned doctors and get their treatment done. This initiative of yours would be appreciable.

Anticipating a positive response,

Yours faithfully,

ABC
Principal
(ABC School)

5. principalgloriaschool@gmail.com

Invitation for attending the carinval

Dear Madam

With extreme pride and pleasure, we would like to invite your students to attend and participate in the carnival being organised by our school on 8th April, 20XX. The carnival will begin at 11 o'clock in the morning. The purpose of this carnival is to raise funds to help the victims of the recent floods in our state. There will be a lot of interesting games and rides. Attractive food stalls have also been arranged.

We request you to kindly grace the occasion with your presence.

Thanking You,
Yours obediently,
Sarita
(Head Girl)
Vidyasagar Public School

Examiner's Comment

- Some candidates gave personal ids while some gave incorrect email ids.
- Some candidates failed to provide necessary information.
- Some candidates only invited the Principal while the invitation was for the students of the neighbouring school.

Suggestions for Students

- Read and learn the format of an email.
- Focus on the details/information to be added.

6. To : principal@ bhairavschool.com

Subject : Invitation for Sending Team for Inter-School Quiz Competition

Respected Sir/Ma'am,

This is to inform you that our school has been honoured to host the Inter-School Quiz Competition of the district this year. Ms. R Shastri, MLA, has kindly consented to be the Chief Guest.

A notice giving details of the event is attached to the mail. You are requested to arrange to send a team of three students to participate on behalf of your school.

You are requested to provide the names as well as the contact details of the students as well as staff members by 28th March, 20XX. For further details, kindly contact the undersigned.

Thanking you,

With Regards
Ravi Saroha
(Head Boy)
Sunlight Public School
Mobile no. 99885XXXXX
Encl. a/a

7. To : rmsouthcity@gmail.com
Subject : Teachers' Day Celebration

Dear Sir/Ma'am,

Teachers' Day is around the corner and we, the residents of the South City Complex, would like to express our gratitude to our teachers by hosting a brief cultural programme on the 5th September between 5.00 p.m. to 7.00 p.m. There are about 25 teachers in our complex and we would be grateful if you allow us the use of the foyer in the Supermarket for the celebration. We also request you to please sponsor a cup of tea and light refreshments for the teachers and a few guests, about 40 in all.

We look forward to a favourable response.

Thanking you,
Yours sincerely,
Ashish Roy
Secretary, Youth Club, South City Society

8. To : inspectorsharma10@yahoo.com
Subject : Miscreants in the area

Respected Sir/Ma'am,

This is to inform you that we, the residents of Siddhartha Nagar, have written this mail to bring to your notice that a few guys are riding their bikes very rashly in the evening hours in the main road of the colony. As you know that this is the time when children play on the road and elderly go for an evening walk these rash drivers can lead to accidents and mishaps. In fact, many of these people are seen bullying and harrassing women, children and even the elderly. Therefore, we request you to look into the matter and help us make our locality safe for all.

Thanking you,

Yours sincerely,
Vaibhav Kumar

9. To : theweek@subscriptionenquiring.com
Subject : Subscription enquiring for 'Nature for All'

Dear Sir/Ma'am,

This is to inform you that I, the President of the Nature Club of Springdales School, Dhaula Kuan, New Delhi, I happened to go through a copy of your magazine at your stall in the recently concluded Book Fair at Pragati Maidan. I found your magazine very interesting and wanted to subscribe to it for our school library so that students can benefit from it. Kindly send me the details of the cost of its subscription and the various plans available for the same. I would appreciate if you could give us some discount over and above the regular subscription rates as we would be using it for educational purposes.

Looking forward to your correspondence.

Yours faithfully,
Naveen Kaul
(President, Nature Club)
Springdales School
New Delhi-110010

10. To : ahmedsac@gmail.com

Subject : Poor service quality in the city

Dear Mr. Ahmed,

This is to inform you that I recently bought Fiat Palio from your store in Nagole with Receipt no. 1100XX. Recently, I faced small problem with car AC and brought the car for maintenance. But to my utter surprise, the showroom staff told me that service is not available in their showroom and they asked me to take the car to the nearby service center.

After much struggle, when I reached the service centre no one was there. I decided to wait when luckily one very rude staff told me that they are busy and are not going to take my car for service. Such a behaviour was shocking. Dejected I had to drive the car to another service centre where they took my car for service. However, even here I was left unsatisfied. The AC which was faulty had been removed and the car was very dirty. Further, I was charge a hefty amount for refusal. This had completely ruined the reputation that your organisation held.

Such a poor behaviour and service was not expected. Hence, I request you to look into the matter, improve it and get my car serviced again. I hope for a early redressal.

Thanks and regards,

Pranit Chopra

CHAPTER TEST

1. You purchased a pair of shoes from an outlet of a well-known brand. The sole of the shoes cracked within a month of your using them. Write an e-mail to Customer Care Department of the company asking them to replace your shoes.
2. Write an e-mail to a English Daily requesting them to sponsor the Debating Competition to be held at your school. You are Jeevan/Jasper of Class X, Air Force School.
3. Write an e-mail to your School Counsellor requesting her to take a session on the topic 'How to choose the right stream in Class XI'. Invent necessary details.
4. Your school is conducting an Inter-Class Talent Search.Write an email to the Principal of a neighbouring school requesting him/her to send a team of teachers to judge the event.
5. Your school is organising an Inter-House Basketball Competition. Write an email to a prominent basketball coach of your city who has agreed to be the referee at the event, giving all relevant details.
6. Write an email to a publication house asking for help in printing posters and pamphlets for advertising the charity drive organised by your school for the underprivileged children.

09

Comprehension Passage

Comprehension is defined as the understanding of a passage or a text.

A comprehension passage, then, is a text set for testing the reader's ability to comprehend or understand the meaning of the matter and to comprehend the style as well as the theme of the passage.

The comprehension passage of about 500 words is generally taken from a famous story or novel. Different types of questions are asked from the passage to test the students' vocabulary and the ability to understand the excerpt/content.The first question comprising 3 parts will be set to test vocabulary. The second question contains short answer type questions.

The last question will consist of a summary that will test the candidate's ability to distinguish main ideas from supporting details and to extract salient points to re-express them. Candidates will be given clear indications of what they are to summarise and of the length of the summary.

Marks are awarded for the candidates' ability to express and form logical sentence. In case of linguistic errors, marks are deducted.

Guidelines to Attempt Comprehension

Keep the following points in mind while attempting an unseen comprehension

1. First, read the passage carefully and study the questions properly.
2. Second, give a second reading to the passage. This reading should be thorough as it will help you identify the answers.
3. Underline the words/phrases related to the questions.
4. While writing the answers, remain precise and to-the-point. Do not make general or vague statements.
5. Write the answers in your own language and expression. Never copy the exact language of the passage.

PYQs Previous Years' Questions

1. Read the following passage carefully and answer the questions that follow. ***ICSE 2023***

1 That huge bell never stopped ringing It got us out of bed, it **summoned** us for meals, it rang between class periods, it sent us unwillingly to bed.

2 One morning, it failed to ring or rather, there was no bell to ring. Someone had removed it and it wasn't found till late in the afternoon.

3 What a glorious day! As there was no bell to rouse us, everyone got up late, and there was no morning PT. Some of us missed breakfast too. The teachers got confused and mixed up their classes. How could the school manage without it? Confusion reigned.

4 Of course, no one owned up. It could have meant expulsion. Some suspicion fell on the Sports Captain because of our **aversion** to morning PT but nothing could be proved.

5 No one was very anxious to find the bell - we were quite happy without it but it was finally discovered hanging from a branch of one of the trees.

6 'It may have been Mr. Sharma,' surmised Brian. Mr. Sharma, our Maths teacher, was known to walk in his sleep. And sleepwalkers did funny things sometimes.

7 'It could be Mool Chand himself,' suggested Cyrus Satralkar.

8 Mool Chand was the school chowkidar, who also had the job of banging the brass bell at appointed times. 'Why would he throw it away?'

9 'He must be as fed up with ringing it as we are of hearing it'. This was my theory. 'Perhaps, he wants a rise in salary.'

10 The identity of the culprit remained a mystery. Happily, the senior Hockey team went on a winning spree against all corners, and our month-end exits were **restored**.

11 But soon there was another sensation.

12 A girl was admitted to our class!

13 The boys were scandalised. No girl had ever studied in our school before. We protested.

14 'What's the problem?' asked Mr. Knight, our class master. 'Haven't you seen a girl before?'

15 'But – but. Sir...' Tata was our spokesman. 'How will we concentrate on our studies?'

16 'When did you ever concentrate on your studies, Tata?'

17 'Are we going co-ed, sir?' Adams wanted to know.

18 'Not at all,' said Mr. Knight. 'This is a special case. She is the school accounts manager's daughter, and he can't afford the Girls school fees. So, I'm sure you'll make her feel very welcome.'

19 The accountant was a popular man who also ran the school's tuck shop and allowed most of us a certain amount of credit. All our objections faded away.

20 At first, Sunita, our new entrant, was a bit of a distraction because, although she was very shy and demure, she had lovely curly hair, bright eyes, pink cheeks and a smile for everyone. All the boys were very polite and attentive to her and Brian in particular was always ready to help her.

– Collection of Stories, Ruskin Bond

(i) For each word given below, choose the correct meaning (as used in the passage) from the options provided.

1. summoned *(line 2)*

(a) totalled (b) ordered
(c) requested (d) shout

2. aversion *(line 14)*

(a) hatred (b) fear
(c) politeness (d) creation

3. restored *(line 33)*

(a) helped (b) returned
(c) permit (d) victory

(ii) Answer the following questions briefly in your own words.

(a) Why did no one confess to having removed the missing bell?

(b) Why did suspicion fall on the Sports Captain?

(c) What made Brian think that it was Mr. Sharma?

(d) Which sentence in the passage tells you that Mr Knight thought poorly of Tata's academic performance?

(e) Why was the accountant a popular man?

(iii) In not more than 50 words, describe the effects of the lost bell.

Ans. (i) 1. (b) ordered

2. (a) hatred

3. (b) returned

(ii) (a) No one confessed to having removed the missing bell because it would have meant expulsion from the school.

(b) Suspicion fell on the Sports Captain because of the students' aversion to morning PT.

(c) Brian thought that it was Mr. Sharma who had removed the bell because he was known to walk in his sleep and sleepwalkers did funny things.

(d) The sentence in the passage that tells us that Mr. Knight thought poorly of Tata's academic performance is: 'When did you ever concentrate on your studies, Tata?'

(e) The accountant was a popular man because he ran the school's tuck shop and allowed most of the students a certain amount of credit.

(iii) When the bell was lost, it was a glorious day for the students. Without the bell, everyone got up late and there was no morning PT. The scheduled time was in shambles as children missed breakfast, teachers got confused and mixed up their classes. Since the school couldn't manage without it, there was a lot of confusion.

2. Read the following passage carefully and answer the questions that follow. ***ICSE Specimen Paper 2023, ICSE 2019***

1 He would have gone on worrying and worrying in this way if an unexpected **distraction** had not arrived in the form of a heavily loaded car bumping over the grassy bank, dodging between the coconut trees and raising a cloud of dust in the narrow path before it came to a standstill in front of Mon Repos, the white bungalow that stood empty most of the year. It was the de Silvas, the family that came from Bombay to spend an occasional holiday in it and bring it suddenly to life for a few days. They had bought Mon Repos a year ago from the Vakils who had been one of the first Bombay families to build holiday cottages on the Thul beach. But they had grown too old and **frail** to come often and after the house has stood empty for several years, sold it to the de Silvas who were young and energetic and seemed heartily to enjoy life on the beach. Whenever they came, life changed for the family and the little hut, too. Immediately there was a hubbub, all kinds of excitement and expectations and of course work to be done, employment to be had and wages.

2 Hari, Bela and Kamal stood by their door under the frangipani tree, tense with excitement watching and holding Pinto back as he barked at the unfamiliar sight of a car and stranger till his voice was quite hoarse. There was a commotion in the marshy creek that separated the hut from the house, too herons, egrets, kingfishers and moorhens all flapping into the **dense** greenery of the pandanus, the casuarina and the bhindi trees for shelter.

3 "Do you think they have come here for good?" Bela whispered.

4 "Hunh - who would live here if he had a house in Bombay?" Hari scoffed.

5 'But look how much luggage they've brought - it can't be just for a few days,' Bela said and it was true that an unbelievable number of boxes and bags and baskets were being taken out of the car, out of the boot and off the luggage carrier so that anyone would have thought they had come to stay forever.

Village by the Sea
Anita Desai

(i) For each word given below, choose the correct meaning (as used in the passage) from the options provided.

1. distraction *(line 2)*
   (a) something that stops you from thinking about something else
   (b) something that helps you to think about something else
   (c) something that you use for weight-training
   (d) something that helps you to not be distracted

2. frail *(line 13)*
   (a) strong (b) funny
   (c) fast (d) weak

3. dense *(line 28)*
   (a) stupid (b) very thick
   (c) a kind of tree (d) sparse

(ii) Answer the following questions briefly in your own words.

(a) Who were the Vakils?

(b) Why was the house more suited to the de Silvas?

(c) Who was Pinto?

(d) What effect did the noise have on the natural surrounding?

(e) From Hari's answer to Bela's question, what opinion does Hari have of Bombay?

(iii) In not more than 50 words, describe how the arrival of the de Silvas changed life for the family in the little hut.

Ans. (i) 1. (a) something that stops you from thinking about something else

2. (d) weak
3. (b) very thick

(ii) (a) The Vakils were one of the first Bombay families to build holiday cottages at the Thul beach.

(b) The house was more suited to the de Silvas because they were young and energetic and seemed to heartily enjoy life on the beach.

(c) Pinto was a pet dog that belonged to Hari, Bela or Kamal.

(d) The natural surrounding was disturbed by Pinto's barking. A commotion was caused in the creek that separated the hut from the house.

(e) Hari's opinion of Bombay is that the city is grand. He thinks that no person who has a house there would live anywhere else, especially the place he lived in.

(iii) The arrival of the de Silvas disturbed not only the physical surrounding but also the lives of the family in the little hut. Whenever they came, it caused a commotion. They caused a lot of excitement and hubbub in the place. People in the family expected that some work was to be done and that meant an opportunity for employment and wages.

3. Read the following passage carefully and answer the questions that follow. ***ICSE Specimen Paper 2022 Sem II***

1 Father was standing in the small courtyard, wearing a dhoti and a banian, the dress which, for its very homeliness, Swaminathan **detested** to see him in; it indicated that he did not intend going out in the near future.

2 "Where are you going?"

3 "Nowhere."

4 "Where were you yesterday at this time?"

5 "Here."

6 "You are lying. You were not here yesterday. And you are not going out now."

7 "That is right," Mother added, just appearing from somewhere, "there is no limit to his loafing in the sun. He will die of sunstroke if he keeps on like this." Father would have gone on forever without Mother's encouragement. But now her words spurred him to action. Swaminathan was asked to follow him to his 'room' in his father's dressing-room.

8 "How many days is it since you have touched your books?" Father asked as he blew off the fine layer of dust on Swaminathan's books, and cleared the web that an industrious spider was weaving between a corner of the table and the pile of books.

9 Swaminathan viewed this question as a gross breach of promise.

10 "Should I read even when I have no school?"

11 "Do you think you have passed the B.A.?" Father asked.

12 "I mean, Father, when the school is closed, when there is no examination, even then should I read?"

13 "What a question! You must read."

14 "But Father, you said before the examinations that I needn't read after they were over. Even Rajam does not read." As he uttered the last sentence, he tried to believe it; he clearly remembered Rajan's complaining bitterly of a home tutor who came and **pestered** him for two hours a day thrice a week.

15 Father was apparently deaf to Swaminathan's remarks. He stood over Swaminathan and set him to dust his books and clean his table. Swaminathan vigorously started blowing off the dust from the book covers. He caught the spider carefully and took it to the window to throw it out. He held it outside the window and watched it for a while. It was swinging from a strand that gleamed in a hundred delicate tints.

16 "Look sharp! Do you want a whole day to throw out the spider?" Father asked. Swaminathan suddenly realized that he might have the spider as his pet and that it would be a criminal waste to throw it out. He secretly slipped it into his pocket and, after shaking an empty hand outside the window, returned to his duty at the desk.

17 "Look at the way you have kept your English text! Are you not ashamed of yourself?" Swaminathan picked up the oily red-bound Fourth Reader, opened it, and banged together the covers in order to shake off the dust and then rubbed **violently** the oily covers with his palm.

18 "Get a piece of cloth, boy. That is not the way to clean things. Get a piece of cloth, Swami," Father said, half kindly and half impatiently.

19 Swaminathan looked about and complained, "I can't find any here, father."

20 "Run and see."

This was a welcome suggestion. Swaminathan hurried out. He first went to his grandmother.

"Granny, get me a piece of cloth, quick."

(i) For each word given below, choose the correct meaning (as used in the passage) from the options provided.

1. detested *(line 3)*

(a) detention (b) detained
(c) hateful (d) hated

2. pestered *(line 37)*

(a) tiny insect (b) botheration
(c) annoyed (d) annoyance

3. violently *(line 57)*

(a) cruelly (b) with great energy
(c) loudly (d) with a lot of noise

(ii) Answer the following questions briefly in your own words.

(a) What did father's clothes show?
(b) How did mother encourage father?
(c) What did the dust on Swami's book indicate?
(d) The author says that the father spoke 'half kindly and half impatiently'. What does it indicate?
(e) What attracted Swami to the spider? What does he do with the spider?

(iii) In not more than 50 words, describe how Swami dealt with the spider.

Ans. (i) 1. (d) hated
2. (c) annoyed
3. (b) with great energy

(ii) (a) Father's clothes showed that he was planning to stay at home.
(b) Mother encouraged father by complaining about Swami. She said that Swami loafed in the Sun the entire day.
(c) The dust on Swami's books indicated that Swami had not touched his books in a long while.
(d) The author's statement that his father spoke 'half kindly and half impatiently' shows that his father was really angry.
(e) Swami was attracted to the spider because of the colour of its thread. He does not throw the spider away; rather, keeps it hidden in his pocket.

(iii) After Swami caught the spider, he took it to the window to throw it. But as he held the spider, he watched it along with its thread which was shining in different colours. He did not want to throw it away. So, he hid the spider in his pocket to make it his pet.

4. Read the following passage carefully and answer the questions that follow. ***ICSE 2020 Modified***

1 Attending classes inside a railway carriage seemed unusual enough but the seating arrangements turned out to be unusual, too. At Totto-chan's previous school, each pupil was **assigned** a specific desk. But here they could sit anywhere they liked at any time. However, the most unusual thing of all about this school was the lessons themselves.

2 Schools normally schedule one subject, for example history, during the first period, when everyone in the class just did history; then say, arithmetic in the second period, when you just did arithmetic. But here it was quite different. At the beginning of the first period, the teacher made a list of all the problems and questions in the subjects to be studied that day. Then, she would say, "Now, start with any of these you like."

3 So, whether you started on history or arithmetic or something else didn't matter at all. Someone who liked composition might be writing something, while behind you someone who liked chemistry might be boiling something in a flask over an alcohol burner. This method of teaching enabled the teachers to observe as the children progressed to higher grades, what they were interested in as well as their way of thinking and their character.
It was an **ideal** way for teachers to really get to know their pupils.

4 As for the pupils, they loved being able to start with their favourite subject, the fact that they had all day to cope with the subjects they disliked meant they could usually manage them somehow. So, study was mostly independent, with pupils free to go and consult the teacher whenever necessary. Then, pupils would be given further exercises to work at alone. It was study in the truest sense of the word, and it meant there were no pupils just sitting inattentively while the teacher talked and explained.

5 The first-grade pupils hadn't quite reached the stage of **independent** study, but even they were allowed to start with any subject they wanted. Some copied letters of the alphabet, some drew pictures, some read books, and some even did physical exercises. Just then, the boy sitting behind her got up and walked toward the blackboard with his notebook, apparently to consult the teacher.

6 Totto-chan stopped looking around the room and fixed her eyes on his back as he walked. The boy dragged his leg and his whole body swayed from side to side. Totto-chan wondered at first if he was doing it on purpose, but she soon realised the boy couldn't help it.

7. The boy said brightly, "My name's Yasuaki. What's yours?" She was so glad to hear him speak that she replied loudly, "I'm Totto-chan."

Adapted from Totto-chan

(i) For each word given below, choose the correct meaning (as used in the passage) from the options provided.

1. assigned *(line 4)*

(a) allotted (b) provided
(c) given (d) attached

2. ideal *(line 26)*

(a) great (b) perfect
(c) appropriate (d) general

3. independent *(line 39)*

(a) available (b) free
(c) unbound (d) limited

(ii) Answer the following questions briefly in your own words.

(a) What was unusual about the seating arrangement?

(b) How did the method of teaching help the teacher?

(c) Why did the pupils enjoy their lessons at this school?

(d) What different things did the first-grade pupils do?

(e) Which sentence in the passage tells us that the boy had difficulty walking like the other children?

(iii) In not more than 50 words, describe how the children were taught.

Ans. (i) 1. (a) allotted

2. (c) appropriate

3. (b) free

(ii) (a) In contrast with the normal seating arrangement where every student is allotted a designated place to sit, the students in this school could sit wherever they liked.

(b) As the children studied their favourite subjects, the teachers had a lot of time to observe them and find out more about their interests, their way of thinking and their character. This way the teachers got to know the students well enough to help them go ahead in their studies.

(c) The pupils enjoyed their lessons at this school because they could begin their day by studying their favourite subject. In this way, they could also save the rest of the day to cope up with the subjects they found difficult.

(d) The first grade pupils were not allowed to study independently but were allowed to start with the subject of their choice. So, some of them wrote alphabet, some drew pictures, the others read books and some of them did physical exercises.

(e) "The boy dragged his leg, and his whole body swayed from side to side." This sentence tells us that the boy had difficulty walking like the other children.

(iii) The teacher made the list of all the topics to be studied that day. The children were then allowed to begin the day with the subject of their own choice. They could discuss their difficulties with the teachers anytime they liked. The first grade pupils also followed the same practice.

5. Read the following passage carefully and answer the questions that follow. ***ICSE 2019 Modified***

1 Billy Weaver had travelled down from London and by the time he arrived it was nine o'clock in the night and the moon was coming up.

2 ''Excuse me,'' he asked a porter, ''but is there a cheap hotel nearby?''

3 ''Try The Bell Hotel,'' the porter answered, pointing down the road.

4 Billy thanked him, picked up his suitcase and set out to walk the distance to The Bell Hotel. He had never been to Richmond before. But the man at the Office had told him it was a **splendid** city.

Billy was seventeen years old. He was wearing a new navy-blue overcoat, a new brown hat, and a new brown suit, and he was feeling fine. He walked briskly down the street.

5 He was trying to do everything briskly these days. The big shots up at the Head Office were fantastically brisk all the time. They were amazing.

The road was lonely and dark with a few scattered houses.

Suddenly, in a downstairs window, Billy saw a printed notice propped up against the window glass. It said Bed and Breakfast.

6 He moved a bit closer and peered through the window into the room and the first thing he saw was a bright fire burning in the hearth. On the carpet in front of the fire, a little dog was curled up asleep with its nose tucked into its belly. The room in half-darkness was filled with pleasant furniture. There was a Piano and a big sofa and several plump armchairs; and in one corner he **spotted** a large parrot in a cage. Animals were usually

7 a good sign in a place like this, Billy told himself and it looked to him as though it would be a pretty decent house to stay in.

8 Then, a queer thing happened to him. He was in the act of stepping back and going away from the window when he felt a strange urge to ring the bell!

9 He pressed the bell. He heard it ringing and then at once the door swung open and a woman was standing there.

10 She gave him a warm welcoming smile.

11 ''Please come in,'' she said pleasantly. Billy found himself **automatically** moving forward into the house.

12 ''I saw the notice in the window,'' he said, holding himself back.

13 ''Yes, I know.''

14 ''I was wondering about a room.''

15 ''It's all ready for you, my dear,'' she said. She had a round pink face and very gentle blue eyes.

16 ''How much do you charge?''

17 ''Five dollars a night, including breakfast.''

18 It was fantastically cheap. He could easily afford it.

(i) For each word given below, choose the correct meaning (as used in the passage) from the options provided.

1. splendid *(line 11)*
(a) beautiful (b) ideal
(c) excellent (d) humongous

2. spotted *(line 31)*
(a) attended (b) gazed
(c) drew (d) noticed

3. automatically *(line 44)*
(a) instinctively (b) justly
(c) usually (d) after great thinking

(ii) Answer the following questions briefly in your own words.

(a) How did the porter assist Billy?

(b) Why did Billy want to do everything briskly?

(c) Why did Billy think animals were a good sign in a place like this?

(d) Which sentence tells you that something strange happened to Billy?

(e) How much did the room cost?

(iii) In not more than 50 words, give a brief account of what Billy saw as he looked through the window of the room.

Ans. (i) 1. (c) excellent
2. (d) noticed
3. (a) instinctively

(ii) (a) The porter assisted Billy by guiding him to The Bell Hotel when Billy asked him whether there was any cheap hotel nearby.

(b) Billy wanted to do everything briskly because he admired the senior officers at the Head Office who also did everything briskly.

(c) Billy thought that animals were a good sign in a place like this because the road was lonely and dark. Further, the pet animals there made him feel that it would be a decent place to live in.

(d) The sentence which tells us that something strange happened to Billy begins in line 24 with the words, "Then, a queer .... ."

(e) The room cost five dollars a night, including breakfast.

(iii) When Billy looked through the window, he saw a bright fire burning in the hearth with a little dog asleep on the carpet in front of it. The room's furniture included a piano, a big sofa and several plump armchairs. A large parrot was in a cage in one corner.

6. Read the following passage carefully and answer the questions that follow. ***ICSE 2018 Modified***

1 Granny knew I'd been in the train for two nights, and she had a huge breakfast ready for me.

2 Later, she told me there'd been a letter from Uncle Ken.

3 'He says he's the manager in Firpo's hotel in Simla,' she said. 'The salary is very good. It's a steady job and I hope he keeps it'.

4 Three days later, Uncle Ken was on the veranda steps with his bedding roll and **battered** suitcase.

5 'Have you given up the hotel job?' asked Granny. 'No,' said Uncle Ken. 'They have closed down.'

6 'I hope it wasn't because of you.'

7 'No, Aunt Ellen. The bigger hotels in the hill stations are closing down.'

8 'Well, never mind. Come along and have your lunch.'

9 Over lunch, Uncle Ken talked very seriously about ways and means of earning a living.

10 'There is only one taxi in the whole of Dehra', he **mused**. 'Surely, there is business for another?'

11 'I'm sure there is,' said Granny. 'But where does it get you? In the first place, you don't have a taxi. And in the second place, you can't drive.'

12 'I can soon learn. There's a driving school in town. And I can use Uncle's old car.'

'I don't think it will run now,' said Granny.

13 'Of course, it will. It just needs some oiling and greasing and a spot of paint.'

14 'All right, learn to drive.'

So, Uncle Ken joined the driving school.

15 After a month, Uncle Ken announced that he could drive and that he was taking the car out for a trial run.

16 'You haven't got your license yet,' said Granny.

17 'Oh, I won't take it far,' said Uncle Ken. 'Just down the road and back again.'

18 He spent all morning cleaning up the car. Granny gave him money for a can of petrol.

19 After tea, Uncle Ken said, 'Come along, Ruskin, hop in and I will give you a ride. Bring Mohan along too.'

20 'Mohan and I needed no urging. We got into the car beside Uncle Ken.

21 'Now don't go too fast, Ken,' said Granny anxiously. 'You are not used to the car as yet.'

22 Uncle Ken nodded and smiled and gave two sharp toots on the horn. He was feeling pleased with himself.

23 Driving through the gate, he nearly ran over a cat. Miss Kellner, coming out for her evening rickshaw ride, saw Uncle Ken at the wheel of the car and ran indoors again.

24 Uncle Ken drove straight and fast tootling the horn without a break.

25 At the end of the road there was a roundabout.

26 'We'll turn here,' said Uncle Ken, 'and then drive back again.'

27 He turned the steering wheel, we began going round the roundabout, but the steering wheel wouldn't turn all the way, not as much as Uncle Ken would have liked it to......

28 So, instead he went on-and straight through the Maharaja of Jetpur's garden wall.

29 It was a single-brick wall, and the car knocked it down and **emerged** on the other side without any damage to the car or any of its occupants. Uncle Ken brought it to a halt in the middle of the Maharaja's lawn.

30 Running across the grass came the Maharaja himself. When he saw that it was Uncle Ken at the wheel, the Maharaja beamed with pleasure.

31 'Delighted to see you, old chap!' he exclaimed. 'Jolly decent of you to drop in again. How about a game of tennis?'

(i) For each word given below, choose the correct meaning (as used in the passage) from the options provided.

1. battered *(line 9)*

(a) worn out (b) damaged
(c) thrown (d) filled

2. mused *(line 19)*

(a) said funnily (b) said thoughtfully
(c) said sarcastically (d) said sadly

3. emerged *(line 62)*

(a) entered (b) exited
(c) joined (d) to come out

(ii) Answer the following questions briefly in your own words.

(a) Why did Granny hope Uncle Ken would keep his job at Firpo's hotel?

(b) When Uncle Ken arrived with his luggage, Granny remarked that she hoped the hotel had not closed down because of him. What does this remark tell you about Uncle Ken?

(c) Why did Uncle Ken think that driving a taxi in Dehra would be profitable?

(d) Which sentence tells you that the narrator and his friend were waiting to be invited for a drive in a car?

(e) Why did Miss Kellner run indoors when she saw Uncle Ken at the wheel of the car?

(iii) In not more than 50 words, describe what happened after the car went through the wall.

Ans. (i) 1. (a) worn out

2. (b) said thoughtfully

3. (d) to come out

(ii) (a) Granny hoped that Uncle Ken would keep his job at Firpo's hotel as it was a steady job with a good salary.

(b) This remark tells us about Uncle Ken that he was not good at work or maybe he had created some problem due to which the hotel had closed down.

(c) Uncle Ken thought that driving a taxi in Dehra would be profitable because there was only one taxi service in the whole of Dehra; thus, there was enough business for another.

(d) The sentence which tells us this is : Mohan and I needed no urging.

(e) Miss Kellner had seen Uncle Ken nearly running over a cat, so she was afraid for her own safety. Thus, she ran indoors when she saw Uncle Ken at the wheel of the car.

(iii) Uncle Ken stopped the car in the middle of Maharaja of Jetpur's lawn. Seeing this, the Maharaja became alarmed and came running to see what had happened. When he saw it was Uncle Ken, whom he knew, he remarked that he was delighted to see his friend and would like to play a game of tennis with him.

7. Read the following passage carefully and answer the questions that follow. ***ICSE 2017 Modified***

1 Every Monday, on his way back from work, Bipin Chowdhury would drop in at New Market to buy books. He had to buy at least five at a time to last him through the week. He lived alone, was not a good mixer, had few friends and didn't like spending time in idle chat. Those who called in the evening got through their business quickly and left. Those who didn't show signs of leaving would be told around eight o'clock by Bipin Babu that he was under doctor's orders to have dinner at eight-thirty. After dinner, he would rest for half an hour and then turn in with a book. This was a routine which had **persisted** unbroken for years.

2 Today, Bipin Babu had the feeling that someone was observing him from close quarters. He turned round and found himself looking at a round-faced, meek-looking man who now broke into a smile.

3 'I don't suppose you recognise me.'

4 Bipin Babu felt ill at ease. It didn't seem that he had ever encountered this man before. The face seemed quite unfamiliar.

5 'Have we met before?' asked Bipin Babu.

6 The man looked greatly surprised. 'We met every day for a whole week. I arranged for a car to take you to the Hudroo falls. My name is Parimal Ghose.'

7 'Ranchi?'

8 Now Bipin Babu realised this man was making a mistake. Bipin Babu had never been to Ranchi. He smiled and said, 'Do you know who I am?'

9 The man raised his eyebrows, and said, 'Who doesn't know Bipin Chowdhury?'

10 Bipin Babu turned towards the bookshelves and said, 'You're making a mistake. I've never been to Ranchi.'

11 The man now laughed aloud.

12 What are you saying, Mr Chowdhury? You had a fall in Hudroo and cut your right knee. I brought you iodine. I had fixed up a car for you to go to Netarhat the next day, but you couldn't because of the pain in the knee. Can't you recall anything? Someone else you know was also in Ranchi at that time, Mr Dinesh Mukherjee. You stayed in a bungalow. You said, you didn't like hotel food. I'll tell you more: you always carried a bag with your books in it on your sightseeing trips. Am I right or not?

13 Bipin Babu spoke quietly, his eyes still on the books.

14 'Which month in Nineteen fifty-eight are you talking about?'

15 The man said, 'October.'

16 'No, sir,' said Bipin Babu. 'I spent October Nineteen fifty-eight with a friend in Kanpur. You're making a mistake. Good day.'

17 But the man didn't go, nor did he stop talking.

18 'Very strange. One evening I had tea with you on the veranda of your bungalow. You spoke about your family. You said, you had no children and that you had lost your wife a **decade** ago.'

19 When Bipin Babu had paid for the books and was leaving the shop, the man was still looking at him in utter disbelief.

20 Bipin Babu's car was safely parked in Bertram street. He told the driver as he got into the car, 'Just drive by the Ganga, will you, Sitaram.' Driving up the Strand Road, Bipin Babu regretted having paid so much attention to the **intruder**. He had never been to Ranchi. He had an excellent memory.

21 Unless he was losing his mind!

(i) For each word given below, choose the correct meaning (as used in the passage) from the options provided.

1. persisted *(line 12)*

(a) accepted (b) forced

(c) continued (d) stated

2. decade *(line 56)*
(a) a period of ten years
(b) a period of fifty years
(c) a period of five years
(d) a period of indefinite time
3. intruder *(line 64)*
(a) criminal (b) trespasser
(c) interferer (d) joker

(ii) Answer the following questions briefly in your own words.
(a) How did Bipin Chowdhury find time to read five books a week?
(b) How did he get rid of visitors who stayed late?
(c) Which sentence tells you that Bipin was uncomfortable?
(d) What strong argument did Bipin Babu give to prove that he was not in Ranchi at that time?
(e) What does Bipin Babu regret?

(iii) What memories of the trip does Parimal Ghose evoke to prove that Bipin Babu was indeed in Ranchi? Answer in not more than 50 words.

Ans (i) 1. (c) continued
2. (a) a period of ten years
3. (b) trespasser

(ii) (a) Bipin Chowdhury found time to read five books a week as every day after dinner at eight thirty he would pick up a book to read and finish it before he went off to sleep.
(b) He used to get rid of visitors who stayed late by telling them that he was under doctor's order to have dinner at eight-thirty and he could no longer spend time with them.
(c) The sentence 'Bipin Babu fell ill at ease' tells us that he felt uncomfortable.
(d) The strong argument given by Bipin Babu was that in October 1958, he was with a friend in Kanpur. He said that he had never been to Ranchi.
(e) Bipin Babu regrets having paid so much attention to the stranger who was giving false claims of having met him.

(iii) Parimal Ghose tried to remind Bipin Babu that it was he who had arranged a car for him when he was in Ranchi in October 1958. He also reminded him that he had brought iodine for him when he had a fall in Hudroo and had cut his right knee. Parimal reminded Bipin of his dislike for hotel food and that he always carried a bag containing books on sightseeing trips.

8. Read the following passage carefully and answer the questions that follow. ***ICSE Specimen Paper 2017***

1 My husband Pele and I were staying in a holiday house overlooking the beautiful, lush rainforests of Indonesia. The glass walls framed a fine view across the Bagon Valley to what had been the summer palace of President Suharto.

2 The first morning we **strolled** hand-in-hand up a winding pathway, heading to the main building for breakfast. But once we arrived at the dinning room, I realised we'd forgotten our money, so I volunteered to run back to the house. Making my way down the path, I turned the last corner only to find a giant bird, similar to an emu, standing outside our front door.

3 "Hey baby, what are you doing?" I cooed, moving slowly so as not to frighten it.

4 Having a deep, abiding **fascination** with all creatures great and small, I wanted a closer look. This was my first mistake.

5 As I came within a few meters, he took a big breath and let out a nasty hiss, stopping me in my tracks.

6 "That's not very friendly," I said, clueless. He hissed again and I promptly made the second mistake of turning and running, instead of backing away slowly. As I rounded the corner, I heard his razor-sharp claws scrabbling on the cobblestones.

7 "Oh!"

8 His steps sounded like a drum as they hit the ground, quickly coming too close for comfort. I suddenly changed direction and headed into the trees. Dodged in and out of the **foliage**. I hoped my tactic would fool him. A crash behind me indicated no such luck.

9 Jumping over a small bush, I found myself out in the open and not far from the dining room. Picking up speed, I bolted over the plants and rockeries surrounding the perimeter and dashed through the gate. When I turned to close it, the bird was nowhere to be seen.

10 I didn't realise it at the time, but I had just come face-to-face with a cassowary, a bird also found in Australia's North Queensland rainforests. Cassowarys weigh 55 kilos or more, stand about 180 centimeters tall and have saber-like toenails that can open a human from chin to groin like a zipper and kill humans.

11 "What's wrong?" Pele asked as I stumbled back into the dining room.

12 "A big bird chased me all the way from the house," I replied.

13 "What?" he asked incredulously. "You're scared of a bird?"

14 "It's as big as me and very mean," I said in a rather sulky voice.

15 "Oh, all right," he laughed. "I'll come with you."

16 Much to Pele's amusement, I stayed behind him on the path and held onto the back of his shirt as we approached the corner of the house.

17 "See! There it is. Look at the size of the thing!"

18 Pele chuckled at the hysteria in my voice. "It's all right," he soothed.

19 Calmly and confidently he walked toward the cassowary.

20 "Shoo! Go on, get out," he said.

21 He made actions with his arms as if it were a pigeon on a window ledge. The response of the cassowary was the same as before: a big hiss and a step forward.

22 "Hmm," said Pele and stopped, not so sure of himself. He tried again. "Go on."

23 The cassowary then ran a few paces at us, hissing aggressively, so we quickly retreated around a corner of the house. Pele picked up a rock the size of his hand and threw it hard, hitting the bird squarely in the chest. It didn't budge.

24 "What are we going to do?" I pleaded. This time, Pele picked up a cane chair.

25 "Stay behind and I'll keep him back. When we get to the door, open it."

26 Again, I held on to the back of his shirt and we started towards the door. This greatly displeased the already annoyed cassowary. Charging at us he ripped at the chair with those lethal claws. Pele stopped to steady the chair - and possibly his resolve.

27 Pele threw the chair at the bird and slammed the door shut.

28 Ducking the flying cane, the bird ran straight at the glass wall, only to bounce off.

29 But it didn't slow down at all. Pecking and scratching at the glass, it continued the assault with a sickening ferocity.

30 It was another 15 minutes before the bird weakened and slowed its attack. Thirty minutes later, we quietly opened the door and crept back to the main building.

(i) For each word given below, choose the correct meaning (as used in the passage) from the options provided

1. strolled *(line 6)*
(a) walk in a leisurely way
(b) run
(c) walk with a limp
(d) jog slowly

2. fascination *(line 15)*
(a) repulsed by something
(b) the desire to want something
(c) attract interest towards something
(d) search for something

3. foliage *(line 29)*
(a) the leaves of a plant or tree
(b) forest
(c) a patterned placement of flowers
(d) grassy land

(ii) Answer the following questions briefly in your own words.

(a) What was Pele's wife's first mistake when she saw the bird?
(b) How did the bird react to the lady's third mistake?
(c) What did she do after this reaction of the bird?
(d) Describe the Cassowary.
(e) Why did Pele find the situation amusing at first? Why did he change his attitude?

(iii) With close reference to the last paragraph of the extract and in not more than 50 words, describe how the couple got into their room when they were together.

Ans (i) 1. (a) walk in a leisurely way
2. (c) attract interest towards something
3. (a) the leaves of a plant or tree

(ii) (a) Pele's wife's first mistake after seeing the bird was to come near it to have a closer look at it.
(b) The bird got more aggressive with the lady's actions and mistakes.
(c) As she saw the bird running aggressively after her, the lady speedily ran towards the dining room and shut its door.
(d) Cassowary is a bird found in Australia's North Queensland rainforests. They weigh 55 kilos or more, stand about 180 centimeters tall and have

saber-like toenails that can open a human from chin to groin like a zipper and kill them.

(e) Pele found the situation amusing at first because he felt that his wife was getting scared of a bird which could not harm them in any way.

He changed his attitude when he realised that the bird was not friendly but was hostile to their advances. It aggressively reacted to their presence and was running after them.

(iii) When the couple came across the Cassowary, the bird reacted aggressively to their presence. It hissed and started stalking towards the couple who got sacred. To divert the bird, Pele threw a rock at it but in vain. Then, using a chair as a shield, the couple ran towards their room. While they reached the room, the bird clawed the chair so Pele threw it at the bird and closed the door to their room.

9. Read the following passage carefully and answer the questions that follow. ***ICSE 2016 Modified***

1 For some time, Mother had greatly envied us our swimming, both in the daytime and at night, but as she pointed out when we suggested she join us, she was far too old for that sort of thing. Eventually, however, under constant pressure from us, Mother paid a visit into town and returned to the villa coyly bearing a mysterious parcel. Opening this, she astonished us all by holding up an extraordinary shapeless garment of black cloth, covered from top to bottom with hundreds of frills and pleats and tucks.

2 'Well, what do you think of it?' Mother asked.

3 We started at the odd garment and wondered what it was for.

4 'What is it?' asked Larry at length.

5 'It's a bathing-costume, of course', said Mother. 'What on Earth did you think it was?'

6 'It looks to me like a badly-skinned whale,' said Larry, **peering** at it closely.

7 'You can't possibly wear that, Mother,' said Margo, horrified, 'why, it looks as though it was made in nineteen-twenty.'

8 'What are all those frills and things for?' asked Larry with interest.

9 'Decoration, of course', said Mother indignantly.

10 'What a jolly idea! Don't forget to shake the fish out of them when you come out of the water.'

11 'Well, I like it, anyway,' Mother said firmly, wrapping the monstrosity up again, 'and I'm going to wear it.'

12 'You'll have to be careful you don't get waterlogged, with all that cloth around you,' said Leslie seriously.

13 'Mother, it's awful; you can't wear it,' said Margo. 'Why on earth didn't you get something more up-to-date?'

14 'When you get to my age, dear, you can't go around in a two-piece bathing suit … you don't have the figure for it.'

15 'I'd love to know what sort of figure that was designed for,' remarked Larry.

16 'You really are hopeless, Mother,' said Margo despairingly.

17 'But I like it … and I'm not asking you to wear it,' Mother pointed out angrily.

18 'That's right, you do what you want to do,' agreed Larry, 'don't be put off. It'll probably suit you very well if you can grow another three or four legs to go with it.'

19 Mother snorted indignantly and swept upstairs to try on her costume. Presently, she called to us to come and see the effect and we all trooped up to the bedroom. Roger the dog was the first to enter, and on being greeted by this strange apparition clad in its voluminous black costume rippling with frills, he retreated hurriedly through the door, backwards, barking **ferociously**. It was some time before we could persuade him that it really was Mother, and even then he kept giving her vaguely uncertain looks from the corner of his eye. However, in spite of all opposition, Mother stuck to her tent-like bathing-suit, and in the end we gave up.

20 In order to celebrate her first entry into the sea, we decided to have a moonlight picnic down at the bay, and sent an invitation to Theodore, who was the only stranger that Mother would tolerate on such a great occasion. The day for the great **immersion** arrived, food and wine were prepared, the boat was cleaned out and filled with cushions and everything was ready when Theodore turned up.

(i) For each word given below, choose the correct meaning (as used in the passage) from the options provided:

1. peering *(line 18)*

(a) stalking (b) looking

(c) nooding (d) scolding

2. ferociously *(line 55)*
(a) angrily (b) aggressively
(c) violently (d) All of these

3. immersion *(line 63)*
(a) drown (b) put in water
(c) overwhelm (d) confuse

(ii) Answer the following questions briefly in your own words.
(a) Why did mother not join swimming in the beginning?
(b) Briefly describe mother's swimming costume.
(c) What did Larry think it was?
(d) Which sentence tells you that Margo thought it was old-fashioned?
(e) What was Leslie's concern?

(iii) In not more than 50 words, describe what happened after mother went upstairs to try on her costume.

Ans (i) 1. (b) looking
2. (d) All of these
3. (b) put in water

(ii) (a) Mother did not join swimming in the beginning as she was far too old for that sort of thing.
(b) The swimming costume was an extraordinary shapeless garment of cloth covered from top to bottom with hundreds of frills, pleats and tucks.
(c) Larry thought it was a badly-skinned whale.
(d) The sentence, "Why on earth didn't you get something more up to date?" tells us that Margo thought it was old-fashioned.
(e) Leslie was concerned that their mother might get waterlogged with all that cloth around her.

(iii) Soon after mother went upstairs to try on her costume, she called them to see the effect. Roger, the dog, entered first but was so shocked at seeing mother in the costume that he failed to recognise her and ran away. In spite of all opposition from the family, mother stuck to her bathing suit and so, they accepted it.

10. Read the following passage carefully and answer the questions that follow. ***ICSE 2015 Modified***

1 Lying in bed, Swami realised with a shudder that it was Monday morning. It looked as though only a moment ago it had been the last period on Friday; already Monday was here. He hoped that an earthquake would reduce the school building to dust but that good building–Albert Mission School had withstood similar prayers for over a hundred years now. At nine o'clock Swaminathan wailed, "I have a headache." His mother said, "Why don't you go to school in a bullock cart?"

2 "So that I may be completely dead at the other end? Have you any idea what it means to be **jolted** in a cart?"

"Have you any important lessons today?"

3 "Important! Bah! That geography teacher has been teaching the same lesson for over a year now, and we have arithmetic, which means for a whole period we are going to be beaten by the teacher.... Important lessons!"

4 And mother generously suggested that Swami might stay at home.

5 At 9:30, when he ought to have been lining up in the school prayer hall, Swami was lying on the bench in Mother's room. Father asked him, "Have you no school today?"

6 "Headache," Swami replied.

7 "Nonsense! Dress up and go."

8 "Headache."

9 "Loaf about less on Sundays and you will be without a headache on Monday."

10 Swami knew how **stubborn** his father could be and changed his tactics. "I cannot go so late to class."

11 "I agree, but you' ll have to; it is your own fault. You should have asked me before deciding to stay away."

12 "What will the teacher think if I go so late?"

13 "Tell him you had a headache and so are late."

14 "He will beat me if I say so."

15 "Will he? Let us see. What is his name?"

16 "Mr. Samuel."

17 "Does he beat the boys?"

18 "He is very violent, especially with boys who come late. Some days ago, a boy was made to stay on his knees for a whole period in a corner of the class because he came late, and that after getting six cuts from the cane and having his ears twisted, I wouldn't like to go late to Mr. Samuel's class."

19 "If he is so violent, why not tell your headmaster about it?"

20 "They say that even the headmaster is afraid of him. He is such a violent man."

21 And then, Swami gave a lurid account of Samuel's violence; how when he started caning, he would not stop till he saw blood on the boy's hand, which he made the boy press to his forehead like a vermillion marking. Swami hoped that his father would be made to see that he couldn't go to his class late. But Father's behaviour took an unexcepted turn. He became excited. "What do these people mean by beating our children? They must be driven out of service. I will see..."

22 The result was he proposed to send Swami late to his class as a kind of challenge. He was also going to send a letter with Swami to the headmaster. No amount of protest from Swami was of any **avail**. Swami had to go to school.

23 By the time he was ready Father had composed a long letter to the headmaster, put in an envelope and sealed it.

24 "What have you written Father?" Swaminathan asked apprehensively.

25 "Nothing for you. Give it to your headmaster and go to your class."

26 Swami's father did not know the truth, that actually Mr. Samuel was a very kind and gentle man.

(i) For each word given below, choose the correct meaning (as used in the passage) from the options provided.

1. jolted *(line 12)*
(a) shaken (b) doubtful
(c) confused (d) irritated

2. stubborn *(line 31)*
(a) angry (b) adamant
(c) accurate (d) admirable

3. avail *(line 63)*
(a) join (b) agree
(c) use (d) find

(ii) Answer the following questions briefly in your own words.

(a) What did Swami wish for a Monday morning? Why was his wish unlikely to be answered?

(b) Which sentence tells us that Swami's father was completely unsympathetic to his son's headache?

(c) In what way was Swami's mother's response different from his father's?

(d) Why did Swami give a colourful account of Mr Samuel to his father?

(e) In what way did father's behaviour take an unexpected turn?

(iii) In not more than 50 words, describe how Swami tried to prove that Mr Samuel is a violent man.

Ans (i) 1. (a) shaken
2. (b) adamant
3. (c) use

(ii) (a) On Monday morning, Swami wished for an earthquake to occur that would completely demolish the school building. For over a hundred years, the students had wished the same for the school but nothing happend. So, his wish was unlikely to be answered.

(b) When Swami told his father that he had a headache, his father said "Nonsense! Dress up and go." This sentence tells that his father was completely unsympathetic to his son's headache.

(c) When Swami informed his mother of his headache, she suggested him to stay at home and miss school. In this way, his mother's response was different from his father's who seemed adamant on sending his son to school.

(d) Swami gave a colourful account of Mr. Samuel to his father in order to skip school for the day. Swami told his father that his teacher Mr. Samuel would beat him with his (Samuel's) cane if he turned up late for class.

(e) Swami had given a false account of his teacher, Mr. Samuel, to his father, thinking that he would allow him to miss school after hearing it. However, his father's behaviour took an unexpected turn when he decided to send Swami late as a challenge. Also, he sent a note to the Headmaster through Swami.

(iii) Swami said to his father that if he reached late to school his teacher Mr. Samuel would beat him. He also narrated an incident of a boy who was made to stay on his knees for a whole period because he came late. Only after beating him with the cane and twisting his ears, did Mr. Samuel make him sit.

11. Read the following passage carefully and answer the questions that follow. ***ICSE 2014 Modified***

1 Richard Parker was so named because of a clerical error. A panther was terrorising the Khulna district of Bangladesh, just outside the Sundarbans. It had recently carried off a little girl. She was the seventh

person killed in two months by the animal. And it was growing bolder. The previous victim was a man who had been attacked in broad daylight in his field. The beast dragged him off into the forest and his **corpse** was later found hanging from a tree. The villagers kept a watch nearby that night, hoping to surprise the panther and kill it, but it never appeared.

2 The Forest Department hired a professional hunter. He set up a small, hidden platform in a tree near a river where two of the attacks had taken place. A goat was tied to a stake on the river's bank. The hunter waited several nights. He assumed the panther would be an old, wasted male with worn teeth, incapable of catching anything more difficult than a human. But it was a sleek tiger that stepped into the open one night: a female with a single cub. The goat bleated. Oddly, the cub, who looked to be about three months old, paid little attention to the goat. It raced to the water's edge, where it drank eagerly. Its mother followed it. Of hunger and thirst, thirst is the greater urge. Only after the tiger had **quenched** her thirst, did she turn to the goat to satisfy her hunger.

3 The hunter had two rifles with him: one with real bullets, the other with immobilising darts. This animal was not a man-eater, but was so close to human habitation that she might pose a threat to the villagers, especially as she was with cub. He picked up the gun with the darts. He fired as the tiger was about to attack the goat. The tiger **reared** up and snarled and raced away. But immobilising darts don't bring on sleep gently, they knock the creature out without warning. A burst of activity on the animal's part makes it act all the faster.

4 The hunter called his assistants on the radio. They found the tiger about two hundred yards from the river. She was still conscious. Her back legs had given way and her balance on her front legs was shaky. When the man got close, she tried to get away but could not manage it. She turned on them, lifting a paw that was meant to kill. It only made her lose her balance. She collapsed and the Pondicherry Zoo had two new tigers. The cub was found in a bush close by, meowing with fear.

5 The hunter, whose name was Richard Parker, picked it up with his bare hands and remembering how it had rushed to drink in river, named it Thirsty. But the shipping clerk at the Howrah train station was evidently a man both confused and diligent. All the papers received with the cub clearly stated that its name was Richard Parker, that the hunter's first name was Thirsty and that his family name was None Given. Richard Parker's name stuck. I don't know if the hunter was ever called Thirsty None Given!

(i) For each word given below, choose the correct meaning (as used in the passage) from the options provided.

1. Corpse *(line 8)*

(a) injured body (b) dead body
(c) rotting meat (d) boneless creature

2. quenched *(line 25)*

(a) satisfied (b) filled
(c) drunk (d) completed

3. reared *(line 33)*

(a) nurtured (b) gave birth
(c) got up (d) slept

(ii) Answer the following questions briefly in your own words.

(a) Why does the author say that the panther 'was getting bolder'?

(b) Why did the Forest Department hire a professional hunter?

(c) What did the hunter expect to encounter? What did he actually encounter?

(d) What did the tiger do before turning to attack the goat? Why did it do that?

(e) What name did the hunter give to the cub? Why?

(iii) In not more than 50 words, narrate how the hunter and his assistants captured the tiger and her cub.

Ans (i) 1. (b) dead body

2. (a) satisfied

3. (c) got up

(ii) (a) The panther was getting bolder as it had killed seven persons in two months. Very recently, it carried off a little girl and the previous victim had been a man who was attacked in broad daylight in his field.

(b) The villagers kept a watch for the panther hoping to surprise and kill it but it never appeared. So, the Forest Department hired a professional hunter to track and kill it.

(c) The hunter expected that the panther would be an old, wasted male with worn teeth, incapable of catching anything more difficult than a human; but, what he actually encountered was a sleek tigress with a cub.

(d) The tiger followed the cub to the water's edge and drank water thirstly before she turned to the goat to satisfy her hunger because thirst is a greater urge than hunger.

(e) The hunter named the cub 'Thirsty' as he remembered how the cub had rushed to drink water in the river.

(iii) A panther was terrorising the village and killed many people. So, a professional hunter was hired. He set up a platform near a river and tied a goat nearby. However, instead of the panther, a tigress with a cub appeared, quenched their thirst and then approached the goat. The hunter used an immobilising gun which made the tigress lose her balance and the cub was found in a bush close by.

12. Read the following passage carefully and answer the questions that follow. ***ICSE 2013 Modified***

1 There were other boys in Manjari village, but Bisnu was the only one who went to school. His mother would not have fussed if he had stayed at home and worked in the fields. That was what the other boys did, all except lazy Chittru, who preferred fishing in the stream or helping himself to the fruit from other people's trees. But Bisnu went to school. He went because he wanted to. No one could force him to go and no one could stop him from going. He had set his heart on receiving a good schooling. He wanted to read and write as anyone in the big world and so he walked to school every day.

2 A colony of langoors lived in the forest. They fed on oak leaves, acorns, and other green things and usually remained in the trees, coming down to the ground only to play or sun themselves. They were beautiful, supple-limbed animals, with black faces and silver-grey coats and long, sensitive tails. They leapt from tree to tree with great **agility**. The young ones wrestled on the grass like boys.

3 A dignified community, the langoors did not have the cheekiness or dishonest habits of the red monkeys of the plains; they did not approach dogs or humans. But they had grown used to Bisnu's comings and goings and did not fear him. Some of the older ones would watch him quietly, a little puzzled. They did not go near the town; because the boys threw stones at them. And anyway, the forest gave them all the food they required. Coming from another direction was a second path, and at the junction of the two paths Sarru was waiting for him. Sarru came from a small village about three miles from Bisnu's and closer to the town.

4 They **hailed** each other and walked along. They often met at this spot, keeping each other company for the remaining two miles.

5 'There was a panther in our village last night', said Sarru.

6 This information interested but did not excite Bisnu. Panthers were common enough in the hills and did not usually present a problem except during the winter months, when their natural prey was scarce.

7 'Did you lose any animals?' asked Bisnu.

8 'No, it tried to get into the cowshed but the dogs set up the alarm. We drove it off.' 'It must be the same one which came around last winter. We lost a calf and two dogs in our village.'

9 'Wasn't that the one that left the shikaris wounded? I hope it hasn't become a cattle-lifter.'

10 'It could be the same. It has a bullet in its leg. These hunters are the people who cause all the trouble. They think it's easy to shoot a panther. It would be better if they missed altogether, but they usually wound it.'

11 'And then, the panthers too slow to catch the barking-deer and starts on our own animals.' 'Were lucky it didn't become a man-eater. Do you remember the man-eater six years ago? I was very small then. My father told me all about it. Ten people were killed in our valley alone.'

12 'What happened to it?'

13 'I don't know. Some say it poisoned itself when it ate the headman of the village.'

14 Bisnu laughed. 'No one liked that old **villain**. They linked arms and scrambled up the stony path to school.'

(i) For each word given below, choose the correct meaning (as used in the passage) from the options provided.

1. agility *(line 19)*

(a) flexibility (b) energy
(c) quickness (d) actively

2. hailed *(line 33)*

(a) come to (b) greeted
(c) waved (d) called for

3. villain *(line 62)*

(a) criminal (b) evil man
(c) intruder (d) immoral

(ii) Answer the following questions briefly in your own words.

(a) How was Chittru different from other boys?

(b) What was Bisnu's ambition?

(c) What information did Sarru give Bisnu?
(d) How did the information affect Bisnu?
(e) Why did the panther become a cattle-lifter?

(iii) In not more than 50 words, describe what Sarru tells Bisnu.

Ans (i) 1. (c) quickness
2. (b) greeted
3. (b) evil man

(ii) (a) Chittru was different because he was lazy and preferred fishing in the stream or breaking fruits off other people's trees. He squandered his time loafing here and there while other boys worked in the field.

(b) Bisnu's ambition was to receive a good schooling. He went on his own accord to school, not forced by anyone, to read and write, so that he could get well educated like other children in the big world.

(c) Sarru informed Bisnu about the sudden visit of a panther to his village, the previous night.

(d) The information interested Bisnu but did not excite him because panthers were a common affair in hills.

(e) The panther had become a cattle-lifter because once it was wounded by the shikaris, who had aimed a bullet in his leg. The panther had consequently become slow paced. Unable to hunt fast running barking deer, it started killing cattle.

(iii) Sarru informed Bisnu of a panther's visit to his village. He mentioned how the panther was shot in the leg which made it slow to hunt deers. He also narrated an old story of a panther who was a man-eater. He joked that it poisoned itself when it ate the headman of the village.

13. Read the following passage carefully and answer the questions that follow. ***ICSE 2012 Modified***

1 It was a dull autumn day and Jill Pole was crying behind the gym.

2 She was crying because they had been **bullying** her. This is not going to be school story, so I shall say as little as possible about Jill's school, which is not a pleasant subject. It was Co- educational, a school for both boys and girls, what used to be called a 'mixed' school; some said it was not nearly so mixed as the minds of the people who ran it. These people had the idea that boys and girls should be allowed to do what they liked. And unfortunately what ten or fifteen of the biggest boys and girls liked best was bullying the others. All sorts of horrid things went on, which at an ordinary school would have been found out and stopped in half a term, but at this school they weren't. Or even if they were, the people who did them were not **expelled** or punished. The Head said they were interesting psychological cases and sent for them and talked to them for hours. And if you knew the right sort of things to say to the Head, the main result was that you became rather a favourite than otherwise.

3 That was why Jill Pole was crying on that dull autumn day on the damp little path which runs between the back of the gym and the shrubbery. And she hadn't nearly finished her cry when a boy came round the corner of the gym whistling, with his hands in his pockets. He nearly ran into her.

4 'Can't you look where you're going?' said Jill Pole.

5 ''All right,'' said the boy, ''you needn't start—'' and then he noticed her face, 'I say, Jill,' he said, ''What's up?''

6 Jill only made faces; the sort you make when you're trying to say something, but find that if you speak you'll start crying again.

7 ''It's them, I suppose—as usual,'' said the boy grimly, digging his hands farther into his pockets.

8 Jill nodded. There was no need for her to say anything, even if she could have said it. They both knew.

9 ''Now, look here,'' said the boy, ''it's no use...''

10 He meant well, but he did talk rather like someone beginning a lecture. Jill suddenly flew into a temper (which is quite a likely thing to happen if you have been interrupted in a cry).

11 ''Oh, go away and mind your own business,'' she said. ''Nobody asked you to come **barging** in, did they? And you're a nice person to start telling us what we all ought to do, aren't you? I suppose you mean we ought to spend all our time sucking up to them and currying favour and dancing attendance on them like you do.''

12 'Oh, Lord !' said the boy, sitting down on the grassy bank at the edge of the shrubbery and very quickly getting up again because the grass was soaking wet. His name unfortunately was Eustace Scrubb, but he wasn't a bad sort.

13 'Jill' he said. 'Is that fair?'

14 ''I d-don't know and I don't care,'' sobbed Jill.

15 Eustace saw that she wasn't quite herself yet and very sensibly offered her a peppermint. He had one too.

Presently Jill began to see things in a clearer light. "I'm sorry, Eustace," she said presently.

(i) For each word given below, choose the correct meaning (as used in the passage) from the options provided:

1. bullying *(line 3)*

(a) to be violent (b) to dominate
(c) to serve (d) to be angry

2. expelled *(line 17)*

(a) punished (b) exited
(c) ordered to leave (d) terminated

3. barging *(line 46)*

(a) running (b) interrupting
(c) continuing (d) harassing

(ii) Answer the following questions briefly in your own words.

(a) Why was Jill crying?
(b) Why do you think she was crying behind the gym?
(c) Who does 'them' refer to in line 24?
(d) Why did Jill fly into a temper?
(e) Which sentences tell us that both Jill and Eustace Scrubb had suffered similarly?

(iii) What kind of school did the children go to? Write your answer in not more than 50 words.

Ans (i) 1. (b) to dominate
2. (c) ordered to leave
3. (b) interrupting

(ii) (a) Jill was crying because the senior boys and girls of her school had been bullying her.

(b) She was crying behind the gym because she did not want anyone to notice her. She wanted to vent out her anger and not be humiliated by crying in front of others.

(c) 'Them' refer to the ten or fifteen of the biggest boys and girls of Jill's school who teased and bullied her.

(d) Jill flew into a temper because she had been interrupted and interfered without her will while she was crying and venting out her feelings.

(e) Line 34 and 35
"I suppose ....like you do."

(iii) The school where the children went was a co-educational school. The people who ran it had the idea that boys and girls should be allowed to do what they liked. As a result, some big boys and girls bullied the others. They were neither expelled nor punished and were treated as interesting psychological cases.

14. Read the following passage carefully and answer the questions that follow. ***ICSE 2011 Modified***

I rested for a moment at the door of Anand Bhavan, on Market Road, where coffee drinkers and tiffin eaters at their tables sat **transfixed** uttering low moans on seeing me. I wanted to assure them, "Don't fear, I am not out to trouble you. Eat your tiffin in peace, don't mind me...You, nearest to me, hugging the cash box, you are craven with fear, afraid even to breathe."

Go on, count the cash, if that's your pleasure. I just want to watch, that's all...If my tail trails down to the street, if I am blocking your threshold: it is because, I'm told, I'm eleven feet tip to tail. I can't help it. I'm not out to kill....I'm too full—found a green pasture teeming with food on the way. Won't need any for several days to come, won't stir, not until I feel hungry again. Tigers attack only when they feel hungry, unlike human beings who slaughter one another without purpose or hunger...'

To the great delight of children, schools were being hurriedly closed. Children of all ages and sizes were running **helter-skelter** screaming joyously, 'No school, no school. Tiger, tiger!' They were shouting and laughing and even enjoyed being scared. They seemed to welcome me. I felt like joining them and bounded away from the restaurant door and trotted along with them at which they cried. "The tiger is coming to eat us. Let us get back to the school."

I followed them through their school gate while they ran up and shut themselves in the school hall securely. I ascended the steps of the school, saw an open door at the far end of a veranda and walked in. It happened to be the headmaster's room, I believe, as I noticed a very dignified man jumping on his table and heaving himself up into an attic, I walked in and flung myself on the cool floor, having a partiality for cool stone floors, with my head under the large desk which gave me the feeling of being back in the Mempi cave....

As I drowsed, I was aware of cautious steps and hushed voices all around. I was in no mood to bother about anything. All I wanted was a little moment of sleep; the daylight was dazzling. In half sleep I heard the doors of the room being shut and blotted and locked. I didn't care. I slept.

While I slept a great deal of consultation was going on. I learnt about it later through my master, who was in the crowd, the crowd which had gathered after making sure that I had been properly locked up — and was watching. The headmaster seems to have remarked some days later, 'Never dreamt in my wildest mood that I'd have to yield my place to a tiger ....' A wag had retorted, 'Might be one way of maintaining better discipline among the boys. 'Now that this brute is safely locked up, we must decide,' began a teacher. At this moment my master pushed his way through the crowds and **admonished**, 'Never use the words "beast" or "brute". They're ugly words coined by humans in their arrogance. The human being thinks all other creatures are "beasts". Awful word!'

(i) For each word given below, choose the correct meaning (as used in the passage) from the options provided:

1. transfixed *(line 3)*
(a) fixed (b) moved
(c) settled (d) stable

2. helter-skelter *(line 22)*
(a) up and down (b) here and there
(c) complete chaos (d) without any thought

3. admonished *(line 58)*
(a) scared (b) told off
(c) scolded (d) irritated

(ii) Answer the following questions briefly in your own words.

(a) What reassurance did the tiger give to the coffee drinkers?
(b) In what way are tigers different from human beings?
(c) Why were the children delighted?
(d) What did the headmaster say some days later?
(e) What was the wag's response?

(iii) In not more than 50 words, describe the tiger's activities from the time it followed the school children till it slept.

Ans (i) 1. (a) fixed
2. (b) here and there
3. (c) scolded

(ii) (a) The tiger reassured the coffee drinkers not to fear him and that he would not trouble them, as he was too full with enough food. He said that neither he was going to kill his prey nor would he have any need to kill for the next 7 days.

(b) Unlike human beings, the tigers attack or kill their prey only when they are hungry and they do not slaughter one another without any purpose.

(c) As there was a tiger roaming at large in the town, the schools were being closed hurriedly. This made the children delighted.

(d) Some days later, the headmaster remarked that not at even in his wildest mood had he expected a tiger coming to his place. He was also surprised at the incident just as the others were.

(e) In reply to the headmaster's remark, the wag witily commented that may be a tiger coming to school was one of the ways of maintaining better discipline among the students.

(iii) Following the school children, the tiger went to the school, climbed up the steps and found the headmaster's room open. He entered and lied down on the cool floor and went off to sleep. Even when he was aware of footsteps outside, he didn't bother to get up and preferred to sleep without caring much for anything else.

15. Read the following passage carefully and answer the questions that follow. ***ICSE 2010 Modified***

1 They pass me everyday, on their way to school-boys and girls from the surrounding villages and the outskirts of the hill station. There are no school buses plying for these children : they walk.

2 For many of them, it's a very long walk to school.

3 Ranbir, who is ten, has to climb the mountain from his village, four miles distant and two thousand feet below the town level. He comes in all weathers, wearing the same pair of cheap shoes until they have almost fallen apart.

4 Ranbir is a cheerful soul. He waves to me whenever he sees me at my window. Sometimes he brings me cucumbers from his father's field. I pay him for the cucumbers; he uses the money for books or for small things needed at home.

5 Many of the children are like Ranbir- poor, but slightly better off than what their parents were at the same age. They cannot attend the expensive residential and private schools that abound here, but must go to the government aided schools with only basic facilities. Not many of their parents managed to go to school. They spent their lives working in the fields or delivering milk in the hill station.

6 The lucky ones got into the army. Perhaps Ranbir will do something different when he grows up.

7 He has yet to see a train but he sees planes flying over the mountains almost every day.

8 "How far can a plane go?" he asks.

9 "All over the world," I tell him. "Thousands of miles in a day. You can go almost anywhere."

10 "I'll go round the world one day," he vows. "I'll buy a plane and go everywhere!" And may be he will. He has a determined chin and a **defiant** look in his eye. Up to a few years ago, very few girls in the hills or in the villages of India went to school. They helped in the home until they were old enough to be married, which wasn't very old. But there are now just as many girls as there are boys going to school.

11 Bindra is something of an extrovert-confident 14 year old who chatters away as she hurries down the road with her companions. Her father is a forest guard and knows me quite well. I meet him on my walks through the deodar woods behind Landour. And I had grown used to seeing Bindra almost every day. When she did not put in an appearance for a week, I asked her brother if anything was wrong.

12 'Oh, nothing,' he says, "she is helping my mother cut grass.

13 Soon the monsoon will end and the grass will dry up. So we cut it now and store it for the cows in winter."

14 "And why aren't you cutting grass too?"

15 "Oh, I have a cricket match today," he says and hurries away to join his team-mates. Unlike his sister, he puts pleasure before work!

16 Cricket, once the game of the **elite** has become the game of the masses. On any holiday, in any part of this vast country, groups of boys can be seen making their way to the nearest field, or open patch of land, with bat, ball and any other cricketing gear that they can cobble together. Watching some of them play; I am amazed at the quality of talent, at the finesse with which they bat or bowl. Some of the local teams are as good, if not better, than any from the private schools, where there are better facilities. But boys from these poor or lower middle-class families will never get the **exposure** that is necessary to bring them to the attention of those who select state or national teams. They will never get near enough to the men of influence and power. They must continue to play for the love of the game or watch their more fortunate heroes' exploits on television.

(i) For each word given below, choose the correct meaning (as used in the passage) from the options provided.

1. defiant *(line 34)*

(a) proud (b) challenging
(c) mocking (d) enraged

2. elite *(line 56)*

(a) privileged (b) educated
(c) wealthy (d) authoritative

3. exposure *(line 67)*

(a) to bring out the reality
(b) to suffer from something
(c) to get an opportunity
(d) to come out of hiding

(ii) Answer the following questions briefly in your own words.

(a) In what way are the children better off than their parents?
(b) What was Ranbir's ambition?
(c) How has the fate of girls changed?
(d) In what way was her brother different from Bindra?
(e) Why is the narrator amazed?

(iii) In not more than 50 words, relate what difficulties the children face in their daily lives. How does the author feel about it?

Ans (i) 1. (b) challenging

2. (a) privileged

3. (c) to get an opportunity

(ii) (a) The children of the mountains are better off than their parents as they at least go to the government schools while their parents had not attended any school. Their lives were spent in working in the fields or delivering milk in the hill stations.

(b) Ranbir's ambition was to buy a plane and go all over the world, flying in it.

(c) A few years back, very few girls in the hills or in the villages went to school. They helped at home till they were old enough to be married but now a proportionate number of girls and boys went to school.

(d) Bindra's brother was different from her as he gave more importance to pleasure than to work. While Bindra helped her mother in cutting grass, her brother played cricket. She was hardworking and responsible towards her household duties.

(e) The narrator is amazed at the quality of talent which the village boys display while playing cricket. He also admires the finesse with which they bat or ball.

(iii) The children do not get buses to go to school. They have to walk. Some children walk up the hills. However, their condition is better than their parents who could not get the opportunity to study. Girls, earlier, didn't get education and got married at an early age. Now, they are getting education. Many children are talented enough to get selected for state and national teams but don't get exposure. Yet, they are better off than their parents.

16. Read the following passage carefully and answer the questions that follow. ***ICSE 2009 Modified***

1 At school, everybody seemed to be overwhelmed by the thought of the examinations. It was weeks since anybody had seen a smile on Shankar's face. Somu had become brisk and businesslike. The Pea took time to grasp jokes and seldom made any either. And as for Rajam, he came to school at the stroke of the first bell, took down everything the teacher said, and left at the stroke of the last bell, hardly uttering a dozen words to anybody. Mani was beginning to look worried and took every opportunity to take Shankar aside and have his doubts (that arose from time to time as he **plodded** through his texts) cleared. He dogged the steps of the school clerk. There was a general belief in the school that the clerk was omniscient and knew all the question papers of all the classes. One day, Mani went to the clerk's house and laid a neat bundle containing fresh brinjals at his feet. The clerk was pleased and took Mani in and seated him on a stool.

2 The clerk looked extremely **amiable** and Mani felt that he could ask anything at that moment and get it. The clerk was murmuring something about his cat, a lank ill-fed thing, that was nestling close to him. Most of what he was saying did not enter Mani's head. He was waiting feverishly to open the topic of question papers. The clerk had meanwhile passed from cats to eye-flies; but it made little difference to Mani, who was waiting for the other to pause for breath to launch his attack. 'You must never let these eye-flies buzz near your eyes. All cases of eyesore can be traced to it. When you get eyesore the only thing you can do is to take a slice of raw onion ...'

3 Mani realised that the other would not stop and butted in, 'There is only a week more for the examinations, sir .....'

4 The clerk was slightly puzzled: 'Yes. Indeed, a week more .... You must take care to choose only the juicy variety, the large juicy variety, not the small onion.....'

5 'Sir,' Mani interrupted, ignoring the juicy variety, 'I am much worried about my examination.' He tried to look pathetic.

6 'I am glad. If you read well, you will pass,' said the Oracle.

7 'You see, sir, I am so worried, I don't sleep at nights, thinking of the examination ..... If you could possibly tell me something important ....I have such a lot to study ..... I don't want to study unnecessary things that may not be necessary for the examination. He meandered thus. The clerk understood what he was driving at, but said, 'Just read all your portions and you will pass.' Mani realised that diplomacy was not his line. He asked bluntly, 'Please tell me, sir, what questions are we getting for our examination?'

8 The clerk denied having any knowledge of the question papers. Mani flattered him by asking, if he did not know the questions, who else would. By just a little more of the same judicious flattery the clerk was moved to give what Mani believed to be 'valuable hints'. In spite of the fact that he did not know what the first form texts were the clerk ventured to advise, 'you must pay particular attention to Geography. Maybe you will have to practice map-drawing a lot.

9 And in Arithmetic make it a point to solve at least five problems every day, and you will be able to tackle Arithmetic as easily as you swallow plantains.'

10 'And what about English?'

11 'Oh, don't worry about that. Have you read all your lessons?'

12 'Yes, sir,' Mani replied without **conviction**.

13 'It is all right then. You must read all the important lessons again and if you have time, yet again and that will be ample.'

14 These answers satisfied Mani greatly. On his way home, he smiled to himself and said that the four annas he had invested on brinjals was not after all a waste.

(i) For each word given below, choose the correct meaning (as used in the passage) from the options provided.

1. plodded *(line 11)*

(a) worked laboriously
(b) asked continuously
(c) revised
(d) wasted time

2. amiable *(line 19)*

(a) kind (b) sympathetic
(c) friendly (d) lively

3. conviction *(line 68)*

(a) confidence (b) ego
(c) perseverance (d) comparison

(ii) Answer the following questions briefly in your own words.

(a) What effect did the coming examinations have on Shankar, Somu, The Pea and Rajam?
(b) Which word in the passage describes the clerk as all knowing?
(c) Why did Mani give the clerk fresh brinjals?
(d) What did the clerk believe was the reason for eyesore? What was the remedy?
(e) Why did Mani try to look pathetic?

(iii) What did Mani really want to know? What valuable hints was he given? Write your answer in not more than 50 words.

Ans (i) 1. (a) worked laboriously
2. (c) friendly
3. (a) confidence

(ii) (a) Everybody was agitated at the thought of the examinations. Nobody had seen a smile on Shankar's face for weeks. Somu had become more active and practical. The Pea seldom cracked jokes and Rajam would enter the school at the stroke of first bell and leave the school at the stroke of the last bell hardly uttering a word to anybody.

(b) 'Omniscient' is the word that describes the clerk as all knowing.

(c) It was a general belief in the school that the clerk knew all the question papers of all the classes. Mani took fresh brinjals for him to bribe him and coax him into telling him what questions they were getting for their examination.

(d) According to the clerk, the eyesore could be traced when the flies buzzed near ones eyes. The remedy was to put few drops of a raw juicy onion in the diseased eye.

(e) Mani tried to look pathetic so that the clerk would feel pity on him and give him some 'valuable hints'.

(iii) Mani wanted to know the important questions he was to get for his examinations. He was advised to pay particular attention to Geography, practise map-drawing a lot and practise atleast five problems of Arithmetic everyday. He was also advised to read all important lessons of English again and again.

17. Read the following passage carefully and answer the questions that follow. ***ICSE 2008 Modified***

1 Sita went to her grandfather and sat down beside him.

2 'When you are hungry, tell me,' she said 'and I will make the bread.'

3 'Is your grandmother asleep?'

4 'Yes. But she will wake soon. The pain is deep.'

5 The old man stared across the river, at the dark green of the forest, at the leaden sky and said, 'If she is not better by morning, I will take her to the hospital in Shahganj. They will know how to make her well. You may be on your own for two or three days. You have been on your own before.'

6 Sita nodded **gravely**—she had been alone before; but not in the middle of the rains with the river so high. But she knew that someone must stay behind. She wanted Grandmother to get well and she knew that only Grandfather could take the small boat across the river when the current was so strong.

7 Sita was not afraid of being left alone but she did not like the look of the river. That evening it began to rain again. Big pellets of rain were scarring the surface of the river. But it was warm rain and Sita could move about in it. She was not afraid of getting wet, she rather liked it. In the previous month, when the monsoon shower had arrived, washing the dusty leaves of the tree and bringing up the good smell of the Earth, she had exulted in it, had run about shouting for joy. She was used to it now, even a little tired of the rain, but she did not mind getting wet. It was **steamy** indoors and her thin dress would soon dry in the heat from the kitchen fire.

8 She walked about barefooted, barelegged. She was very sure on her feet. Her toes had grown accustomed to gripping all kinds of rocks, slippery or sharp and though thin, she was surprisingly strong.

9 Black hair, streaming across her face. Black eyes. Slim brown arms. A scar on her thigh: when she was small, visiting her mother's village, a hyena had entered the house where she was sleeping, fastened on

to her leg and tried to drag her away but her screams had roused the villagers and the hyena had run off.

10 She moved about in the pouring rail, chasing the hens into a shelter behind the hut. A harmless brown snake, flooded out of its hole, was moving across the open ground. Sita took a stick, picked the snake up with it and dropped it behind a cluster of rocks. She had no quarrel with snakes. They kept down the rats and the frogs. She wondered how the rats had first come to the island—probably in someone's boat or in a sack of grain.

11 She disliked the huge black scorpions who left their waterlogged dwellings and tried to take shelter in the hut. It was so easy to step on one and the sting could be very painful. She had been bitten by a scorpion the previous monsoon and for a day and a night she had known fever and great pain. Sita had never killed living creatures but now, whenever she found a scorpion, she crushed it with a rock! When, finally, she went indoors, she was hungry. She ate some **parched** gram and warmed up some goat's milk.

12 Grandmother woke once and asked for water and Grandfather held the brass tumbler to her lips.

13 The roof was leaking and a small puddle formed on the floor. Grandfather kept the kerosene lamps alight. They did not need the light but somehow it made them feel safer.

14 It rained all night.

(i) For each word given below, choose the correct meaning (as used in the passage) from the options provided.

1. gravely *(line 12)*
(a) smoothly (b) seriously
(c) angrily (d) funnily

2. steamy *(line 29)*
(a) hot (b) suffocating
(c) crazy (d) Both (a) and (b)

3. parched *(line 59)*
(a) cooked (b) roasted
(c) dried (d) wet

(ii) Answer the following questions briefly in your own words.

(a) Why was Sita willing to stay alone?
(b) What had made Sita like the first monsoon shower?
(c) Why did Sita have a scar on her thigh?
(d) Which word in the passage tells us that Sita did not need to fear the snake?
(e) Why did she think snakes were useful?

(iii) What kind of a girl was Sita? Describe her in 50 words.

Ans (i) 1. (b) seriously
2. (d) Both (a) and (b)
3. (c) dried

(ii) (a) Sita was willing to stay alone because she knew that someone had to stay behind at home. Moreover, she was used to living alone by her own. She also wanted her grandmother to get well and knew that only grandfather could take the small boat across the river to the hospital when the current was so strong.

(b) Sita felt excited and joyous when the first monsoon shower washed the dusty leaves of the trees, thereby, bringing up the good smell of the Earth.

(c) Sita had a scar on her thigh as when she was small, a hyena had entered their house and had hurt her while trying to drag her out.

(d) The word is 'harmless'.

(e) Sita thought snakes were useful for killing rats and frogs and keeping their population down.

(iii) Sita was a young and considerate girl. She was helpful and caring. She looked after her sick grandmother devotedly. The rains thrilled and delighted her. She was not at all afraid of snakes though she hated the scorpions as she had suffered intensely when bitten.

18. Read the following passage carefully and answer the questions that follow. ***ICSE 2007 Modified***

1 The boy was idling in the market-place on the look out for mischief. All at once, he saw it beckoning him. Workmen had been slating the church spire and their ladders stretched invitingly from Earth to steeple.

2 All children like scrambling up to high places to see if the world looks any different from an apple tree or a stable loft. Over and above his love for climbing, Michael had a longing to do things that had never been done before. As he gazed at the spire, crowned by a golden ball and weather-vane, an idea crept into his mind— he would be the first person in Flushing to stand on the golden ball beneath the weather-vane!

3 He glanced around. No one was looking; Michael began to swarm up the ladder. At the top of the tower, there rose a slated spire crowned by a golden ball and weather-vane. At last, Michael found himself squatting on top of the ball, holding on by the vane. Presently, he heard workmen moving below. He did

not peer over or speak. He was not going to be hauled down before Flushing had seen him. The voices died away and Michael sat resting.

4 At last, he felt ready to **startle** the town. He pulled himself to his feet and keeping tight hold of the weather-vane, managed to stand on top of the ball. It was well that he had a cool head and iron nerves.

5 Someone must have cast a **casual** glance up at the vane and seeing his little figure, cried out. In a minute or two Michael was delighted to see the market-place full of people who had rushed out of their shops and houses to gaze at the dizzy sight. It was splendid to have all those eyes and hearts glued upon you!

6 But Michael did not intend to stay there until he was fetched down, to be handed over to his father and cuffed before the crowd. After a while, he prepared to descend of his own free will.

7 He leaned over the ball. The ladder had gone. The workmen had taken it away! A sudden feeling of sickness and giddiness came over Michael. He mastered it. To wait for rescue was a humiliating end to his escapade. He would come down alone, even if it cost him his life.

8 The spire at the base of the ball was only half slated and Michael saw some hope of gaining a foothold on the old part. He clasped his arms round the top of the ball and let his body swing down; he was just able to feel the first slate with his toes. Those toes were shod with iron toe-caps, for Michael was hard on his shoes. Michael kicked with his marmoured toes till the slate crashed and fell in; then, he got a foothold on the wooden laths beneath.

9 He rested for a minute, with aching arms and a stiff body. He must change his grip on the ball, which was too big to slide his arms down; he must get clear of it and somehow **grasp** the spire beneath. One false move and he would be hurled to death on the cobbles below.

10 Slowly, he began to slide his hands together at the top of the ball and then downward over its bulging face. Every inch was packed with peril; every inch pushed him backward towards death. It seemed to him that he would be too weak to hold on when the time came for him to grasp the spire.

11 But at last, the steady, deadly creeping of his fingers brought him to a point where he could bend forward. With a sudden snatch, he caught the base of the ball.

12 The next moment, he was kicking out it stairway in the old tiles and swarming swiftly down. He reached the foot of the spire, lifted the trapdoor of the tower, ran down the steps and was caught by his father in the organ loft.

(i) For each word given below, choose the correct meaning (as used in the passage) from the options provided.

1. startle *(line 22)*
(a) to shock someone
(b) to make someone laugh
(c) to scare someone
(d) to irritate someone

2. casual *(line 26)*
(a) spontaneous (b) by chance
(c) coincidence (d) normal

3. grasp *(line 54)*
(a) give (b) take
(c) hold (d) keep

(ii) Answer the following questions briefly in your own words.

(a) What was Michael doing in the market-place? What attracted his attention?

(b) What did Michael long to do? What did he plan to do to accomplish this?

(c) How did Michael display 'a cool head and iron nerves'?

(d) Which sight filled Michael's heart with delight and why?

(e) Why did Michael not wait for rescue?

(iii) With close reference to the last five paragraphs of the extract and in not more than 50 words, trace Michael's descent from the top of the ball to the foot of the spire.

Ans (i) 1. (a) to shock someone
2. (b) by chance
3. (c) hold

(ii) (a) Michael was passing his time in the market place, idling around looking for something naughty to do. He got attracted by the ladders of the workmen who had been slating the church spire. These ladders were very invitingly stretched from Earth to steeple.

(b) Michael longed to do things that had never been done before. He wanted to be the first person in this town of Flushing to stand on the golden ball beneath the weather vane.

(c) Michael displayed 'a cool head and iron nerves' by pulling himself to his feet and standing on the top of the ball and by keeping a tight hold on the weather vane.

(d) The sight of the market place full of people rushing out of their shops and houses to gaze at the dizzy sight filled Michael's heart with delight. He felt wonderful to have so many eyes and hearts fixed on him.

(e) Michael did not wait for rescue because that would have been a shameful end to his brave act. He would have been handed over to his father and cuffed before the crowd. So, he decided to come down alone even if it cost him his life.

(iii) Michael clasped his arms around the top of the ball and let his body swing down till his foot reached the slatted spire. He kicked with his iron toe-caps till the slate crashed in. Michael then got a foothold on the wooden laths below. Slowly, he slid his hands at the top of the ball and reached its base. Kicking out the stairway, he slipped down.

19. Read the following passage carefully and answer the questions that follow. ***ICSE 2006 Modified***

1 There came to our town some years ago a showman who owned an institution called the Gaiety Land. Overnight, our Gymkhana Grounds became **resplendent** with banners and streamers and coloured lamps. From all over the district, crowds poured into the show. Within a week of opening, in gate money, they collected five hundred rupees a day. Gaiety Land provided us with all sorts of fun and gambling and side-shows. For a couple of annas, in each booth, we could watch anything from performing parrots to crack motor cylists. In addition to this, there were lotteries and shooting galleries, where, for an anna, you always stood a chance of winning a hundred rupees.

2 There was a particular corner of the show which was in great favour. Here, for a ticket costing eight annas, you could be lucky enough to acquire a variety of articles-pin cushions, sewing machines or even a road engine. One evening, they drew a ticket, number 1005 and I happened to own the other half of the ticket. Glancing down the list of articles, they declared that I had become the owner of a road engine!

3 I looked **stunned**, people gathered around and gazed at me as if I were some sort of a curious animal. Some people muttered and giggled, "Fancy anyone becoming the owner of a road engine!" It was not the sort of prize one could carry home at short notice. I asked the showman if he could help me to transport it. He merely pointed at a notice which decreed that all the winners should remove their prizes immediately after the draw and by their own effort.

4 However, they had to make an exception in my case. They agreed to keep the engine at the Gymkhana Grounds till the end of the season and then I would have to make my own arrangements to take it out.

5 When I asked the showman if he could find me a driver, he just smiled and said, "The fellow who brought it here had to be paid a hundred rupees for the job and five rupees a day. I sent him away and made up my mind that if no one was going to draw it, I would just leave it to its fate."

6 "Can't I sell it to some municipality?" I asked innocently. He burst into a laugh. "As a showman, I have enough trouble with municipal people. I would rather keep out of the way." My friends and relatives poured in, to congratulate me on my latest **acquisition**. No one knew precisely how much a road engine would fetch, all the same they felt that there was a lot of money in it.

7 "Even if you sell it as scrap iron, you can make a few thousands," some of my friends declared. Everyday, I made a trip to the Gymkhana Grounds to have a look at my engine. I grew very fond of it.

8 I loved its shining brass parts. I stood near it and patted it affectionately, hovered about it and returned home everyday only at the close of the show. I thought all my troubles were coming to an end. How ignorant I was! How little did I guess that my troubles had just begun!

(i) For each word given below, choose the correct meaning (as used in the passage) from the options provided.

1. resplendent *(line 4)*
   (a) happy (b) bright
   (c) shining (d) majestic
2. stunned *(line 23)*
   (a) shocked (b) irritated
   (c) frozen (d) enraged
3. acquisition *(line 47)*
   (a) deal (b) ownership
   (c) inheritance (d) gift

(ii) Answer the following questions briefly in your own words.

(a) Which two sentences in the first paragraph show that Gaiety Land was popular?

(b) Give three reasons for the popularity of Gaiety Land.

(c) What is meant by "it was not the sort of prize one could carry home at short notice?"

(d) What was the showman's response to the narrator asking for help to transport the road engine?

(e) Why was the showman ready to leave the road engine to its fate?

(iii) In not more than 50 words, describe the reactions of the public, friends and relatives towards the narrator on his winning the road engine.

Ans (i) 1. (b) bright

2. (a) shocked

3. (b) ownership

(ii) (a) The two sentences in the first paragraph that show Gaiety Land was popular are

(a) "From all over the district, crowds poured into the show."

(b) "Within a week of opening, in gate money, they collected five hundred rupees a day."

(b) The three reasons for Gaiety Land's popularity are

(a) The grounds were wonderfully decorated with banners, streamers and coloured lamps.

(b) For a few annas, one could enjoy performing tricks, etc.

(c) For an anna, a person stood a chance to win a hundred rupees.

(c) The road engine was not the kind of prize that could be taken home immediately. Much preparation is involved in transporting it.

(d) The showman only pointed to the notice which said that prizes were to be immediately removed by the winner's own efforts.

(e) Transporting the road engine was too expensive and therefore if no one won it, the showman was ready to just leave it and go.

(iii) When the narrator won the road engine, people gathered around and looked at the narrator as if he had done something strange. Narrator's friends and relatives came to his house to congratulate him. They thought that there was a lot of money in the road engine. Some felt that if he sold it even as a scrap, he could at least make a few thousands.

20. Read the following passage carefully and answer the questions that follow. ***ICSE 2005 Modified***

1 The story of *Robinson Crusoe*, few people know, is based on a real life incident. The son of a cobbler, Alexander Selkirk was a wayward young man, with little respect for authority. Abject conditions at sea and the cruelty of the captains made the sailors miserable in those days. It was not surprising that Alexander became rebellious and malevolent when he became a sailor.

2 In 1704, he was Sailing Master on a ship; when it anchored for repairs near the desolate island of Juan Fernandez about 650 kilometres West of Chile. They were looking for gold, which they often got by plundering other ships. In the days that followed, Alexander hatched a conspiracy. He **instigated** the other sailors to leave the ship and remain on the island.

3 They would declare a mutiny. Perhaps, Alexander reasoned that the Captain would accept their demands if he believed that his men would refuse to sail otherwise. Unfortunately for Alexander, the crew played the Judas. The Captain, getting to know of Alexander's part in the planned mutiny, left him behind on the island as he was a bad influence on the men. He was provided with a few necessities and among them was a copy of the Bible.

4 Alexander, **marooned** on an island populated only by wild cats and goats, became adept at hunting and his food soon comprised of fish, turtles and meat. He also made clothes with goat skin. Although a cobbler's son, he could not make shoes. Running barefoot after goats had hardened the soles of his feet. He read the Bible again and again and slowly took to reading it aloud. He spoke and sang to the cats and learnt to milk goats.

5 Once, during his stay on the island, a Spanish ship anchored near the island and the crew rowed in. Alexander was petrified and hid in the thick foliage. In those days, Spain and England were at daggers drawn. Fortunately, the Spaniards left after a brief rest.

6 In February, 1709, two English ships sailed in to collect fresh water and shoot goats. Alexander rushed to them for succour. He looked strange with his **unkempt** hair, beard and goat skin clothes. His rescuers understood him with great difficulty. His speech had changed a great deal. His vocabulary had shrunk and he had to grope for words. They did, however, manage to understand his story finally. Alexander took a job as a sailor on one of the ships and reached London in 1711. He returned home with a large fortune. However, he ran out of this fortune in two years and had to return to sea. Alexander's adventure became well-known.

7 Eight years later, Daniel Defoe gave the story a new shape with many twists, calling it *The Adventures of Robinson Crusoe*. It was now the story of a man who was shipwrecked on an island and lived alone for an unbelievable twenty eight years.

(i) For each word given below, choose the correct meaning (as used in the passage) from the options provided:

1. instigated *(line 14)*

(a) to anger (b) to irritate
(c) to conspire (d) to commit

2. marooned *(line 26)*

(a) lonely (b) deserted
(c) agitated (d) left to die

3. unkempt *(line 44)*

(a) wild (b) graceful
(c) ungroomed (d) ugly

(ii) Answer the following questions briefly in your own words.

(a) Explain the phrase, 'with little respect for authority'.

(b) Why did Alexander become reckless and malevolent when he became a sailor?

(c) What was the conspiracy that Alexander hatched ? Why did he do so?

(d) How did the crew play the Judas?

(e) Why was Alexander petrified when the crew of the Spanish ship rowed in?

(iii) In about 50 words of your own, give an account of Alexander's adventure on the island.

Ans (i) 1. (c) to conspire
2. (b) deserted
3. (c) ungroomed

(ii) (a) The phrase means having no respect for the superiors. In the passage, Alexander did not respect or obey the captain.

(b) Alexander became rebellious and malevolent due to the harsh conditions, he suffered while at sea. The captains were also rude and cruel, and made the sailors miserable in those days. Thus, it was natural for him to behave in this manner.

(c) Alexander conspired with the other sailors that they would refuse to sail on the ship and remain on the island. They would declare a mutiny and leave the captain alone on the ship.
He did so to compel the captain to accept all their demands.

(d) The crew played the Judas by acting falsely toward him. They betrayed him and sailed with the captain on the ship leaving him all alone on the uninhabited island.

(e) Alexander was petrified because in those days Spain and England were enemies. Had they discovered him, they would have surely killed him.

(iii) Alexander was deserted on an island with a few necessities. He hunted wild animals for food. He wore goat's skin. He also read the Bible.
Once he was frightened to see a Spanish ship anchored near the island. Spain and England were enemies and he thought they would surely kill him on discovery. In 1709, two English ships sailed and he returned home with a large fortune.

CHAPTER TEST

1. Read the passage given below and answer the questions (i), (ii) and (iii) that follow.

1 I often went to the lagoon, which has a four-fathom bank where the tababa (tiger shark) **muster** in hundreds for a day or two every month. Offshore at rising tide, you can watch their great striped bodies sliding and swooping with arrogant ease not six feet under your keel. They range in length from nine to fourteen feet, with an occasional giant of eighteen feet. Their hideous size contrasts nightmarishly with the slack grace of their movements.

2 Thirty-five years ago the Gilbertese were beginning to use steel hooks for shark-fishing but many still claimed that the old-style twelve-inch wooden hook, trained to the right shape on the living ironwood tree was the only thing for tiger shark. The shark hunter's gaff was a glorious club with a ten-pound stone for its head. He fished from a canoe not much longer than a man, with the line made last to it. When a big shark took the hook, the craft lurched suddenly and started careering round in mad circles; or it bounced insanely up and down; or it zigzagged like a misdirected rocket, the fisherman holding on grimly.

3 Half a dozen cockleshells milling round like that, without visible means of propulsion, made a wildly **eccentric** sight from the shore. But the fury of a tiger shark's struggles soon exhausted it and it floated limply to the surface. Then the fisherman hauled the spent brute cautiously alongside and, letting out one piercing howl of pleasure, cracked it on the nose with his club.

4 Usually safety first is the rule when tiger sharks are about, but the feat of one Tarawa man, Teriakai, became a matter of official record. His vital, stocky frame was the equal of a giant's for work. Whenever there was a special job to be done, we always chose Teriakai to do it. Thus, when the captain and chief engineer of a visiting steamer wanted to go out for a sail in threatening weather, we sent Teriakai along to look after them.

5 A northerly storm caught Teriakai and his friends and **capsized** their boat, spilling them into the lagoon eight miles from land, with tiger shark all round.

6 Teriakai immediately hacked the mainsail adrift; buoyed at head and foot by its spars, it made a fine bag under water. "Stay inside this," he said to the captain and engineer "and the tababa won't smell you". Then he put down the anchor and started for shore to get help. "If I get past the tababa" he said, "We shall perhaps be meeting again."

7 He swam straight at the tiger sharks - the captain and engineer watched him - and the devils let him through. Teriakai told me afterwards, "If you stay still in the sea, or swim away in fear, the tababa will charge you. If you swim without fear towards them, they will be afraid and leave you in peace." So he chose his shark, swam lull speed towards it and lo! the line melted away before him. There was nothing to it - except a conarge that passes belief.

8 The swift night of the equator fell. In the welter of waves, Teriakai missed his direction and swam into a maze of reefs off the coast. The breaking seas flung him on cruel edges, rolled him over splintering coral-branches, but he got through, still conscious, swam a mile to shore, walked two more to a white trader's house and collapsed on the veranda.

Adapted from *"A Pattern of Islands"*
by Arthur Grimble

(i) For each word given below, choose the correct meaning (as used in the passage) from the options provided.

1. muster *(line 2)*
   (a) give (b) gather
   (c) gain (d) act

2. eccentric *(line 24)*
   (a) strange (b) common
   (c) beautiful (d) majestic

3. capsized *(line 40)*
   (a) drowned (b) landed
   (c) to cause to overturn
   (d) to turn around in direction

(ii) Answer the following questions in your own words as briefly as possible.

(a) What does the writer say about the size and movement of the sharks?

(b) Why was Teriakai chosen for special jobs?

(c) How did Teraikai ensure the safety of the captain and chief engineer?

(d) What was Teriakai's belief about sharks?

(e) What was the condition of Teriakai after he came out of the water?

(iii) In not more than 50 words, describe how the Gilbertese captured a tiger shark. (Failure to keep within the word limit will be penalised).

2. Read the passage given below and answer the questions (i), (ii) and (iii) that follow.

1 The boy found the kites from Japan hidden in a dark passage of the house. Snehamoy helped him take out the kites from the box, lifting each delicately by its staff and spread them out on the courtyard.

2 They fixed the day of celebration for Biswakarma- the god of machines to be their kite-flying day. But first, they'd have to be ready with rolls of line to fly the kites, lines sharpened with a coating of finely ground glass to cut those of their rivals. A suitable field must be found, one with a good view of the horizon and free of trees to prevent the lines getting tangled up in the branches. Their hearts pounded at the thought of a kite-fight. Like a sensible teacher, Snehamoy sat the boy down with his exercise book. 'If each kite takes five hundred feet of line to fly, how many feet would twenty kites take?' he asked the boy. The boy **frowned**, 'Only five hundred feet for each kite! What if they get tangled with others during a fight and keep circling away needing more and more?'

3 The two spent a whole afternoon asking neighbours for empty glass bottles. Snehamoy's aunt smashed them in her kitchen, then ground the shards in a pestle, **pricking** her thumb in the process. Glue was added to the glass granules and a touch of vermilion dye to have the lines stand out against the blue sky and the clouds. After returning from school, Snehamoy joined the boy in stringing lines from one end of their courtyard to another. Then, like workers, they wrapped their palms in soft cotton cloth, took lavish dips in the pail of abrasive and went from one end of a line to another, carefully applying a uniform layer over it. In the end, they sat back in the kitchen and admired the brilliant maze turning their courtyard into a field of red pepper.

4 For days, pedalling to and fro from school, Snehamoy heard the village buzzing with the impending kite-fight. Rival groups of boys formed teams and were **spurred** on by a shopkeeper who was offering his regular kites free to anyone who was willing to brave the foreign invasion. Yet on the day of the grand contest, as the first of the Japanese kites came out of the box and heaved by its flyers, went up over the school building, there was a pall of silence. It was a giant Baromon, crashing the helmet of a samurai warrior between its teeth. Scarlet and ochre, it hung still, face up, refused to be cowed by the stiff breeze.

5 Standing in a circle with the boys, Snehamoy strung the kites, gaze fixed on the sky. Like characters in a play, they made their appearance one by one. The Tsugara whirred like an airplane through a clever loop fixed on its back. The crowd went into a roar over the kabuki faces, which floated in the sky like stained glass windows lit by the afternoon sun. Soon the lines were crossing and tangling up the kites with a steady stream of taunts spurring on the flyers. The boy reached inside the kite box and scooped out more. Instantly the field buzzed with humming and whistling kites shaped as cicadas, gnats, dragonflies and dancing carps. It felt like a carnival and drew the crowd's applause.

Adapted from *The Japanese Wife - Kunal Basil*

(i) For each word given below, choose the correct meaning (as used in the passage) from the options given below.

1. frowned *(line 17)*
   (a) to show displeasure
   (b) to be angry
   (c) to be depressed
   (d) to be suspicious

2. pricking *(line 13)*
   (a) slicing (b) eating
   (c) poking (d) puncturing

3. spurred *(line 28)*
   (a) angered (b) encouraged
   (c) fought (d) stopped

(ii) Answer the following questions in your own words as briefly as possible.

(a) Where did the boy find the kites? Describe the first kite which was heaved into the sky.

(b) How did Snehamoy and the boy decide how much line each kite would need?

(c) What effect did the impending kite-fight have on the villagers?

(d) How did the kites flown by Snehamoy and the boy add to the atmosphere of joy and brightness?

(e) What was used to make the line? How was it made?

(iii) In not more than 50 words of your own, describe the efforts made by Snehamoy and his companion to make the line before the kite-fight. (Failure to keep within the word limit will be penalised.)

10

Tenses (Verb Forms)

The tense of a verb in a sentence refers to when the said action takes place.

According to this, there are three kinds of tenses. They are

1. **Present** (the time that is now)
2. **Past** (the time that is gone)
3. **Future** (the time that is to come)

Each tense has four sub-types. They are

(i) Simple Tense
(ii) Continuous Tense
(iii) Perfect Tense
(iv) Perfect Continuous Tense

Present Tense

1. Simple Present Tense

The Simple Present Tense is used to state an action that is a happening at the moment, a habit or a universal fact.

For example,

- She plays in the park.
- She doesn't play in the park.
- Does she play in the park?

2. Present Continuous Tense

The Present Continuous Tense form of a verb tells us that an action is in progress at the time of speaking.

For example,

- She is playing in the park.
- She is not playing in the park.
- Is she playing in the park?

3. Present Perfect Tense

The Present Perfect Tense form of a verb tells us about an action that began in the past and has been completed recently.

For example,

- She has played in the park.
- She has not played in the park.
- Has she played in the park?

4. Present Perfect Continuous Tense

The Present Perfect Continuous Tense form of a verb is used to talk about an action that started in the past and is still continuing in the present.

For example,

- She has been playing in the park.
- She has not been playing in the park.
- Has she not been playing in the park?

Past Tense

1. Simple Past Tense

The Simple Past Tense is used to show an action that had started and was completed at a specified time in the past.

For example,

- She played in the park.
- She didn't play in the park.
- Did she play in the park?

2. Past Continuous Tense

The Past Continuous Tense form of a verb tells us that an action was in progress at some point in the past.

For example,

- She was playing in the park.
- She wasn't playing in the park.
- Was she playing in the park?

3. Past Perfect Tense

The Past Perfect Tense form of a verb tells us that one action was complete before another action began in the past.

For example,

- She had played in the park.
- She hadn't played in the park.
- Had she played in the park?

4. Past Perfect Continuous Tense

The Past Perfect Continuous Tense denotes an action that had continued for some time in the past before being completed at some other point in the past itself.

For example,

- She had been playing in the park.
- She hadn't been playing in the park.
- Had she been playing in the park?

Future Tense

1. Simple Future Tense

The Simple Future Tense tells us that an action will take place in the future.

For example,

- She will play in the park.
- She will not play in the park.
- Will she play in the park?

2. Future Continuous Tense

The Future Continuous Tense form of a verb tells us that an action will start in the future and continue for some time in the future.

For example,

- She will be playing in the park.
- She will not be playing in the park.
- Will she be playing in the park?

3. Future Perfect Tense

The Future Perfect Tense form of a verb denotes that an action will complete before a point of time in future.

For example,

- She will have played in the park.
- She will not have played in the park.
- Will she have played in the park?

4. Future Perfect Continuous Tense

The Future Perfect Continuous Tense denotes an action that will continue till a specific point of time in the future.

For example,

- She will have been playing in the park.
- She will not have been playing in the park.
- Will she have been playing in the park?

PYQs Previous Years' Questions

1. Fill in each of the numbered blanks with the correct form of the word given in brackets. Do not copy the passage but write in correct serial order the word or phrase appropriate to the blank space.
ICSE 2023

Example

(0) One night four college students ………… (be) out partying late and did not study for the test scheduled for the next day.

Answer: were

In the morning, they **(1)** ………… ***(think)*** of a plan. They **(2)** ………… ***(make)*** themselves look dirty with grease and dirt. Then they **(3)** ………… ***(go)*** to the Dean and **(4)** ………… ***(say)*** they **(5)** ………… ***(go)*** out to a wedding last night and on their way back the tyre of their car burst and they had to push the car all the way back.
The Dean thought for a minute and said that they could have the re-test after three days. They **(6)** …… ***(thank)*** him and said they would be ready. On the day of the test, they were made to sit in separate rooms. They agreed as they **(7)** ………… ***(prepare)*** well. But they **(8)** ………… ***(get)*** a rude shock!

Ans.

1. thought	2. made	3. went
4. said	5. had gone	6. thanked
7. had prepared	8. got	

2. Fill in each of the numbered blanks with the correct form of the word given in brackets. Do not copy the passage but write in correct serial order the word or phrase appropriate to the blank space.
ICSE Specimen Paper 2023, ICSE 2019

Example

(0) I .... (slow) the car as I saw the new house.

Answer: slowed

I **(1)** .... ***(pull)*** up into the driveway **(2)** .... ***(observe)*** the way they had **(3)** .... ***(build)*** up the balcony. I **(4)** .... ***(forgot)*** that the bricks of the house **(5)** .... ***(be)*** chocolate brown. The new people **(6)** .... ***(make)*** the tiny balcony into a study room. I **(7)** .... ***(stare)*** at this house, **(8)** .... ***(remember)*** my childhood there.

Ans. 1. pulled 2. to observe 3. built 4. had forgotten 5. were 6. had made 7. stared 8. remembering

3. Fill in the blanks with the correct forms of the words provided after the blanks. **ICSE Specimen Paper 2022 Sem II**

When Ranji **(0)** .... ***(see)*** the pool, he did not hesitate to **(1)** .... ***(get)*** into it. He had often **(2)** .... ***(go)*** swimming, alone or with friends, when he had **(3)** .... ***(live)*** with his parents in a thirsty town in the middle of the Rajputana Desert. There, he had **(4)** .... ***(know)*** only sticky, muddy pools where buffaloes wallowed and women washed clothes.

Example: (0) saw

Ans. 1. get 2. gone 3. lived 4. known

4. Fill in each of the numbered blanks with the correct form of the word given brackets. Do not copy the passage but write in correct serial order the word phrase appropriate to the blank space. **ICSE 2020 Modified**

Example (0) taught

By the time she was three, Matilda had **(0)** .... ***(teach)*** her to read by **(1)** .... ***(study)*** newspapers and magazines **(2)** .... ***(throw)*** around the house. At the age of four, she **(3)** .... ***(read)*** fast and well and she naturally began **(4)** .... ***(hanker)*** after books. The only book in the whole of enlightened household was something called Easy Cooking, **(5)** .... ***(belong)*** to her mother, and when she had read this cover-to-cover and had **(6)** .... ***(learn)*** all the recipes by heart, she **(7)** .... ***(decide)*** she **(8)** .... ***(want)*** something interesting.

Ans. 1. studying 2. thrown 3. read 4. hankering 5. belonging 6. learnt 7. decided 8. wanted

Examiner's Comment

- Some candidates made spelling mistake by writing 'studying' as 'studing'.
- In the fifth blank, many candidates wrote which belonged making it an adjective clause when the question was about tenses.

Suggestion for Students

- Frequently practice passages on tenses so as to identify the correct use of tense in the given context.Understand the difference between the use of 'since' and 'for'.

5. Fill in each of the numbered blanks with the correct form of the word given in brackets. Do not copy the passage but write in correct serial order the word or phrase appropriate to the blank space. **ICSE 2019**

Example (0) roamed

Once upon a time, in the days when genies and giants **(0)** .... ***(roam)*** the land, there **(1)** .... ***(live)*** a farmer **(2)** .... ***(name)*** Baba Ayub. He lived with his family in a little village by the name of Maidan Sabz. Because he had a large family to feed, Baba Ayub **(3)** .... ***(see)*** his days **(4)** .... ***(consume)*** by hard work. Every day, he **(5)** .... ***(labour)*** from dawn to sundown, **(6)** .... ***(plough)*** his field and **(7)** .... ***(turn)*** the soil and **(8)** .... ***(tend)*** to his meagre pistachio trees.

Ans. 1. lived 2. named 3. saw 4. consumed 5. laboured 6. ploughing 7. turning 8. tending

6. Fill in each of the numbered blanks with the correct form of the word given in brackets. Do not copy the passage but write in correct serial order the word or phrase appropriate to the blank space. **2018**

Example (0) beginning

Alice was **(0)** .... ***(begin)*** to get very tired of **(1)** .... (*sit*) by her sister on the bank and of having nothing to do. Once or twice, she had **(2)** .... ***(peep)*** into the book her sister was reading, but it **(3)** .... ***(have)*** no pictures or conversations in it, "and what is the use of a book," **(4)** .... ***(think)*** Alice, "without pictures or conversations?" Alice wondered whether the pleasure of **(5)** .... ***(make)*** a daisy- chain would be worth the trouble of getting up and picking the daisies, when suddenly a white rabbit with pink eyes **(6)** .... (***run***) close by her. Alice did not think this was very remarkable, until the rabbit actually **(7)** .... ***(take)*** a watch out of its waistcoat-pocket, and **(8)** .... ***(look)*** at it, and then hurried on.

Ans. 1. sitting 2. peeped 3. had
4. thought 5. making 6. ran
7. took 8. looked

7. Fill in each of the numbered blanks with the correct form of the word given in brackets. Do not copy the passage but write in correct serial order the word or phrase appropriate to the blank space. **ICSE 2017**

Example (0) started

My mother **(0)** .... ***(start)*** school when she **(1)** .... ***(be)*** six and **(2)** .... ***(stop)*** the same term. She was unusual in the village as she had a father and brother who **(3)** .... ***(encourage)*** her to go to school. She was the only girl in a class full of boys and claims she was brighter than the boys. But every day, she **(4)** .... ***(will)*** leave behind her girl cousins **(5)** .... ***(play)*** at home and she **(6)** .... ***(envy)*** them. There **(7)** .... ***(seem)*** to be no point in **(8)** .... ***(go)*** to school just to end up doing housework.

Ans. 1. was 2. stopped
3. had encouraged 4. would
5. playing 6. would envy
7. seemed 8. going

8. In the following passage, fill in each of the numbered blanks with the correct form of the word given in brackets. Do not copy the passage but write in correct serial order the word or phrase appropriate to the blank space. **ICSE Specimen Paper 2017**

Example:
(0) discussed.

The other day we **(0)** .... ***(discuss)*** the attitudes of people in our country. "Why **(1)** .... ***(be)*** most of them rude and aggressive?" Pritam asked. Sanjana **(2)** .... ***(say)*** that it **(3)** .... ***(be)*** because there **(4)** .... ***(be)*** too many people and one had to fight for everything. Nirode **(5)** .... ***(insist)*** that it **(6)** .... ***(be)*** the climate. We **(7)** .... ***(be)*** as efficient and polite as Europeans if only our weather **(8)** .... ***(be)*** better.

Ans. 1. are 2. said 3. was
4. were 5. insisted 6. was
7. will be 8. is

9. Fill in each of the numbered blanks with the correct form of the word given in brackets. Do not copy the passage but write in correct serial order the word or phrase appropriate to the blank space. **ICSE 2016**

Example

He had been **(0)** ...... ***(sit)*** on the bank of a small irrigation canal.

(0) sitting

He was **(1)** .... ***(gaze)*** at a couple of heron **(2)** .... ***(fish)*** in the muddy water when he **(3)** .... ***(feel)*** something bump his elbow. **(4)** .... ***(look)*** around, he **(5)** .... ***(find)*** at his side a little goat, jet black and soft as velvet with lovely grey eyes. Neither her owner nor her mother **(6)** .... ***(be)*** around. She continued to **(7)** .... ***(nudge)*** Mukesh, so he **(8)** .... ***(look)*** in his pocket for nourishment.

Ans. 1. gazing 2. fishing
3. felt 4. Looking
5. found 6. was
7. nudge 8. looked

10. Fill in each of the numbered blanks with the correct form of the word given in brackets. Do not copy the passage but write in correct serial order the word or phrase appropriate to the blank space. **ICSE 2015**

Example

One morning, I (0) ... ***(see)*** the python curled up on the dressing table.

(0) saw

He was **(1)** ..... ***(gaze)*** at his own reflection in the mirror. I **(2)** ...... ***(go)*** for grandfather but by the time we **(3)** .... ***(return)*** to the room, the python **(4)** .... ***(move)*** on. He was seen in the garden and once the cook saw him **(5)** .... ***(crawl)*** up the ladder to the roof. Then, we **(6)** ..... ***(find)*** him on the dressing table again **(7)** ...... ***(admire)*** himself in the mirror. "He's trying to look better for Aunt Mabel", I said. I **(8)** ...... ***(regret)*** this remark immediately because grandmother overheard and held up my pocket money for the rest of the week!

Ans. 1. gazing 2. went
3. returned 4. had moved
5. crawling 6. found
7. admiring 8. regretted

11. Fill in each of the numbered blanks with the correct form of the word given in brackets. Do not copy the passage but write in correct serial order the word or phrase appropriate to the blank space. **ICSE 2014**

Example

From his perch behind the clock, Hugo could **(0)** .... ***(see)*** everything.

(0) see.

He rubbed his fingers nervously against the small notebook in his pocket and **(1)** .... ***(tell)*** himself to be patient. The old man in the toy booth **(2)** .... (argue) with the girl. She **(3)** .... ***(be)*** about Hugo's age and he often saw her go into the booth and **(4)** .... ***(disappear)*** behind the counter. The old man **(5)** .... ***(look)*** agitated today. Had he figured out some of his toys were **(6)** .... ***(miss)*** ? Well, there was nothing to be **(7)** .... ***(do)*** about that now. The old man and the girl argued some more and finally she closed her book and **(8)** .... ***(run)*** off.

Ans. 1. told 2. was arguing 3. was 4. disappear 5. looked 6. missing 7. done 8. ran

12. Fill in each of the numbered blanks with the correct form of the word given in brackets. Do not copy the passage but write in correct serial order the word or phrase appropriate to the blank space. **ICSE 2013**

Example

A woman **(0)**........... ***(wait)*** at an airport one night, with several long hours before her flight.

(0) was waiting

She **(1)** .... ***(hunt)*** for a book in the airport shops, **(2)** .... ***(buy)*** a bag of cookies and found a place to sit. She **(3)** .... ***(engross)*** in her book but happened to see that the man sitting beside her, bold as could be, grabbed a cookie or two from the bag in between which she tried to ignore to avoid a scene. So, she **(4)** .... ***(munch)*** the cookies and watched the clock, as the gutsy thief diminished her stock. She **(5)** .... ***(get)*** more irritated as the minutes ticked by, thinking, "If I wasn't so nice, I **(6)** .... ***(black)*** his eye." With each cookie she took, he took one too. When only one was left, she wondered what he would do. With a smile on his face, a nervous laugh, he **(7)** .... ***(take)*** the last cookie and broke it in half. He offered her half as he ate the other half. She had never known she could be so angry and turned to gather her belongings. As she reached for her baggage, she gasped with surprise; there was her bag of cookies in front of her eyes. If mine are here, she moaned in despair, the others were his, he **(8)** .... ***(try)*** to share.

Ans. 1. hunted 2. bought 3. was engrossed 4. munched 5. was getting 6. would blacken 7. took 8. was trying

13. Fill in each of the numbered blanks with the correct form of the word given in brackets. Do not copy the passage but write in correct serial order the word or phrase appropriate to the blank space. **ICSE 2012**

Example

My guide **(0)** .... ***(tell)*** me if I wanted to meet these people I would have to walk two miles.

(0) told

We finally **(1)** .... ***(reach)*** a village where I **(2)** .... ***(meet)*** a lady whose age I **(3)** .... ***(can)*** not immediately make out. My translator **(4)** .... ***(find)*** it difficult to interpret the lady's words because her dialect was quite different. She **(5)** .... ***(be)*** a dark-skinned and dark-haired lady. She must have been around seventy years old but there was no grey in her hair. She obviously could not afford to dye her hair. So, what was her secret? Nobody **(6)** .... ***(know)***. It must have been a 'secret' common to all for not one person in that whole village **(7)** .... ***(has)*** a trace of grey hair! I **(8)** .... ***(think)*** about it for a long time.

Ans. 1. reached 2. met 3. could 4. found 5. was 6. knew 7. had 8. thought

14. Fill in each of the numbered blanks with the correct form of the word given in brackets. Do not copy the passage but write in correct serial order the word or phrase appropriate to the blank space. **ICSE 2011**

Example

We were not **(0)** .... ***(allow)*** to talk during the lecture.

(0) allowed

The children **(1)** .... ***(sit)*** in a neat circle and **(2)** .... ***(begin)*** **(3)** .... ***(copy)*** their multiplication tables. Most **(4)** .... ***(scratch)*** in the dirt with sticks they had **(5)** .... ***(bring)*** for that purpose. The more fortunate **(6)** .... ***(has)*** slate boards that they **(7)** .... ***(write)*** on with sticks **(8)** .... ***(dip)*** in a mixture of mud and water.

Ans. 1. sat 2. began 3. copying 4. were scratching 5. brought 6. had 7. were writing 8. dipped

15. In the following passage, fill in each of the numbered blanks with the correct form of the word given in brackets. Do not copy the passage but write in correct serial order the word or phrase appropriate to the blank space. **ICSE 2010**

Example (0) given

But just when I had almost **(0)** .... ***(give)*** up hope, I was **(1)** .... ***(strike)*** with a brilliant idea : my birthday was due fairly soon and if I **(2)** .... ***(deal)*** with the family skillfully, I **(3)** .... ***(feel)*** sure, I could not only get a boat but a lot of other equipments as well. I **(4)** .... ***(suggest)*** to the family that, instead of **(5)** .... ***(let)*** them choose my presents, I **(6)** .... ***(may)*** tell them the things that I **(7)** .... ***(want)*** most. In this way, they could be sure of not **(8)** .... ***(disappoint)*** me.

Ans. 1. struck 2. dealt 3. felt
4. suggested 5. letting 6. might
7. wanted 8. disappointing

16. In the following passage, fill in each of the numbered blanks with the correct form of the word given in brackets. Do not copy the passage but write in correct serial order the word or phrase appropriate to the blank space. **ICSE 2009**

Example (0) spoke

As she **(0)** .... ***(speak)***, I **(1)** .... ***(rise)*** and **(2)** .... ***(go)*** to the centre blackboard. I **(3)** .... ***(find)*** the chalk **(4)** .... ***(write)*** in block letters the title of the book. Then, I **(5)** .... ***(put)*** the chalk down and went to **(6)** .... ***(sit)*** beside her, to **(7)** .... ***(hold)*** her hand. The day had barely **(8)** .... ***(begin)***.

Ans. 1. rose 2. went 3. found
4. to write 5. put 6. sit
7. hold 8. begun

17. In the following passage, fill in each of the numbered blanks with the correct form of the word given in brackets. Do not copy the passage but write in correct serial order the word or phrase appropriate to the blank space. **ICSE 2008**

Example (0) was

There **(0)** .... ***(be)*** some confusion in the doorway. A man **(1)** .... ***(get)*** into the compartment **(2)** .... ***(stammer)*** an apology. Then, the door **(3)** .... ***(bang)*** and the world was **(4)** .... ***(shut)*** out again. I **(5)** .... ***(return)*** to my berth. The guard **(6)** .... ***(blow)*** his whistle and we **(7)** .... ***(move)*** off. Once again, I **(8)** .... ***(have)*** a game to play.

Ans. 1. got 2. stammering 3. banged
4. shut 5. returned 6. blew
7. moved 8. had

18. In the following passage, fill in each of the numbered blanks with the correct form of the word given in brackets. Do not copy the passage but write in correct serial order the word or phrase appropriate to the blank space. **ICSE 2007**

Example (0) am convinced

I **(0)** .... ***(convince)*** that my father **(1)** .... ***(remember)*** by all those who value integrity. He **(2)** .... ***(be)*** a man of learning and also saw to it that he **(3)** .... ***(teach)*** his pupils with passion and patience. He, at times, **(4)** .... ***(use)*** to lose his temper but that was because he always **(5)** .... (want) his pupils to learn and learn well. As a person, he was honest and simple. His greatness **(6)** .... ***(lie)*** in the fact that he **(7)** .... ***(have)*** a pure heart, devoid of malice. Such a man is always valued and **(8)** .... ***(be)*** very rare to find.

Ans. 1. will be remembered
2. was 3. taught 4. used
5. wanted 6. lay 7. had
8. is

19. In the following passage, fill in each of the numbered blanks with the correct form of the word given in brackets. Do not copy the passage but write in correct serial order the word or phrase appropriate to the blank space. **ICSE 2006**

Example (0) giving

Mid-afternoon while **(0)** .... ***(give)*** my report to Mrs. Biggs, I **(1)** .... ***(hear)*** a loud thumping **(2)** .... ***(come)*** from the direction of her store room.

"What **(3)** .... ***(be)*** all that noise downstairs?" I asked.

"Probably a rat. I don't hear anything," she replied.

I ran downstairs and **(4)** .... ***(open)*** the store room door. There was Mr. Biggs **(5)** .... ***(look)*** very dusty and very disgruntled; he wanted to know why Mrs. Biggs **(6)** .... ***(shut)*** him up for hours. He had gone into the store room in search of a walking stick and Mrs. Biggs, **(7)** .... ***(see)*** the door open, had promptly **(8)** .... ***(bolt)*** it.

Ans. 1. heard 2. coming
3. is 4. opened
5. looking 6. had shut
7. seeing 8. bolted

20. In the following passage, fill in each of the numbered blanks with the correct form of the word given in brackets. Do not copy the passage but write in correct serial order the word or phrase appropriate to the blank space. ***ICSE 2005***

Example (0) returned

After Christopher Columbus **(0)** .... ***(return)*** from his famous voyage across the Atlantic, the King of Spain **(1)** .... ***(wish)*** to celebrate the great event and honour the man who **(2)** .... ***(make)*** himself a national hero. He **(3)** .... ***(do)*** so by holding a banquet in honour of the explorer. To this banquet, he **(4)** .... (invite) many of the nobles of the King's Court. Some of them **(5)** .... ***(be)*** jealous of the success Columbus **(6)** .... ***(achieve)***. One of them sat next to Columbus. He turned towards Columbus and said, "Of course, you **(7)** .... ***(be)*** a brave man but it doesn't take much intelligence to do what you have done. After all, anyone can take a ship and sail on and on till he **(8)** .... ***(reach)*** land."

Ans. 1. wished 2. had made
3. did 4. invited
5. were 6. had achieved
7. are 8. reaches

11

Prepositions

A preposition is a word which shows the relationship of the nouns (or the pronouns) with the other words in the sentence.

Role of a Preposition

Prepositions are important when constructing sentences. Prepositions are usually short words and they are generally placed directly in front of nouns. For example,

1. He kept the water bottle on the table.
   (The preposition 'on' shows the relationship between *water bottle* and *table*.)
2. The school is between the church and the confectionary shop.
   (The preposition 'between' shows the relationship between *the church* and the *confectionary shop*.)

Some Prepositions and Their Uses

Common Prepositions	Their Uses	Examples
On	• to refer to specific days and dates (time) • to refer to a surface (place) • to refer to devices (agent)	• He will meet you after dance class on Monday. • The kitten is sleeping on the ground. • Right now, she is watching her favourite show on the TV.
At	• to refer to a specific time • to indicate a place	• He called me at 8 o'clock yesterday. • I will see you at the venue.
In	• to specify day, month, season, year (time) • to indicate a location (place) • used while doing something (agent) • to indicate color, shape and size	• The session will begin in March. • Your dog is running in the park. • She went to Chennai in a hurry. • This shirt comes in four colours.
To	• to refer to a time period • to indicate the direction	• You have to be there from 1 p.m. to 2:30 pm. • My cousins went to watch a game.
For	• to indicate the duration or time • to indicate the receiver • to indicate the purpose of an action	• We walked around for an hour. • She bought this bag for me. • We use the hall for dance practice.
With	• to indicate agent • to indicate being together	• I wrote to her with my favourite pencil. • He ordered a coffee with the brownie.
By	• to indicate an end point of time • to indicate proximity (place) • to indicate means or a method (agent)	• They should arrive by tomorrow. • She was standing by her brother. • I request you to send this file by mail.

Common Prepositions	Their Uses	Examples
Since	• to indicate that something started in the past and continues till now	• No one has seen him since the last weekend.
From	• to show the time or point in time when something starts • to show who sent something/somebody • to show the range of something	• Tickets for the game are available from this week. • He received a mail from his estranged father. • The store sells everything from pins to computers.
After	• to refer to a later time • to indicate place next to • following somebody	• She will arrive home after a month. • My name comes after his in the list. • He ran after her when she left.
Before	• to refer to timed events • to refer to place	• I like to practice my violin before the evening tea. • Remember to get off the bus before the school.
Until/till	• to show when something will happen, begin or end	• Until I see it, I won't believe it.
During	• to denote the length of time in which something happens	• During the holidays, I wrote many poems.
Beside	• means next to or at the side of	• The building beside the school is being demolished today.
Besides	• means in addition to	• Besides him, who did you tell?
Of	• to indicate relating to, belonging to • to indicate measurement • to indicate being part of something	• The poet is a close acquaintance of mine. • The cost of 2 kgs of onion is 50 rupees. • The lid of the box has fallen down.

PYQs Previous Years' Questions

1. Fill in the blanks with appropriate words. *ICSE 2023*

(i) A bird .... hand is worth two in the bush.

(ii) The boy is crazy .... football.

(iii) She was tired .... fighting and struggling all the time.

(iv) He opted .... of the race.

(v) We borrowed the bikes .... our uncle.

(vi) The police station is .... the right.

(vii) I looked at the stars .... the telescope.

(viii) There was an accident ....the crossroads.

Ans. (i) in (ii) about (iii) of
(iv) out (v) from (vi) on
(vii) through (viii) at

2. Fill in the blanks with appropriate words. *ICSE Specimen Paper 2023*

(i) Please wash .... the curry stain from your dress.

(ii) She turned .... the offer to work at the factory.

(iii) The burglars broke .... the house when the family was away.

(iv) I shall compete .... him.

(v) She agreed .... my proposal.

(vi) She would like to come .... foot.

(vii) The Vishwas Group of Companies has taken .... the cosmetic market completely.

(viii) He agreed to carry .... the manager's orders.

Ans. (i) away (ii) down (iii) into
(iv) with (v) to (vi) on
(vii) over (viii) out

3. Choose the correct option to fill in the blanks: *ICSE Specimen Paper 2022 Sem II Modified*

(i) He was frightened so he hid .... the cupboard.

(ii) They built a bridge .... a turbulent stream.

(iii) His intelligence will carry him .... all his difficulties.

(iv) She called .... her teacher to help her to sort out her difficulties.

Ans. (i) behind/inside (ii) across (iii) through
(iv) up

4. Fill in the blanks with appropriate words. *ICSE 2020*

(i) It has been raining .... two hours.

(ii) He just scrapped .... his examination.

(iii) Mrs. Kapoor was bent .... attending the meeting.

(iv) She is proud and looks .... on her colleagues.

(v) Rahul plays football .... his grandfather.

(vi) The mother was sitting .... the sick child all night.

(vii) Monica is leaning .... the wall.

(viii) Rosie is very good .... art and craft.

Ans. (i) for (ii) through (iii) upon
(iv) down (v) with (vi) beside
(vii) against (viii) at

Examiner's Comment

- Most candidates were not aware of the uses of prepositions and thus made common errors like using 'since' in place of 'for', 'over' in place of 'upon', 'on/by' in place of 'against', etc.

Suggestions for Students

- Understand the difference between easily confused prepositions like 'since' and 'for'.
- Read the entire sentence before deciding upon the preposition to be filled in the blank.

5. Fill in each blank with an appropriate word. *ICSE 2019*

(i) The puppy was hiding .... the sofa.

(ii) Stop worrying .... your future.

(iii) When I stepped .... the lift, I found it had stopped working.

(iv) We had to use a bridge to go .... the river.

(v) I have lived in this town .... ten years.

(vi) Please switch .... all lights and fans when you leave the room.

(vii) Ronnie is married .... my cousin.

(viii) The gift came .... a birthday card.

Ans. (i) beneath (ii) about (iii) into
(iv) across (v) for (vi) off
(vii) to (viii) with

6. Fill in each blank with an appropriate word. *ICSE Specimen Paper 2019*

(i) He hid the stolen goods .... the floor boards.

(ii) The teacher knew all .... the problem.

(iii) The boy sat still .... the night waiting to be called.

(iv) My grandmother would have fallen .... if I had not caught her hand.

(v) The sailor held on to the mast of the boat for fear of being blown .... in the storm.

(vi) All the boarders were taken .... a walk today.

(vii) Even though she slept .... several mattresses, she still felt the hard pea.

(viii) Anup and Arun have quarrelled .... a silly matter.

Ans. (i) under (ii) about (iii) throughout (iv) off (v) away (vi) on (vii) on (viii) over

7. Fill in each blank with an appropriate word. **ICSE 2018**

(i) The poet's mother was stung .... a scorpion.

(ii) "Please write .... what I tell you; otherwise, you will forget," the teacher said.

(iii) The dog was hiding .... the bed, barking at the stranger.

(iv) Sheila's grandmother found it difficult to climb .... the steep staircase.

(v) The soldier fought bravely .... his country.

(vi) There is no use crying .... split milk.

(vii) I don't know what they were arguing .... but I could hear angry voices.

(viii) The school playground is out .... bounds for the pupils of the primary school.

Ans. (i) by (ii) down (iii) under (iv) up (v) for (vi) over (vii) about (viii) of

8. Fill in each blank with an appropriate word. **ICSE 2017**

(i) She shouted angrily .... the disobedient boy.

(ii) I asked them to provide us .... a guide.

(iii) The tree grew at a dangerous slant and had to be cut ....

(iv) My daughter believes .... fairies.

(v) He drew a beautiful diagram .... the board.

(vi) She battled her way .... the crowd.

(vii) We were asked to gather .... the teacher.

(viii) They had to climb .... the steep pathway to reach the top.

Ans. (i) at (ii) with (iii) down (iv) in (v) on (vi) through (vii) around (viii) up

9. Fill in the blanks with appropriate words:

ICSE Specimen paper 2017

(i) Her parents live .... New Delhi.

(ii) Joe's parents are sick .... his behaviour.

(iii) Colonel Gurmeet congratulated the soldiers .... their victory.

(iv) The planet was seen .... the telescope.

(v) The news of his promotion came .... the next day.

(vi) He is not afraid .... the consequences.

(vii) He rushed .... the class as he was late.

(viii) The school is famous .... its sports achievements.

Ans. (i) in (ii) of (iii) on (iv) through (v) on (vi) of (vii) to (viii) for

10. Fill in each blank with an appropriate word. **ICSE 2016**

(i) There was a steep rise .... onion prices.

(ii) Air pollution is responsible for the spread .... bronchitis.

(iii) He was .... pressure to complete the work.

(iv) John jumped .... the river to rescue the child.

(v) His teacher is very pleased .... him.

(vi) Ali took .... his cap and wiped his face.

(vii) The old woman could not get .... the shock.

(viii) He should not get .... with such rudeness.

Ans. (i) in (ii) of (iii) under (iv) into (v) with (vi) off (vii) over (viii) away

11. Fill in the blank with an appropriate word. **ICSE 2015**

(i) He found the key just .... the front door.

(ii) I could not accompany my cousin .... the trip because I had fever.

(iii) The noise prevented us .... sleeping.

(iv) The young man put the flute .... his lips and began to play.

(v) Ashok leaned .... the wall tiredly.

(vi) The paper dart went gliding .... the air.

(vii) The cyclist rode quickly .... the path.

(viii) The young child carried the heavy bucket .... the stairs.

Ans. (i) near (ii) on (iii) from (iv) to (v) against (vi) into (vii) on (viii) up

12. Fill in the blank with an appropriate word. *ICSE 2014*

(i) The teacher spoke .... for Raju when he was wrongly accused of stealing money.

(ii) We can visit her in the hostel .... 3 pm and 5 pm on Saturday.

(iii) The Sinhas have lived in New Delhi .... 1943.

(iv) Little children are often afraid .... the dark.

(v) Sneha has applied .... a scholarship.

(vi) It took Ahmed many months to get .... the loss of his friend.

(vii) She turned .... the generous offer made by the manager.

(viii) We were asked to take .... our footwear as we were entering a place of worship.

Ans. (i) up (ii) between (iii) since
(iv) of (v) for (vi) over
(vii) down (viii) off

13. Fill in the blank with an appropriate word. *ICSE 2013*

(i) She takes a lot of trouble .... her work.

(ii) Our English friends have taken .... Indian food quite quickly.

(iii) He got an A .... the Mathematics test.

(iv) He jumped .... the river to save his friend from drowning.

(v) Always be prepared .... a surprise test.

(vi) She hid .... the cupboard and gave everyone a fright.

(vii) She is fond .... pets.

(viii) The brothers quarrelled .... themselves for their father's property.

Ans. (i) for (ii) to (iii) in
(iv) into (v) for (vi) inside
(vii) of (viii) among

14. Fill in the blank with an appropriate word. *ICSE 2012*

(i) He was touched .... pity when he heard the tale.

(ii) There is always a demand .... good tailors.

(iii) The mother prevented her child .... going out in the rain.

(iv) The baby crawled .... the table and hid there.

(v) Once upon a time, the great King ruled .... all these villages and towns.

(vi) She is the smarter .... the two.

(vii) Sheila insists .... wearing that dress, although her mother thinks it is too short for her.

(viii) The teacher complained .... him when she met his mother in the market.

Ans. (i) with (ii) for (iii) from
(iv) under (v) over (vi) of
(vii) upon (viii) against

15. Fill in the blank with an appropriate word. *ICSE 2011*

(i) He congratulated me ...... my great achievement.

(ii) The poor man is afflicted .... arthritis.

(iii) She is blind .... the faults of her husband.

(iv) The boss had many complaints .... Shyam.

(v) You must prepare .... the examination.

(vi) She is not aware .... the danger.

(vii) Ravi was accurate .... his calculations.

(viii) They hid the money .... the carpet.

Ans. (i) on (ii) with (iii) to
(iv) against (v) for (vi) of
(vii) in (viii) under

16. Fill in the blank with an appropriate word. *ICSE 2010*

(i) I refrained .... telling Reeta the truth.

(ii) The leader counted .... the cooperation of his colleagues.

(iii) The public was cautioned .... pickpockets.

(iv) Janaki escorted her daughter to the cinema theatre as she was anxious .... her safety.

(v) Their path was beset .... difficulties yet they succeeded.

(vi) The mouse crept stealthily .... the cheese.

(vii) It was good .... you to invite Sheila for the picnic.

(viii) Smoking .... public places is now banned.

Ans. (i) from (ii) on (iii) against
(iv) about (v) with (vi) towards
(vii) of (viii) in

17. Fill in the blank with an appropriate word. *ICSE 2009*

(i) I prevailed .... him to join the gymnasium.

(ii) The curious child eagerly begged .... an answer to the riddle.

(iii) He was bent .... coming first in the examinations.

(iv) The theory exam was followed .... a group discussion.

(v) I ran .... my teacher at the show last night.

(vi) She is extremely anxious .... an interview next week.

(vii) What a contrast .... the two siblings!

(viii) The brother fought .... their father's property.

Ans. (i) upon (ii) for (iii) on/upon (iv) by (v) into (vi) about (vii) between (viii) over/for

18. Fill in the blank with an appropriate word. **ICSE 2008**

(i) The elderly man prepared himself for a life .... retirement.

(ii) Do you take his word .... mine?

(iii) Rohini is very concerned .... her father's health.

(iv) Altaf had many books and papers scattered all .... the room.

(v) The Phoenix is a legendary bird that rises .... its ashes.

(vi) The police pulled the briefcase from .... the table.

(vii) The mob rushed onto the pavement; everyone seemed angry........... everyone else.

(viii) The old woman looked .... the cupboard, searching for the photograph.

Ans. (i) after (ii) over (iii) about (iv) over (v) from (vi) under (vii) with (viii) inside

19. Fill in the blank with an appropriate word. **ICSE 2007**

(i) Truth always prevails .... the long run.

(ii) Sujata stood .... the river and saw the ship pass by.

(iii) She took some money .... her father to buy a video game.

(iv) Shilpa gave me a rare gift .... my birthday.

(v) Deepak was very upset .... me.

(vi) Michelle is longing .... meet me.

(vii) It has been a long time .... I have met my sister.

(viii) The worker asked .... his wages.

Ans. (i) in (ii) beside (iii) from (iv) on (v) with (vi) to (vii) since (viii) for

20. Fill in the blank with an appropriate word. **ICSE 2006**

(i) He refused to put .... with their interference in his affairs.

(ii) She has been going .... the script for days.

(iii) It is our duty to protest .... injustice.

(iv) He soon became accustomed .... the harsh weather.

(v) Dilip went out .... his way to help the poor.

(vi) He was able to put .... his ideas so cleverly that he impressed everyone.

(vii) He persists .... teasing the other children in the class.

(viii) I have been waiting for you .... four o'clock.

Ans. (i) up (ii) through (iii) against (iv) to (v) of (vi) across (vii) on (viii) since

21. Fill in the blanks with an appropriate word. **ICSE 2005**

(i) The safari parks of South Africa abound .... wild animals.

(ii) The young man excels ..... both music and dance.

(iii) She is a diligent student, worthy .... praise.

(iv) I saw .... his plan and realised that he was going to cheat us.

(v) I was .... the impression that the meeting had been cancelled.

(vi) Always be true .... yourself.

(vii) The villagers lodged a complaint .... the corrupt officials.

(viii) I can rely .... my sister for help.

Ans. (i) with (ii) in (iii) of (iv) through (v) under (vi) to (vii) against (viii) on

12

Conjunction

Conjunctions

Conjunctions are one or more words used to join phrases, clauses or sentences to form new sentences.

Conjunctions can be divided into four categories. They are

Coordinating Conjunctions

Coordinating conjunctions join two words, clauses or sentences of equal importance. There are seven coordinating conjunctions, which are and, but, for, or, yet, so, nor.

e.g.

(a) They were poor yet happy.

(b) She called and told me about her situation.

(c) I could not attend the wedding for I had fever.

(d) Do the chores or clean your room.

Subordinating Conjunctions

A subordinating conjunction introduces the subordinate clause in a sentence and joins it with the main clause.

Some common subordinating conjunctions are though, although, since, after, as, because, before, lest, than, till, until, if, while, when, whether.

e.g.

(a) I did as I was expected to dance.

(b) I was there when children were performing.

(c) You can call whenever you need help.

(d) I bought the book though it was very expensive.

Correlative Conjunctions

A correlative conjunction is a pair of words that is used to join two or more clauses or sentences of equal importance.

Some common correlative conjunctions are both…and, not only…but also, either…or, neither…nor, no sooner…than, hardly…when, such…that.

e.g.

(a) I will either eat salad or drink milk for dinner.

(b) No sooner had they completed the work, than they demanded the wages.

(c) Not only her dress but also her jewellery is extraordinary.

(d) Keshav scores good marks because he is both hardworking and intelligent.

Compound Conjunction

A compound conjunction is two or more words used together to join two clauses or sentences.

Some common compound conjunctions are in order that, even if, as well as, as though.

(a) The notice was published in order that all might know the facts.

(b) Such an act would not be kind even if it were just.

(c) He walks as though he were slightly lame.

(d) The principal as well as the teachers attended the Independence Day function.

Transformation of Sentences Using Different Conjunctions

If/Unless

'If' and 'Unless' are used for conditional sentences. Both of them join the subordinate clause with the principal clause. However, 'Unless' means ' If not'. Hence, the affirmative sentence (principal clause) is converted into negative and *vice-versa* while changing the sentence containing 'If ...' into those containing 'Unless ... '.

But, if both subordinate and principal clause are negative, then while using 'unless', no changes are made.

Consider the following sentences

"If you keep trying, you will succeed."

"Unless you keep trying, you will not succeed."

If we reverse the order of clauses in both of the above sentences, the conjunction will be joining the two clauses thereby eliminating the need for 'comma' as,

You will succeed <u>if</u> you keep trying.

Or You will not succeed <u>unless</u> you keep trying.

e.g.

(a) Unless you teach me, I shall not pass.
If you teach me, I shall pass.

(b) Sheela will be selected for the competition only if she goes for the auditions.
Unless she goes for auditions, Sheela will not be selected for the competition.

(c) Unless they work harder, they have no chance of passing the test.
If they don't work harder, they have no chance of passing the test.

(d) If your friends get here before 7 o'clock, we can take them out for dinner.
Unless your friends get here before 7 o'clock, we cannot take them out for dinner.

As soon as/Hardly/Scarcely ..... when /No sooner ..... than

All of them are used to denote actions that happen one after another. e.g.

(a) As soon as he heard the bell, he ran towards the door.

- No sooner did he hear the bell than he ran towards the door.
- Hardly had he heard the bell when he ran towards the door.

Note With 'No sooner......than', both Past Perfect Tense and Past Indefinite Tense can be used in the subordinate clause, while the main clause is in Simple Past Tense.

e.g.

(b) No sooner did she meet him than she told her friend about him.

- Hardly had she met him when she told her friend about him.
- As soon as she met him, she told her friend about him.

(c) No sooner had I joined the company than my team lead resigned.
As soon as I joined the company, my team lead resigned.

Note 'No sooner' and 'hardly' are adverbs and when a sentence begins with an adverb, the law of inversion applies. Hence, the **'helping verb'** is put before the **'subject'**.

PYQs Previous Years Questions

I. 1. Join the following sentences to make one complete sentence **without using** ***and***, ***but*** or ***so***. Choose the correct option. ***ICSE 2023***

(i) He jumped up. He ran away.
  (a) He jumped up before he ran away.
  (b) Jumping up, he ran away.
  (c) He ran away after jumping.
  (d) He ran away because he jumped up.

(ii) He has failed many time. Still, he hopes to succeed.
  (a) He succeeds after he failed many times.
  (b) Despite of failing, he hopes to succeed.
  (c) In spite of many failures, he hopes to succeed.
  (d) He failed many times even though he hopes to succeed.

(iii) Do not be a jeweller. Do not be a goldsmith.
  (a) Be neither a jeweller nor a goldsmith.
  (b) Be both a jeweller and a goldsmith.
  (c) Either be a jeweller or a goldsmith.
  (d) Be a jeweller as well as a goldsmith.

(iv) A cottager and his wife had a hen. The hen had an egg every day.
  (a) Everyday, a hen laid an egg for a cottager and his wife.
  (b) A cottager and his wife had a hen who laid an egg every day.
  (c) The cottager and his wife had an egg every day because they had a hen.
  (d) A cottager and his wife had a hen which laid an egg every day.

2. Join the following sentences to make one complete sentence **without using** ***and***, ***but*** or ***so***. Choose the correct option. ***ICSE Specimen Paper 2023***

(i) The delegates arriver. The meeting started immediately.
  (a) No sooner did the delegates arrive than the meeting started.
  (b) No sooner did the delegates arrive, the meeting started.
  (c) No sooner the delegates arrived than the meeting started.
  (d) The delegates arriving, the meeting started.

(ii) We lost our ticket. We lost our luggage.
  (a) We lose our ticket as well as our luggage.
  (b) Having lost our ticket we lost our luggage.
  (c) We lost our ticket as well as our luggage.
  (d) We lost our ticket and we lost our luggage.

(iii) He cultivates orchids. He displays them at the flower show.
  (a) He cultivates orchids to display at the flower show.
  (b) He cultivates orchids for displayed at the flower show.
  (c) He cultivates orchids to play with at the flower show.
  (d) He cultivates orchids, but displays them only at the flower show.

(iv) He ran away. He had seen the Principal coming.
  (a) No sooner did he see the Principal coming, he ran away.
  (b) He ran to see the Principal coming.
  (c) By seeing the Principal coming, he ran away.
  (d) Seeing the Principal coming, he ran away.

3. Choose the correct option to join the following sentences **without using 'and', 'but'** or **'so'**: ***ICSE Specimen Paper 2022 Sem II***

(i) He plays cricket. He plays tennis.
  (a) He plays not only cricket but also tennis.
  (b) He plays either cricket or tennis.
  (c) He plays cricket as well as tennis.
  (d) He plays neither cricket nor tennis.

(ii) Submit your project. Only then can you appear for the test.
  (a) Until you submit your project, you can appear for the test.
  (b) Until you appear for the test, you cannot submit your project.
  (c) Unless you submit your project, you can appear for the test.
  (d) Unless you submit your project, you cannot appear for the test.

(iii) The man was running fast. The police caught him.
  (a) Although the man was running fast, the police caught him.
  (b) The police caught the man in spite he was running fast.
  (c) Despite his running fast, the man caught the police.
  (d) The man was running fast although the police caught him.

(iv) Sheena drew a picture. Her mother put it up on the fridge.
  (a) Her mother put a picture on the fridge that Sheena drew.

(b) Sheena drew a picture that her mother put on the fridge.
(c) He mother drew a picture that Sheena put on the fridge.
(d) Her mother put on the picture that Sheena drew.

4. Join the following sentences to make one complete sentence **without using** ***and, but*** or ***so.*** *ICSE 2020*

(i) Sarah and Tyra are twins. They look exactly alike.
(a) Because they are twins, Sarah and Tyra look exactly alike.
(b) They are twins, hence, Sarah and Tyra look exactly alike.
(c) For they are twins, Sarah and Tyra look exactly alike.
(d) Given that they are twins, Sarah and Tyra look exactly alike.

(ii) Rohan does not like to play cricket. He does not like to play hockey either.
(a) Rohan neither likes to play cricket or hockey.
(b) Rohan neither like to play cricket nor hockey.
(c) Rohan does not like to play either cricket or hockey.
(d) Rohan like to play neither cricket or hockey.

(iii) Sania pushed as hard as she could. The door would not open.
(a) Though Sania pushed as hard as she could yet, the door would not open.
(b) Though Sania pushed as hard as she could, she could not open the door.
(c) Though Sania pushed as hard as she could, the door would not open.
(d) Though Sania pushed as hard as she could, the door did not open.

(iv) The school bus drove through the gate. The clock was striking eight at that moment.
(a) When the bus drove through the gate, the clock struck eight.
(b) As soon as the bus drove through the gate, the clock struck eight.
(c) After the bus drove through the gate, the clock struck eight.
(d) Both (a) and (b)

5. Join the following sentences to make one complete sentence **without using** ***and, but*** or ***so.***

(i) He was very ill. He did not take any medicine.
(a) Although he was very ill, he did not take any medicine.
(b) Even when ill, he did not take medicine.
(c) He was very ill yet he did not take any medicine.
(d) Both (a) and (c)

(ii) You come back from your holiday. We will discuss the problem.
(a) When you come back from your holiday, we will discuss the problem.
(b) As soon as you came back from your holiday, we will discuss the problem.
(c) When you came back from your holiday, we will discuss the problem.
(d) Only when you come back from your holiday, will we discuss the problem.

(iii) He remained absent on Friday. It was foolish of him.
(a) It is foolish of him to be absent on Friday.
(b) It was foolish of him to remain absent on Friday.
(c) It was considered foolish of him that he remained absent on Friday.
(d) It was foolish of him to be absent.

(iv) Rahul ran all the way to the bus stop. He missed the bus.
(a) When Rahul ran all the way to the bus stop, he missed the bus.
(b) Although Rahul ran all the way to the bus stop, he missed the bus.
(c) Even if Rahul runs all the way to the bus stop, he will miss the bus.
(d) When Rahul runs all the way to the bus stop, he misses the bus.

6. Join the following sentences to make one complete sentence **without using** ***and, but*** or ***so.***
ICSE Specimen Paper 2019

(i) He practised everyday. He came first in the race.
(a) As he practiced every day, he came first in the race.
(b) He came first in the race after practicing every day.
(c) Because he practised every day, he came first in the race.
(d) Both (a) and (c)

(ii) She did such intricate embroidery. Her eyesight was affected.
(a) Her eyesight was affected while doing intricate embroidery.
(b) Her eyesight was affected because she did such intricate embroidery.
(c) Her eyesight was affected when she was doing intricate embroidery
(d) Her eyesight was affected whenever she was doing intricate embroidery

(iii) Molly has a very good vocabulary. She reads a lot.
- (a) As Molly reads a lot, she certainly has a good vocabulary.
- (b) Molly has a very good vocabulary since she reads a lot.
- (c) Molly has a very good vocabulary as she reads a lot.
- (d) both (b) and (c)

(iv) They broke open door. They saw everything was in a mess.
- (a) When they broke open the door, they saw everything was in mess.
- (b) As soon as they break open the door, they saw everything was in mess.
- (c) Hardly had they broke open the door, they saw everything was in mess.
- (d) No sooner did they broke open the door, that they saw everything was in mess.

7. Join the following sentences to make one complete sentence <u>**without using**</u> ***and, but*** or ***so***. ***ICSE 2018***

(i) They have to go to bed early every night. They are allowed to stay up late on Saturdays.
- (a) They have to go to bed every night except on Saturdays.
- (b) On Saturday, they are allowed to stay up late or otherwise they have to go to bed every night.
- (c) They have to go to bed early every night except Saturdays, when they are allowed to stay up late.
- (d) None of the above

(ii) The children were delighted. The exams had been cancelled.
- (a) The children were delighted why the exams had been cancelled.
- (b) The exams had been cancelled because the children were delighted.
- (c) The children were delighted that the exams had been cancelled.
- (d) The exams had been cancelled as if the children were delighted.

(iii) We are not allowed to play in the Sun. We are not allowed to play in the rain.
- (a) We are not allowed to play in the Sun or the rain.
- (b) We are not allowed to play in the Sun because of the rain.
- (c) And in the rain, we are not allowed to play or in the Sun.
- (d) In the rain and in the Sun, we are allowed to play.

(iv) This is the place. The dog was rescued from its cruel owner.
- (a) This is the place when the dog was rescued from its cruel owner.
- (b) This is the place where the dog was rescued from its cruel owner.
- (c) The dog was rescued from this place from its cruel owner.
- (d) All of the above

8. Join the following sentences to make one complete sentence <u>**without using**</u> ***and, but*** or ***so***.

(i) This is the hospital. I was born here.
- (a) This is the hospital where I was born.
- (b) I was born in this hospital.
- (c) I was born in that hospital.
- (d) Both (a) and (b)

(ii) The children have been sick for a week. They were unable to go to school.
- (a) Having been sick for a week, the children were unable to go to school.
- (b) Being sick for a week, the children didn't go to school.
- (c) The children were unable to go to school as they were sick.
- (d) Having been sick for a week, that the children were unable to go to school.

(iii) Mrs. Kumar has been a teacher for thirty years. She will now retire.
- (a) Mrs. Kumar who has been a teacher for thirty years will now retire.
- (b) As Mrs. Kumar has been a teacher for thirty years, she will now retire.
- (c) It is time for Mrs. Kumar to retire.
- (d) Mrs. Kumar has been a teacher for thirty years for now she will retire.

(iv) We have had no respect for nature. Now, we are suffering from the effects of global warming.
- (a) Since we have no respect for nature, we are suffering from the effects of global warming.
- (b) Because we have no respect for nature, we are suffering from the effects of global warming.
- (c) As we have no respect for nature, we are suffering from the effects of global warming.
- (d) All of the above

9. Join the following sentences to make one complete sentence <u>**without using**</u> ***and, but*** or ***so.***
ICSE Specimen Paper 2017

(i) Sonia asked a riddle. I was unable to solve it.
- (a) Sonia asked a riddle which I was unable to solve.

(b) I was unable to solve Sonia asked me.
(c) Sonia asked a riddle which I am unable to solve.
(d) Sonia asked a riddle which I will be unable to solve.

(ii) John helped Thomas. Thomas will always be grateful.
(a) Thomas has always been grateful to John for his help.
(b) Thomas will always be grateful to John for his help.
(c) Thomas is grateful to John for his help.
(d) Thomas needs to be grateful to John for his help.

(iii) Rajan is a great Cricketer. He is also popular.
(a) Apart from being a great cricketer, Rajan is popular.
(b) Rajan is a great cricketer, yet he is popular.
(c) Apart from being a great cricketer, Rajan is also popular.
(d) Besides being a great cricketer, Rajan is popular.

(iv) Adnan sang a wonderful song. It became a hit.
(a) Adnan sings a wonderful song which will become a hit.
(b) Adnan sang a wonderful song which became a hit.
(c) Adnan sang a wonderful song which is going to become a hit.
(d) Adnan sings a wonderful song which became a hit.

10. Join the following sentences to make one complete sentence **without using** ***and*, *but*** or ***so*.**

(i) My grandfather is very old. He is very active.
(a) My grandfather is old yet active.
(b) Even though my grandfather is old, he is active.
(c) Beside being old, my grandfather is active.
(d) Apart from being old, my grandfather is active.

(ii) Mala is not in the classroom. Mala is not in the library.
(a) Mala is neither in the classroom nor the library.
(b) Mala is neither in the classroom nor in the library.
(c) Mala is not in the classroom or the library.
(d) Mala cannot be found in the classroom or the library.

(iii) She was so excited about her performance. She could not sleep at night.
(a) She was too excited about her performance that she could not sleep at night.
(b) She was so excited about her performance that she cannot sleep at night.
(c) She was too excited about her performance to sleep at night.
(d) She was very excited about her performance and sleep at night.

(iv) Mumbai is very densely populated. It is one of the major cities in the country.
(a) As Mumbai is very densely populated, it is one of the major cities in the country.
(b) Mumbai is very densely populated as it is one of the major cities in the country.
(c) As Mumbai is very densely populated yet, it is one of the major cities in the country.
(d) Although Mumbai is very densely populated, it is one of the major cities in the country.

11. Join the following sentences to make one complete sentence **without using** ***and*, *but*** or ***so*.**

(i) He had learnt to cycle. He has yet to learn to swim.
(a) Though he had learnt to cycle, he had yet to learn to swim.
(b) Though he will have learnt to cycle, he had yet to learn to swim.
(c) Though he had learnt to cycle, he is yet to learn to swim.
(d) Though he learnt to cycle, he had to learn to swim.

(ii) The child helped her mother to make breakfast. She washed the tomatoes.
(a) The child helped her mother to make breakfast as she washed the tomatoes.
(b) The child helped her mother to make breakfast for she washed the tomatoes.
(c) The child helped her mother to make breakfast by washing the tomatoes.
(d) The child helped her mother to make breakfast in washing the tomatoes.

(iii) They bought a new car. They can travel long distances.
(a) They bought a new car so that they can travel to long distances.
(b) They bought a new car to travel long distances.
(c) They bought a new car for they wanted to travel long distances.
(d) They bought a new car such that they can travel long distances.

(iv) Sunita opened her purse. She found the money missing.
(a) When Sunita opened her purse, she found the money missing.
(b) When Sunita opened her purse, she did not find the money.
(c) When Sunita opens her purse, she finds the money missing.
(d) Although Sunita opened her purse, she found the money missing.

12. Join the following sentences to make one complete sentence **without using** ***and, but*** or ***so.*** ICSE 2012

(i) The minister was wise. The king did not trust him.
(a) Although the minister was wise, yet the king did not trust him.
(b) Although the minister was wise, but the king did not trust him.
(c) Although the minister was wise, the king did not trust him.
(d) All of the above

(ii) We reached the port. The storm came on.
(a) As we reached the port, the storm came on.
(b) Since we reached the port, the storm came on.
(c) While we reached the port, the storm came on.
(d) As soon as we reached the port, the storm came on.

(iii) One should not borrow money. One should not lend money.
(a) One should neither borrow or lend money.
(b) One should either borrow nor lend money.
(c) One should neither borrow and lend money.
(d) One should neither borrow nor lend money.

(iv) She will win the prize. She deserves it.
(a) She deserves to win the prize and she will.
(b) She will win the prize because she deserves it.
(c) She will win the prize but she doesn't deserve it.
(d) None of the above

13. Join the following sentences to make one complete sentence **without using** ***and, but*** or ***so.*** ICSE 2010

(i) You will surely be late. Hurry up!
(a) Unless you hurry up, you will be late.
(b) Unless you hurry up, you will not be late.
(c) Unless you hurry up, you will barely be late.
(d) Unless you hurry up, you will surely not be late.

(ii) The trekkers got lost due to the heavy fog. They had misplaced their map as well.
(a) Not only did the trekkers get lost due to the heavy fog but they also misplaced their map.
(b) Not only did the trekkers get lost due to the heavy fog but they misplaced their map.
(c) Both the trekkers get lost due to the heavy fog and they also misplaced their map.
(d) Both the trekkers got lost due to the heavy fog and they misplaced their map.

(iii) She has to apologise. He will not meet her again if she does not do so.
(a) He will meet her again unless she apologises.
(b) He will not meet her again if she apologises.
(c) He will not meet her again unless she apologises.
(d) He will meet her again if she does not apologise.

(iv) I wear this expensive outfit very sparingly. I bought it last month.
(a) I wear this expensive outfit very sparingly while I bought last month.
(b) I wear this expensive outfit very sparingly which I bought last month.
(c) I wear this expensive outfit very sparingly where I bought last month.
(d) I wear this expensive outfit very sparingly when I bought last month.

14. Join the following sentences to make one complete sentence **without using** ***and, but*** or ***so.*** ICSE 2009

(i) Swarna asked me a question. I was unable to answer it.
(a) I was unable to answer the question which Swarna asked me.
(b) I was unable to answer the question that Swarna asked me.
(c) Swarna asked me a question which I was unable to answer.
(d) All of the above

(ii) You helped Tania. She will always be grateful.
(a) Tania will always be grateful for your help.
(b) You helped Tania because she was grateful.
(c) Tani will always be grateful because you helped her.
(d) Both (a) and (c)

(iii) I heard you won a prize. I am extremely delighted.
(a) I am extremely delighted to hear that you won a prize.
(b) I am extremely delighted to hear which you won a prize.
(c) I am extremely delighted to hear when you won a prize.
(d) I am extremely delighted to hear and you won a prize.

(iv) There was heavy traffic. We reached the stadium on time.
(a) Though there was heavy traffic, but we reached the stadium on time.
(b) Though there was heavy traffic, yet we reached the stadium on time.
(c) Though there was heavy traffic, we reached the stadium on time.
(d) All of the above

II. Re-write the following sentences according to the instructions given after each. Make other changes that may be necessary but do not change the meaning of each sentence. Choose the correct options.

1. If the boys do not reach the school on time, they will be punished.
   (Begin: Unless...) ***ICSE 2023***
   (a) Unless the boys reach the school on time, they will not be punished.
   (b) Unless the boys are punished, they will not reach the school on time.
   (c) Unless the school punished the boys, they will not reach on time.
   (d) Unless the boys reach the school on time, they will be punished.

2. As soon as he reaches him, his friends call him.
   (Begin: Hardly...) ***ICSE 2023***
   (a) Hardly does he reach home when his friends call him.
   (b) Hardly had he reached home than his friends call him.
   (c) Hardly, he reaches home, his friends call him.
   (d) Hardly when he reaches home than his friends call him.

3. Unless the train arrives on time, we shall miss the concert.
   (Begin: If...) ***ICSE Specimen Paper 2023***
   (a) If the train arrives on time, we shall miss the concert.
   (b) If the train does not arrive on time, we shall miss the concert.
   (c) If the train arrived on time, we shall miss the concert.
   (d) If the train does not arrive on time, we shall not miss the concert.

4. As soon as he finishes his work, he starts playing.
   (Begin: Hardly...) ***ICSE Specimen Paper 2023***
   (a) Hardly his work is finished, he starts playing.
   (b) Hardly he finishes his work, he starts playing.
   (c) Hardly he has finished his work and he starts playing.
   (d) Hardly does he finish his work, when he starts playing.

5. As soon as the whistle blew, the game stopped.
   (Begin: No sooner...) ***ICSE Specimen Paper Sem II 2022***
   (a) No sooner did the whistle blow, the game stopped.
   (b) No sooner than the whistle blew, the game stopped.
   (c) No sooner did the whistle blew than the game stopped.
   (d) No sooner did the whistle blow than the game stopped.

6. As soon as the teacher enters, she is greeted by her students.
   (Begin: No sooner...) ***ICSE 2020 Modified***
   (a) No sooner did the teacher enter the class than she greets her students.
   (b) No sooner does the teacher enter the class than she was greeted by her students.
   (c) No sooner does the teacher enter the class than she is greeted by her students.
   (d) No sooner did the teacher enter the class than she was greeted by her students.

7. Sheela will be selected for the competition only if she goes for the auditions.
   (Begin: Unless...) ***ICSE 2020 Modified***
   (a) Unless she goes for auditions, Sheela will be selected for the competition.
   (b) Unless she auditions, Sheela will not be selected for any competition.
   (c) Unless she goes for auditions, Sheela is not going be selected for the competition.
   (d) Unless she goes for auditions, Sheela will not be selected for the competition.

8. As soon as the Sun rose over the hills, the fog disappeared.
   (Begin: No sooner...) ***ICSE 2019 Modified***
   (a) No sooner does the Sun rise over the hills then the fog disappeared.
   (b) No sooner had the Sun rise over the hills that the fog disappeared.
   (c) No sooner did the Sun rise over the hills than the fog disappeared.
   (d) No sooner did the Sun rise over the hills, the fog disappeared.

9. If your friends get here before 7 o'clock, we can take them out for dinner.
   (Rewrite using 'Unless') ***ICSE 2019 Modified***
   (a) Unless your friends get here before 7 o'clock, we can take them out for dinner.
   (b) Unless your friends get here before 7 o'clock, we will not take them out for dinner.
   (c) Unless your friends get here before 7 o'clock, we will take them out for dinner.
   (d) Unless your friends get here before 7 o'clock, we cannot take them out for dinner.

10. As soon as her song was over, I knew that she had won the competition.
    (Begin: No sooner...) ***ICSE Specimen Paper 2019***

(a) No sooner did her song got over that I know that she had won the competition.
(b) No sooner was her song over than I knew that she had won the competition.
(c) No sooner did her song was over than I knew that she had won the competition.
(d) No sooner was her song over that I knew that she had won the competition.

11. As soon as the bell rang, the children ran out.
(Begin: No sooner…) ***ICSE Specimen Paper 2019***
(a) No sooner did the bell ring than the children run out to play.
(b) No sooner does the bell ring then the children run out to play.
(c) No sooner did the bell ring that the children run out to play.
(d) No sooner does the bell ring than the children run out to play.

12. She laid the table after she had finished the cooking.
(Begin: When…) ***ICSE 2018 Modified***
(a) When she finished the cooking, she laid the table.
(b) When she has finished cooking, she laid the table.
(c) When she had finished the cooking, she laid the table.
(d) When she had finished the cooking, she had laid the table.

13. As soon as the sports meet ended, the children ran on the field.
(Begin: Hardly…) ***ICSE 2018 Modified***
(a) Hardly did the sports meet ended that the children ran on the field.
(b) Hardly does the sports meet ended when the children ran on the field.
(c) Hardly had the sports meet ended when the children ran on the field.
(d) Hardly had the sports meet ended then the children ran on the field.

14. We had not even walked one kilometer when they stopped us.
(Begin: Hardly…) ***ICSE Specimen Paper 2017***
(a) Hardly had we walked one kilometer that they stopped us.
(b) Hardly had we walked one kilometer when they stopped us.
(c) Hardly did we walked one kilometer when they stopped us.
(d) Hardly did we walked one kilometer that they stopped us.

15. Put your tools away, the children may fall over them
(Use: lest…) ***ICSE Specimen Paper 2017***
(a) Put your tools away lest the children should not fall.
(b) Put your tools away lest the children should fall.
(c) Put your tools away lest the children can fall.
(d) Put your tools away lest the children should not have fallen.

16. If Mary catches the first bus, she will be in time for school.
(Begin: Unless…) ***ICSE 2016***
(a) Unless Mary catches the first bus, she will be in time for school.
(b) Unless Mary catches the first bus, she will not be in time for school.
(c) Unless Mary caught the first bus, she would not be in time for school.
(d) Unless Mary will not catch the first bus, she will not be in time for school.

17. Hardly had the teacher left the room when all the children started making a noise.
(Begin: No sooner…) ***ICSE 2016***
(a) No sooner did the teacher left the room that the children started making a noise.
(b) No sooner had the teacher left the room than the children started making a noise.
(c) No sooner did the teacher left the room than the children started making a noise.
(d) No sooner had the teacher left the room then the children started making a noise.

18. As soon as Sunita sat down to study, the lights went off.
(Begin: No sooner…) ***ICSE 2015 Modified***
(a) No sooner did Sunita sat down to study than the lights went off.
(b) No sooner had Sunita sat down to study that the lights went off.
(c) No sooner does Sunita sat down to study then the lights went off.
(d) No sooner had Sunita sat down to study than the lights went off.

19. As soon as the function got over, the crowd dispersed.
(Begin: Hardly had…) ***ICSE 2015 Modified***
(a) Hardly did the function got over than the crowd dispersed.
(b) Hardly had the function got over when the crowd dispersed.
(c) Hardly had the function got over then the crowd dispersed.
(d) Hardly did the function got over when the crowd dispersed.

20. As soon as we lit the candle, the power supply was restored.

(Begin: No sooner...) ***ICSE 2014 Modified***

(a) No sooner did we light the candle than the power supply was restored.

(b) No sooner has we light the candle that the power supply was restored.

(c) No sooner did we light the candle then the power supply was restored.

(d) No sooner had we light the candle than the power supply was restored.

21. My mother said I could go with you only if I returned home by five o'clock.

(Use: as long as) ***ICSE 2013 Modified***

(a) My mother told me I can go with you as long as I returned home by five o'clock.

(b) My mother said I could go with you as long as I returned home by five o'clock.

(c) My mother says that I could go with you as long as I return home by five o'clock.

(d) My mother said I could go with you as long as I be at home by five o'clock.

22. As soon as the Chief Guest had seated himself, the play began.

(Begin: No sooner...) ***ICSE 2012 Modified***

(a) No sooner did the Chief Guest seated himself that the play began.

(b) No sooner had the Chief Guest seated himself than the play began.

(c) No sooner had the Chief Guest seated himself that the play began.

(d) No sooner does the Chief Guest seated himself then the play began.

23. The children will sit out in the garden, if the weather is cool.

(Begin: The children won't...) ***ICSE 2011 Modified***

(a) The children won't sit in the garden as the weather is hot.

(b) The children won't sit out in the garden if the weather is hot.

(c) The children will sit out in the garden if the weather is hot.

(d) The children won't sit out in the garden when the weather is hot.

24. The child disappeared as soon as the bus stopped.

(Begin: Hardly...) ***ICSE 2011 Modified***

(a) Hardly did the bus stopped when the child disappeared.

(b) Hardly had the bus stopped that the child disappeared.

(c) Hardly had the bus stopped when the child disappeared.

(d) Hardly does the bus stopped then the child disappeared.

25. Unless Ria takes care of her health, she will not be able to look after her family.

(Begin: Ria must...) ***ICSE 2010 Modifed***

(a) Ria must take care of her health, or she will not be able to look after her family.

(b) Ria must take care of her health yet, she will not be able to look after her family.

(c) Ria must take care of her health, otherwise, she will not be able to look after her family.

(d) Ria must take care of her health, if not she will not be able to look after her family.

13

Transformation of Sentences

A sentence can be expressed in a number of ways. These number of ways may include the usage of different words of similar meanings, or using the words figuratively or using different syntaxes of sentences. Transformation means changing one form of a sentence into another without altering its meaning or sense. There are different ways of transforming a sentence form into another.

I. Sentences

Types of Sentences

Interchange of Sentences

You are often asked to interchange the type of sentences in the following ways

Affirmative ⇌ Negative

(By using antonym)

e.g. (i) Apurva is an industrious girl. → Apurva is not a lazy girl.

(ii) I don't understand why this happens. → I fail to understand why this happens.

Assertive ⇌ Interrogative

e.g. (i) You can wait for a minute.
Can't you wait for a minute?

(ii) Who doesn't know Hindi in India?
Everybody knows Hindi in India.

Assertive ⇌ Exclamatory

e.g. (i) This is a very beautiful sight.
What a beautiful sight this is !

(ii) How wonderfully she has done it !
She has done it wonderfully.

Interchange of Simple/ Complex/ Compound Sentences

Simple ⇌ Compound

e.g. (i) In spite of several attempts, he could not get the visa for Australia. (*Simple*)

He attempted several times but he couldn't get the visa for Australia. (*Compound*)

(ii) I will have lunch and come with you. (*Compound*)

After having lunch, I will come with you. (*Simple*)

Simple ⇌ Complex

e.g. (i) In spite of several attempts, he couldn't get the visa for Australia. (*Simple*)

Though he attempted several times, he couldn't get the visa for Australia. (*Complex*)

(ii) He carried an umbrella because he did not want to get drenched in the rain. (*Complex*)

He carried an umbrella for not getting drenched in the rain. (*Simple*)

Change of Adverbs

- too ——— to/ so ——— that
- though/in spite of (despite)

e.g. (i) Manpreet is too humble to disobey her mother.
Manpreet is so humble that she can not disobey her mother.

(ii) Though Sejal was ill, she came for the class.
Despite being ill, Sejal came for the class.

Complex ⇌ Compound

(i) He carried an umbrella that he might not get drenched in the rain. (*Complex*)

He did not want to get drenched in the rain, so he carried an umbrella. (*Compound*)

(ii) He promised to return my notes but he didn't. (*Compound*)

Although he had promised to return my notes, he didn't. (*Complex*)

Synthesis of Sentences

Definition

Synthesis means the combination of a number of sentences into one new sentence.

The following are the chief ways of combining two or more simple sentences into one long sentence.

By Using a Participle

- He got up early. He went on a walk.
  Getting up early, he went on a walk.
- She was irritated by her. She put on headphones.
  Irritated by her, she put on headphones.

By Using a Noun or a Phrase in Opposition

- This is my father. His name is Frank.
  This is my father, Frank.

By Using a Preposition with a Noun or Gerund

- He performed so well. She was pleasantly surprised.
  On seeing him perform so well, she was pleasantly surprised.
- He is quite sick. He went to work.
  In spite of being quite sick, he went to work.

By Using the Absolute Construction

- The chair was broken. He threw it.
  The chair being broken, he threw it.
- The exam was cancelled. He was elated.
  The exam being cancelled, he was elated.

By Using an Infinitive

- Man works day and night. He has to support his family.
  Man works day and night to support his family.
- She will go to Kanpur. She will see her father.
  She will go to Kanpur to see her father.

By Using an Adverb or Adverbial Clause

- Great people serve their country. Their service is selfless.
  Great people serve their country selflessly.

II. Degrees of Camparison

Change of Degree

Change of degree means transformation of one degree of adjective into another while retaining the same meaning of the sentence.

Let us try to understand the rules of transforming one form of degree of comparison into another.

Superlative Degree to Positive and Comparative

When we use superlative degree to estimate the quality of an object, we mean to say that it has the highest degree of that particular quality among all the objects being compared.

This means 'no other' object has that quality to the same degree.

Therefore, in positive degree, we use 'No other' and in comparative 'all other' or 'any other'. e.g.

(i) **Superlative** She is the tallest girl in the class.

Positive No other girl in the class is as tall as her.

Comparative She is taller than any other girl in the class.

(ii) **Superlative** Russia is the largest country in the world.

Positive No other country in the world is as large as Russia.

Comparative Russia is larger than any other country in the world.

Positive Degree to Comparative Degree

Consider the following sentence

Radhika is as intelligent as Siya.

This means that both have equal levels of intelligence. The sentence in comparative degree will thus be

Siya is not more intelligent than Radhika.

Note: When the positive and the comparative degree are used to compare only two things or persons, the adjective cannot be transformed into superlative degree.

Remember In case of conversion from positive degree to comparative degree and *vice versa*, the sentence begins with the second entity being compared. Moreover, an affirmative sentence is changed into negative sentence and *vice versa*.

III. Active and Passive Voice

Change of Persons

Subject	Object
I	me
we	us
you	you
he	him
she	her
they	them
Name (Jay/Mayur)	Name remains as it is (Jay/Mayur)

Change of Verb According to Tense

Tense or Modal + Base		Active Voice	Passive Voice
Simple	Present Past Future	beat/beats beat shall/will beat	am/is/are beaten was/were beaten shall /will be beaten
Continuous	Present Past Future	am/is/are beating was/were beating shall/will be beating	am/is/are being beaten was/were being beaten Not applicable
Perfect	Present Past Future	have/has beaten had beaten shall/will have beaten	have/has been beaten had been beaten shall/will have been beaten
Perfect Continuous	Present Past Future	Not applicable	Not applicable
	Can/may/must, etc. + base	can/may/must, etc. beat	can/may/must, etc. be beaten

Changes with Modals

- When a sentence in active voice has a modal auxiliary (can, could, may, might, etc.), the modal verb does not change its form and the sentence is changed into passive voice in the following manner
  ACTIVE – Subject + modal + first form of verb + object
  PASSIVE – Object + modal + be + first form of verb + by + subject

e.g. Shaurya ***can*** cook many international cuisines. *(Active)*

Many international cuisines ***can be*** cooked by Shaurya. *(Passive)*

My father could visit me in the evening today. *(Active)*

I could be visited by my father in the evening today. *(Passive)*

Other Changes

Interrogative Sentences

In interrogative sentences, the 'auxiliary' or the 'wh-word' that forms the question remains at its place, the question mark also remains at the end of the sentence. The rest of the changes (like interchange of places of subject and object) take place the same way as in the case of assertive sentences.

Note: Only **'who'** changes to 'by whom' since it acts as the subject itself.

Yes-No Type Questions

Active Voice	Passive Voice
Do you like apples?	Are apples liked by you?
Has she done her homework?	Has her homework been done by her?

Wh-Type Questions

(a) **What** do you need? (*Active voice*)

What is needed by you? (*Passive voice*)

I need a **phone**. (*Active voice*)

A **phone** is needed by me.(*Passive voice*)

(b) Where did she purchase this bag from? (*Active voice*)

From where was this bag purchased by her? (*Passive voice*)

Imperative Sentences

1. To convert orders into Passive voice, 'let' is used followed by 'be + past participle'.
   e.g. Open the door.
   Let the door be opened.
2. To convert requests/advice/suggestions into Passive voice, the sentence is started with 'you'.
   e.g. (a) Please pass the book.
   You are requested to pass the book.
   (b) Help the ones in need.
   You should help the ones in need.

IV. Direct and Indirect Speech

Rules for Changing Simple Direct Speech into Indirect Speech

Rules	Direct Speech	Indirect Speech
• Remove separating comma, inverted commas and use the connector 'that'.	He said, "I do not like pasta."	He said that he did not like pasta.
• When there is an object in Reporting verb, change 'said to' into 'told' and 'says to' into 'tells'.	He said to me, "You have been a great help."	He told me that I had been a great help.
	He says to me, "My teacher is highly educated."	He tells me that his teacher is highly educated.
• When there is no object in Reporting verb, 'said' and 'says' remain the same.	Sheeba said, "I work in an MNC."	Sheeba said that she worked in an MNC.
	Kamya says, "I will go to the party."	Kamya says that she will go to the party.

Changes in Reported Speech when Reporting Verb is in Past Tense

Change of Verb Forms	Change of Pronouns	Time, Place Expressions and Other Changes
is, am, are — was, were	1st person → according to the subject	now — then
has, have — had	2nd person → according to the object	ago — before
$V_3 - V_2$	3rd person → unchanged	today — that day
did — had + IIIrd form of the verb	2nd person → changed to 3rd person if the reporting verb has no object	last night—the previous night or the night before
was, were — had been		next week — the following week
will — would		here – there
shall — should		hither — thither
can — could		this — that
		thus — so
		come — go

Tensewise Conversion of Direct into Indirect Speech

Direct Speech	Indirect Speech
Simple Present Tense	Simple Past Tense
Present Continuous Tense	Past Continuous Tense
yts16 Present Perfect Tense	Past Perfect Tense
Present Perfect Continuous Tense	Past Perfect Continuous Tense
Simple Past Tense	Past Perfect Tense
Past Continuous Tense	Past Perfect Continuous Tense
Past Perfect Tense	Past Perfect Tense
Simple Future Tense (Will/Shall)	Should/Would
Future Continuous Tense (Shall Be/Will Be)	Should Be/Would Be
Future Perfect Tense (Shall/Will + Have)	Would + Have

Rules for Changing Interrogative Sentences into Indirect Speech

Interrogative sentences are of two types

(i) Yes-No type questions or verbal questions

(ii) Wh-type questions

Yes-No Type Questions

When the reported speech is a yes-no type question, the conjunction 'if' or 'whether' is used and the interrogative sentence (or question) is converted into an assertive sentence.

The other changes (tense, pronouns, etc.) are made as usual and the question mark is removed.

Most importantly, the reporting verb is changed from 'says' and 'said' to 'asks' and 'asked', respectively.

e.g. She said to me, "Do you want to play?"

She asked me if I wanted to play.

Wh-Type Questions

No conjunction is used as the Wh-word itself works as a conjunction to join the reporting verb with the reported speech.

All other changes are made in the same manner as the yes-no type questions.

e.g. Mother said to him, "What do you want for dinner?"

Mother asked him what he wanted for dinner.

Rules for Changing Imperative Sentences into Indirect Speech

- In case of imperative sentences, the preposition 'to' is used in place of conjunction after the reporting verb.
- Depending upon the type of imperative sentence (i.e. order, suggestion, advice, request, etc.), the reporting verb is changed into ordered, suggested, advised, requested, etc.
- In case of negative imperative sentences (such as don't play there), 'to' is put after 'not' that follows reporting verb.

In case of sentences beginning with 'Let's', the reporting verb is changed to proposed or suggested.

e.g. The officer said to her, "Please vacate this area."
The officer requested her to vacate that area.

Rules for Changing Exclamatory Sentences into Indirect Speech

We replace the reporting verb with 'exclaimed with joy', 'exclaimed with sorrow', 'exclaimed with surprise', etc. according to the sense of the reported speech.

e.g. Rima said, "Yay! We won the competition."
Rima exclaimed with joy that we had won the competition.

Nominalisation

Nominalisation is a type of word formation in which a verb or an adjective or a common noun is used as or transformed into a noun generally, abstract noun.

e.g. guide (Verb) → guidance (Abstract noun)
smart (Adjective) → smartness (Abstract noun)
child (Common noun) → childhood (Abstract noun)

Transforming a Verb in a Sentence into its Noun Form

A noun can be a subject or an object in a sentence. Therefore, when we are changing the 'verb' in a sentence into its 'noun' form, we need to provide another verb that may suit the context of the sentence and that may not harm its syntax or its meaning.

Let us consider following examples to learn this:

- You need to justify your answer.
  If we have been asked to use the noun form of the verb 'justify', i.e. 'justification', then the sentence will be :
- You need to give justification for your answer.

Or

- Your answer needs justification.

You can understand that both the sentences have the same meaning as the original sentence. But the syntax of both is different.

Therefore, if you comprehend the sentence with the context with which the words are used, you will be able to change their construction using different parts of speech.

Transforming an Adjective in a Sentence into its Noun Form

Consider the following example :

- The little boy gave a **brave** performance.
  We know that an adjective qualifies a noun. So, when we change adjective into abstract noun, the noun which is being qualified by it must either change its position or be provided with a suitable preposition to receive its effect. Sometimes, another suitable 'verb' also needs to be supplied in order to complete the sense of the sentence.

The above sentence can be rewritten as :

- The little boy exhibited **bravery** in his performance.

Or

The little boy's performance exhibited **bravery**.

PYQs Previous Years' Questions

Objective Questions

1. Re-write the following sentences according to the instructions given after each. Make other changes that may be necessary, but do not change the meaning of each sentence. Choose the correct options. *ICSE 2023*

(i) He said to me, "I don't believe you."
(Begin : He said ....)
(a) He said he doesn't want to believe in me.
(b) He said that he didn't believe me.
(c) He said that he didn't believe in me.
(d) He said I don't believe you.

(ii) Some boys were helping the wounded man.
(Begin : The wounded ....)
(a) The wounded man was helping some boys.
(b) The wounded man were helping some boys.
(c) The wounded man was being helped by some boys.
(d) The wounded boys were helping the man.

(iii) He is as wise as Solomon.
(Use : 'wiser')
(a) Solomon was wiser than he is.
(b) He and Solomon are wiser.
(c) Solomon was the wisest.
(d) Solomon was not wiser than he is.

(iv) She is weak but she is courageous.
(Begin: Despite ......)
(a) Despite of being weak she is courageous.
(b) Despite being weak, she is courageous.
(c) Despite being courageous, she is not weak.
(d) Despite weak, she is courageous.

(v) We will never forget what we saw.
(Begin: Never......)
(a) Never forget what we see.
(b) Never will we forget what we had seen.
(c) Never will we see what we forget.
(d) Never will we forget what we saw.

(vi) Jaswant's grandfather is too old to take up this job,
(Use. ....so.........that...)
(a) Jaswant's grandfather is so old that he could not take up his job.
(b) Jaswant's grandfather is so old that he cannot take up this job.
(c) Jaswant's grandfather is so old that he could take up this job.
(d) Jaswant's grandfather is so old that he can take up this job.

2. Re-write the following sentences according to the instructions given after each. Make other changes that may be necessary but do not change the meaning of each sentence. Choose the correct options. *ICSE Specimen Paper 2023*

(i) The captain said, "It gives me great pleasure to be here this evening."
(Begin: The captain......)
(a) The captain said that it was giving him great pleasure to be there that evening.
(b) The captain said that it gives me great pleasure to be there this evening.
(c) The captain said that it gave him great pleasure to be here this evening.
(d) The captain said that it gave him great pleasure to be there that evening.

(ii) He has applied many times. He has never been selected.
(Begin: In spite......)
(a) In spite of applying many times, he had never been selected.
(b) In spite applying many times, he has never been selected.
(c) In spite of applying many times, he has never been selected.
(d) In spite never being selected, he has applied many times.

(iii) Very few managers are as honest as James.
(End: ....managers)
(a) James is more honest than other managers.
(b) James is more honest than most other managers.
(c) James is honest than many other managers.
(d) James is most honest among other managers.

(iv) I accept your offer.
(Use: acceptable)
(a) Your offer is acceptable to me.
(b) Your offer was acceptable to me.
(c) Your offer is acceptable.
(d) Your acceptable offer came to me.

(v) As soon as he finishes his work, he starts playing.
(Begin: Hardly......)
(a) Hardly his work is finished, he starts playing.
(b) Hardly he finishes his work, he starts playing.
(c) Hardly he has finished his work and he starts playing.
(d) Hardly does he finish his work, when he starts playing.

(vi) I have never seen Mr. Joe lose his temper.
(Begin: Never......)
(a) Never I have seen Mr. Joe lose his temper.
(b) Never did I see Mr. Joe lose his temper.
(e) Never have I seen Mr. Joe losing his temper.
(d) Never ever did I see Mr. Joe lose his temper.

3. Read each sentence with its instructions. Choose the correct answer from the options provided beneath each: ***ICSE Specimen Paper 2022 Sem II***

(i) He came to the party.
(Add Question tag)
(a) Isn't it? (b) Didn't he?
(c) Wasn't it? (d) Wasn't he?

(ii) The teacher said, "Akhtar, why were you absent yesterday?"
(Begin: The teacher asked Akhtar...)
(a) The teacher asked Akhtar why he was absent yesterday.
(b) The teacher asked Akhtar why were you absent yesterday.
(c) The teacher asked Akhtar why are you absent yesterday.
(d) The teacher asked Akhtar why he had been absent the previous day.

(iii) In spite of the water logging, the traffic was heavy.
(Begin: Despite...)
(a) Despite the water logging, the traffic was heavy.
(b) Despite of the water logging, the traffic was heavy.
(c) Despite the traffic being heavy, there was water logging.
(d) Despite of water logging, there was heavy traffic.

(iv) Mother was too angry to argue with the shop keeper.
(Remove 'too'.)
(a) Mother was too angry so that she could not argue with the shop keeper.
(b) Mother was so angry to argue with the shop keeper.
(c) Mother was so angry that she could not argue with the shop keeper.
(d) Mother was so angry not to argue with the shop keeper.

(v) Everybody put up their hands.
(Begin: There was nobody...)
(a) There was nobody who put up their hands.
(b) There was nobody who did not put up their hands.
(c) There was nobody whom put up their hands.
(d) There was nobody who should put up their hands.

(vi) We celebrated grandfather's hundredth birthday.
(Begin : Grandfather...)
(a) Grandfather's hundredth birthday was celebrated by us.
(b) Grandfather celebrated his hundredth birthday.
(c) Grandfather was celebrated on his hundredth birthday.
(d) Grandfather celebration was on his hundredth birthday.

(vii) Kaushik has the best handwriting in the class.
(Begin: No one...)
(a) No one has the better handwriting than Kaushik in the class.
(b) No one has the better handwriting in the class than Kaushik.
(c) No one in the class has better handwriting than Kaushik.
(d) No one's handwriting in the class is better than Kaushik.

4. Re-write the following sentences according to the instructions given after each sentence. Make other changes that may be necessary but do not change the meaning of the given sentence. ***ICSE 2020 Modified***

(i) The librarian orders books for the school library every year.
(Begin: Books ....)
(a) Books for the school library are ordered by the librarian every year.
(b) Books in the school library is ordered by the librarian every year.
(c) Books of the school library will be ordered by the librarian every year.
(d) Books for the school library need to be ordered by the librarian every year.

(ii) No one will deny that the children have worked very hard this year.
(Begin: Everyone ....)
(a) Everyone needs to agree that the children did work very hard this year.
(b) Everyone will agree that the children have worked very hard this year.
(c) Everyone can agree that the children have worked very hard this year.
(d) Everyone will have to agree that the children worked very hard this year.

(iii) She is so busy that she finds no time to entertain her friends.
(Rewrite using 'too')
(a) She is too busy that she cannot find time to entertain her friends.
(b) She is too busy and so she cannot find time to entertain her friends.
(c) She is too busy to find time for the entertainment her friends.
(d) She is too busy to find time to entertain her friends.

(iv) In spite of the very hot weather, Kevin stepped out to buy.
(Begin: Despite ....)
(a) Despite the very hot weather, Kevin stepped out to buy.
(b) Despite of the very hot weather, Kevin stepped out to buy.
(c) Despite of the very hot weather and Kevin stepped out to buy.
(d) Despite the hot weather, Kevin will step out to buy.

(v) I would rather eat fruit than a lot of unhealthy junk food.
(Begin: I prefer ....)
(a) I prefer eating fruit as compared to a lot of unhealthy junk food.
(b) I prefer eating fruit to a lot of unhealthy junk food.
(c) I will prefer to eat fruit any day to unhealthy junk food.
(d) I prefer to eat fruit to a lot of unhealthy junk food.

(vi) The tree was cut down ruthlessly.
(Begin: They ....)
(a) They will cut down the tree ruthlessly.
(b) They ruthlessly cut down the tree.
(c) They are going to cut down the tree ruthlessly.
(d) They cut down the tree ruthlessly.

5. Re-write the following sentences according to the instructions given after each one. Make other changes that may be necessary but do not change the meaning of the given sentence. ***ICSE 2019 Modified***

(i) The old women said to Arun, "Can you help me cross the street?"
(Begin : The old women asked Arun ....)
(a) The old woman asked Arun whether he could help her cross the street.
(b) The old woman asked to Arun whether he could help her cross the street.
(c) The old woman asked Arun if he can help her cross the street.
(d) The old woman asked Arun whether he can help her cross the street.

(ii) It rained so heavily that they could not go for the picnic.
(Rewrite : Using 'too .... to')
(a) It rained too heavily for them so they could not go to the picnic.
(b) It rained too heavily for them to go to the picnic.
(c) It rained too heavily to go to the picnic.
(d) It rained too heavily for the picnic.

(iii) The school captain was elected by the students of Classes XI and XII.
(Begin : The students ....)
(a) The students elected the school captain.
(b) The students of Classes XI and XII will elect the school captain.
(c) The students of Classes XI and XII elected the school captain.
(d) The students of Classes XI and XII needed to elect the school captain.

(iv) Greenland is the largest island in the world.
(Rewrite : Using 'larger')
(a) There is no island larger than Greenland in the world.
(b) Greenland is larger than any other island in the world.
(c) There is no island that is larger than Greenland.
(d) There is no larger island than Greenland in the world.

(v) How cruel Shylock was to demand his pound of flesh!
(Begin : It was cruel ....)
(a) It was cruel of Shylock to demand his pound of flesh.
(b) It was cruel to demand his pound of flesh on the part of Shylock.
(c) It was cruel on the part of Shylock to demand his pound of flesh.
(d) Both (a) and (c)

(vi) Arun was asked by his mother to explain the missing buttons on his shirt.
(Rewrite : Using 'explanation')
(a) Arun's mother asked him to give her an explanation about the missing buttons on his shirt.
(b) Arun's mother gave her an explanation about the missing buttons on his shirt.
(c) Arun's mother needed him to give her an explanation about the missing buttons on his shirt.
(d) Arun's mother required an explanation about the missing buttons on his shirt.

6. Rewrite the following sentence according to the instructions given after each. Make other changes that may be necessary but do not change the meaning of each sentence. ***ICSE Specimen Paper 2019***

(i) "Will you lend me the book tomorrow?" Priya asked her classmate.
(Begin: Priya asked her classmate if.......)
(a) Priya asked her classmate if he would lend her the book the next day.
(b) Priya asked her classmate if he would lent her the book tomorrow.
(c) Priya asked her classmate if he will lend her the book the day after.
(d) Priya asked her classmate if he can lend her the book the day after.

(ii) The teacher scolded him for coming late.
(Begin: He......................................)
(a) He is going to the scolded for coming late.
(b) He was scolded by the teacher for coming late.
(c) He is going to be scolded for being late by the teacher.
(d) He got scolded by the teacher for he was late.

(iii) It was so hot that the P.T. period could not be held.
(Begin: It was too ....)
(a) It was too hot for the P.T. period to be held.
(b) It was too hot so the P.T. period could not be held.
(c) It was too hot for the P.T. period.
(d) It was too hot to play outside in the P.T. period.

(iv) Our school sent up the best exhibit to the Town Hall.
(Re-write using : 'better')
(a) No other school did a better exhibit than our school to the town hall.
(b) No other school sent up a better exhibit than our school to the town hall.
(c) No other school could sent up a better exhibit than us to the town hall.
(d) No other school can sent up a better exhibit to the town hall.

(v) Visitors under eighteen were not allowed into the hall.
(Begin: Only visitors ....)
(a) Only visitors above eighteen were allowed into the hall.
(b) Only visitors who are above eighteen years were allowed in the hall.
(c) Only visitors above eighteen years of age were allowed into the hall.
(d) Only visitors who were allowed into the hall were above eighteen years of age.

(vi) They were asked to combine all their ideas into one document.
(Re-write using: 'combination')
(a) They asked for a combination of all their ideas into one document.
(b) They were asked for a combination of all their ideas into one single document.
(c) They are going to be asked for a combination of all ideas into a document.
(d) They are asked for a combination of all their ideas as one document.

7. Re-write the following sentences according to the instructions given after each one. Make other changes that may be necessary but do not change the meaning of the given sentence. ***ICSE 2018 Modified***

(i) He is old but still he works hard.
(Begin : Despite ....)
(a) Despite of being old, he still works hard.
(b) Despite old age, he still works hard.
(c) Despite him being old, he works hard.
(d) Despite being old, he still works hard.

(ii) The delivery boy was requested to bring the parcel the next day.
(Rewrite using direct speech ....)
(a) I asked the delivery boy, "Could you bring the parcel tomorrow?"
(b) I said to the delivery boy, "Could you bring the parcel the next day?"
(c) I says to the delivery boy, "Could you bring the parcel tomorrow?"
(d) I asked the delivery boy, "Can you bring the parcel tomorrow?"

(iii) I prefer playing a game to watching television.
(Begin : I would rather ....)
(a) I would rather play a game over watching television.
(b) I would rather play a game to watch television.
(c) I would rather play a game and not watch television.
(d) I would rather play a game than watch television.

(iv) Every family has a black sheep.
(Begin : There is no ....)
(a) There is no family where there is no a black sheep.
(b) There is no family without a black sheep.
(c) There is no family with the lack of a black sheep.
(d) There is no family with a black sheep.

(v) I have never worn a more ill-fitting suit.
(End : .... ever worn.)
(a) This is an ill-fitted suit that I have ever worn.
(b) This is the most ill-fitted suit that I have ever worn.
(c) This is the ill-fitted suit that I don't think is ever worn.
(d) This is the most ill-fitted suit to be ever worn.

(vi) Anil is too fast a runner not to come first in the race.
(Begin : Anil is so ....)
(a) Anil is so fast a runner that he came first in the race.
(b) Anil is so fast in the race that he came first in the race.
(c) Anil is so fast a runner that he came first.
(d) Anil is so fast in running that he came first in the race.

8. Re-write the following sentences according to the instructions given after each one. Make other changes that may be necessary but do not change the meaning of the given sentence. ***ICSE 2017 Modified***

(i) Not many people read for pleasure these days.
(Begin : A few ....)
(a) A few people only read for pleasure these days.
(b) A few people read for pleasure these days.
(c) A few people read only for pleasure these days.
(d) A few people will read for pleasure these days.

(ii) Since her childhood, Meera has been good in Mathematics.
(End : .... childhood)
(a) Meera is good in Mathematics since her childhood.
(b) Meera had been good in Mathematics since her childhood.
(c) Meera has been good in Mathematics since her childhood.
(d) Meera was good in Mathematics even in her childhood.

(iii) "We have had no rain since January", Ramu said.
(Begin : Ramu said that they ....)
(a) Ramu said that they had no rains since January.
(b) Ramu said they had no rains since January.
(c) Ramu said that they had had no rains for long.
(d) Ramu said that they had had no rains since January.

(iv) It is dangerous as well as illegal to drive a motorcycle without a helmet.
(Begin : It is not ....)
(a) It is not safe or legal for you to be driving a motorcycle without a helmet.
(b) It is not safe or legal to drive a motorcycle without a helmet.
(c) It is not considered safe or legal to drive a motorcycle without a helmet.
(d) It was not safe or legal to drive a motorcycle without a helmet.

(v) He had plenty of wealth but he was not happy.
(Begin : In spite ....)
(a) In spite of being wealthy, he was not happy.
(b) In spite being wealthy, he was happy.
(c) In spite of being wealthy, he was happy.
(d) In spite of being wealthy yet, he was not happy.

(vi) He was so tired that he could not stand.
(Use : too ....)
(a) He is too tired to stand.
(b) He was too tired to stand.
(c) He considered it too tiring to stand.
(d) He was too tired to even consider standing.

(vii) Every one of them was an experienced mountaineer.
(Begin : There was no ....)
(a) There was no inexperienced mountaineer among them.
(b) There was no one inexperienced in mountaineering among them.
(c) There is no inexperienced mountaineer between them.
(d) There was no inexperienced mountaineer between them.

(viii) I have never seen a film as bad as this.
(Begin : This is ....)
(a) This is the worst film I ever saw.
(b) This is the worst film to be ever seen.
(c) This is the worst film I have ever seen.
(d) This is the worst film to see.

9. Rewrite the following sentence according to the instructions given after each. Make other changes that may be necessary but do not change the meaning of each sentence. ***ICSE Specimen Paper 2017***

(i) The memory is so vivid that I will never forget it.
(Use too in place of so)
(a) The memory is too vivid to be forgotten.
(b) The memory is too vivid for me to forget.
(c) The memory is too vivid that I cannot forget it.
(d) The memory is too vivid for me to have forgotten.

(ii) That need not happen.
(Rewrite: using does)
(a) That does not need to have happened.
(b) Does that need to have happened?
(c) That does need not happened.
(d) That does not happen.

(iii) Food and sleep were all we cared about.
(Begin: All....)
(a) All we care about was sleep or food.
(b) All we care about is food and sleep.
(c) All we cared about was food and sleep.
(d) All we cared about was food or sleep.

(iv) We sat there face to face with our accuser.
(Begin: There.............)
(a) There we sat face to face with our accuser.
(b) There we sat with our accuser.
(c) There we sat with the accuser while facing each other.
(d) There face to face we sat with our accuser.

(v) Herbert consulted his parents before accepting the job offer.
(Begin: Herbert did not ....)
(a) Herbert forgets to consult his parents before accepting the job offer.
(b) Herbert did not forget to consult his parents after accepting the job offer.
(c) Herbert did not forget to consult his parents before accepting the job offer.
(d) Herbert had forgotten to consult his parents before accepting the job offer.

(vi) It was the last time he saw his wife.
(Begin: Never.......................)
(a) Never did he see his wife after that.
(b) Never he has seen his wife since last time.
(c) Never has he seen his wife since last time.
(d) Never was he able to see his wife since last time.

10. Rewrite the following sentences according to the instructions given after each one. Make other changes that may be necessary but do not change the meaning of the given sentence. ***ICSE 2016***

(i) The book was so interesting that I could not put it down.
(Begin : The book was too ....)
(a) The book was too interesting to put down.
(b) The book was too interesting to be putting down.
(c) The book was too interesting.
(d) The book was too interesting to be put down.

(ii) The Principal said, "All the prizes will be distributed tomorrow."
(Begin : The Principal said that ....)
(a) The Principal said that the prize distribution would be done the next day.
(b) The Principal exclaimed that the prize distribution will be done the next day.
(c) The Principal told that the prize distribution would be done the next day.
(d) The Principal said that the prize distribution will be done tomorrow.

(iii) Last night's dinner was cooked for us by father.
(Begin : Father ....)
(a) Father cooked for us last night.
(b) Father cooked dinner last night for us.
(c) Father cooked dinner for us last night.
(d) Father decided to cook dinner for us last night.

(iv) Inspite of having high fever, the girl came to school.
(Begin : Despite ....)
(a) Despite of having high fever, the girl came to school.
(b) Despite of high fever, the girl come to school.
(c) Despite having high fever, the girl will come to school.
(d) Despite having high fever, the girl came to school.

(v) I prefer going out with friends to staying alone at home.
(Begin : I would rather ....)
(a) I would rather go out with friends than stay alone at home.
(b) I would rather go out with friends to staying alone at home.
(c) I would rather go out with friends over staying alone at home.
(d) I would rather go out with friends than staying alone at home.

(vi) This is the funniest movie I have ever seen.
(Begin : Never ....)
(a) Never did I see such a funny movie.
(b) Never had I seen such a funny movie.
(c) Never have I seen such a funny movie.
(d) Never will I see such a funny movie.

11. Re-write the following sentences according to the instructions given after each one. Make other changes that may be necessary but do not change the meaning of the given sentence. ***ICSE 2015 Modified***

(i) Arun gave Ramesh some excellent advice.
(Begin: Ramesh was ....)
(a) Ramesh gave some excellent advice to Arun.
(b) Ramesh was given some excellent advice by Arun.
(c) Ramesh was to give some excellent advice to Arun.
(d) Ramesh was given some excellent advice on the behalf of Arun.

(ii) Has Alia written to you?
(Begin: Have you ....)
(a) Have you received the letter/letters from Alia?
(b) Have you received any letter/letters on the behalf of Alia?
(c) Have you received any letter/letters from Alia?
(d) Have you received any letter/letters?

(iii) The monsoon is the best season in our country.
(Re-write using 'good' ....)
(a) No other season is as good as monsoon in our country.
(b) Our country saw many good seasons while the best of all is monsoon.
(c) Many other seasons are as good as monsoon.
(d) Our country saw many good seasons still the best of all is monsoon.

(iv) Harish was so tired that he could not keep his eyes open.
(Begin: Harish was too ....)
(a) Harish was too tired to open his eyes.
(b) Harish was too tired to keep his eyes open.
(c) Harish is too tired to even keep his eyes open.
(d) Harish was too tired that he can keep his eyes open.

(v) Father said to Sunil, "I can help you with your homework."
(Begin: Father told Sunil ....)
(a) Father told Sunil that he could help him with his homework.
(b) Father told Sunil that he can help him with his homework.
(c) Father said to Sunil that he could help him with his homework.
(d) Father says to Sunil that he can help him with his homework.

(vi) Naresh goes to a school which has over a thousand students.
(Begin: There ....)
(a) There is a school with over a thousand students and Naresh is one of them.
(b) There is a school which has over a thousand students and Naresh is one of them.
(c) There is a school wherein Naresh studies and it has over a thousand students.
(d) Both (a) and (b)

12. Re-write the following sentences according to the instructions given after each one. Make other changes that may be necessary, but do not change the meaning of the given sentence. ***ICSE 2014 Modified***

(i) The bee is more industrious than all other creatures.
(Use 'most industrious')
(a) The bee is the most industrious of all.
(b) The bee is the most industrious.
(c) The bee is the most industrious of all creatures.
(d) The bee is most industrious of creatures.

(ii) The old woman was too slow to catch the bus.
(Begin : The old woman was so ....)
(a) The old woman was so slow to catch the bus.
(b) The old woman was so slow that she could never catch the bus.
(c) The old woman was so slow that she could not catch the bus.
(d) The old woman was so slow to not catch the bus.

(iii) "I'll do it tomorrow," he promised.
(Re-write in indirect speech)
(a) He promised to do it the next day.
(b) He promised that he will do it the next day.
(c) He promised that he would do it tomorrow.
(d) He promised to do it tomorrow.

(iv) Though Reema got an expensive gift, she was not happy.
(Begin : In spite ....)
(a) In spite getting an expensive gift, Reema was not happy.
(b) In spite of getting an expensive gift, Reema was happy.
(c) In spite of getting an expensive gift, Reema did not seem happy.
(d) In spite of getting an expensive gift, Reema was not happy.

(v) I prefer reading a book to watching a movie.
(Begin : I would rather ....)
(a) I would rather read a book to watch a movie.
(b) I would rather read a book over watching a movie.
(c) I would rather read a book than watch a movie.
(d) I would rather read a book and watch a movie.

(vi) I have never seen Mr. Roy lose his temper.
(Begin : Never ....)
(a) Never have I seen Mr. Roy lose his temper.
(b) Never will I see Mr. Roy lose his temper.
(c) Never had I seen Mr. Roy lose temper.
(d) Never am I going to see Mr. Roy lose his temper.

(vii) She found your keys in the garage.
(Begin : The keys ....)
(a) The keys are to be found in the garage by her.
(b) The keys will be found in the garage by her.
(c) The keys were going to be found in the garage by her.
(d) The keys were found in the garage by her.

13. Re-write the following sentences according to the instructions given after each one. Make other changes that may be necessary but do not change the meaning of the given sentence. ***ICSE 2013 Modified***

(i) These windows need cleaning again.
(Begin : These windows will ....)
(a) These windows will have to be cleaned again.
(b) These windows need to be cleaned again.
(c) These windows are going to be cleaned again.
(d) These windows will be cleaned again.

(ii) It doesn't matter which chemical you put into the mixture first, the results will be the same.
(Use : difference)
(a) It doesn't make any difference which chemical you put into the mixture first, the results will be the same.
(b) It makes any difference which chemical you put into the mixture first, the results will be the same.
(c) It doesn't make much difference which chemical you put into the mixture first, the results will be the same.
(d) It doesn't make a difference which chemical you put into the mixture first, the results will be the same.

(iii) Who does this pen belong to?
(Begin : Do you know ....)
(a) Do you know to who does this pen belong?
(b) Do you know to whom does this pen belong?
(c) Do you know to which man does this pen belong?
(d) Do you know to whom does this pen belong to?

(iv) Heavy rain has caused the cancellation of the outdoor garden party.
(Begin : Due ....)
(a) Due to heavy rains, the outdoor garden party was cancelled.
(b) Due to heavy rains, the outdoor garden party is cancelled.
(c) Due to heavy rains, the outdoor garden party will be cancelled.
(d) Due to heavy rains, the outdoor garden party has been cancelled.

(v) I've never seen so many people in this building before.
(Begin : This is ....)
(a) This is the first time when I am seeing so many people in this building.
(b) This is the first time when I saw so many people in this building.
(c) This is the first time when I will be seeing so many people in this building.
(d) This is the first time when I will see many people in this building.

(vi) If we light the fire, the rescuers will see us.
(Begin : We will ....)
(a) We will see the rescuers if we light the fire.
(b) We will be seen by the rescuers if we light the fire.
(c) We will be seen if we light the fire.
(d) We are going to see the rescuers if we light the fire.

(vii) Only a few books were remaining on the shelf when we left.
(Begin : Most ....)
(a) Most of the books are removed from the shelf when we left.
(b) Most of the books were removed from the shelf when we left.
(c) Most of the books are going to be removed from the shelf when we left.
(d) Most of the books need removal from the shelf when we left.

14. Re-write the following sentences according to the instructions given after each one. Make other changes that may be necessary but do not change the meaning of the given sentence. ***ICSE 2012 Modified***

(i) My mother left a month ago.
(Begin : It has ....)
(a) It has been a month since my mother left.
(b) It has been a month to my mother leaving.
(c) It has been a month when my mother left.
(d) It has been a month since my mother had gone.

(ii) Anil was wrong to lose his temper.
(Begin : Anil ought ....)
(a) Anil ought not to lose his temper.
(b) Anil ought to lose his temper.
(c) Anil ought not to lose temper.
(d) Anil ought to lose temper.

(iii) Rajiv said to Arjun, "Is this the book you were reading yesterday?"
(Begin : Rajiv asked Arjun if ....)
(a) Rajiv asked Arjun if this was the book he is reading the day before.
(b) Rajiv asked Arjun if that was the book he read the day before.
(c) Rajiv asked Arjun if this was the book he had been reading the day before.
(d) Rajiv asked Arjun if that was the book he had been reading the day before.

(iv) Only a foolish person would be taken in by this trick.
(Begin : None ....)
(a) None other than a foolish person would be taken from this trick.
(b) None other than a foolish person will be taken by this trick.
(c) None other than a foolish person would be taken in by this trick.
(d) None but a foolish person would be taken in by this trick.

(v) Everybody has heard of Gandhiji.
(Begin: Who ....?)
(a) Who heard of Gandhiji?
(b) Who will not have heard of Gandhiji?
(c) Who is that who has not heard of Gandhiji?
(d) Who has not heard of Gandhiji?

(vi) He will issue the cheque only when he hears from the head office.
(Begin : On ...., ...)
(a) On being heard from the head office, he will issue the cheque.
(b) On hearing from the head office, he issued the cheque.
(c) On hearing from the head office, he will issue the cheque.

(c) On hearing from the head office, he will issue the cheque.

(d) On hearing from the head office, he is going to issue the cheque.

(vii) Father will send you a message if his flight is cancelled.

(Begin : Should ....)

(a) Should the flight get cancelled, father will send you a message.

(b) Should the flight gets cancelled, father is going to send you a message.

(c) Should the flight gets cancelled, father sends you a message.

(d) Should the flight cancel, father will send you a message.

15. Re-write the following sentences according to the instructions given after each one . Make other changes that may be necessary but do not change the meaning of the given sentence. ***ICSE 2011 Modified***

(i) This horse is better trained than yours.

(Begin : Your ....)

(a) Your horse is well trained as this.

(b) Your horse is not well trained as this.

(c) Your horse is not as well trained as this.

(d) Your horse is such as well trained as this.

(ii) The thief ran so fast that the police could not catch him.

(Re-write using : too ....)

(a) The thief ran too fast for the police to catch him.

(b) The thief ran too fast such that the police could catch him.

(c) The thief ran too fast for the police.

(d) The thief runs too fast for the police to catch him.

(iii) Her attitude often annoys me.

(Re-write using : annoyance ....)

(a) Her attitude often causes annoyance.

(b) Her attitude is the cause annoyance to me.

(c) Her attitude often causes annoyance to me.

(d) Her attitude often results in annoyance.

(iv) There is no success without effort.

(Begin : Whenever ....)

(a) Whenever you make an effort, you get success.

(b) Whenever you will make an effort, you will get success.

(c) Whenever you made an effort, you succeeded.

(d) Whenever anyone makes an effort, he/she get success.

(v) "Please teach me to cycle", she asked her brother.

(Re-write in indirect form)

(a) She requested her brother to teach her to cycle.

(b) She asked her brother to teach her to cycle.

(c) She told her brother to teach her to cycle.

(d) She commanded her brother to teach her to cycle.

(vi) The peasants regarded him as a thief and called him a villain.

(End : .... the peasants)

(a) He is regarded as a thief and is called a villain by the peasants.

(b) He was regarded as a thief and called a villain by the peasants.

(c) He was to be regarded as a thief and called a villain by the peasants.

(d) He is a thief and a villain according to the peasants.

16. Re-write the following sentences according to the instructions given after each one. Make other changes that may be necessary, but not change the meaning of the given sentence. ***ICSE 2010 Modified***

(i) His arrogance was the cause of his losing the election.

(Re-write the sentence using 'arrogant')

(a) He lost the election because he was arrogant.

(b) He loses the election as he was arrogant.

(c) He will lose the election because he was arrogant.

(d) He lost the election because of his arrogant.

(ii) If you are not a member, you cannot borrow books.

(Begin : Only ....)

(a) Only members are allowed to borrow books.

(b) Only some members are allowed to borrow books.

(c) Only all members are allowed to borrow books.

(d) Only members are those who are allowed to borrow books.

(iii) It is a pity our vacation is not longer.

(Begin : I wish ....)

(a) I wish if our vacation was longer.

(b) I wish for our vacation to be longer.

(c) I wish our vacation was longer.

(d) both (b) and (c)

(iv) Raju did not complete the exercise on time.
(Re-write the sentence adding a question tag)
(a) Raju could finish the exercise in time, couldn't he?
(b) Raju did finish the exercise in time, could he?
(c) Raju could finish the exercise in time, didn't he?
(d) Raju didn't finish the exercise in time, did he?

(v) Rohan was so terrified of being left alone in the house that he started screaming.
(Begin : So ....)
(a) So terrified Rohan was of being left alone in the house that he started screaming.
(b) So terrified was Rohan that he started screaming of being left alone in the house.
(c) So terrified is Rohan of being left alone in the house that he starts screaming.
(d) So terrified was Rohan of being left alone in the house that he started screaming.

(vi) The teacher asked, "How many of you think the answer is correct?"
(Re-write the sentence using indirect speech)
(a) The teacher desired to know how many of us thought that the answer was correct.
(b) The teacher asked to know how many of us thought that the answer was correct.
(c) The teacher wanted to know how many of us thought that the answer was correct.
(d) The teacher suggested to know how many of us thought that the answer was correct.

(vii) Sunil is the fastest runner in the school.
(End : .... as Sunil.)
(a) No other runner in the school is as fast as Sunil.
(b) No other runner in the school is faster than Sunil.
(c) No other runner in the school can win over Sunil.
(d) No other runner in the school is fast as Sunil.

Subjective Questions

1. Re-write the following sentences according to the instructions given after each one. Make other changes that may be necessary but do not change the meaning of the given sentence. ***ICSE 2009 Modified***

(i) Study hard now or you will regret it.
(Begin : Unless ....)

Ans. Unless you study hard, you will regret it.

(ii) The boy asked, "Why are you lying on the road in this manner?"
(Begin : The boy asked why he ....)

Ans. The boy asked why he was lying on the road in that manner.

(iii) Megha is too tall to crawl under the table.
(Begin : Megha is so ....)

Ans. Megha is so tall that she cannot crawl under the table.

(iv) He arrived in school on time even though he stopped for a bite on the way.
(Use 'In spite of' instead of even though)

Ans. In spite of stopping for a bite on the way, he arrived in school on time.

(v) She opened the kitchen door and a cockroach ran out.
(End with 'cockroach')

Ans. As she opened the kitchen door, she saw a running cockroach.

(vi) Arjun was a better speaker than his brother.
(Begin : His brother ....)

Ans. His brother was not as good a speaker as Arjun.

(vii) Asha missed her examination because of her illness.
(Begin : Her illness ....)

Ans. Her illness caused Asha to miss her examination.

(viii) As soon as the curtain came down, the applause rang out.
(Begin : No sooner ....)

Ans. No sooner the curtain came down than the applause rang out.

2. Re-write the following sentences according to the instructions given after each one. Make other changes that may be necessary but do not change the meaning of the given sentence. ***ICSE 2008 Modified***

(i) "Have you walked alone, this long distance today?" he asked Sumita.
(Begin : He asked Sumita if ....)

Ans. He asked Sumita if she had walked alone that long distance that day.

(ii) The detective interrogated the suspect closely for over three hours.
(Begin : The suspect ....)

Ans. The suspect was interrogated closely for over three hours by the detective.

(iii) I suddenly realised that the room was too small for the three of us to share.
(Begin : I suddenly realised that the room was so ....)

Ans. I suddenly realised that the room was so small that it could not be shared by the three of us.

(iv) In spite of all her efforts, Susan did not succeed.
(*Begin : Despite* ....)

Ans. Despite all her efforts, Susan did not succeed.

(v) As soon as the bell rang, the children rushed out of class.
(*Begin : No sooner* ....)

Ans. No sooner did the bell ring than the children rushed out of class.

(vi) Sachin stood first in class and he also excelled at debate.
(*Begin : Not only* ....)

Ans. Not only did Sachin stand first in the class but also excelled at debate.

(vii) She was the only person capable of being House Captain.
(*Use : capability* ....)

Ans. She was the only person with the capability of being the House Captain.

(viii) Rohan was the tallest boy in the basketball team.
(*Re-write using 'taller'* ....)

Ans. Rohan was taller than any other boy in the basketball team.

3. Re-write the following sentences according to the instructions given after each one. Make other changes that may be necessary, but do not change the meaning of the given sentence. ***ICSE 2007 Modified***

(i) Anne paid a heavy price for her recklessness.
(*Begin : It* ....)

Ans. It was a heavy price that Anne paid for her recklessness.

(ii) No sooner had Ram narrated the story than he was praised.
(*Begin : Hardly* ....)

Ans. Hardly had Ram narrated the story when he was praised.

(iii) Tanuja is a very friendly girl and is always cheerful.
(*Begin : Besides* ....)

Ans. Besides being very friendly, Tanuja is always cheerful.

(iv) They had to put off the garden party because of the heavy rain.
(*Begin : The heavy* ....)

Ans. The heavy rain made them put off the garden party.

(v) Margaret said to me, "Please do not forget to meet me tomorrow."
(*Begin : I was* ....)

Ans. I was requested by Margaret not to forget to meet her the next day.

(vi) In spite of my warning Dev, he ignored me.
(*Begin : Though* ....)

Ans. Though I had warned Dev, he ignored me.

(vii) The business talks failed because neither side was willing to compromise.
(*Begin : Since* ....).

Ans. Since neither side was willing to compromise, the business talks failed.

(viii) They were very afraid and so they could not speak.
(*Begin : Being* ....)

Ans. Being very afraid, they could not speak.

4. Re-write the following sentences according to the instructions given after each one. Make other changes that may be necessary but do not change the meaning of the given sentence. ***ICSE 2006 Modified***

(i) As soon as the Chief Guest arrived, the band started playing.
(*Begin : No sooner* ....)

Ans. No sooner did the Chief Guest arrive than the band started playing.

or

No sooner had the Chief Guest arrived than the band started playing.

(ii) He went to the library and to the bank.
(*Begin : Not only* ....)

Ans. Not only did he go to the library but also to the bank.

(iii) Though he is very poor, he helps others in need.
(*Begin : In spite* ....)

Ans. In spite of his poverty, he helps others in need.

(iv) He does not intend to leave the company.
(*Use : intention*)

Ans. He has no intention of leaving the company.

(v) "Do you want some more ice-cream or a slice of cake?" asked my aunt.
(*Begin : My aunt asked* ....)

Ans. My aunt asked me if/whether I wanted some more ice-cream or a slice of cake.

(vi) They are painting a mural on the front wall.
(*Begin : A mural* ....)

Ans. A mural is being painted on the front wall by them.

(vii) Tansen was the best singer in Akbar's court.

(Use : better ....)

Ans. Tansen was better than any other singer in Akbar's court.

(viii) You remembered to buy a loaf of bread, didn't you?

(Begin : You didn't ....)

Ans. You didn't forget to buy a loaf of bread, did you?

5. Re-write the following sentences according to the instructions given after each one. Make other changes that may be necessary but do not change the meaning of the given sentence.

ICSE 2005 Modified

(i) Jasdeep has probably forgotten his mother's birthday.

(Begin : In ....)

Ans. In all probability, Jasdeep has forgotten his mother's birthday.

(ii) Mr Sharma advised the children not to go out in the cold.

(End with : "................................", said Mr Sharma)

Ans. "Do not go out in the cold", said Mr Sharma.

(iii) For more information, please contact the secretary of the club.

(Begin : Should ....)

Ans. Should you need more information, contact the secretary of the club.

(iv) He could not take part in the singing competition as he had a sore throat.

(Use : prevented)

Ans. His sore throat had prevented him from taking part in the singing competition.

(v) Ritika returned to school a week ago.

(Begin : It has been ....)

Ans. It has been a week since Ritika returned to school.

(vi) She was beautiful and humble.

(Begin : Not only ....)

Ans. Not only was she beautiful but also humble.

(vii) Both the players are not adequately prepared for the tournament.

(Begin : Neither ....)

Ans. Neither of the players is adequately prepared for the tournament.

(viii) A fragrant flower is the loveliest creation of nature.

(Begin : No other ....)

Ans. No other creation of nature is as lovely as a fragrant flower.

SECTION TEST

10 Verbs (Verbs Form)

1. Fill in the blanks in the passage given below with the appropriate form of the verb given in brackets. Do not write the passage but write the verbs in correct order.

As I entered the room, the first thing that **(1)** ………… ***(strike)*** me as odd, was the candle still **(2)** ………… ***(burn)*** on the table. The curtains had been **(3)** ………… ***(draw)*** back and the room was bright. No one in their right minds **(4)** ………… ***(keep)*** a candle **(5)** ………… ***(burn)*** in broad daylight. The large French windows overlooked the lawn **(6)** ………… ***(bath)*** in sunlight. Marie had probably **(7)** ………… ***(catch)*** my odd stare at the table and so **(8)** ………… ***(move)*** over and blew the candle out. She then glanced at the window and went over to open them.

2. Fill in the blanks in the passage given below with the appropriate form of the verb given in brackets. Do not write the passage but write the verbs in correct order.

After they **(1)** ………… ***(walk)*** for a while, they **(2)** ………… ***(see)*** an isolated cottage. They **(3)** ………… ***(peep)*** through the broken window, **(4)** ………… ***(look)*** for someone who **(5)** ………… ***(guide)*** them back to the main road. They **(6)** ………… ***(find)*** that the cottage **(7)** ………… ***(be)*** dirty, cobwebs **(8)** ………… ***(hang)*** across the roof and it seemed to be unoccupied. They were disappointed.

3. Fill in the blanks in the passage given below with the appropriate form of the verb given in brackets. Do not write the passage but write the verbs in correct order.

One day, I **(1)** ………… ***(be)*** in the lunch line, and there I saw a pile of apples. The teacher-in-charge **(2)** ………… ***(stare)*** at me and said, "Just **(3)** ………… ***(take)*** one. God **(4)** ………… ***(watch)***". So, I **(5)** ………… ***(take)*** an apple, and the tine **(6)** ………… ***(move)*** along. At the next table, there **(7)** ………… ***(be)*** a pile of chocolate chip cookies. I **(8)** ………… ***(not know)*** what to do. "Psst," the kid behind me whispered. Take all you want.

4. Fill in the blanks in the passage given below with the appropriate form of the verb given in brackets. Do not write the passage but write the verbs in correct order.

The other day, we **(1)** ………… ***(discuss)*** the setting up of a Debating Club in our school. We **(2)** ………… ***(talk)*** about the club and how many students **(3)** ………… ***(be)*** interested in you. Then we (4) ………… ***(begin)*** to talk about the rules and regulations **(5)** ………… ***(govern)*** the club. None of us could **(6)** ………… ***(agree)*** and we began **(7)** ………… ***(argue)***. Finally, our English teacher **(8)** ………… ***(have)*** to be informed, and she came and broke up the meeting.

5. Fill in the blanks in the passage given below with the appropriate form of the verb given in brackets. Do not write the passage but write the verbs in correct order.

We decided to travel by car and **(1)** ………… ***(leave)*** the house early. We **(2)** ………… ***(be)*** on the road for two hours when our car **(3)** ………… ***(hit)*** a stone that **(4)** ………… ***(he)*** in the middle of the road. The car **(5)** ………… ***(go)*** off the road but we **(6)**

11 Prepositions

1. Fill in each blank with a suitable word. (Do not write the sentence)

(i) The school board then agreed ………… the course of action.

(ii) The benefits ………… providing students with lunch at school, far outweigh the logistical challenges.

(iii) Most students benefit ………… interactions with fellow students outside school hours.

(iv) The latest set of losses resulted ………… the captain losing her job.

(v) Celine clashed …… her boss in the last meeting.

(vi) They clashed ……… the tone of the presentation.

(vii) I forgot ………… buy the medicine in time.

(viii) I completely forgot …… the strike the next day.

2. Fill in each blank with a suitable word. (Do not write the sentence)

(i) The new supervisor is not very popular ….. her direct reports.

(ii) Most people are known …. the company they enjoy.

(iii) The manager impressed ….. his subordinates, the need for more sales.

(iv) Bamana was so sick after the party, that the doctor had to be called ….

(v) A cholera epidemic has broken ..... in the state.
(vi) Conviction will carry you ..... difficult times.
(vii) Jakob is very good .... repairing things.
(viii) The lead runner was running so fast that the rest of the field couldn't keep ..... with it.

3. Fill in each blank with a suitable word. (Do not write the sentence)
(i) She turned ...... the offer to work at the factory.
(ii) To everyone's surprise, he turned ...... at the party.
(iii) He broke .... in the middle of his speech at the function.
(iv) The burglars broke .... the house when the family was away.
(v) He agreed to carry .... the manager's orders.
(vi) Sita's daughter carried .... the family business when Sita went abroad.
(vii) He ran .... from home at the age of ten.
(viii) I ran .... my old friend in the market place.

4. Fill in each blank with a suitable word. (Do not write the sentence)
(i) If we set ...... early, we can return before sunset.
(ii) He left the company for good and set .... his own business.
(iii) The teacher jumped .... a conclusion and punished the child.
(iv) Ramesh jumped .... my offer of a job.
(v) I am a simple man and have no use .... much money.
(vi) My father lost the use .... his right arm in an accident.
(vii) Rahul decided to carry .... with tennis and give up ohlev ball.
(viii) Dinanath is a good worker and is always ready to carry .... his masters orders.

5. Fill in each blank with a suitable word. (Do not write the sentence)
(i) We failed to agree .... a common plan of action.
(ii) When I explained my plan of action to him, he did not agree .... me.
(iii) The Principal does not approve .... indiscipline.
(iv) I need his approval .... I can start the work.
(v) An explanation about the evolution of species is given .... Chapter 2.
(vi) The answers to these questions are given .... page 44.
(vii) One fine day, he set ...... on his adventurous trip.
(viii) As soon as he entered the room, he set .... his heavy bag.

12 Conjuction

1. Join the following sentences to make one complete sentence without using and, but or, so
(i) She is pretty. She is intelligent.
(a) She is pretty as well as intelligent.
(b) She is pretty beside intelligent.
(c) She is pretty also intelligent.
(d) She is pretty much intelligent.
(ii) Martin is not tall. His father is not tall.
(a) Neither Martin nor his father is tall.
(b) Either Martin or his father is tall.
(c) Neither Martin or his father is tall.
(d) Either Martin nor his father is tall.
(iii) They wanted to win. They worked hard for that reason.
(a) They worked hard to win.
(b) They work hard to win.
(c) They worked harder to win.
(d) They worked hardest to win.
(iv) Jane is quite friendly. Her brother is rather reserved.
(a) Jane is quite friendly while her brother is rather reserved.
(b) Jane is quite friendly whereas her brother is rather reserved.
(c) Jane is quite friendly also her brother is rather reserved.
(d) Jane is quite friendly whether her brother is rather reserved.

13 Transformation of Sentences

1. Rewrite the following sentences according to the instructions given after each. Make other changes that may be necessary but do not change the meaning of each sentence.
(i) What a difficult question it was!
(Begin : It ....)
(a) It was a difficult question.
(b) It was a very difficult question.
(c) It was not a very difficult question.
(d) It was not a difficult question.
(ii) You are not supposed to create any disturbance here.
(Begin : Are you ....)

(a) Are you not supposed to create any disturbance here?
(b) Are you supposed to create any disturbance here?
(c) Are you creating any disturbance here?
(d) Are you not creating any disturbance here?

(iii) Can the cat ever sing? (Begin : The cat ....)
(a) The cat can ever sing. (b) The cat can sing.
(c) The cat can never sing. (d) None of the above

(iv) He could not parachute down in the Taj Mahal. (Begin : Could ....)
(a) Could he ever parachute down in the Taj Mahal?
(b) Could he never parachute down in the Taj Mahal?
(c) Could he not parachute down in the Taj Mahal?
(d) Could he parachute down in the Taj ahal?

(v) How irritating his voice was! (Use : very)
(a) His voice is very irritating.
(b) His voice was irritating.
(c) His voice was very irritating.
(d) His voice very is irritating.

(vi) How could anybody cool down the sun? (Use : nobody)
(a) Nobody can cool down the sun.
(b) Nobody but could cool down the sun.
(c) Nobody could cool down the sun.
(d) Nobody but can cool down the sun.

(vii) These pieces of furniture are not of superior quality. (Use : inferior)
(a) These pieces of furniture are of inferior quality.
(b) These pieces of furniture is of inferior quality.
(c) These pieces of furniture are inferior.
(d) These pieces of furniture is inferior.

(viii) All these instruments were not known to us earlier. (Use : unknown)
(a) All these instruments are unknown to us earlier.
(b) All these instruments are not unknown to us earlier.
(c) All these instruments were unknown to us earlier.
(d) All these instruments were not unknown to us earlier.

(ix) No one could infer what his last lines meant. (Begin : It ....)
(a) It is difficult for anyone to infer the meaning of his last lines.
(b) It was difficult for no one to infer the meaning of his last lines.
(c) It was difficult for anyone to infer the meaning of his last lines.
(d) It is difficult for no one to infer the meaning of his last lines.

(x) Everybody will admit that he did his best. (Use : deny)
(a) No one will not deny that he did his best.
(b) No one will deny that he did his best.
(c) Everyone will deny that he did his best.
(d) Everyone will not deny that he did his best.

(xi) There have been people who have already written about this earlier. (Begin : You are not the ....)
(a) You are not the only person to write about this.
(b) You are not the last person to write about this.
(c) You are not the former person to write about this.
(d) You are not the first person to write about this.

(xii) I am listening to such a miraculous and enchanting music for the first time. (Begin : I have not ....)
(a) I have not listened to such a miraculous and enchanting music before.
(b) I have not listen to such a miraculous and enchanting music before.
(c) I have not been listening to such a miraculous and enchanting music before.
(d) All of the above

(xiii) Can you imagine how the people at places having – 24°C temperature survive? (Begin : You .....)
(a) You can imagine how people at places having – 24 °C temperature survive.
(b) You can imagine how people at places not having – 24 °C temperature survive.
(c) You cannot imagine how people at places having – 24 °C temperature survive.
(d) None of the above

(xiv) He never expected to receive such a nice gift from his friends. (Begin : It was ....)
(a) It was beyond him to receive such a nice gift from his friends.
(b) It was beyond his expectation to receive such a nice gift from his friends.
(c) It was beside his expected to receive such a nice gift from his friends.
(d) It was beside his expectation to receive such a nice gift from his friends.

(xv) Radhika is unable to accept this shocking news. (Use : cannot)
(a) Radhika cannot accept this shocking news.
(b) Radhika cannot deny this shocking news.
(c) Radhika cannot reject this shocking news.
(d) Radhika cannot criticise this shocking news.

ICSE Fully Solved

SAMPLE PAPER 01

Time : 2 hrs
Marks : 80

English Language Paper 1

General Instructions

1. Answer to this paper must be written on the paper provided separately.
2. You will not be allowed to write during first 15 minutes. This time is to be spent in reading the question paper.
3. The time given at the head of this paper is the time allowed for writing the answers.
4. Attempt all five questions.
5. The intended marks for questions or parts of questions are given in brackets [ ].
6. You are advised to spend not more than 30 minutes in answering Question 1 and 20 minutes in answering Question 2.

Question 1

(Do not spend more than 30 minute on this question)

Write a composition (300-350 words) on any one of the following. **[20]**

(i) Write an original short story entitled 'Treasure Hunting'.

(ii) Imagine that you have witnessed a fire that razed an area near your colony. Narrate the incident in your own words. What were the sounds and sights that you experienced during the incident? How did the experience make you feel?

(iii) How do you prefer to spend your spare time? Describe your favourite activity. What are the sounds, sights, smells and feelings that you associate with the activity?

(iv) 'Money causes more harm than good.'
Express your views either for or against this statement.

(v) Study the picture given below. Write a story, a description or an account of what it suggests to you. Your composition may be about the subject of the picture or you may take suggestions from it; however, there must be a clear connection between the picture and your composition.

Question 2

Select any one of the following.
(Do not spend more than 20 minutes on this question) **[10]**

(i) Though your city attracts a lot of tourists often they are disappointed to see the unruly traffic and the state of the roads. Write a letter to the Municipal Commissioner complaining about the hardships suffered by the visitors.

(ii) Write a letter to your father informing him of your success in winning a prize in a debate competition.

Question 3

(i) You are Richa/ Jatin Mehra, the Head Girl/ Boy of Mother Teresa School, Kochi. Your Principal has asked you to put up a notice, asking House Captains to submit names of volunteers for 'Save Water Campaign' for which a march is to be held on 20th August, 20XX. **[5]**

(ii) Write an e-mail addressing the Principal of the neighbouring school requesting him/ her to send students to participate in the march. **[5]**

Question 4

Read the following passage carefully and answer the questions that follow.

Sher Singh's brother lay in the hut with a severe pain in his stomach. His mother wrung out rags in boiling water and lay them on his stomach. But the pain did not lessen. In fact, he was doubled up with it. Sher Singh knew that he was dying. So, he decided to carry him to a hospital at Kalaghat.

Sher Singh's father could not be traced because he was at that time out with a photographic expedition. He was known as Sher Singh Bahadur because of his **prowess** and hunting skill. Sher Singh's mother took an old sari and made a sling for him to put around his forehead and down his back. She lifted Kunwar, now doubled with pain and put him into it.

It was already evening. All the huts of Laldwani lay in a strong orange glow. Soon, Sher Singh entered the forest. The rough grass was dotted with thorn and sal trees. He took a path rutted with cart wheels. His bare toes disappeared into silk-soft dust. But he stopped at once because of some jungle sense. He saw a cobra contracting and hissing with its hood spreading to show the spectacle mark on the back. He was frozen but the cobra slid off into the matted grass.

Kunwar was twitching with pain and groaning. Sher Singh did not stop. A minute's delay could mean much. Around him lay primeval forest in which the struggle of vegetation and life continued as they had done since the beginning of the world. The jungle was infested with animals and the beasts of prey. After walking a distance, he saw the bear tracks in the dust. Fearing he quickened his pace. Kunwar was **delirious.** Sher Singh's muscles thrilled with piercing pain. He lay against a tree for some rest.

It was then he heard the deluge and squeal of elephants. Below him lay the broad river bed shining like ivory in the moonlight. The elephants had disappeared. Sher Singh crossed the shallow river water. But he was really afraid to cross the second river.

Towards midnight he heard the second river ahead of him. The snow had melted and it was roaring. Unfortunately, the bridge had been washed away. Only a fierce crest of water showed where it lay submerged. He set Kunwar down and gave him some water. Sher Singh, then, gathered grass and plaited it into a rope. He tied the rope round his brother and himself so they would keep together.

Then he entered the water just above the bridge. The river seized and flattened them. At first, he couldn't move but edged slowly finding the split ends of bamboo. The deluge deafened him, timber banged and bruised him. He could not even breathe in the spray and the water was also very cold. He didn't know if his brother lived or died. However, he kept the child's head above the water. Inch by inch, he got along. He was deaf, blinded, frozen, drowned-it went on and on.

When Sher Singh awoke, he found that he was in a bullock cart, then a truck.

"Where have you come from, boy?"

"Laldwani."

"You carried him alone ? Across the river in flood ?"

They were at the hospital.

Sher Singh felt shy to go in the hospital. He had no money. But he laboured all day in loading the coal and bought a little flour, some mustard oil and chillies. Presently the doctor called for him. He himself came out.

"Sher Singh Bahadur, are you here ?"

"My father is not here," replied the boy, with eyes in tears.

"But I am Sher Singh."

"You are the boy who brought the child Kunwar in from Laldwani ?"

"Yes."

Then a smile broke all over the doctor's great, gentle face, so he looked like a brown man. "Sher Singh Bahadur!" he said. "Your brother will live. Come and see."

(i) For each word given below, choose the correct meaning (as used in the passage) from the options provided. **[2]**

1. prowess *(line 10)*
   (a) strength (b) knowledge
   (c) skill (d) ability
2. delirious *(line 30)*
   (a) confused (b) ill
   (c) sensitive (d) dangerous

(ii) Which word in the passage means the opposite of word 'relinquished'? **[1]**

(a) deluge (b) seized
(c) plaited (d) banged

(iii) Answer the following questions briefly in your own words.

(a) What made Sher Singh decide that he must take his brother to hospital if he was to be saved? **[2]**

(b) What was Sher Singh's father known for in his area? **[2]**

(c) Even though Sher Singh hadn't reached the second river, why did he fear to cross? **[2]**

(d) How did the deluge affect Sher Singh? **[2]**

(e) Why did the doctor come out? **[1]**

(iv) In not more than 50 words, describe how Sher Singh carried his brother to the hospital. **[8]**

Question 5

(i) Fill in each of the numbered blanks with the correct form of the word given in brackets. Do not copy the passage but write in correct serial order the word or phrase appropriate to the blank space. **[4]**

Example;

(0) is

One of the defects of our civilisation ***(o)*** .... (be) that it ***(1)*** .... (do not know) what to ***(2)*** .... (do) with its knowledge. Science as we ***(3)*** .... (see) has given us powers fit for gods, yet we ***(4)*** .... (use) them like small children. For example, we ***(5)*** .... (do not know) how to manage our machines. Machines were made to be man's servants, yet he ***(6)*** .... (grow) so dependent on them that they ***(7)*** .... (be) in a fair measure to ***(8)*** .... (become) his master.

(ii) Fill in the blanks with appropriate words. **[4]**

(1) How shall I go .... solving the problem?

(2) She has just come .... a fortune.

(3) Where can we dispose .... this rubbish?

(4) The prisoner broke .... under questioning.

(5) I now call .... the chairman to speak.

(6) It is one of the best collections I have come ....

(7) I can't make .... what he means.

(8) Can we agree .... a course of action?

(iii) Join the following sentences to make one complete sentence ***without using*** **and, but** or **so**. Choose the correct option. **[4]**

(1) One should not borrow money. One should not lend money.

(a) One should not borrow or lend money.

(b) One should neither borrow nor lend money.

(c) One should not borrow money nor lend it.

(d) One should neither borrow or lend money.

(2) There was a heavy traffic. We reached the conference on time.

(a) Though there was heavy traffic we reached the conference on time.

(b) There was heavy traffic, even then we reached the conference on time.

(c) Despite the heavy traffic, we could reach the conference on time.

(d) Although there was heavy traffic, yet we reached the conference on time.

(3) The English teacher gave a novel to Ravi. She wanted him to review it.

(a) The English teacher gave a novel to Ravi so that he could review it.

(b) Ravi was given a novel to review by the English teacher.

(c) The English teacher gave a novel to Ravi to review.

(d) Ravi was given a novel so that he could review it.

(4) I finished my homework. I went to play.

(a) Having finished my home work, I went to play.

(b) After finishing my homework, I went to play.

(c) I went to play after I finished my homework.

(d) As soon as I finished my homework, I went to play.

(iv) Choose the correct option to rewrite the following according to the instructions given after each sentence. **[8]**

(1) If a fire breaks out, use the emergency exit.
(Begin : In case of ....)

(a) In case of a fire breaking out, use the emergency exit.

(b) In case of fire use the emergency exit.

(c) In case of breakout of fire, you need to use the emergency exit.

(d) In case of fire, the emergency exit is to be used.

(2) He succeeded in completing the assignments although he was ill.
(Use : Despite ....)

(a) Despite of being ill, he succeeded in completing the assignments.

(b) Despite of illness, he succeeded in completing the assignments.

(c) Despite his illness, he succeeded in completing the assignments.

(d) Despite being ill, he succeeded in completing the assignments.

(3) Sam did not realise that he had committed an error.

(Begin : Little ………..)

(a) Little did Sam realise that he had committed an error.

(b) Little had Sam realised that he had committed an error.

(c) Little Sam realised that he committed an error.

(d) Little has Sam realised that he has committed an error.

(4) ''How do you dare to remain absent without leave?'' said the teacher to the boy.

(Begin with : The teacher asked the boy how ………..)

(a) The teacher asked the boy how he remained absent without leave.

(b) The teacher asked the boy how he has dared to remain absent without leave.

(c) The teacher asked the boy how he dare remain absent without leave.

(d) The teacher asked the boy how he dared to remain absent without leave.

(5) Amazing discoveries have been made by the explorers.

(Begin with : Explorers ………..)

(a) Explorers have made amazing discoveries.

(b) Explorers made discoveries that are amazing

(c) Explorers have made discoveries that amaze people

(d) Explorers made amazing discoveries.

(6) Unfortunately, he failed in the first attempt.

(Use : 'succeed' instead of 'failed')

(a) Fortunately, he could succeed in the first attempt.

(b) Unfortunately, he did not succeed in the first attempt.

(c) Unfortunately, he has not been able to succeed in the first attempt.

(d) Unfortunately, he could not succeed in the first attempt.

(7) Do they believe in the existence of God?

(End with : 'exists')

(a) Do they not believe that God exists?

(b) Do they believe that God exists?

(c) Do God exists?

(d) Can you believe that God exists?

(8) The price of milk has risen recently.

(End with : 'milk')

(a) There is a price rise in the case of milk.

(b) There is a rise of the price of milk.

(c) There is a rise in the price of milk.

(d) There has been a rise in the price of milk.

Answers

1. (i) **Treasure Hunting**

Siya and Aarohi were digging in their backyard when their spades hit a hard, wooden object. The girls' house stood in a once deserted area, a famous place for pirates to hide their stolen treasures. Their relatives had often teased them of living over treasures, but Siya and Aarohi never dreamt of anything of the sort.

When the girls began their playful digging in their backyard, they had not expected to find anything. So, they were highly excited by their present find. In order to not damage the object, both girls went down on hands and knees to gently uncover the object. Finding something like this in their backyard was too incredible to believe!

As they brushed the coarse grains of sand away from what resembled the lid of a box, they saw the words 'Redhound' inscribed in bold capital letters on it. When the box was finally loose, they saw that it had carvings along the sides and on its lid. They opened it, hoping to find gold, pearls and diamonds. Unfortunately, they found a whole pile of old letters tied neatly in a bunch. Siya searched deeper into the box and found a ruby ring and a gold necklace. Even though it was not much, the girls rushed into their house to tell their parents of the good news

The following day, some archaeologists were called to the site. After various observations and tests, they managed to say that the box was indeed a rare treasure. The letters were written by a pirate captive who lived almost two hundred years ago and they told of how he lost the woman he loved.

Since the girls had found the box in their backyard, they could keep their find. Siya and Aarohi could not be happier. Their parents were also happy for them.

(ii) **A Fire**

I had never seen a house on fire before, only filmed reports of it on the television. So, one evening when I heard the siren screams of a few fire-engines rushing past my house, I dashed into the street and joined a growing crowd of curious people. Even at a distance, I could recognise that the affected houses were in an area where one of my acquaintance lived.

What a terrible scene greeted my eyes! The fire was raging through the shabbily built houses. Flames leaped up hungrily to devour the wooden sheds. Every now and then tongues of fire would shoot up almost skyhigh, sprinkling bright red sparks of fire about. Fiery wooden beams crashed and glowed brightly. Thick black smoke spread all around.

Dozens of firemen from the four fire-engines were engaged in putting out the fire. The rushing water from several hoses soaked the houses but it did not seem to have any effect on the flames. Soon, a few firemen with hoses in their hands were seen climbing up tall ladders of the fire-engines. The continuous flooding from the top finally brought the fire under control. Where it had been red there was only black — the charred remains of ruined houses.

While all eyes were transfixed on the inferno, the plight of the victims did not escape the eyes of the spectators. Firemen were seen dragging wailing women away from the burning houses to a safe area. Frightened children clutched to their mothers. Some of the men simply stared speechlessly as they witnessed their homes reduced to ashes.

It took only thirty minutes before the whole area was razed to the ground. No one could salvage anything. The only consolation was the fact that no lives were sacrificed. It was a heart wrenching incident that I witnessed. I wish I had never seen it. You never know what is going to happen in the very next moment! May God bless us all and keeps everyone safe!

(iii) As a student, I am quite busy on weekdays. However, at weekends, I have much free time. In that time, I like playing some sports such as badminton or tennis with my friends. Sports not only makes me stronger but also connects me with my friends. We sometimes go bicycle riding also.

Another thing I like to do in my free time is gardening with my mother. She plants a fair bit of flowers and I enjoy helping her take care of them. It is a pleasure to feel the soil, prune the plants, remove the weeds and do the little things that help the plants grow better. It always fills me with wonder to watch seedlings germinate, sprout leaves and eventually grow to produce beautiful flowers.

Pottering around in the garden also taught me many things about the insects, butterflies, snails, caterpillars, centipedes, millipedes and other small creatures that inhabit the place. These creatures are mostly harmless and watching them go about their 'chores' always fascinates me.

Other than these, I also like to read to books in my spare time. I have a big bookshelf with many kinds of books but I prefer science books. Through these books, my knowledge is gradually increased. I also love to listen to music. Sometimes, I dance when listening to my favorite songs. Music really paints my life. Last but not the least, I spend my free time on surfing on Internet. I can chat with my friends or log on websites to read online news. With Internet, I get updates about many places without having to go anywhere. This is all how I spend my spare time.

(iv) **Money Causes more Harm than Good**

For the Motion

Good morning to one all present here. We all know that some people around us wonder why we cannot live in a world where everyone is equal and where there is no greed our jealousy resulting from status differences. Unfortunately they overlook the fact that our desire to have higher status than others is part of our human nature and nothing can change it. Man's desire to rise ahead of others is too strong and money is the only thing that man completes for. Hence, I stand in favour of the motion 'Money does more harm than good.'

It's good to have money and the things that money can buy but it's good to check up once in a while and make sure that you have not lost the things that money cannot buy. Money comes and goes but what stays our memories with our family and friends. Over abundance of money brings increased sorrows, war, crimes and robbery. However, people are finally realising that money cannot bring them the happiness they crave for.

There are things that are far more important than having money, things like spending time with family and loved ones and enjoying your career. Time is more valuable than money. You can get more money but you cannot get more time. If one has to work 15 hours a day and never get time to spend with family, friends and spend the money, that what good does it do?

While money cannot buy happiness, it certainly let you choose your own form of misery. Money is necessary, but it is not the only thing. And once our basics are covered, we find that we have richness in being together and enjoying the simple things. We certainly have to be careful to set up our priorities correctly to avoid regrets letter in the life. Money can help fulfill a host of materials needs. But learning to be content is far more important. Money can buy status but it can't buy friendship or even save you from a sticky situation. However, time invested in love and quality friendship last eternally. In the end, I would only like to say earning money is important but running behind it is not correct.

Against the Motion

Good morning to one and all present here. Today, I stand against the motion 'Money causes more harm than good.'

In my opinion, money is an essential commodity that helps us in our life. Without money, people will stop working with eagerness. When there is equality everywhere, the determination to work will decrease. A person who works hard will get the same benefit as the person who is lazy which will be wrong. Ultimately, everyone will stop working and there will be a halt at progress and there will be no development.

I would like to state that even though money is not everything, it is something very important. Beyond the basic needs, money helps us in achieving our goals and supporting the people we care about the most – family and friends. We can have better education, health care with money. In addition this, adventure and fun increases when you have money.

It helps us get some of life's intangibles freedom or independence, the opportunity to make the most of our skills and talents, the ability to choose our own course in life, financial security and much more. Furthermore, money is a means to trade our skills for what we need. When we have money, we can develop any skill we want by learning at reputed institutes. This will give us better work opportunities.

Moreover, it is the money that creates respect and honour for someone. It is the money that takes the most shrewed one. Money can give us the power to make a difference in the lives of others. Thus, I would like to I really through a Universal token such as money, just like it is a requirement of life as an individual to be surrounded by air to breathe.

(v) The image shows of a farmer waiting for rain to come to sow his fields. A drought-like situation can be seen.

Droughts refer to conditions when particular regions face scarcity of water because of low or no rainfall. It is one of the most prevalent problems in India. A lot of areas in the country get hit by drought every year. They include Western Rajasthan and the Kutchtch regions of Gujarat. The main factor for this is the geographical location of these areas due to which monsoon season in these are occurs for a very short duration. Many factors contribute to the problem of drought which includes deforestation, global warming, human activities, etc.

Agriculture in India is often attributed as gambling with monsoons because of its almost exclusive dependency on precipitation from monsoons. The failure of these monsoons leads to a series of droughts. The most impacted section of the society is the marginal farmers, landless labourers and persons from the economically backward section. When drought occurs, there is a lack of better prices and exploitation of the farmers by middlemen, all of which have led to a series of suicides committed by farmers across India.

However, droughts can be predicted and prevented well in advance. The Meteorological Department can easily predict the quantity and duration of rainfall with a fair degree of accuracy. As a result, the Government authorities have ample time to cope with this problem. They can counter the intensity and impact of droughts by a series of preventive as well as curative measures.

Executing a rainwater harvesting project with community cooperation, teaching drought management techniques to communities, increasing the forest cover by plantation, researching arid cultivation technologies to implement them in drought-prone areas can be useful. Finally, the farmers must be introduced to crop insurance schemes so that they do not suffer a great loss.

To sum it up, drought is a difficult situation with which we have to deal with. When the severity is high, it becomes all the more difficult to manage it. Thus, it is essential to take effective measures to deal with it.

2. (i) 4, Satellite Area,
Malgudi

7th June, 20XX

The Municipal Commissioner,
M.G. Road, Malgudi

Dear Sir/Ma'am,

This is to draw your kind attention to the hardships suffered by the visitors due to the unruly traffic and the bad condition of the roads in our city.

Though our city attracts a lot of tourists, they often find it disappointing to see the way the traffic operates on the roads. The people driving the vehicles always seem to be in a hurry. They turn erratic on the road and do not exactly follow the traffic signal. Reckless riding by the scooterists endangers the road scene. The truck drivers are generally drunk and largely are the biggest risk to the lives of people. Tourists find this unruly traffic difficult to cope with.

Besides, the condition of the city roads is menacing. The roads are littered with potholes and open manholes which can be dangerous. At many places, pavements are occupied by vendors which pose different kinds of problems to the pedestrians as well as the traffic.

A few strict steps like imposing heavy fines and for felting the licence of the offenders could help in curbing the people from going haywire on the roads. A constant vigil by the traffic police may improve the conditions on the roads. Civil authorities must take immediate steps to mend roads and remove the hurdles there on.

Hope something substantial will be done to help retain the tourist status of our city.

Thanking you,

Yours sincerely,
Aman Khurana

(ii) 216, Chandni Chowk,
Delhi

26th February, 20XX

My dear father,

I hope this letter finds you in the best of your spirits and health. I am hale and hearty here. You will be very glad to know that this year's top prize for the best debator has come to me. It is a silver trophy beautifully casted with the name of the school engraved on it.

The debate was on 'Inter-school' level. Three other boys from different schools took part in it. The topic of discussion was 'Whether Municipalisation of Secondary School Education would be Beneficial.'

All the three boys spoke in favour of it. They said that municipalisation of secondary education was the only way to bring about reforms in the system of education. According to them, it was proper to pass over secondary education to Municipal authorities to enable them to correlate the primary and secondary education. This would, they argued, channelise education from primary stage to higher secondary stage in one single stream which will make for a uniform progress.

Their argument convinced many. My teachers felt restless when I stood up to speak. I started with a feeble voice but soon it became forceful. I smashed their arguments by saying whether my friends, in order to channelise education in one stream, would like to municipalise college education as well? My arguments went home and the audience seemed convinced. I was highly applauded. My rivals were silent and I was declared the winner.

I was later told by my teacher that the manner of my speech was forceful as were my arguments. The boys and teachers of my school were very happy because I had brought honour to them. The function ended happily.

Yours affectionately,
Rishi

3. (i) Save Water!
Lets participate in a march with a cause
Date : 20th August, 20XX Saturday
Time : 11 : 00 am onwards
Venue : School grounds
All house captains are required to give the names of volunteers by 14th August, 20XX.

(ii) principal.bc@xyzschool.com

Dear Sir/ Ma'am,

Mother Teresa School, Kochi is going to organise a one-act play in the march on 20th August, 20XX for 'Save Water Campaign'. You are requested to send a team of children to participate in the march for the cause.

It will be a great opportunity for students of both the schools to interact with one another and create awareness among the people.

Kindly send the names of the participants by 14th August, 20XX.

Thanking you,
Regards
PQR
(Principal)
Mother Teresa School

4. (i) (1) (a) strength (2) (a) confused (ii) (b) seized

(iii) (a) Sher Singh's brother was doubled up with pain. Despite his mother's efforts, the pain did not lessen. Sher Singh knew that his brother was dying. So, he decided to carry him to a hospital at Kalaghat.

(b) In his area, Sher Singh's father was known for his hunting skills as a famous Shikari and for his bravery.

(c) Sher Singh feared to cross the second river even before he actually reached this river because he knew that at that time the river was in flood due to melting snow.

(d) The deluge deafened Sher Singh. Timber banged and bruised him. He could not even breathe in the spray and the water was also very cold.

(e) The doctor come out as he wanted to see and admire the one who had brought Kunwar to him for treatment.

(iv) Sher Singh carried his brother through the dense jungle. His muscles thrilled with piercing pain but he did not lose hope. However, the snow had melted and the river was roaring. The bridge had been washed away but Sher Singh made a rope and tied it around his brother and himself. The river seized and flattened them. The flood deafened him, the timber banged and bruised him. However, he crossed all the hurdles and reached the hospital.

5. (i) 1. does not know 2. do
3. have seen 4. use
5. do not know 6. has grown
7. are 8. become

(ii) (1) about (2) off
(3) off (4) down
(5) upon (6) across
(7) out (8) on

(iii) (1) (b) One should neither borrow nor lend money.
(2) (a) Though there was a heavy traffic, we reached the conference on time.
(3) (c) The English teacher gave a novel to Ravi to review.
(4) (a) Having finished my homework, I went to play.

(iv) (1) (b) In case of fire use the emergency exit.
(2) (d) Despite being ill, he succeeded in completing the assignments.
(3) (a) Little did Sam realise that he had committed an error.
(4) (d) The teacher asked the boy how he dared to remain absent without leave.
(5) (a) Explorers have made amazing discoveries.
(6) (d) Unfortunately, he could not succeed in the first attempt.
(7) (b) Do they believe that God exists?
(8) (c) There is a rise in the price of milk.

ICSE Unsolved

SAMPLE PAPER 02

Time : 2 hrs
Marks : 80

English Language Paper 1

General Instructions

1. Answer to this paper must be written on the paper provided separately.
2. You will not be allowed to write during first 15 minutes. This time is to be spent in reading the question paper.
3. The time given at the head of this paper is the time allowed for writing the answers.
4. Attempt all five questions.
5. The intended marks for questions or parts of questions are given in brackets [ ].
6. You are advised to spend not more than 30 minutes in answering Question 1 and 20 minutes in answering Question 2.

Question 1

(Do not spend more than 30 minute on this question)

Write a composition (300-350 words) on any one of the topics given below. **[20]**

(Do not spend more than 30 minutes on this question)

(i) Write an original story which illustrates the truth of the statement 'If winter comes, can spring be far behind.'

(ii) Relate an incident from your experience that brings out the following message– 'Practice as if you're the worst, perform as if you're the best.'

(iii) Which is the most beautiful place in India– is it a village, a city, a town, a mountain or a beach? Describe the beauty of the place. What are the sights, sounds smells and feelings that you associate with that place? What did you feel like when you were there? Or if you haven't been there, what captures your mind and makes you plan to go there?

(iv) 'Capital Punishment.' Express your views either for or against the statement.

(v) Study the picture given below. Write a story, description or an account of what it suggests to you. Your composition may be about the subject of the picture or may take suggestions from it, but there must be a clear connection between the picture and your composition.

Question 2

Select any one of the following.
(Do not spend more than 20 minutes on this question) **[10]**

(i) Imagine that you have a friend in America who has planned to visit India. Advise him in a letter about what time of the year he should come, what he can bring with him and places he should aim to visit. You can also tell him you would be delighted if he spends a few days with you.

(ii) Write a letter to the Chairman, State Electricity Board pointing out the shortage of electricity in your city.

Question 3

(i) You are the President of a children's club in your locality. You and your team are planning to organise a programme to celebrate Teachers' Day. Write a notice to be put up in the local Supermarket giving details of the programme to create an awareness of the event. **[5]**

(ii) Write an e-mail to the General Manager of the Supermarket seeking permission to display the notice and requesting a sponsorship for the event. **[5]**

Question 4

Read the following passage carefully and answer the questions that follow.

A sound of quick steps broke the silence of the moor. Crouching among the stones, we started intently at the silver-tipped bank in front of us. The steps grew louder and through the fog, as through a curtain, there stepped the man whom we were awaiting. He looked round him in surprise as he emerged into the clear, starlit night.

Then he came swiftly along the path, passed close to where we lay, went on up the long slope behind us. As he walked he glanced continually over either shoulder, like a man who is ill at ease.

'Hist!' cried Holmes and I heard the sharp click of a cocking pistol. 'Look out. It's coming.' There was thin, crisp, continuous patter from somewhere in the heart of the crawling bank. The cloud was within fifty yards of where we lay and we glared at it, all three, uncertain what horror was about to break from the heart of it. I was at Holmes' elbow and I glanced for an instant at his face.

It was pale, exultant, his eyes shining brightly in the moonlight. But suddenly, they started forward in rigid, fixed stare and his lips parted in amazement. At the same instant, Lestrade gave a yell of terror and threw himself face downwards upon the ground. I sprang to my feet; my inert hand grasping my pistol, my mind paralysed by the dreadful shape which handspring out upon us from the shadows of the fog.

A hound it was, an enormous coal-black hound, but not such a hound as mortal eyes have ever seen. Fire burst from its mouth, its eyes glowed with a smoldering glare, its muzzle and develop were outlined in **flickering** flame. Never in the **delirious** dream of a disordered brain could anything more savage, more appealing, more hellish, be conceived than that dark form and savage face which broke upon us out of the wall of fog.

With long bounds the huge black creature was leaping down the track, following hard upon the footsteps of our friend. So paralysed were we by the apparition that we allowed him to pass before we had recovered our nerve.

Then Holmes and I fired together, the creature gave a hideous howl, which showed that one at least had hit him. He did not pause, however, but bounded onwards. Far away on the path we saw Sir Henry looking back, his face white in the moonlight, his hands raised in horror, glaring helplessly at the frightful thing which was hunting him down.

But that cry of pain from that hound had blown all our fears to the wind. If he was vulnerable, he was mortal, if he could wound him we could kill him. Never have I seen a man run as Holmes ran that night in front of us. As we flew up the track, we heard scream from Sir Henry and the deep roar of the hound. I was in time to see the beast spring upon its victim, hurl him to the ground and worry at his throat.

But the next instant Holmes had emptied five barrels of his revolver into the creature's flank. With a last howl of agony and a vicious snap in the air, it rolled upon its back, four feet pawing furiously and then fell limp upon its side.

(i) For each word given below, choose the correct meaning (as used in the passage) from the options provided. **[2]**

(1) flickering *(line 32)*

(a) twinkling (b) shining
(c) seeing (d) burning

(2) delirious *(line 32)*

(a) confused (b) angry
(c) irritated (d) suspicious

(ii) Which word in the passage means the opposite of the word 'resilient'? **[1]**

(a) crouching (b) exultant
(c) enormous (d) vulnerable

(iii) Answer the following questions in your own words.

(a) Mention two reasons given in the passage which show that the man who had come through the fog was not sure of himself. **[2]**

(b) Would you say that Holmes, Lestrade and Watson were mentally prepared for the horrible creature which emerged from the fog? Give reasons for your answer. **[2]**

(c) Why did Holmes and Watson shoot the hound only after it had passed them? **[2]**

(d) Watson says that Sherlock Holmes and he were no longer afraid of the hound after they had shot at it. Why? **[2]**

(e) Was the hound able to get his victim? How does the text reveal it? **[1]**

(iv) In not more than 50 words, describe the chain of events after Lestrade threw himself on the ground. **[8]**

Question 5

(i) Fill in each of the numbered blanks with the correct form of the word given in brackets. Do not copy the passage but write in correct serial order the word or phrase appropriate to the blank space. **[4]**

Example

(0) **were playing**

One lonely evening, my Grandpa ***(o)***........... (play) an interesting game of chess with his old friend who ***(1)*** .... (come) to ***(2)*** .... (visit) him. When the game ***(3)*** .... (be) over, my Grandpa ***(4)*** .... (realise) that his friend ***(5)*** .... (die) seven years ago. "I ***(6)*** .... (enjoy) the game," ***(7)*** .... (assert) his old friend. And according to my Grandpa, that friend ***(8)*** .... (come) every day for six months now.

(ii) Fill in the blanks with appropriate words. **[4]**

(1) The magistrate convicted him .... murder.

(2) He was touched ...... pity when he heard the tale.

(3) He has no hope .... recovery.

(4) I entrusted him .... all my wealth.

(5) He was in great need .... money.

(6) The Germans fought .... the English in the Second World War.

(7) The new chapter begins .... page 20.

(8) They didn't want the news of their engagement ..... till it was officially announced.

(iii) Join the following sentences to make one complete sentence without using ***and***, ***but*** or ***so***. Choose the correct option. **[4]**

(1) She slipped out of class. The professor was delivering a lecture.

(a) She slipped out when the professor was delivering the lecture.

(b) She slipped out as the professor was delivering the lecture.

(c) She slipped out as soon as the professor started delivering the lecture.

(d) She slipped out before the professor delivered the lecture.

(2) She purchased a new car. It runs on electricity.

(a) She purchased a new car as it runs on electricity.

(b) She purchased a new car which runs on electricity.

(c) She purchased a new car which is supposed to run on electricity.

(d) She purchased a new car running on electricity.

(3) The thief entered the room. He found it empty.

(a) As the thief entered the room, he found it empty.

(b) Though the thief entered the room, he found it empty.

(c) When the thief entered the room, he found it empty.

(d) The thief entered the room to find it empty.

(4) He has some weaknesses. He is the darling of everyone. **[4]**

(a) Although he is the darling of everyone, he has some weaknesses.

(b) Although he is the darling of everyone, yet he has some weaknesses.

(c) In spite of being the darling of everyone, he has some weaknesses.

(d) Despite of becoming the darling of everyone, he has some weaknesses.

(iv) Choose the correct option to rewrite the following according to the instructions given after each sentence. **[8]**

(1) It is probable he will never come back.

(Begin: In ....)

(a) In all probability, he will never come back.

(b) In probability, it is expected he will never come back.

(c) In all probability, he is to never come back.

(d) In all probability, he stated that he will never come back.

(2) He got back his property ten years later.

(Use 'restored')

(a) Ten years later, his property was restored to him.

(b) His property restored to him ten years later.

(c) The property was restored to him after ten years.

(d) His property was restored albeit ten years later.

(3) Our forces have been defeated last month.

(Begin: It has been ....)

(a) It has been declared that our forces are defeated last month.

(b) It has been found that our forces have been defeated last month.

(c) It was found that our forces have been defeated last month.

(d) It is stated that our forces have been defeated last month.

(4) The captain told him to leave the office.

(Use 'order')

(a) The captain ordered him to leave the office.

(b) He was ordered to leave the office.

(c) The captain ordered for him to leave the office.

(d) The captain ordered to leave the office.

(5) He kept flying ahead of us, cackling loudly, until Larry has thoroughly exasperated.

(Begin: Larry ....)

(a) Larry flew ahead of us as he was thoroughly exasperated, cackling loudly.

(b) Larry was flying ahead of us, until he was thoroughly exasperated, cackling loudly.

(c) Larry kept flying ahead of us, cackling loudly; he was thoroughly exasperated.

(d) Larry kept flying ahead of us, cackling loudly, until he was thoroughly exasperated.

(6) He tricked the gun under his arm and stamped irritably on to the bridge.

(End: .... his arm.)

(a) The man had rushed towards the bridge with the gun tucked under his arm.

(b) The man was rushing towards the bridge with the gun tucked under his arm.

(c) The man rushed towards the bridge with the gun tucked under his arm.

(d) The man rushed with the gun tucked under his arm towards the bridge.

(7) I had just settled down to do my homework assignment when lights went off.

(Begin: Hardly ....)

(a) Hardly I settled down to do my homework assignment then the lights went off.

(b) Hardly I had settled down to do my homework assignment than the lights went off.

(c) Hardly did I settle down to do my homework assignment that the lights went off.

(d) Hardly had I settled down to do my homework assignment that the lights went off.

(8) He said, "I will not listen to such gossip and scandal."

(Begin: He said that ....)

(a) He said that he would not listen to such gossip and scandal.

(b) He said that he is not listening to such gossip and scandal.

(c) He said that he will not listen to such gossip and scandal.

(d) He said that he is not going to listen to such gossip and scandal.

ICSE Unsolved

SAMPLE PAPER 03

Time : 2 hrs
Marks : 80

English Language Paper 1

General Instructions

1. Answer to this paper must be written on the paper provided separately.
2. You will not be allowed to write during first 15 minutes. This time is to be spent in reading the question paper.
3. The time given at the head of this paper is the time allowed for writing the answers.
4. Attempt all five questions.
5. The intended marks for questions or parts of questions are given in brackets [ ].
6. You are advised to spend not more than 30 minutes in answering Question 1 and 20 minutes in answering Question 2.

Question 1

(Do not spend more than 30 minute on this question)

Write a composition (300-350 words) on any one of the following: **[20]**

(Do not spend more than 30 minutes on this question)

(i) Write an original short story entitled 'An Unexpected Fortune'.

(ii) 'The development of artificial intelligence will help humanity.'
Express your views either for or against this statement.

(iii) What do you prefer – reading, sleeping, playing or cooking?
Describe your favourite activity. What are the sounds, sights, smells and feelings that you associate with the activity? Why do you like it more than the others?

(iv) Have you had an experience that led to a renewed faith in humanity? Give an account in your own words that led to the renowned faith and explain how the experience made you feel.

(v) Study the picture given below. Write a story, description or an account of what it suggests to you. Your composition may be about the subject of the picture or you may take suggestions from it; however, there must be a clear connection between the picture and your composition.

Question 2

Select any one of the following.
(Do not spend more than 20 minutes on this question) **(10)**

(i) Write a letter to your high-school English teacher thanking him/her for teaching you English so well that you are very confident in speaking as well as writing in English on any topic easily.

(ii) You are fond of reading and like to visit the Public Library. However, your coaching timings clash with the timings of the library. Write a letter to the

Librarian requesting him/her to extend the timings of the library. Explain why you choose the library and how you will benefit from the change of time.

Question 3

(i) Your school is conducting an exhibition of working models. Write a notice to be put in your school informing students about the event and inviting them to participate. **[5]**

(ii) Write an e-mail addressing the Principal of the neighbouring school requesting him/ her to send students to participate in the exhibition. **[5]**

Question 4

Read the following passage carefully and answer the questions that follow.

The worst days of any summer are the rainy ones. We spend all year looking forward to nice weather and long, hot days. All of winter, with its dreary gray days and bitter cold, we dream of those endless days at the beach, laying on the sand and soaking in the bright and burning sun. And then, summer comes, and it rains.

As a child, I would wake up to rainy summer days and come close to crying. It wasn't fair. We suffered through months of school and miserable weather for those **scant** ten weeks of freedom and balmy weather. Any day that I could not spend at the beach or playing ball with my friends seemed like a punishment for something I didn't even do. On those rainy summer days, I had nothing to do and could only sit inside, staring out at the rain like a Dickensian orphan. I was an only child, so there was no one else to play with.

My father worked from home, so I was not truly alone, but he could not actively play with me since he was technically at work. It was those days that I would resign myself to whatever was on television or any books that I could find lying around. I'd crawl through the day and pray each night that the rain would not be there the next day.

As an adult, though, my opinion of summer rain has changed. When you have to work every day, summer is not as eagerly anticipated. Mostly, the days run together, bleeding into each other so that they no longer seem like separate entities and instead feel like continuations of the same long day. Everything seems monotonous and dull, and an **ennui** or listlessness kicks in. Such a mindset makes you cheer for anything new or different.

I spend the winter dreaming of summer and the summer dreaming of winter. When summer comes, I complain about how hot it is. And then I look forward to the rain, because the rain brings with it a cold front, which offers a reprieve admittedly one that is all too short from the torture of hot and humid days. Rainy days are still the worst days of the summer, but summer rain today means positively beautiful and considerably cooler weather tomorrow.

(i) For each word given below, choose the correct meaning (as used in the passage) from the options provided. **[2]**

(1) scant *(line 11)*

(a) adequate (b) few
(c) many (d) enough

(2) ennui *(line 31)*

(a) laziness (b) listlessness
(c) boredom (d) confusion

(ii) Which word in the passage means the opposite of the word 'harsh'? **[1]**

(a) dreary (b) balmy
(c) winter (d) monotonous

(iii) Answer the following questions briefly, in your own words.

(a) Why does the author call the rainy days the worst days of any summer? **[2]**

(b) What does the author mean by the phrase Dickensian orphan used in the passage? **[2]**

(c) How has the author's opinion about the summer rain changed as an adult? **[2]**

(d) What does the author feel about the changing seasons – summer to winter and vice-versa? **[2]**

(e) Based on the description of the climatic features given in this passage, identify the region to which the author belongs. **[1]**

(iv) In about 50 words, describe the author's childhood experience of summer rain. **[8]**

Question 5

(i) Fill in each numbered blanks with the correct form of the word given in brackets. Do not copy the passage but write in correct serial order the word or phrase appropriate to the blank space. **[4]**

Example

(0) **published**

The study, *(0)* .... (publish) in the journal, *(1)* .... (reveal) that the legs are those of an adult woman of about 40 years of age. Dr Buckley's chemical analysis also *(2)* .... (establish) that the materials used to *(3)* .... (embalm) the legs are consistent with 13th Century BC mummification traditions, which when taken in conjunction with the findings of the other specialists involved, led to the identification.

Professor Fletcher said: "This *(4)* .... has been (b) the most exciting project to be part of, and a great privilege to be working alongside with some of the world's leading experts in this area. Both Stephen and myself have a long history *(5)* .... (study) Egypt's royal mummies, and the evidence we've been able to *(6)* .... (gather) about Nefertari's remains not only *(7)* .... (complement) the research we've been doing on the queen and her tomb but really does allow us to add another piece to the jigsaw of what is actually *(8)* .... (know) about Egyptian mummification."

(ii) Fill in the blanks with appropriate words. **[4]**

(1) I am sorry .... the mistake.

(2) .... his being innocent of the crime, the judge sentenced him to one year imprisonment.

(3) The robbers fell .... amongst themselves over the sharing of the loot.

(4) The completion of the railway line has been held .... owing to the workers' strike.

(5) The passenger car sales showed a decline .... 7% to 5.6%

(6) All is not well .... the automobile sector.

(7) Mr. Murugan has been in this college .... 2010.

(8) When she parted .... her parents, her eyes were full of tears.

(iii) Join the following sentences to make one complete sentence **without using and, but** or **so**:

Choose the correct option. **[4]**

(1) A man is drowning. He shouted for help.

(a) The man shouted for help as he was drowning.

(b) The man should for help for he was drowning.

(c) The man was drowning when he shouted for help.

(d) After the man started drowning, he shouted for help.

(2) Rahul ran all the way to the bus stop. He missed the bus.

(a) Although Rahul ran all the way to the bus stop yet, he missed the bus.

(b) Although Rahul ran all the way to the bus stop, he missed the bus.

(c) Even when Rahul ran all the way to the bus stop, he missed the bus.

(d) Despite of Rahul running all the way to the bus stop, he missed the bus.

(3) He thought Ritu was honest. He lend her the money.

(a) He thought Ritu was honest therefore, he lent her the money.

(b) He thought Ritu was honest yet, he lent her the money.

(c) He lent Ritu the money as he thought she was honest.

(d) Both (b) and (c)

(4) He has won the first prize. I am pleased to announce it.

(a) I am pleased to announce that he has won the first prize.

(b) It gives me pleasure in announcing that he has won the first prize.

(c) I am pleased to announce him as the first prize winner.

(d) I am pleased to announce that he had got the first prize.

(iv) Choose the correct option to rewrite the following according to the instructions given after each sentence. **[8]**

(1) As soon as we lit the candle, the power supply was restored.

(Begin: No sooner...)

(a) No sooner did we light the candle than the power supply was restored.

(b) No sooner had we light the candle that the power supply was restored.

(c) No sooner did we light the candle then the power supply was restored.

(d) No sooner had we light the candle than the power supply was restored.

(2) Father will send you a message if his flight is cancelled.

(Begin: should ......)

(a) Should his flight is cancelled, father shall send you a message.

(b) Should his flight be cancelled, father will send you a message.

(c) Should his flight cancel, father will send you a message.

(d) Should his flight be cancelled, father will need to send you a message.

(3) No sooner had the match finished than it began to rain.

(rewrite sing 'hardly')

(a) Hardly did the match finish that it began to rain.

(b) Hardly had the match finished then it began to rain.

(c) Hardly had the match finished when it began to rain.

(d) Hardly did the match finished than it began to rain.

(4) He had plenty of wealth but he was not happy.

(Being: In spite...)

(a) In spite of the plenty of wealth, he is not happy.

(b) In spite of his wealth, he is not happy.

(c) In spite of wealth, he was not happy.

(d) In spite of the plenty of wealth, he was not happy.

(5) Everything comes if a man works hard.

(End: hardworking man)

(a) Everything comes to a hardworking man.

(b) Everything can come to a hardworking man.

(c) Everything will be coming to a hardworking man.

(d) Everything will come to a hardworking man.

(6) Very few countries are as hot as India.

(Use hotter' instead of 'hot')

(a) India is hotter than many other countries.

(b) No other country is hotter than India.

(c) Many other countries are not hotter than India.

(d) India is hotter when compared to other countries.

(7) Crossing the road carelessly is dangerous.

(Begin: It...)

(a) It is dangerous to carelessly cross the road.

(b) It is considered dangerous to cross the road carelessly.

(c) It is dangerous to be careless while crossing the road.

(d) It is dangerous to cross the road carelessly.

(8) The President rose to speak and there was silence.

(Begin: When...)

(a) When the President rose to speak, there was silence.

(b) When there was silence, the President rose to speak.

(c) When the President had risen to speak, everyone was silent.

(d) When there was silence, the President has risen to speak.

ICSE Solved

Latest Specimen Question Paper

Time : 2 hrs
Marks : 80

English Language Paper 1

General Instructions

1. Answer to this paper must be written on the paper provided separately.
2. You will not be allowed to write during first 15 minutes. This time is to be spent in reading the question paper.
3. The time given at the head of this paper is the time allowed for writing the answers.
4. Attempt all five questions.
5. The intended marks for questions or parts of questions are given in brackets [ ].
6. You are advised to spend not more than 30 minutes in answering Question 1 and 20 minutes in answering Question 2.

Question 1

(Do not spend more than 30 minutes on this question.)

Write a composition (300-350 words) on any one of the following: **[20]**

(i) Write an original short story entitled: 'A Narrow Escape'.

(ii) Have you ever forgiven someone when it was hard to do so?

Explain what helped you to forgive them, and the positive impact it had.

What did you learn from the experience?

(iii) *'Competition hampers the overall development of students.'*

Express your views either for or against this statement.

(iv) You are taking a leisurely stroll in a beautiful garden.

Describe what you see around you, adding details about the sounds and the scents.

(v) Study the picture given below. Write a story or a description or an account of what it suggests to you. Your composition may be about the subject of the picture or you may take suggestions from it; however, there must be a clear connection between the picture and your composition.

Question 2

(Do not spend more than *20 minutes on this question.)*

Select ***any one*** of the following. **[10]**

(i) You recently read an interesting book that impacted you deeply. Write a letter to your friend highlighting the parts that impressed you. Explain two ways in which you would like to make changes in your behaviour or actions based on what you have read.

(ii) As someone who enjoys gardening, you would like other students in your school to experience its benefits. Write a letter to the principal of your school seeking permission to start a club for students to learn about gardening. Give specific reasons for your request and explain why the club would meet after school hours.

Question 3

(i) Your school is hosting an interschool debate competition. Write a notice informing the students at your school about the event. **[5]**

(ii) Write an e-mail to the principal of a neighbouring school informing him/her of the interschool debate competition being held at your school and requesting him/her to send a team of students to participate. **[5]**

Question 4

Read the following passage carefully and answer the questions that follow :

Tiger Talk :

It was still a busy hour in the city when I entered Market Road. People ran for their lives at the sight of me. As I progressed through, shutters were pulled down, and people hid themselves under culverts, on trees, behind pillars. The population was melting out of sight. At the circus I had had no chance to study human behaviour. Outside the circus ring they sat in their seats placidly while I cowered before Captain's whip. I got a totally wrong notion of human beings at that angle. I had thought that they were ***sturdy*** and fearless. But now I found them fleeing before me like a herd of deer, although I had no intention of attacking them. When I paused in front of a tailor's shop, he abandoned his machine and shut himself in a cupboard, wailing, 'Alas, I am undone, won't someone shoot that tiger?' A prisoner between two constables, who had been caught for murder and was just emerging from the Court House, got his chance to escape when the constables fled, abandoning him with his handcuffs. I tore a horse from its *jutka* and enjoyed the sight of the passengers spilling out of it and running for their lives. A couple of street dogs invited destruction when they barked madly, instead of minding their business.

Later, I learnt from my master of the chaos that befell the city when it became known that Captain had been destroyed and that I was somewhere in the city. Sheer hopelessness seems to have seized the townspeople. They withdrew to their homes and even there remained nervous. All doors and windows everywhere were shut, bolted, and sealed. Some even thought that I was some extraordinary creature who might pass through the walls and lie in wait on the roof or in the loft or ***basement***. Poor people living in huts had real cause to Worry : I could have taken any of their homes apart. But why should I? One could understand their fears, but why should those living in brick and cement feel nervous? It was due to their general lack of a sense of security and an irrational dread of losing their assets. Why should a simple tiger have any interest in them either to destroy or to safeguard?

I rested for a moment at the door of Anand Bhavan, on Market Road, where coffee drinkers and tiffin eaters at their tables sat transfixed, uttering low moans on seeing me. I wanted to assure them, 'Don't fear, I am not out to trouble you. Eat your tiffin in peace, don't mind me ... You, nearest to me, hugging the cash box, you are craven with fear, afraid even to breathe. Go on, count the cash, if that's your pleasure. I just want to watch, that's all ... If my tail trails down to the street, if I am blocking your threshold, it is because, I'm told, I'm eleven feet tip to tail. I can't help it. I'm not out to kill ... I'm too full—found a green pasture teeming with food on the way. Won't need any for several days to come, won't stir, not until I feel hungry again. Tigers attack only when they feel hungry, unlike human beings who slaughter one another without purpose or hunger ...'

— A Tiger in the School, R. K. Narayanan

(i) For each word given below choose the correct meaning (as used in the passage) from the options provided: **[2]**

1. sturdy (line 10)
   (a) brave (b) strong
   (c) compassionate (d) fixed
2. basement (line 34)
   (a) room at the top of the house
   (b) library
   (c) the ground floor
   (d) a room at the bottom of the house

(ii) Which word in the passage means the opposite of the word 'liabilities'? **[1]**
(a) threshold (b) chaos
(c) assets (d) cash box

(iii) Answer the following questions briefly in your own words.
(a) Which sentence in the passage tells us that the people were fast disappearing? **[2]**
(b) Why was the prisoner lucky on that day? **[2]**
(c) What reason does the tiger give to explain why people in brick and cement houses are nervous? **[2]**
(d) The passage describes a man who is shivering with fear and clutching his cash box. What kind of a person do you think he was? **[2]**
(e) How would you have reacted if a tiger walked into the street outside your school? **[1]**

(iv) In not more than 50 words, describe the tiger's thoughts on how differently people behave inside and outside the circus. **[8]**

Question 5

(i) Fill in each of the numbered blanks with the correct form of the word given in brackets. Do not copy the passage but write in correct serial order the word or phrase appropriate to the blank space. **[4]**

Example : (0) Rikki-tikki .... (know) better than to waste time in staring.

Answer : knew

Rikki-tikki was angry. He sat back on his tail and hind legs, and .... ***(1)*** (look) all round him, ... ***(2)*** (chatter) with rage. But Nag and Nagaina .... ***(3)*** (disappear) already into the grass. When a snake misses its stroke, it never .... ***(4)*** (say) anything or .... ***(5)*** (give) any sign of what it means to do next. Rikki-tikki did not care to follow them, for he did not .... ***(6)*** (feel) sure that he .... ***(7)*** (can) manage two snakes at once. So, he trotted off to the gravel path, and sat down to think. It .... ***(8)*** (is) a serious matter for him.

(ii) Fill in the blanks with appropriate words. **[4]**

(1) My sister and I get .... very well with each other.

(2) Mini plays basketball .... her friends every day.

(3) It has been twenty years .... she graduated from college.

(4) Growing up, we were looked .... and brought up by our grandparents.

(5) Most students take the bus .... school as it reaches the premises on time.

(6) The cricket match was put .... because of torrential rains.

(7) Roy backed .... of the competition at the last minute.

(8) I have been training under her .... the past two years.

(iii) Join the following sentences to make one complete sentence **<u>without using</u>** ***and, but*** or ***so***. Choose the correct option. **[4]**

1. We placed our order late. We received the food on time.
   (a) Despite placed our order late, the food was received on time.
   (b) Despite placing our order late, we received the food on time.
   (c) Despite we placed our order late, the food was received on time.
   (d) Despite of us placing our order late, we receiving the food on time.
2. The music stopped. The audience left the auditorium.
   (a) Hardly had the music stopped so the audience left the auditorium.
   (b) Hardly had the music stopped then the audience left the auditorium.
   (c) Hardly had the music stopped since the audience left the auditorium.
   (d) Hardly had the music stopped when the audience left the auditorium.
3. You cannot enter the club. You do not have a membership.
   (a) You cannot enter the club unless you have a membership.
   (b) You cannot enter the club since you have a membership.
   (c) You cannot enter the club whereas you have a membership.
   (d) You cannot enter the club if you have a membership.
4. She was very late. She could not catch the train.
   (a) She was to late to catch the train.
   (b) She was so late to catch the train.
   (c) She was too late to catch the train.
   (d) She was as late so as to catch the train.

(iv) Choose the correct option to rewrite the following according to the instructions given after each sentence. **[8]**

1. The burglar ran away the moment he saw the guard.
   (Begin with: No sooner...)
   (a) No sooner has the burglar seen the guard, he ran away.
   (b) No sooner than the burglar saw the guard, he ran away.
   (c) No sooner did the burglar see the guard when he ran away.
   (d) No sooner had the burglar seen the guard than he ran away.
2. The parents have trained their children well.
   (Begin with: The children ...)
   (a) The children were trained well by their parents.
   (b) The children is being trained well by their parents.

(c) The children had been trained well by their parents.

(d) The children have been trained well by their parents.

3. My cousins returned home one month ago.

(Begin with: 'It has'...)

(a) It has been one month for my cousins' return home.

(b) It has been one month since my cousins returned home.

(c) It has been one month when my cousins returned home.

(d) It has been one month ago that my cousins returned home.

4. Your form will be accepted if it is submitted on time.

(Use: 'unless')

(a) Your form will be accepted unless it is submitted on time.

(b) Unless your form is submitted on time, it will not be accepted.

(c) Unless the form is accepted, it should be submitted on time.

(d) Your form will be accepted unless it is not submitted on time.

5. The house needs a thorough cleaning again.

(Use: thoroughly)

(a) The house needs a thoroughly cleaning again.

(b) The house needed a cleaning thoroughly again.

(c) The house needs to be cleaned thoroughly again.

(d) The house needed to be thoroughly clean yet again.

6. My sister offered me a new job in her company.

(Begin with: A new job...)

(a) A new job was offered to me by my sister in her company.

(b) A new job has been offered to me by my sister in her company.

(c) A new job had been offered to me by my sister in her company.

(d) A new job was being offered to me by my sister in her company.

7. ''I am going to watch my friend's play tomorrow,'' she said.

(Begin with: She said...)

(a) She said that she is going to watch her friend's play tomorrow.

(b) She said that she will be going to watch her friend's play tomorrow.

(c) She said that she was going to watch my friend's play the following day.

(d) She said that she was going to watch her friend's play the following day.

8. Nithin is more talented than most of the professional musicians I know.

(Use: few)

(a) Professional musicians I know have few talents as Nithin.

(b) Few professional musicians I know are as talented as Nithin.

(c) Few professional musicians I know are not as talented as Nithin.

(d) Professional musicians I know do not have as few talents as Nithin.

Answers

1. (i) **A Narrow Escape**

I was returning to India after having completed my studies from abroad. The yearning to meet my parents and friends grew with every passing minute as I boarded the plane. Seated next to me was a boy who was about five years old. He was going to visit his grandma in India and was travelling alone. Next to him were two old ladies in their late fifties who despite their gray hair, were bubbling with excitement and chattering excitedly causing some distraction. No sooner had the plane taken off from London Airport than the boy jumped out of his seat removing his seat belt and started roaming about in the plane. He was very candid and spoke to everyone in the plane. The old ladies called the boy and gave him two chocolates. The air-hostess brought some snacks and tea which was indeed very tempting. After having my refreshment, I settled down to complete a novel that I had brought with me. I had almost completed my novel when I heard the captain requesting passengers to fasten the safety belts as we were about to land at the Palam airport. Just then, a young man seated behind me got up and caught hold of the boy, pointing a gun to his temple. He warned us to stick to our chairs. Entering the cockpit, he ordered the pilot not to land the plane. Suddenly, one of the old ladies collapsed on the floor. Seeing this, the other lady shouted at the hijacker for having caused a heart attack.

The hijacker's attention was momentarily diverted. Sensing this, a well-built young man, sitting in the front passage near the hijacker, knocked the gun out of his hand. Wild and noisy disorder prevailed for a while as others pounced on the unarmed hijacker, freeing the boy in the process. He was overpowered and everybody heaved a sigh of relief. The plane finally landed at the airport and the hijacker was promptly arrested.

We were all accorded a warm welcome from the waiting crowd which had gathered at the airport as news of the hijacking had spread. The child leaped into the open arms of his grandmother who hugged him lovingly. It was indeed a narrow escape for all of us.

(ii) I love reading books. I read books whenever I get time. Recently, I finished the book 'Harry Potter and the Prisoner of Azkaban'. It is my favourite book. I have already read it three whole times. So, obviously, I told my best friend Shubh about it. He got so excited after hearing about it that he immediately asked me for the book.

I gave the book to him on Sunday two weeks ago in the evening, and told him to be careful with it and return it in a week. On the next Wednesday, however, he informed me in school that he lost it. I was furious. I got so angry that I told him that we were not friends anymore. I stopped talking to him altogether. My anger was so obvious that my mom questioned me about what had happened. I told her everything and she smiled. She said to me, "Forgive him. I will buy you another copy." I had not expected that. I thought that she would be angry with me. She left a few moments later and I did not pay any more attention to her words.

But soon, I started feeling very lonely. I spent the entire day last Sunday feeling sorrowful. When I saw him the next day, Shubh had a bandage on his head. Before I could stop myself, I ran to him and asked what happened. He was shocked by my concern. He replied with his voice full of emotions, "I walked straight into a pillar and hurt myself." Seeing him so distraught, I hugged him and forgave him.

He asked me why I had forgiven him and I told him that I missed him. We both smiled and sat together for the rest of the day.

When I reached home, my mother was pleasantly surprised to see me so happy. She smiled and said, "I am glad you heeded my words." I replied guilty, "I didn't. I missed him." I continued telling her what happened the day before.

"Mother, last night I read a story. In it, there were a couple of friends who had been fighting for years, never admitting their mistakes and apologising. One of those friends dies after a car accident and, during his funeral, his friend cried a lot and regretted that they never patched up. I don't want to live my life with such bitterness and especially for such a trivial matter. Moreover, you promised to buy me another copy so it is a win-win." My mother laughed heartily hearing this and gave me a hug.

(iii) **For the Motion**

Respected judges and my honourable opponents; today, I am here to present my views against the motion 'Competition hampers the overall development of students'.

Children, placed in a competitive setting, are often left feeling disappointed, defeated, and bad about themselves. Worse yet, competition can be destructive to self-esteem, especially if children feel like they do not measure up or that they are not being recognised for their efforts.

In a competitive culture, a child is told that it isn't enough to be good. They must triumph over others. But the more they compete, the more they need to compete to feel good about themselves. However, winning doesn't build character, it simply lets a child gloat temporarily. By definition, not everyone can win a contest. If one child wins, another cannot. Competition, thus, leads children to envy winners and to dismiss losers.

Competition further leads to depression among students. We need to understand that every student is not a genius.

Every student has their own skills and preferences, and we must influence them according to their knowledge. The depression may cost their life and, sometimes, they lose control which leads to making wrong decisions. Failure in a competition can further reduce confidence and enthusiasm in a student's life.

Thus, competitions are neither healthy nor productive for students of young age and can hinder their growth and development.

Against the Motion

Respected judges and my honourable opponents; today, I am here to present my views in favour of the motion 'Competition hampers the overall development of students'.

One of the biggest advantages of being involved in a competition is that it prepares students for a real-life scenarios which provides students knowledge different from one acquired from education. It involves creating the best decision-making process and approaching for involvement in different curriculum activities. This also helps in developing skills, growth and overall development.

Competition is good for everyone as long as it is healthy. Such competition inspires students to do their best – not just good enough. When students compete, they become more inquisitive, research independently and learn to work with others. They strive to do more than is required. These abilities prepare children for future situations of all kinds. Whether it's applying to college, seeking a promotion or finding a cure for cancer, the ability to be competitive can give them an important edge.

A competition can be healthy when it provides feedback to students about their performance and improvement, when winning is not the sole or primary objective and when students get to learn about themselves under challenging situations. Under these circumstances, competition can teach invaluable lessons that children do not typically learn in the classroom. Competition teaches critical thinking, decision-making and problem solving. Without those skills, countries can't compete in a global economy. In a supportive environment, it can teach a child to accept failure without compromising their self-esteem.

One of the biggest mistakes some parents make is protecting their child from failure. Failure is not a bad thing. It might feel uncomfortable but it is a wonderful opportunity to learn. In fact, learning from failures not only motivates students to work harder and improve a skill, but it also can help them become more capable adults who do not crumble the first time things get tough. Children can learn how to lose and still feel good about their efforts.

All in all, healthy competition can teach students that it's not always the best that they are successful; rather, those who work hard and stick it out are the real winners in the end. The key is to find healthy ways to compete.

(iv) A morning walk is very rewarding. It is only at this time in the cities that the roads are not crowded. There is hardly any traffic. One can enjoy a walk in the lap of nature. As one walks, one's worries and anxieties vanish away. The sheer delight of the movement is enough to make the day.

I go for morning walk with my friends to a nearby garden where we take two or more rounds. As we set out from our home, we see the street deserted except for a few walkers like us. There are couples in track suits walking briskly along. There are also groups of elderly men gossiping and laughing among themselves. Youngsters are seen wearing ear phones and jogging to their favourite songs. In the quietness of the morning, I can hear the chirping of the birds, parrots and pigeons. They are seen flying from one branch of a tree to another. Amidst the sheet of thin white fog, the colourful flowers in the garden give solace to the heart and a feast to the eyes. The fragrance of the sweet smelling flowers fills my mind with freshness. The pure fresh air of the morning, devoid of the poisonous gases exhaled by the innumerable vehicles running to and fro in the city streets, gives a boost to the body to battle the day's hectic schedule. Gradually, penetrating through the dense fog, the first rays of the Sun shine across the park. Now, the body begins to respond well to the movements of the limbs and the flow of fresh, cool air one breathes. The momentum now sets in and the legs appear to walk effortlessly. One foot glides over the other as if trying to be the first to land ahead.

Words are insufficient to describe the feelings one undergoes during winter morning leisure walks in gardens.

(v) Education is an essential tool for bright future for all of us. We can achieve anything good in the life using the tool of education. Higher level of education helps people in earning social and family respect and unique recognition. Education time is a crucial part of life for everyone personally and socially. It provides a person a unique standard in the life and feeling of well being. Education provides ability to solve any big social and family and even national and international level problems. No one of us can unseen the importance of education in the life in every aspect.

It turns the minds towards positivity in the life and removes all the mental problems and negativity.

It changes the people's thought by bringing positive thoughts and removing negative thoughts. Our parent plays a great role in turning our mind towards education from childhood. They try their best to give us good education from the popular educational institutions. It provides us opportunity to gain technical and highly skilled knowledge as well as enlarge our views all over the world. Best ways to enhance the skill and knowledge level is to get practiced of reading news paper, seeing educational programmes on TV, reading books of good authors, etc. Education makes us more civilized and better educated. It helps us in making better position in the society and achieves dreamed position in the job.

It makes us able to become a good doctor, engineer, officer, pilot, teacher, etc. in the life whatever we want to become. Regular and proper study leads us towards success by making a goal of life. Earlier the education system was so tough and people from all castes were not able to get education according to their own wish. It was very tough to get admission in the proffered colleges because of high cost. But now it has become so simple and easy to go ahead in the education.

2. (i) 229/C, Garima Houses

Moti Nagar, Delhi

17th June, 20XX

My dear Rhea,

How are you? I hope you are doing well. I am fine as well. I am enjoying this summer vacation a lot. Remember how we talked about developing and working on good habits? I choose reading books. I have read five books this holiday. My parents are so happy that I am developing this interest. They even suggested me a couple of books. In fact, the last book I read was suggested to me by my mother. It was a very interesting book too.

I am writing to tell you about it. The book is C. B. Divakaruni's 'The Palace of Illusions'. It is a reimagining of the great Indian epic – the 'Mahabharata'. I learned a lot from this book especially the need to learn how to survive in difficult conditions. The princess Panchali was taught how to survivc in a forest. Although it seemed odd for a princess, I learned later on that it was integral because she had to spend thirteen years in the forest with her husbands. So, I will learn such things too so that if I ever get stuck in such a situation.

I also learned the importance of keeping one's mouth shut so as to not make promises that one can't keep and to speak up for the right things. If you know the story of the 'Mahabharata', I am sure you understand what I am referring to. I would suggest you to read this book as it will teach you a lot about life.

I can't wait to start another book and then discuss them with you. See you on the first day of school after the vacations.

Yours affectionately,

Kritika

(ii) To

The Principal,

ABC Public School

17th June, 20XX

Respected Sir/Ma'am,

Most respectfully, I beg to state that I am a student of your institution willing to start a new initiative for encouraging other students for gardening. For that purpose, I have thought about forming a students' club where interested students will take part and learn about gardening once every week.

I have harboured an interest in gardening since childhood when I used to see my mother taking care of the plants in my home. Current state of the world requires an in-depth knowledge of nature and surroundings. The easiest way of overcoming the burdens like pollution, excessive temperature etc. is planting more trees and making the surrounding green.

So, I want to encourage other students as well in this initiative. I am hopeful that our little contribution and sincere attitude towards nature can bring great changes in future.

Kindly, grant permission for going forward with this initiative.

Thanking you,

Yours faithfully,

Chandni Gupta

3. (i)

War of Words
Inter-School Debate Competition
on 16th November, 20XX
from 10:00 a.m. to 2:00 p.m.
at Sinha Auditorium, DKV Public School
All the students from Classes IX and X who wish to participate are to submit their names to Savita ma'am on or before 7th November, 20XX.

(ii) principal@skvs.org

Invitation to participate in the Inter-School Debate Competition

Dear Sir,

This is to inform you about the Inter-School Debate Competition 'War of Words' being organised by our school on 16th November, 20XX from 10:00 a.m. to 2:00 p.m. It will be organised at the Sinha Auditorium in the main building of our school.

We request you to motivate and send a team of five students of your school to participate in the competition.

Participation from your school will make a huge impact on the student community.

Anticipating a positive response from you in accepting our invitation,

Thanking you,

Yours faithfully,

Praful Shah

Secretary, Student Council

4. (i) 1. (b) strong

2. (d) a room at the bottom of the house

(ii) (c) assets

(iii) (a) 'As I progressed through, shutters were pulled down, and people hid themselves under culverts, on trees, behind pillars' – is the sentence that tells us that people were fast disappearing.

(b) The prisoner was lucky on that day because he got chance to escape when the two constables fled by abandoning him with his handuffs.

(c) The tiger explained that people in brick and cement houses are nervous due to their general lack of security and an irrational dread of losing their assets.

(d) The person who was shivering with fear and clutching his cash box appear to be giving much importance to money and he could not leave his money in any situation.

(e) If I saw a tiger on the street outside our school, I would definitely be stunned and puzzled with fear.

After some minutes, I would try to find a safe shelter for going away from the sight of the tiger to protect myself.

(iv) Inside the circus, the tiger had no chance to study human behaviour. Outside the circus ring, others sat in their seats placidly while the tiger cowered before captain's ship. He thought humans are sturdy and fearless. But outside he got the true view of humans who were fleeing like deer in front of him as they got scared. The tiger had no intention of attacking anyone but everyone was afraid of him.

5. (i)

1. looked	2. chattering
3. had disappeared	4. says
5. gives	6. feel
7. could	8. was

(ii)

(1) along	(2) with
(3) since	(4) after
(5) to	(6) off
(7) out	(8) for

(iii) 1. (b) Despite placing our order late, we received the food on time.

2. (d) Hardly had the music stopped when the audience left the auditorium.

3. (a) You cannot enter the club unless you have a membership.

4. (c) She was too late to catch the train.

(iv) 1. (d) No sooner had the burglar seen the guard than he ran away.

2. (d) The children have been trained well by their parents.

3. (b) It has been one month since my cousins returned home.

4. (b) Unless your form is submitted on time, it will not be accepted.

5. (c) The house needs to be cleaned thoroughly again.

6. (a) A new job was offered to me by my sister in her company.

7. (d) She said that she was going to watch her friend's play the following day.

8. (b) Few professional musicians I know are as talented as Nithin.

ICSE

Solved Question Paper 2024

Time : 2 hrs
Marks : 80

English Language Paper 1

General Instructions

1. Answer to this paper must be written on the paper provided separately.
2. You will not be allowed to write during first 15 minutes. This time is to be spent in reading the question paper.
3. The time given at the head of this paper is the time allowed for writing the answers.
4. Attempt all five questions.
5. The intended marks for questions or parts of questions are given in brackets [ ].
6. You are advised to spend not more than 30 minutes in answering Question 1 and 20 minutes in answering Question 2.

Question 1

Write a composition (300 - 350) words on **any one** of the following. **[20]**

(i) Write an original short story entitled 'A Strange Visitor'.

(ii) Narrate an incident from your experience in which your parents had entrusted you with a difficult task. Give details of the task, how you carried it out and your feelings at the end.

(iii) Describe how you speed your time on a holiday afternoon. Why do you think it is necessary to have these times of quietness and solitude ?

(iv) Express your views either for or against the statement ' Junk food should be banned'.

(v) Study the picture given below. Write a story or a description or an account of what it suggest to you. Your composition may be about the subject of the picture, or you may take suggestions form it; however, there must be a clear connection between the picture and your composition.

Question 2

Select **any one** of the following. **[10]**

(Do not spend more than 20 minutes on this question)

(i) Your friend was absent from school on a day when an unfortunate incident took place for which you were blamed. Write a letter to your friend giving details about the incident, your role in it and how the matter was finally resolved.

(ii) You wish to stage a play to create awareness about the importance of saving electricity. Write a letter to the Manager of a nearby shopping mall / supermarket requesting permission to use the space in front of the shopping mall/supermarket to stage the play. Give him / her details about your requirements and state why the play will be beneficial to the shoppers.

Question 3

(i) Your school is hosting an Inter-School Dance Competition. Write a notice to be put up on your school notice board informing the students about the event. **[5]**

(ii) Write an e-mail to the Principal of a neighbouring school to request him / her to send their dance teacher to act as a judge for the competition. **[5]**

Question 4

Read the following passage carefully and answer the questions that follow.

Ashamanja Babu lived in a small flat in Bhowanipore. A Clerk in the registry department of Lajpat Rai Post office, Ashamanja Babu was fortunate as he could walk to his office in seven minutes flat without having to fight his way into the buses and trains of Calcutta. He lived a rather carefree life as he was not the kind of person to sit and brood about what might have been had Fate been kinder to him. On the whole, he was quite content with his lot. Two Hindi films and fish twice a week-these were enough to keep him happy. The only thing that **perturbed** him at times was his lack of companionship. A bachelor with few friends and relatives, he often wished he had a dog to keep him company. It need not be a huge Alsation like the one owned by the Talukdars, who lived two houses down the lane; it could be any ordinary little dog which would follow him around morning and evening. Wag its tail when he came home from work and obey his orders faithfully. Ashamanja Babu's secret desires were that he would speak to his dog in English, ' Stand up ', ' Sit down', ' Shake hands' - How nice it would be if his dog obeyed such commands ! That would make him really happy.

On a cloudy day marked by a steady drizzle, Ashamanja Babu went to the market in Hashimara to buy some oranges. At one end of the market, beside a **stunted** Kul tree, sat a man. As their eyes met, the man smiled. Was he a beggar ? His clothes made him look like one. Ashamanja Babu noticed at least five sewning-on patches on his trousers and jacket. But the man didn't have a begging bowl. Instead, by his side was a shoe - box with a little pup sticking its head out of it.

'Good morning !' said the man in English. Ashamanja Babu was obliged to return the greeting. 'Buy dog ? Dog buy ? Very good dog.' The man had taken the pup out of the box and had put it down on the ground . Very cheap. Very good . Happy dog?

The pup shook the raindrops off its coat, looked at Ashamanja Babu and wagged its minuscule two inch tail. Ashamanja Babu moved closer to the pup.

Crouched on the ground and stretched out his hand. The pup gave his ring finger a lick with its pink tongue. Nice, Friendly dog.

'How much? What price?

'Ten rupees'

A little haggling and the price came down to seven rupees. Ashamanja Babu paid the money, put the pup back in the shoe box, closed the lid to save it form the drizzle, and turned homewards, forgetting all about the oranges.

–Ashamanja Babu's Dog by Satyajit Ray

(i) For each word given below choose the correct meaning (as used in the passage) from the options provided. **[2]**

1. perturbed *(line 11)*
   (a) frightened (b) unsettled
   (c) confused (d) mocked
2. stunted (line 27)
   (a) prevented form growing
   (b) prepared for tricks
   (c) prevented form taking action
   (d) allowed to do stunts

(ii) Which word in the passage means the opposite of the word 'expensive' ? **[1]**
(a) Carefree (b) Ordinary
(c) Cheap (d) Haggling

(iii) Answer the following questions briefly in your own words.
(a) What kept Ashamanja Babu happy? **[2]**
(b) What does this tell you about him? **[2]**
(c) What is that one other thing he needed to complete his hapiness? **[1]**
(d) Why did Ashamanja Babu think the man was a beggar? **[2]**
(e) Why did Ashamanja Babu forget about his oranges? **[2]**

(iv) In not more than 50 words, narrate the series of events form the time the puppy was taken out of the box till it was paid for. **[8]**

Question 5

(i) Fill in each of the numbered blanks with the correct form of the word given in brackets. Do not copy the passage but write in correct serial order the word or phrase appropriate to the blank space. **[4]**

Example: Next day my uncle (0) .... (speed) a lot of time.

Answer: (0) spent

He *(1)* .... (select) clothes for me, and my aunt *(2)* .... (give) my face a scrub and *(3)* .... (groom) me. My uncle *(4)* .... (follow) me about *(5)* .... (utter) several pieces of advice before *(6)* .... (let) me out, 'You must never scowl even if the Sun *(7)* .... (hit) you in the eyes. You must try *(8)* .... (look) pleasant. **[4]**

(ii) Fill in the blanks with appropriate words.

(1) There's a black cat sitting .... the wall.
(2) The horse jumped .... the hedge.
(3) Mother goes .... the market every day.
(4) Several people have climbed Mount Everest .... recent years.
(5) I often go to school .... my friend.
(6) I have left my keys .... home.
(7) Instead of talking , prove your worth .... doing something.
(8) I have not slept .... yesterday.

(iii) Choose the correct option to make one complete sentence **without using and but or so**. **[4]**

1. The magician took pity on the mouse. He turned it into a cat.
   (a) Showing pity on the mouse he turned it into a cat.
   (b) Taking pity on the mouse he turned it into a cat.
   (c) The magician turned the mouse into a cat by taking pity .
   (d) Taking pity on the mouse the magician turned it into a cat.
2. This work must be completed. There is a deadline.
   (a) Since this work must be completed, there is a deadline.
   (b) This work must be completed because there is a deadline.
   (c) This work must be completed though there is a deadline.
   (d) This work must be completed when there is a deadline.
3. He fled somewhere. His pursuers could not follow him.
   (a) He fled where his pursuers could not follow him,
   (b) He pursued somewhere his followers could be flee.
   (c) He fled somewhere when his pursuers could not follow him.
   (d) He fled where his pursuers cannot follow him.
4. He began late. He finished first.
   (a) He finished first and began late
   (b) He began first but finished late.
   (c) Though he finished late, he began first.
   (d) Though he began late, he finished first.

(iv) Choose the correct option and rewrite the sentence according to the instruction given after each. **[8]**

Arun and Nikhil had climbed the mountain.

(Add a question tag)

   (a) Arun and Nikhil had climbed the mountain, didn't they ?
   (b) Arun and Nikhil had climbed the mountain, had they ?
   (c) Arun and Nikhil had climbed the mountain, hadn't they ?
   (d) Arun and Nikhil had climbed the mountain, did they ?
2. The children have broken the window pane. *(Begin The window pane ………...)*
   (a) The window pane had been broken by the children.
   (b) The window pane has been broken by the children.
   (c) The window pane has not been broken by the children.
   (d) The window pane had not been broken by the children.
3. The apples are so cheap that they cannot be good. *(Use : 'too')*
   (a) The apples are too cheap and good.
   (b) The apples are to cheap as well as good.
   (c) The apples are too good to be cheap.
   (d) The apples are two cheap to be good.
4. She is very clever and beautiful *(Use : 'not only')*
   (a) Not only is she very clever but also beautiful.
   (b) Not only was she beautiful and she was also clever.
   (c) Not only is she clever she was also very beautiful.

(d) Not only was she very beautiful but is also clever.

5. I prefer a simple vanilla ice cream to fancy desserts.

(Begin : I would rather ………)

(a) I would rather have a simple vanilla ice cream to fancy desserts.

(b) I would rather have a simple vanilla ice cream than fancy desserts.

(c) I would rather prefer a simple vanilla ice cream than fancy desserts.

(d) I would rather have a vanilla ice cream than a fancy dessert.

6. He asked, " When do you intend to make the payment ? "

(Begin : He asked ……...)

(a) He asked when he did intend to make the payment.

(b) He asked when she is intending to make the payment.

(c) He asked when I intended to make the payment.

(d) He asked when they are intending to make the payment.

Question 6

If the rain does not stop, Mariam will not be able to do the laundry. *(Begin : Unless ………)*

(a) Unless the rain does not stop, Mariam will not be able to do the laundry.

(b) Unless Mariam does the laundry, the rain will not stop.

(c) Unless the rain stop, Mariam will not be able to do the laundry.

(d) Unless the rain stops, Mariam will not be able to do the laundry.

Question 8

This is the best move I have ever seen.

(Begin : Never ………………...)

(a) Never had I seen a good movie than this.

(b) Never I have seen a better movie than this.

(c) Never have I seen a better movie than this.

(d) I have never seen a good movie as this.

Answers

1. (i) **A Strange Visitor**

It was a bleak and a sad day for I was knee deep in debt and no resource to pay for it. Unfortunately, I had unconsciously become a part of a fraud scheme and had given up all my savings in it. Due to my job, I had been unable to look into the scheme and was satisfied that I was getting huge returns. Consequently, I had lived a modest but a fulfilling life. My happiness was snatched a few months back when the reality came out and I found that the organisers of the scheme had racked up many debts in my name. Further, only I could pay for it as the scammers were nowhere to be found.

Much like other days, that day also, my mind was filled with these thoughts and my mistakes. With sadness, anger and many other emotions, I went outside to look around. It was a cold frosty morning. The fields were white and scenic but cold. I lived in rural Ireland which was very quiet. By the side of my house, there is a large stone and that's nothing unusual as Ireland is full of large stones. Some stones are said to be Fairy Stones which is believed to take living form to help those in need.

However, that day someone was sitting on the stone. As I went near the person, I saw that it was a very charismatic looking man. He was not anyone I knew and he did not look like he was of this time as he wore funny clothes. He looked to be freezing, so I asked him if he was ok but he didn't reply. I asked him if he was hungry, no response. I asked him into the house to warm himself by the fire. I went in before him and left the door open behind me.

After a few moments he came in, stood at the door, looked around and sat on the stool near the open fire.

I made him a cup of hot tea and offered him some baked bread and a few biscuits. He sat there and seemed to enjoy his tea but he did not speak a word to me.

After he had finished his tea, I took his cup from him and asked if there was anything else he would like. Just as he smiled, there was a knock at the front door. As I opened it, there was no one there so I turned around to try to get the man to speak again. However, he was gone. I was baffled. Where had he gone? There was only one way out, that was past me by the front door. As I was wondering, I saw a pouch on the stool. Much to my surprise, it contained 20 gold coins. I think the man forgot it, so I kept the coins for him. My situation has improved since then but the man did not come back.

(ii) I remember one incident where my parents gave me a difficult task to do which I was nervous about. It was about driving a car. I had been taking driving lessons at that time for a few weeks and was fairly good at it.

I used to go for my lessons thrice a week and was getting a hang of it. During one of those lessons, my father accompanied me and sat at the backseat while I was practising my skills. I felt somewhat nervous and intimidated but I ended up doing quite well in that lesson and my father also gave me a reassuring smile when we headed back home after the lesson.

The next day was Sunday and my parents had decided to go for a small outing to the City Mall for some lunch and shopping. I was excited and started getting dressed up for the outing. After I was dressed, I went downstairs to the living room to take out the keys to lock the house. As I was looking for the house keys in the drawer, my father asked me to take out the car keys as well. I took both the keys and gave the car keys to him. To my surprise, my father told me that he didn't need the car keys as it would be me who would be driving today. I felt a little anxious as it would be my first time driving my parents in a car. But I took the keys from him and said that I would love to drive, without giving any hint that I was nervous about it. We left the house and I started driving slowly but attentively. I gained a fair speed after a few minutes and got a little confident. The rest of the drive went smoothly and we reached the mall in 15 minutes. I felt relieved that I did well without facing any obstacles. My parents gave me a proud and reassuring smile as they got out of the car and patted my back for the drive.

(iii) In this highly busy and competitive world, no one has free time. I also do not have much time to relax. However, when I get a chance I tend to utilise it to take a breather and spent some time relaxing. The concept of relaxing on a holiday afternoon means different things for different people. For me, it means a variety of things depending upon my mood. Generally, these things range from painting to watching a movie.

There are days when I am inspired by the attractive doodles and paintings on pinterest. With much enthusiasm, one day, I decided to do mandala art of Goddess Saraswati. For the same, I gathered my art supplies that I needed and sat to work. It was a tiring process which took me 3 whole holiday afternoons to complete but that art piece now resides in my grandparents house as a framed photo.

Sometimes, you would find me watching latest movies on my home projector. I would sit on my couch, arrange for my food and randomly pick a movie which is generally either a comedy or a horror movie.

Spending my time doing nothing but giving my mind a break is essential for me. And I think it should a necessity for everyone. These times of quietness and solitude help us reenergize for the coming days. If we do not take a break and do what makes us happy, our lives can take us on the path of burn-out or a situation wherein we are physically and mentally exhausted. In such situations, we do not wish to do anything and suffer from many lifestyle diseases.

Thus, a break from the hustle and bustle of life is required by our mind and body. In this break, we need to do what we want to do without anyone ordering us around or nagging us. This is our moment of peace, relaxation and joy away from the stress of life. Giving yourself the gift of 'me time' is important for your well-being all year, but especially if you're feeling particularly stressed out.

(iv) **Junk Food Should be Banned**

For the Motion

Good morning to esteemed judges and respected opponents. I stand here today to advocate for the banning of junk food in our society.

Wise people, including our parents, have often been quoted to say that health is wealth. It is only the foolish who choose not to listen.

Before we consider the merits of banning something particular, we must investigate its long-term effects on the human body. Junk food is an umbrella term that refers to highly processed and calorie- dense foods that are low in nutritional value. These foods often contain high levels of unhealthy ingredients such as sugar, salt, unhealthy fats, and artificial additives. These food items affect the human body in a number of ways. The short term effects include energy spikes and crashes, bloating, constipation, and dehydration. Various scientific studies and researches have associated junk food with many other lifelong illnesses including obesity, diabetes, heart disease, hypertension, tooth decay and cavities, and even nutritional deficiencies.

Respected audience, I would like you to consider the following question: Why do we eat food?

Is it to make our life functions slower? To ensure that we live shorter, diseased lives full of pain and medicines? If so, then I invite all of you to continue eating the poison that is called junk food, because that is the only path that it will lead you on. Eating junk food is similar to giving an open invitation to all the diseases in the world.

If, on the other hand, you are reasonable individuals, then you will be aware of the fact that all living beings eat food to gain energy and to cultivate a strong body which can fight off diseases and ensure a painless existence.

Unfortunately, youngsters cannot be trusted to make the right decisions for themselves. Hence, it is essential that the decision to stop partaking in this particular form of poison be taken for them. Considering the significant risk to the health and wellbeing of humans as individuals and as a society, I support the complete ban of all non-nutritious junk foods in a vision to create a healthier society.

Thank you.

Against the Motion

Good morning to one and all. Ladies and gentlemen, esteemed judges, and respected opponents, I stand here today to advocate against the banning of junk food in our society.

I agree with my opponent in the fact that junk food is often harmful to health and that it has practically nothing to say for its lack of nutritional value.

I would also agree that it is in fact a slow poison! However, while it may not be nutritious and conducive to a healthy lifestyle, for many people it is the only choice. The rushed lifestyle of the modern world does not allow people the time to carefully choose ingredients according to their nutritional value and cook it. Many people only have the time to cook two minute noodles before rushing off to work. Would you stand in front of them and proclaim that just because they are not eating anything healthy, they cannot eat anything at all?

Junk food does serve a purpose after all. It may not be nutritious but it does fill the stomach. For the people with limited time and limited choices, junk food stands for comfort.

Although it is imperative that we cultivate good eating habits, unfortunately the ability to have a nutritious meal is not a necessity; it is a luxury. As the residents of a country whose 7% population is below poverty line, it would be a grave injustice to pass laws in favour of those who can afford luxuries.

Therefore, I call upon your humanity and condemn the complete ban of junk foods.

Thank you

(v) A few weeks back I paid a visit to my Grandma's village which is located on the outskirts of a city. I was mesmerised by seeing the straw and clay houses and the swings on the trees where children were playing and having fun. The whole atmosphere was very lively and energetic and surprisingly calm at the same time. I felt relaxed to be away from the noisy city and being around nature.

After having some delicious lunch that my Grandma had prepared especially for me, I went out for a quick stroll around the village. The cool breeze under the shade of the trees felt really pleasant and comforting.

As I was walking, I came across a bunch of small children sitting under a huge banyan tree. I walked towards them and saw that they were all sitting in a circle around a Carrom board which was placed on the ground near the tree's trunk. The children saw me approaching, looked at me and smiled. They asked me if I wanted to play to which I politely said no. I asked them about the Carrom board and to whom it belonged. The children rejoiced and said that they bought the Carrom board at the village fair with the money that my Grandma had given them. It was their first time playing with it. I felt such joy after hearing that my generous Grandma had given these kids money so that they could buy themselves this game to play together. The children then started to arrange all of the pucks together in a circle in the middle of the board. They also played rock, papers, scissors to decide who would play the first shot. The excitement of the children made me appreciate the little things in life and to enjoy every moment as it comes.

2. (i) XYZ Apartments
Delhi
8th February, 20XX

Dear Vayu,

I hope you are fine now. I missed you a lot during the exhausting day. I know you must be very curious to know about why I called the day exhausting. Well, something happened and I was wrongly blamed. While going to the playground in a queue during recess, Ravi fell down the stairs which resulted in many serious injuries. When we all were asked about how it happened, Stuti blamed me saying that I was just behind him and must have pushed him as a revenge for the humiliating prank he did on me. I was shocked by such a blame. I agree I was angry but we had resolved the issue way before which many of our classmates pointed out.

Now, without further questioning, the school decided to call my parents. When they arrived, my parents were informed about the situation and my punishment- they were rusticating me. Calmly, my father reminded them of the CCTV cameras, which had recently been installed. He asked to show him the footage so that he can see for himself if I really did this.

The school authorities were shocked that they had not thought of this. They hurriedly got the footage which clearly showed that I, in fact, was not immediately behind Ravi and that he had slipped on a banana peel. Looking at the truth, everyone was apologetic towards me. However, I was and still am hurt at the blame.

The issue, though resolved, has shown me who are my true friends.

I just hope you were there today to see how bad it was. Get well soon so that we can visit Ravi.

Yours friendly
PQR

(ii) 16, ABC Apartments
Nashik
1st June, 20XX

The Manager,
XYZ Shopping Mall
Nashik

Dear Sir/Ma'am,

It is with great pleasure that I have written this letter to inform you on behalf of 'Live Happy Youth Club' that we are organising a small play to create awareness about the importance of saving electricity. For the same,
I would request you to permit us to use the space in front of the shopping mall.

The play, though appears to be social, will increase footfall in your mall. While shopping is the main concern, event like ours will also include the entertainment aspect encouraging more and more people to visit the mall. Further, it will boost your overall sales.

I hope that you would consider our request and permit us to stage our play in your premises.
Hoping for a positive response.

Thanking you,

Yours faithfully,

PQR

(Secretary, Live Happy Youth Club)

3. (i) DAZZLING DANCERS

Inter-School Dance Competition

Date 31st January, 20XX

Time : 11:00 a.m. onwards

Venue : Auditorium, XYZ School

Come, participate, cheer and witness the dancing extravaganza.

(ii) **To** : principalpqr@gmail.com

Subject : Invitation to judge the Inter School Dance Competition

Sir/Ma'am

With great pleasure, I would lie to inform you that XYZ School, Delhi is going to organise an Inter-School Dance Competition on 31st January, 20XX from 11:00 a.m. onwards in the school auditorium. For the same, we would love to have the dance teacher of your school as a judge the competition.

Kindly accept our invitation and increase the glory of the competition. Hoping for a positive response.

Thanking You,

Yours obediently,

ABC

(Principal)

XYZ School

4. (i) 1. (b) unsettled

2. (a) prevented from growing

(ii) (c) cheap

(iii) (a) Watching two Hindi films and having fish twice a week kept Ashamanja Babu happy.

(b) This tells us that he was a simple man who was content with his life.

(c) Since he was a bachelor, he longed for companionship to complete his happiness. He wished that he had a dog.

(d) Ashmanja Babu thought that the man was a beggar because his clothes had patches sewn on them.

(e) Ashmanja Babu forgot about his oranges because he came across a puppy for sale which he eventually ended up buying.

(iv) The man took the pup out of the box and kept it on the ground. The pup looked at Ashmanja Babu and wagged his tiny tail. Ashmanja Babu bent down and stretched out his hand when the dog licked his ring finger with its pink tongue. He then asked for the price when the man said "ten rupees". After some haggling the price came down to seven rupees.

5. (i) 1. selected 2. gave

3. groomed 4. followed

5. uttering 6. letting

7. hits 8. looking

(ii) (1) on (2) over

(3) to (4) in

(5) with (6) at

(7) by (8) since

(iii) 1. (d) Taking pity on the mouse the magician turned it into a cat

2. (b) This work must be completed because there is a deadline.

3. (a) He fled where his pursuers could not follow him.

4. (d) Though he began late, he finished first.

(iv) 1. (c) Arun and Nikhil had climbed the mountain, hadn't they?

2. (b) The window pane has been broken by the children.

3. (d) The apples are too cheap to be good.

4. (a) Not only is she very clever but also beautiful.

5. (b) I would rather have a simple vanilla ice cream than fancy desserts

6. (c) He asked when I intended to make the payment.

7. (d) Unless the rain stops, Mariam will not be able to do the laundry.

8. (c) Never have I seen a better movie than this.

ICSE Solved

Latest Specimen Question Paper 2025

Time : 2 hrs
Marks : 80

English Language Paper 1

General Instructions

1. Answer to this paper must be written on the paper provided separately.
2. You will not be allowed to write during first 15 minutes.
3. The time is to be spent in reading th question paper.
4. The time given at the head of this paper is the time allowed for writing the answers.
5. Attempt all five questions.
6. The intended marks for questions or parts of questions are given in brackets [ ].
7. You are advised to spend not more than 30 minutes in answering Question 1 and 20 minutes in answering Question 2.

Question 1

(Do not spend more than 30 minutes on this question.)

Write a composition (300-350 words) on ***any one*** of the following. **[20]**

(i) Write an original short story in which a woman, her strange neighbour and a police officer form the main characters.

(ii) Your teacher has asked you to form a group and work on a particular project. Write an account of how you worked together and what each of you learned from the experience.

(iii) "Peer pressure is a force for good."

Express your views either ***for*** or ***against*** this statement.

(iv) Describe the locality in which you live. Give details of the things you see and hear as you walk around your locality. What do you especially like about the place?

(v) Study the picture given below. Write a story or a description on an account of what it suggests to you. Your composition may be about the subject of the picture or you may take suggestions from it; however, there must be a clear connection between the picture and your composition.

Question 2

(Do not spend more than 20 minutes on this question.)

Select ***any one*** of the following. **[10]**

(i) Your uncle was unable to attend your birthday celebration but has sent you one thousand rupees as a gift. Write a letter thanking him, tell him how you will spend the money and why you have made that particular choice.

(ii) The garbage bins in your locality have not been cleared regularly resulting in the overflow of garbage in the area. Write a letter to the Municipal Commissioner of your city/town complaining about the problem. Offer suggestions for the removal of the garbage and cleaning up of the place.

Question 3

(i) Your school is hosting an Art and Craft exhibition. Write a notice informing the pupils at your school about the event. **[5]**

(ii) Write an e-mail to a local artist inviting him/her to inaugurate the exhibition and be the Chief Guest on the occasion. **[5]**

Question 4

Read the following passage carefully and answer the questions that follow.

One day, I found the pond occupied by several buffaloes. Their keeper, a boy a little older than me, was swimming about in the middle. Instead of climbing out on the bank, he would pull himself up on the back of one of his buffaloes, stretch his naked brown body out on the animal's glistening **hide**, and start singing to himself.

When he saw me staring at him from across the pond, he smiled, showing gleaming white teeth on a dark face. He invited me to join him in a swim. I told him I couldn't swim, and he offered to teach me.

His name was Ramu, and he promised to give me swimming lessons every afternoon, and so it was during the afternoons - especially summer afternoons when everyone was asleep-that we usually met. Before long, I was able to swim across the pond to sit with Ramu astride a **contented** buffalo.

Sometimes, I would slip into the water. Emerging in shades of green and khaki, I would sneak into the house through the bathroom and bathe under the tap before getting into my clothes.

One afternoon, Ramu and I found a small tortoise in the mud sitting over a hole in which it had laid several eggs. I presented the tortoise to Grandfather. He had a weakness for tortoises, and was pleased with this addition to his menagerie, giving it a large tub of water all to itself, with an island of rocks in the middle. If one of the dogs bothered it too much, it would draw its head and legs into its shell and defy all its attempts at rough play.

Ramu came from a family of bonded labourers and had received no schooling. But he was well-versed in folklore and knew a great deal about birds and animals.

'Many birds are sacred,' said Ramu, as we watched a blue jay swoop down from a peepul tree and carry off a grasshopper.

Both Ramu and Grandfather were of the opinion that we should be more gentle with birds and animals and should not kill so many of them.

"It is also important that we respect them", said Grandfather. "We must acknowledge their rights. Birds and animals are finding it more difficult to survive, because we are trying to destroy both them and their forests."

Ramu and I spent long summer afternoons at the pond. I still remember him with affection, though we never saw each other again after I left Dehra.

— *Rusty, the Boy from the Hills, Ruskin Bond*

(i) For each word given below, choose the correct meaning (as used in the passage) from the options provided. **[2]**

1. Hide *(line 6)*
   (a) blanket (b) fur
   (c) undisclosed (d) skin

2. Contented *(line 17)*
   (a) cheerful (b) lazy
   (c) satisfied (d) container

(ii) Which word in the passage is the opposite of 'easy'? **[1]**
(a) sneak (b) difficult
(c) labourer (d) survive

(iii) Answer the following questions briefly in your own words.
(a) What did Ramu like to do once he had climbed on the back of a buffalo? **[2]**
(b) What offer did Ramu make to the narrator? **[2]**
(c) Why do you think the narrator would bathe before entering the house? **[2]**
(d) Who was the large tub of water for? **[1]**
(e) How would the tortoise protect itself from the dogs? **[2]**

(iv) Despite the lack of schooling, what did Ramu know? How, according to Ramu and Grandfather, should we treat birds and animals? Answer in not more than fifty words. **[8]**

Question 5

(i) Fill in each of the numbered blanks with the correct form of the word given in brackets. Do not copy the passage but write in correct serial order the word or phrase appropriate to the blank space. **[4]**

Example:

(0) The Sun .... (shine) bright outside.

Answer: shone

It was hot in the railway compartment and the fan .... (1) (not work).

The elderly lady .... (2) (use) up all her water because she had cheerfully shared it with her fellow passengers. She knew that the train .... (3) (halt) at the station for only three minutes. Calling a shoeshine boy, she said, "Will you help me? I .... (4) (need) a bottle of cold water and here is the money," and she put a twenty rupee note in his hand. The boy snatched the money and .... (5) (disappear) into the crowd on the platform. A fellow passenger .... (6) (cannot believe) what he had witnessed. "What .... (7) (you do)?" He said, "You .... (8) (never see) your money again". Just then, the whistle was heard and the train began to move. At that moment, the child appeared at the window with the water. 'Your water,' he gasped, out of breath. 'And the change.'

(ii) Fill in the blanks with appropriate words. **[4]**

(a) We can cut ...... this field instead of taking the main road.

(b) Passengers are advised ...... standing on the footboard of a moving bus.

(c) They have been working on the project ...... years now.

(d) Ever ...... the accident, he has been afraid of boarding buses.

(e) It is a hard climb ...... the hill.

(f) She turned ...... the offer because she did not like the terms and conditions.

(g) I will need to speak ...... my parents before I sign up for the school trip.

(h) The sports teacher was taken ...... when he heard how enthusiastic the team was.

(iii) Join the following sentences to make one complete sentence **without using *and, but*** or ***so***. Choose the correct option. **[4]**

1. Stay still. We cannot take your photograph otherwise.

(a) Stay still, else we cannot take your photograph otherwise.

(b) Stay still because we can take your photograph otherwise.

(c) Unless you stay still, we cannot take your photograph.

(d) If you stay still, we cannot take your photograph.

2. Roy's mother rang up the school office. She wanted to enquire about the swimming classes at the summer camp.

(a) Roy's mother rang up the school office as she want to enquire about the swimming classes at the summer camp.

(b) Roy's mother rang up the school office to enquire about the swimming classes at the summer camp.

(c) Roy's mother has rung up the school office to enquire about the swimming classes at the summer camp.

(d) Roy's mother rang up the school office wanting enquiry about the swimming classes at the summer camp.

3. I left my keys somewhere. Do you know where they are?

(a) Do you know where I had left my keys?

(b) Do you know where my keys were left behind?

(c) Do you know where I left my keys?

(d) Do you know where I would have left my keys?

4. The captain should not be blamed for the team's defeat. The players should not be blamed for the team's defeat.

(a) The captain should neither be blamed nor the players should be blamed for the team's defeat.

(b) Neither the captain nor the players should be blamed for the team's defeat.

(c) The captain should not be blamed for the team's defeat as the players should not be blamed for the team's defeat.

(d) The captain should not be blamed for the team's defeat but the players too should not be blamed for the team's defeat.

(iv) Choose the correct option to rewrite the following according to the instructions given after each sentence. **[8]**

1. The audience broke into loud applause as soon as he finished speaking. *(Begin with: No sooner...)*

(a) No sooner he finished speaking that the audience broke into loud applause.

(b) No sooner had he finish speaking when the audience broke into loud applause.
(c) No sooner did he finish speaking than the audience broke into loud applause.
(d) No sooner the audience broke into loud applause than he finished speaking.

2. The news surprised everyone in my family. *(Begin with: The news took ...)*
(a) The news took everyone in my family by surprise.
(b) The news took everyone in my family with surprise.
(c) The news took with surprise everyone in my family.
(d) The news took everyone in my family for a surprise.

3. Yesterday was so much fun. *(End with a question tag)*
(a) Yesterday was so much fun, would you say?
(b) Was yesterday much fun?
(c) Yesterday was so much fun, isn't it?
(d) Yesterday was so much fun, wasn't it?

4. I wouldn't eat that food if I was not really hungry. *(Use: 'unless')*
(a) Unless I eat that food I will remain really hungry.
(b) I wouldn't be really hungry unless I ate that food.
(c) I wouldn't eat that food unless I was not really hungry.
(d) I wouldn't eat that food unless I was really hungry.

5. It is so hot and humid that I cannot sleep. *(Use: too)*
(a) It is hot and humid too sleep.
(b) It is too hot and humid to sleep.
(c) It is hot and humid too so I cannot sleep.
(d) It is too hot and humid such that I cannot sleep.

6. I prefer going out with friends to staying alone at home. *(Begin with: I would rather...)*
(a) I would rather go out with friends than stay alone at home.
(b) I would rather prefer going out with friends than staying alone at home.
(c) I would rather prefer to go out with friends than stay alone at home.
(d) I would rather go out with friends to staying alone at home.

7. "Why were you absent yesterday?", the teacher asked me. *(Begin with: The teacher asked me why...)*
(a) The teacher asked me why was I absent yesterday.
(b) The teacher asked me why I had been absent yesterday.
(c) The teacher asked me why I had been absent the day before.
(d) The teacher asked me why was I absent the day before.

8. Very few dancers are as graceful as she is. *(Begin with: She is...)*
(a) She is one of the most graceful dancers.
(b) She is the most graceful dancer.
(c) She is more graceful than all the other dancers.
(d) She is more graceful than a few other dancers.

Answers

1. (i) **The Mysterious Neighbour**

It was a quiet evening in the residential neighbourhood when Meera noticed something unusual. A new tenant had moved into the house next door–a house that had been vacant for months. She hadn't seen anyone come or go but she could hear strange noises at night, like muffled footsteps and odd sounds coming from the house. Curiosity gnawed at her but she dismissed it as nothing more than overactive imagination.

One evening, as Meera was returning from her walk, she saw the new neighbour standing by his gate. He looked out of place, with a hurried and anxious demeanor. His eyes darted nervously around and Meera felt a strange chill.

"Good evening," she said, trying to break the silence.

The man quickly glanced at her and gave a stiff nod but didn't speak. His odd behavior made Meera uneasy. Over the next few days, she noticed stranger occurrences -unexplained lights at odd hours and the man often seen leaving and returning at strange times. Meera couldn't shake the feeling that something was wrong.

One afternoon, she noticed a police officer standing outside her house. She walked over and learned that there had been a report of suspicious activity at the house next door. The officer had come to investigate. Meera, feeling uneasy, mentioned the strange behaviour of her new neighbour.

The officer's face grew serious. "Ma'am, you're not mistaken. We've been watching that house for some time. The man living there is suspected of involvement in a series of robberies in the area."

Meera's heart raced. Her curiosity had led her into an unexpected and dangerous situation. The officer assured her that the investigation was ongoing but for now, she was safe.

The following week, the house was empty again. The mysterious neighbor had vanished, leaving behind only questions and the quiet echoes of a dangerous secret.

(ii) Our teacher assigned us a project in which we were to form a group and work together. The task was to create a presentation on 'The Impact of Social Media on Society'. At first, I was a bit unsure about working in a group but soon, I realised that the experience would be a great learning opportunity.

We were a group of four members– Riya, Aman, Neha and myself. We began by dividing the work based on our strengths. Riya, who is good at researching, was in charge of gathering information. Aman, who is skilled at creating visuals, handled the design and presentation slides. Neha, being a confident speaker, took responsibility for presenting the final product. I, on the other hand, was in charge of compiling the information and organising the content for the presentation.

At first, we faced some challenges. Since everyone had different schedules, it was difficult to find time to meet. However, we decided to use online tools to collaborate, share ideas and drafts on Google Docs.

This way, we could work independently but still stay connected. Over time, we learned how to communicate effectively and respect each other's opinions. Even though there were disagreements about the design of the slides, we discussed our views openly and found a middle ground that suited everyone.

Through this project, I learned the importance of teamwork and flexibility. Working together taught me to trust my teammates and value their strengths. I also realised that good communication is key to overcoming challenges. Riya learned how to manage time effectively, as she had to balance research with other responsibilities.

Aman discovered that creativity is not just about design but also about how information is presented. Neha gained confidence in public speaking and learned how to engage an audience.

In conclusion, this group project not only helped us gain knowledge about the topic but also improved our collaboration skills.

We each grew individually and as a team and the experience made me realise the value of working together towards a common goal.

(iii) **For the Motion**

The pressure to conform to do what others are doing can be powerful and hard to resist. A person might feel pressured to do something just because others are doing it. The pressure becomes even more powerful when it comes from one's peers or friends. Peer pressure is a phenomenon that can influence a person to do something because one's peers are doing it.

Peer pressure is often painted in a negative light evoking images of young individuals being coerced into harmful behaviours or adopting unhealthy habits. However, when channelled positively, peer pressure can be a powerful force for good. It can encourage individuals to strive for a better performance and adopt healthier lifestyles, thereby fostering personal growth and development.

One of the most significant benefits of positive peer pressure is its ability to motivate individuals towards excellence. In educational settings, the influence of peers who prioritise their studies can be contagious. For instance, students who see their friends dedicating time to homework and preparing diligently for exams are likely to feel motivated to mirror these productive behaviours. This form of peer pressure can create a supportive environment where students push each other to achieve their best, ultimately raising the academic standards of the entire group.

Moreover, peer pressure can promote healthy social behaviours and ethical standards. Young people learn a great deal about social interactions from their peers. When surrounded by friends who respect others, engage in community service and uphold integrity, individuals adopt these positive traits. This leads to a more compassionate and responsible community.

Additionally, peer pressure can be a pivotal force in discouraging negative habits. For example, a group of friends can influence a member to stop smoking or reduce alcohol consumption. The desire to fit in and be accepted can motivate individuals to make healthier lifestyle choices which might be difficult to undertake alone.

However, the positive outcomes of peer pressure depend significantly on the group dynamics and the prevailing attitudes within a peer group. It is crucial for individuals, especially young people, to choose their friends wisely.

Being part of a group that values positive and constructive behaviours can transform peer pressure into a beneficial force that enhances one's life.

In conclusion, peer pressure undoubtedly has the potential to be a force for good. It encourages excellence, promotes ethical behaviour and supports healthy lifestyle choices. Like any tool, the impact of peer pressure depends on how it is used. If leveraged positively, it can lead to personal and communal improvement.

Against the Motion

We all share the need to connect with others, no matter our age. We want a sense of belonging at home and within the community. Being accepted by peers is an important part of adolescence. Teens yearn to fit in and to be seen in a favourable light. As a result, peers often have a strong influence on teen behaviours, choices and actions. More often than not, peer pressure takes a negative turn. Hence, I do not agree with the statement— "Peer pressure is a force for good".

The impact and scope of influence of peer pressure is so adverse that it has a negative impact on an individual.

Friends or peers may encourage engaging in risky things such as doing drugs, reckless driving, alcoholic habit, bunking classes, etc. As a result, one could get distracted and go on a path that ruins one's future.

The impact of peers can be easily found in the age of social media wherein individuals participate in reckless acts to fit in with peers. They try to follow the standard and, in doing so, go against their values and belief systems.

Often, children, enticed with what their friends have, become entitled and show immature behaviour. They even participate in illegal activities to fulfill their need to fit in.

If an individual does not fit in and give in to peer pressure, he/she is often bullied to the point that the person develops mental health problems and even causes self-harm. Now and then, the effect of peer tension on young teenagers is disrupting to the point that they can barely remain in their skin, are separated from loved ones and become discouraged and restless.

Thus, peer pressure is not a force for good.

(iv) Locality refers to the specific geographical area or neighbourhood in which a community of people live and work.

It is a fundamental concept that helps define the character, culture and identity of a particular place. The term is often used to describe the unique features of a specific region as well as the social connections and shared experiences of its residents.

One of the most important aspects of locality is the sense of community that it fosters. Whether it is a small town, a large city neighbourhood or a rural area, a locality can create a strong sense of belonging and shared identity among its residents. This sense of community is often built around common interests, traditions and values which are strengthened by the interactions and relationships between people in the area.

I live in a great residential locality in Delhi. It is society with multiple complexes. There is a huge park nearby with lush greenery and many different kinds of birds. Multiple amenities are easily accessible in my locality. We have three malls which are 10 minutes ride away with many big brands and eateries. There are also many famous street food stalls which offer a diverse range of food options. From vegetarian delights to international cuisines, you'll find it all here. The nearby market is bustling with a variety of snacks, chaat, candies and cuisines. And, the best part? You can enjoy all this in one place from hotdogs and momos to hot and cold beverages like coffees, teas, milkshakes and juices.

Another gem is the local market. From 10:30 a.m. until 8:30 p.m., it's a bustling market with hundreds of retailers selling anything and everything. But, as evening descends, this place undergoes a magical transformation into a foodie's paradise. The aroma of Gulab jamun, Dahi vada, Samosa, Dosa, Pav bhaji, Pani puri, Chinese food and Soft beverages fills the air. You'll also find mobile food vendors here. This market focuses on traditional Indori food. Poha Jalebi merits special mention, as it is the city's king of street food. Poha is available at all times, 24 hours a day, 365 days a year.

Overall, it is a fantastic and well-known street market in my city where people enjoy shopping.

(v) He was the funniest boy I had ever met. He would make everyone laugh even in the most trying times. Blessed with a funny nature, Varun would make everyone forget his/her worries in his company. No amount of sadness could dampen his spirit.

I remember once three of us friends including Roshni and Varun and I had failed the chemistry exam badly. Our parents had been called and we were told that we would have to repeat a year. That was a very hard time but, even then, no look of worry could be spotted on Varun's face or in his behaviour. His cheer remained undiminished even when his father suffered a major financial loss in business. Even during that time, Varun was known to spread cheer around. He always pushed his worries to the backseat and dedicated himself towards making others happy.

However, the loss of Varun's pet Munch, a few months ago, immersed him in grief. That was the only time that robbed him of his smiling face. For days, he did not speak to anyone and shut himself up in his room. We could not see him like that so Roshni and I decided to do something to dispel his gloom.

One day, we all went to his place and rang the doorbell of his house. There, we kept a little box, slightly open from one side and hid ourselves so that he could not see us. When he opened the door, he was surprised to find no one. He picked up the box with a look of amazement on his face. He took the lid off and out came a puppy, quite like Munch. He held it in his hands and started to play with it. It brought his smile back. Then, we all came into the sight and shouted with excitement, 'Surprise!' Indeed, that little effort from our end helped Varun come out of his sorrow. Later, we played with the puppy and, then, went to the park. We played till late in the evening and enjoyed as our friend was back again.

2. (i) XYZ Apartments
PQR City

14th July, 20XX

Dear Uncle,

I hope this letter finds you in the best of health and spirits. I am well and happy here. I have written to tell you that it upset me that you couldn't attend my birthday party. At the same time, I want to thank you for the money (1000 rupees) that you sent me as a birthday gift. I can't tell you how much I appreciate it. It really means a lot to me that you remembered my special day. I've already put your gift to good use. I have given it as fee for an educational tour that our school is organising to Amritsar. We will be going to the Wagah border, the Jallianwallah Bagh, the Golden temple and many other places.

I am grateful for your generosity and support. You've always been an amazing uncle to me and I feel truly blessed to have you in my life.

Thank you again for your kindness and thoughtfulness. I hope we can catch up soon and celebrate properly.

Yours loving,
XYZ

(ii) 202, M.G. Road,
Agra

27th July, 20XX

The Municipal Commissioner,
Municipal Corporation,
Agra

Subject Complaint regarding overflowing garbage and lack of cleanliness in locality

Dear Sir/Ma'am,

Through this letter, I would like to draw your attention to the overflowing garbage and lack of cleanliness in M.G. Road, Agra. It is a matter of great disappointment that in the times when the entire country is striving towards cleanliness and sanitation, our locality presents a picture of dirt. It is not the lack of garbage bins or cleaning staff, but the lack of action on the part of the staff that the bins are always overflowing. As a result, there is a bad odour in the locality and people are becoming prone to diseases.

Hence, I request you to solve this problem and ensure that the locality maintains its cleanliness. For the same, I suggest that garbage vans and staff should come regularly to clean the locality. Further, regular inspection can ensure that the system is effective in its implementation. With your aid, we would be able to move ahead in our path towards cleanliness.

Thanking you,

Yours faithfully,
ABC

3. (i) **SHOW YOUR SKILL!**

Art and Craft Exhibition

25th December, 20XX

9 a.m. to 12 p.m.

School Auditorium

All the students from Class IX to XII are requested to register their names with the Head Girl by 20th December, 20XX.

(ii) **E-mail-id** xyz@gmail.com

Invite to inaugurate the Arts and Crafts exhibition as a Chief Guest

Respected Sir/Ma'am,

With great pleasure and pride, ABC School would like to inform in that it is organising an Arts and Crafts Exhibition on 3rd August, Friday from 10:00 a.m. to 3:00 p.m. in the Assembly Area, ABC School. For the same, we would be honoured if you could inaugurate and grace the exhibition as the Chief Guest.

With your valuable experience and knowledge, students would be motivated to participate in creative activities and take up art as a proper career. Hoping for a positive reply.

Anticipating a positive response,

Yours faithfully,

PQR

4. (i) 1. (d) skin 2. (c) satisfied

(ii) (b) difficult

(iii) (a) Once he had climbed the back of the buffalo, Ramu liked to stretch his naked brown body out on the animal's glistening hide/back and start singing to himself.

(b) Ramu offered to teach the narrator to swim every afternoon.

(c) The narrator would bathe before entering the house to avoid being scolded for swimming in the village pond when everyone was asleep. He thought that his elders become angry so he would sneak into the house through the bathroom and bathe under the tap to get clean first.

(d) The large tub of water was for the tortoise presented by the narrator to his grandfather.

(e) To protect itself from the dogs, the tortoise would draw its head and legs into its shell and defy all the dogs' attempts at rough play.

(iv)

Ramu	came	from	a	family
of	bonded	labourers	and	received
no	schooling.	However,	he	was
well-versed	in	folklore	and	knew
a	great	deal	about	birds
and	animals.	We	should	be
gentle	with	birds	and	animals
and	should	not	kill	them.
It	is	also	important	to
acknowledge	and	respect	their	rights.

5. (i) 1. was not working 2. had used
3. halted/would halt 4. need
5. disappeared 6. could not believe
7. are you doing 8. will never see

(ii) a. across b. against
c. for d. since
e. up f. down
g. to h. back

(iii) 1. (c) Unless you stay still, we cannot take your photograph.
2. (b) Roy's mother rang up the school office to enquire about the swimming classes at the summer camp.
3. (c) Do you know where I left my keys?
4. (b) Neither the captain nor the players should be blamed for the team's defeat.

(iv) 1. (c) No sooner did he finish speaking than the audience broke into loud applause.
2. (a) The news took everyone in my family by surprise.
3. (d) Yesterday was so much fun, wasn't it?
4. (d) I wouldn't eat that food unless I was really hungry.
5. (b) It is too hot and humid to sleep.
6. (a) I would rather go out with friends than stay alone at home.
7. (c) The teacher asked me why I had been absent the day before.
8. (a) She is one of the most graceful dancers.

ICSE

Solved Question Paper 2025

Time : 2 hrs
Marks : 80

English Language Paper 1

General Instructions

1. Answer to this paper must be written on the paper provided separately.
2. You will not be allowed to write during first 15 minutes.
3. The time given at the head of this paper is the time allowed for writing the answers.
4. Attempt all five questions.
5. The intended marks for questions or parts of questions are given in brackets [ ].
6. You are advised to spend not more than 30 minutes in answering Question 1 and 20 minutes in answering Question 2.

Question 1

(Do not spend more than 30 minutes on this question.)

Write a composition (300-350 words) on ***any one*** of the following. **[20]**

(i) Write an original short story in which a poor tailor wins an award which changes his/her life.

(ii) Your friends once played a harmless prank on you. Give an account of what happened, your response to the prank and what you learnt from the experience.

(iii) Describe what you see and hear as you move about the corridors and compound during your school break time. How does the scene change after the bell rings?

(iv) "More collaboration, less competition is the need of the hour." Express your views either ***for*** or ***against*** this statement.

(v) Study the picture given below. Write a story or a description or an account of what it suggests to you. Your composition may be about the subject of the picture, or you may take suggestions from it; however, there must be a clear connection between the picture and your composition.

Question 2

(Do not spend more than 20 minutes on this question.)

Select ***any one*** of the following. **[10]**

(i) Your grandmother has taught you a special skill. Write a letter thanking her. Explain how you will use that skill and why it is important to you.

(ii) There is no bus stop in your locality. Write a letter to the Municipal Commissioner of your town/city complaining about the problem. Offer possible solutions.

Question 3

(i) Your school is hosting an Inter School Story Writing Competition. Write a notice informing the students about the event. **[5]**

(ii) Write an e-mail to a famous person inviting him/her to be the Judge on the occasion. **[5]**

Question 4

Read the following passage carefully and answer the questions that follow.

A little later, when he went to the pump to wash, he saw the school children pouring by with their **satchels** across their shoulders. They all wore the same clothes - grey shorts or skirts and light blue shirts or blouses - faded and mended, and they all had their hair oiled and combed down very flat. Some went by in laughing, racing groups, others had to be led by their mothers or grandparents to the school building. This reminded him of his sisters in the village.

The boys in the kitchen now looked at him with less hostility. Jagu seemed pleased with Hari too, and sometimes handed him a glass of tea in the middle of the day. When he had a few moments to **spare**, Jagu sat down at one of the long wooden tables, drummed loudly on it and sang a song in a dialect Hari did not know. When he caught Hari listening and smiling, he smiled back. Then Hari knew that he too had a village somewhere that he called home. It was just that he was a silent, hardworking, worried man and had no time and no gift for speech.

It was the watch mender, Mr. Panwallah, who was truly a benefactor, the kindest and most helpful of all. One afternoon, during those hot, still hours when there were no customers for a change, Hari was standing in front of the eating house, idly watching the traffic because he was too tired to do anything else, and Mr. Panwallah called to him to come and sit beside him on the bench behind the counter in his shop.

"Want to help?" he asked. "Want to learn how to make a clock tick? I'm just going to open this big grandfather clock sent to me for repair - you'll be able to see the workings plain. Don't often get a piece like this anymore – wall clocks, yes, and electronic gadgets – but you don't often come upon a grandfather clock like this. It's a real piece of luck, being able to show you one of this size." Look, he said, swinging open the door at the back and revealing the machinery to a fascinated Hari who felt as if the door had opened into a new and strange house. Mr. Panwallah showed Hari what was wrong with it, what had made it stop. "Interesting, isn't it? How would you like to learn? Tell you what - I'll take you on as an apprentice. You don't have much to do between two and four, do you? Of course you will have to ask Jagu first. I can pay you a little, not much, and you can help me for two hours a day. Perhaps I can make a watch mender of you."

– Village by the Sea, Anita Desai

(i) For each word given below choose the correct meaning (as used in the passage) from the options provided. **[2]**

1. Satchels *(line 2)*
   - (a) snatching
   - (b) scarves
   - (c) school bags
   - (d) sweaters
2. Spare *(line 13)*
   - (a) share
   - (b) offer
   - (c) thin
   - (d) extra

(ii) Which word in the passage is the opposite of 'closed'? **[1]**

- (a) behind
- (b) fascinated
- (c) opened
- (d) revealing

(iii) Answer the following questions briefly in your own words.

- (a) How were the school children dressed? **[2]**
- (b) In what way was Jagu kind to Hari? **[2]**
- (c) What did the song tell Hari about Jagu? **[2]**
- (d) Which sentence in the passage tells us that Jagu was not a talkative man? **[2]**
- (e) Why were there no customers at that time of the day? **[1]**

(iv) In not more than 50 words describe how Mr. Panwallah introduced Hari to watch mending. **[8]**

Question 5

(i) Fill in each of the numbered blanks with the correct form of the word given in brackets. Do not copy the passage but write in correct serial order the word or phrase appropriate to the blank space. **[4]**

Example :

One day we (0) ……… (lift) the box up.

Answer : (0) lifted

We (1) ……… (find) a dead mouse (2) ……… (lie) among our treasures. It (3) ……… (be) an exciting discovery.

A boy took it up by its tail and (4) ……… (wave) it in front of our faces.

"What shall we do with it?" he (5) ……… (cry).

"It stinks!" someone (6) ……… (shout).

"Throw it out of the window quick!"

He (7) ……… (hesitate). They all (8) ……… (look) at me.

(ii) Fill in the blanks with an appropriate words. **[4]**

(a) My best friend, John is named .... his grandfather.

(b) A grey mist hung .... the fields.

(c) The little girl spoke .... against the bully.

(d) They accused him .... theft.

(e) The police got the fire .... control.

(f) There is a bridge .... the river.

(g) The driver jumped .... the car.

(h) I have not seen my uncle .... last summer.

(iii) Choose the correct option to make one complete sentence **without using *and*, *but*** or ***so***. **(4)**

1. These are fresh mangoes. I bought them yesterday.
   (a) These are fresh mangoes which I bought yesterday.
   (b) These mangoes were fresher when I bought them yesterday.
   (c) These are fresh mangoes which were bought yesterday.
   (d) These are fresh mangoes brought by me yesterday.
2. The debating teams were very happy. They were declared joint champions.
   (a) The debating teams were very happy as they have been declared joint champions.
   (b) The debating teams are very happy as they are declared joint champions.
   (c) The debating teams were very happy as they had been declared joint champions.
   (d) The debating teams will be very happy as they will be declared joint champions.
3. The rain came down. All the people ran away.
   (a) When the rain came down, all the people ran away.
   (b) When it rained, the people ran away.
   (c) The rain had come down all the people ran away.
   (d) The The rain having come, all the people ran away.
4. The disciple was wise. The teacher did not trust him.
   (a) Although the disciple was wise yet the teacher trusted him.
   (b) Although the disciple was not wise the teacher trusted him.
   (c) Although the disciple is wise, the teacher trusted him.
   (d) Although the disciple was wise, the teacher did not trust him.

(iv) Choose the correct option and rewrite the sentence according to the instruction given after each. **[8]**

1. The teacher said, "Come early tomorrow, the examination begins at eight o'clock."
   (Begin: The teacher told us to.........)
   (a) The teacher told us to come early the next day as the examination would begin at eight o'clock.
   (b) The teacher told us to come early tomorrow as the examination begins at eight o'clock.
   (c) The teacher told us the examination will begin at eight o'clock so come early tomorrow.
   (d) The teacher told us to come by eight o'clock as the examination will begin early the next day.
2. Rahul not only plays the guitar but also the drums.
   (Use: 'as well as')
   (a) Rahul plays the guitar as well as the drums.
   (b) Rahul plays the guitar as well the drums.
   (c) Rahul plays the guitar as well as he does the drums.
   (d) Rahul plays the guitar and the drums as well.
3. She said she would not be available.
   (Add a question tag)
   (a) Didn't she say that she would not be available?
   (b) She said she would not be available, did she?
   (c) She said she would not be available, didn't she?
   (d) She said she would not be available, wouldn't she?
4. This is the most beautiful painting in the exhibition.
   (Begin: No other......)
   (a) No other painting is as beautiful as this exhibition.
   (b) No other painting in this exhibition is beautiful.
   (c) No other painting is beautiful as this painting in the exhibition.
   (d) No other painting in the exhibition is as beautiful as this one.
5. I prefer aerobics to yoga.
   (Use: 'rather')
   (a) I would rather do aerobics to yoga.
   (b) I would rather do aerobics than yoga.
   (c) I would rather prefer aerobics than yoga.
   (d) I would rather do yoga than aerobics.

6. The coach taught the children the rules of the game.
   (Begin: The rules.........)
   (a) The rules have being taught by the coach to the children.
   (b) The rules of the game have been taught by the children to the coach.
   (c) The rules of the game is taught by the coach to the children.
   (d) The rules of the game were taught by the coach to the children.
7. No sooner did the film star arrive than the crowd cheered.
   (Begin: As soon as.........)
   (a) As soon as the film star arrived then the crowd cheered.
   (b) As soon as the film star arrives the crowd starts cheering.
   (c) As soon as the crowd cheers the film star arrives.
   (d) As soon as the film star arrived the crowd cheered.
8. School bags are often too heavy for students to carry. *(Use: 'so')*
   (a) School bags are so heavy students cannot carry them.
   (b) School bags are often so heavy that students cannot carry them.
   (c) School bags are often so heavy for students to carry.
   (d) School bags are heavy so students cannot carry them.

Answers

1. (i) Ravi was a poor tailor who lived in a small town. He had a tiny shop where he stitched clothes for the people in his neighbourhood. He worked hard every day but he barely earned enough to buy food for his family. Even though his life was tough, Ravi never complained. He loved his work and always tried to make beautiful clothes. His dream was to become a famous tailor one day but he did not know how to achieve it.

One day, a big announcement was made in the town. A famous fashion company was holding a competition for tailors. The winner would get a big cash prize and a job in the city. Ravi's friends told him to participate but he was unsure. "I am just a simple tailor. How can I win such a big contest?" he said.

His wife, Meena, smiled and said, "You must try. You are talented and this is your chance." Encouraged by her words, Ravi decided to take part. He worked day and night on a special dress. He carefully stitched every piece of fabric, adding beautiful patterns by hand. When he finished, he felt proud of his work. His children also admired the dress and told him he would surely win.

On the day of the competition, Ravi saw many talented tailors with fancy designs. He felt nervous but stayed hopeful. When the judges saw his dress, they were amazed. "This is wonderful! Such fine stitching and unique design," one of them said. After much discussion, Ravi was declared the winner!

Tears filled Ravi's eyes as he accepted the award. The prize money helped him expand his shop, and soon, he got many new customers. A few months later, the fashion company offered him a big job in the city. His life changed forever.

Ravi had once doubted himself but now he knew-hard work, belief and the courage to try could make dreams come true.

(ii) One evening, my friends and I were sitting in the park, talking and laughing. It was a normal day and I had no idea that they were planning to play a prank on me.

Suddenly, my friend Rahul pointed towards a tree and said, "Look! There's a snake!" I froze in fear. I have always been scared of snakes. My heart started beating fast and I quickly moved away. My other friends also pretended to be scared. They ran in different directions, making me even more frightened.

Rahul then shouted, "It's coming towards you!" That was enough for me-I turned around and ran as fast as I could. I didn't stop until I reached the park gate. My friends burst into laughter. Confused, I turned back and saw them holding a rubber snake in their hands. That's when I realised they had tricked me!

At first, I felt embarrassed. But soon, I started laughing too. I had to admit, they got me really well. It was just a harmless joke and they didn't mean to hurt me. Later, we all sat together, and they promised not to scare me like that again. We talked about other funny pranks we had seen or experienced before.

This experience taught me an important lesson. Sometimes, we take things too seriously, but it's okay to laugh at ourselves. I also understood that friends may play pranks, but they do it for fun, not to make us feel bad. However, I also learned that we should be careful while playing pranks so that no one gets truly hurt or scared.

That day, I realised that friendship is about fun, laughter and understanding. Even though I was scared at first, in the end, it became a funny memory that we still talk about and laugh about today. It showed me that the best friendships are filled with joy, trust and unforgettable moments.

(iii) As soon as the bell rings for break time, the quiet classrooms suddenly come alive. Students rush out into the corridors, their footsteps echoing on the tiled floor. Some are laughing and chatting, while others hurry towards the canteen. The air is filled with the mixed sounds of voices, laughter and the clatter of shoes on the ground. Excitement is visible on every face as they enjoy their short break from studies.

In the school compound, small groups of students gather under trees or sit on benches. Some enjoy their lunch, while others share jokes and stories. A few students run across the playground, playing tag or football. Others prefer to relax and watch their friends play. The canteen is the busiest place, with students lining up to buy snacks. The smell of samosas and noodles fills the air, making everyone feel hungry. Some students quickly finish their food to have more time to play.

Teachers walk around, keeping an eye on the students. Some remind the students to keep the place clean, while others chat with their colleagues. Near the water taps, a group of students splash water on each other and laugh loudly. The whole school is full of energy and excitement. Even those who were tired during class now seem refreshed.

Then, the warning bell rings, and everything changes. Students quickly gather their things and start walking towards their classrooms. The noise begins to fade as friends say goodbye and hurry inside. Some students finish the last bites of their food, while others rush to the washroom before class. The playground, once full of movement, becomes empty.

When the final bell rings, silence takes over. The corridors are now quiet, with only a few latecomers running to their rooms. Teachers stand at the doors, waiting for students to settle down. Within minutes, the school returns to its usual calm, and the sound of lessons begins again.

(iv) **For the Motion**

In today's world, people focus too much on competition. Everyone wants to be the best but this often leads to stress and unhealthy rivalry. Instead of competing, we should work together and support each other. More collaboration and less competition can create a better society.

First, collaboration helps in learning and growth. When people work together, they share ideas and knowledge. This leads to better solutions and faster progress. In workplaces, teams achieve more when they cooperate instead of competing. In schools, students can understand concepts better when they help each other.

Second, competition creates pressure and stress. Many students and employees feel anxious because they always have to prove themselves. This can harm their mental health. Instead of focusing on beating others, people should focus on improving their skills through teamwork.

Moreover, collaboration leads to a peaceful and friendly environment. When people work together, they build strong relationships. It reduces jealousy and promotes kindness. Society benefits when people help each other instead of trying to win all the time.

In the modern world, innovation happens through teamwork. Scientists, doctors and engineers work together to solve big problems. If they only competed, they would not make such great discoveries. Even in business, companies succeed when they form partnerships and share ideas.

Some people believe that competition pushes people to do better. However, too much competition can create selfishness and dishonesty. People may focus only on winning instead of learning and growing together. A balance is needed, but in today's world, collaboration should be encouraged more.

In conclusion, working together is better than competing. Collaboration leads to learning, reduces stress and creates a friendly environment. To build a better future, we must support and uplift each other instead of always trying to be better than others.

Against the Motion

Competition is an important part of life. It motivates people to work harder, improve their skills and achieve success. While collaboration is useful, focusing only on teamwork and reducing competition may not always be the best approach.

First, competition encourages progress. When people compete, they try to do better than others. This leads to new inventions, better services and higher-quality products. For example, in business, companies compete to provide the best products, which benefits customers. Without competition, progress may slow down.

Second, competition builds confidence and resilience. In schools, students work hard to score well in exams because they compete with their classmates. This makes them disciplined, focused and goal-oriented. If competition is reduced, many may lose interest in improving themselves.

Moreover, competition prepares people for real-life challenges. In the professional world, people compete for jobs, promotions, and recognition. Those who work hard and prove their skills succeed. If there is no competition, people may not feel the need to develop their talents.

Some argue that collaboration is better because it promotes teamwork and reduces stress. While this is true, collaboration works best when people have already developed their skills through competition. Without competition, collaboration alone may lead to laziness and a lack of innovation.

In conclusion, while collaboration is important, competition should not be reduced. A balance between the two is needed. Healthy competition pushes people to do their best, while collaboration helps in sharing knowledge and working towards a common goal. Instead of removing competition, we should encourage fair and positive competition that benefits everyone.

(v) In a small village, a mother and her children worked in their vegetable garden. Every morning, they stepped into their green fields, caring for their plants with love. Their hard work made the crops grow fresh and healthy. It was not just about growing food; it was about connecting with nature and learning patience.

One bright morning, the family was harvesting brinjals. The mother, dressed in a pink saree, smiled as she handed the vegetables to her children. The boy, wearing a vest, held a basket filled with colourful brinjals. His younger sister, in a blue dress, stood nearby, watching happily. Their faces glowed with joy and satisfaction. They knew that their efforts had borne fruit, and their happiness was pure.

For them, farming was not just work-it was a way of life. They enjoyed growing their own food and felt proud of their efforts. The mother had taught her children that nature rewards those who care for it. With patience and dedication, their small garden provided enough vegetables for their daily meals. Sometimes, they even shared extra produce with neighbours. This created a strong bond among the villagers.

The village believed in working together. People helped each other during planting and harvesting seasons. They knew that unity made life easier and happier. Unlike cities, where people bought everything from markets, villagers valued the food they grew with their own hands. It was fresh, healthy, and free from chemicals. Their connection with the land was deep and meaningful.

As they gathered the last batch of brinjals, the children laughed and played. The mother looked at them with love, knowing she was teaching them valuable lessons-hard work, teamwork, and gratitude for nature.

The picture of this happy family in their green fields shows the beauty of simple living. It reminds us that joy comes not from wealth but from the satisfaction of honest effort, the love of family, and the strength of a close-knit community.

2. (i) Mamura, Sector 66
Noida - 201301

4th March, 20XX

Dear Grandma,

I hope you are doing well. I am writing this letter to thank you for teaching me gardening. I really enjoyed learning how to plant seeds, water them, and take care of the plants.

This skill is very special to me because it connects me to nature and reminds me of you. I will use it to grow my own flowers and vegetables. It will help me keep the environment green and beautiful. Gardening also teaches me patience and hard work. I will always remember the time we spent together in the garden. Thank you for your love and guidance. I feel lucky to have you as my grandmother.

Take care and stay healthy.
With love,
Nilima

(ii) H.No. 45, Greenwood Colony
Rajgarh Road, Guwahati - 781003

4th March, 20XX

The Municipal Commissioner
Guwahati Municipal Corporation
Guwahati - 781001

Subject Request for a Bus Stop in Our Locality

Respected Sir/Madam,

I am writing to bring to your attention the lack of a bus stop in our locality. Many people, including students, office workers, and senior citizens, face great difficulty because of this. We have to walk a long distance to catch a bus, which is very inconvenient, especially during bad weather.

I request you to kindly arrange a bus stop in our area. A suitable place for it would be near Lachit Nagar Point on Rajgarh Road. This will help many people and make travel easier for everyone.

I hope you will consider our request and take action soon. Thank you for your time and support.

Yours sincerely,
Reshmi Saikia

3. (i) **Inter-School Story Writing Competition**

Our school is hosting an Inter-School Story Writing Competition. Students from all classes can participate.

The event will be held on 6th March, 20XX, in the school auditorium. Interested students must register by 5th March, 20XX. For details, contact your class teacher.

(ii) abc@gmail.com

Invitation to Judge Our Public Speaking Competition

Dear Dr. Tharoor,

I hope you are doing well. We are organising an Inter-School Public Speaking Competition on 28th March, 20XX at St. Xaviers College, Gurgaon. We would be honoured if you could be the judge for the event. Your presence and guidance would inspire our students.

Please let us know your availability.

Best regards,
Ravi Shashank
St. Xaviers College

4. (i) 1. (c) school bags
2. (d) extra

(ii) (c) opened

(iii) (a) The school children wore grey shorts or skirts and light blue shirts or blouses. Their clothes were faded and mended, and their hair was oiled and combed flat.

(b) Jagu was kind to Hari by giving him a glass of tea during the day and smiling at him when he noticed Hari listening to his songs.

(c) The song made Hari realise that Jagu also had a village he called home.

(d) "It was just that he was a silent, hard-working, worried man and had no time and no gift for speech."

(e) There were no customers because it was a hot afternoon, a quiet time for business.

(iv)

Mr. Panwallah	called	Hari	to	sit
beside	him	and	showed	him
the	inside	of	a	big
grandfather	clock.	He	explained	what
was	wrong	with	it	and
how	to	fix	it.	He
then	offered	to	take	Hari
as	an	apprentice,	paying	him
a	little	and	patiently	training
him	for	two	hours	daily.

5. (i) 1. found 2. lying 3. was 4. waved
5. cried 6. shouted 7. hesitated 8. looked

(ii) (a) after (b) over (c) out (d) of
(e) under (f) over (g) out of (h) since

(iii) 1. (a) These are fresh mangoes which I bought yesterday.
2. (c) The debating teams were very happy as they had been declared joint champions.
3. (a) When the rain came down, all the people ran away.
4. (d) Although the disciple was wise, the teacher did not trust him.

(iv) 1. (b) The teacher told us to come early tomorrow as the examination begins at eight o'clock.
2. (a) Rahul plays the guitar as well as the drums.
3. (c) She said she would not be available, wouldn't she?
4. (d) No other painting in the exhibition is as beautiful as this one.
5. (b) I would rather do aerobics than yoga.
6. (d) The rules of the game were taught by the coach to the children.
7. (d) As soon as the film star arrived the crowd cheered.
8. (b) School bags are often so heavy that students cannot carry them.